Your Insight & Awareness Book

Your Insight & Awareness Book

Lorraine Nilon

Illustrations by Katherine Close

Your Insight & Awareness Book by Lorraine Nilon
First published 2017 by Insight & Awareness Pty Ltd
www.insightandawareness.com.au
© 2011 Lorraine Nilon

No part of this publication may be reproduced, stored in retrieval systems or transmitted in any form by any means without prior written permission of the copyright owner.

The information contained in this book is in no way intended to offer medical or psychological advice or treatment. The author is neither a psychologist nor a licensed counsellor. All information is designed as suggestions for soul truth exploration. Individuals using this information, do so on their own responsibility. The author neither warrants nor guarantees the level of success to be achieved by the application of the information in this book. The author specifically disclaims any liability arising from how others choose to apply the information in this book. The ultimate efficacy is affected by the reader's willingness to be truthfully honest.

National Library of Australia Cataloguing-in-Publication entry:
Author: Nilon, Lorraine Dawn.
Title: Your Insight and Awareness Book / Lorraine Dawn Nilon
Illustrator Katherine Close
ISBN: 9780992281700 (paperback)
ISBN: 9780992281731 (hard cover)
Subjects: Self. Self-consciousness (Awareness)
Spirituality. Self-actualization (Psychology).
Contributors: Close, Katherine, illustrator.
Dewey Number: 126

Illustrations and cover by Katherine Close
Conceptual design for illustrations—Lorraine Nilon
Conceptual design for illustrations and Assistant to clarity—Leanne McIntyre-Burnes
Figurine illustrations for Images and Illusions, Chapter 25–page 307
Amber and Carley Hennessy (Aged 8)
Editor and Assistant to clarity—Bronwen Prazak
Proofreading and Assistant to clarity—Rachel Dearnley
Author photographed by Paul Mathews

www.insightandawareness.com.au

Also available as an ebook from major ebook vendors.

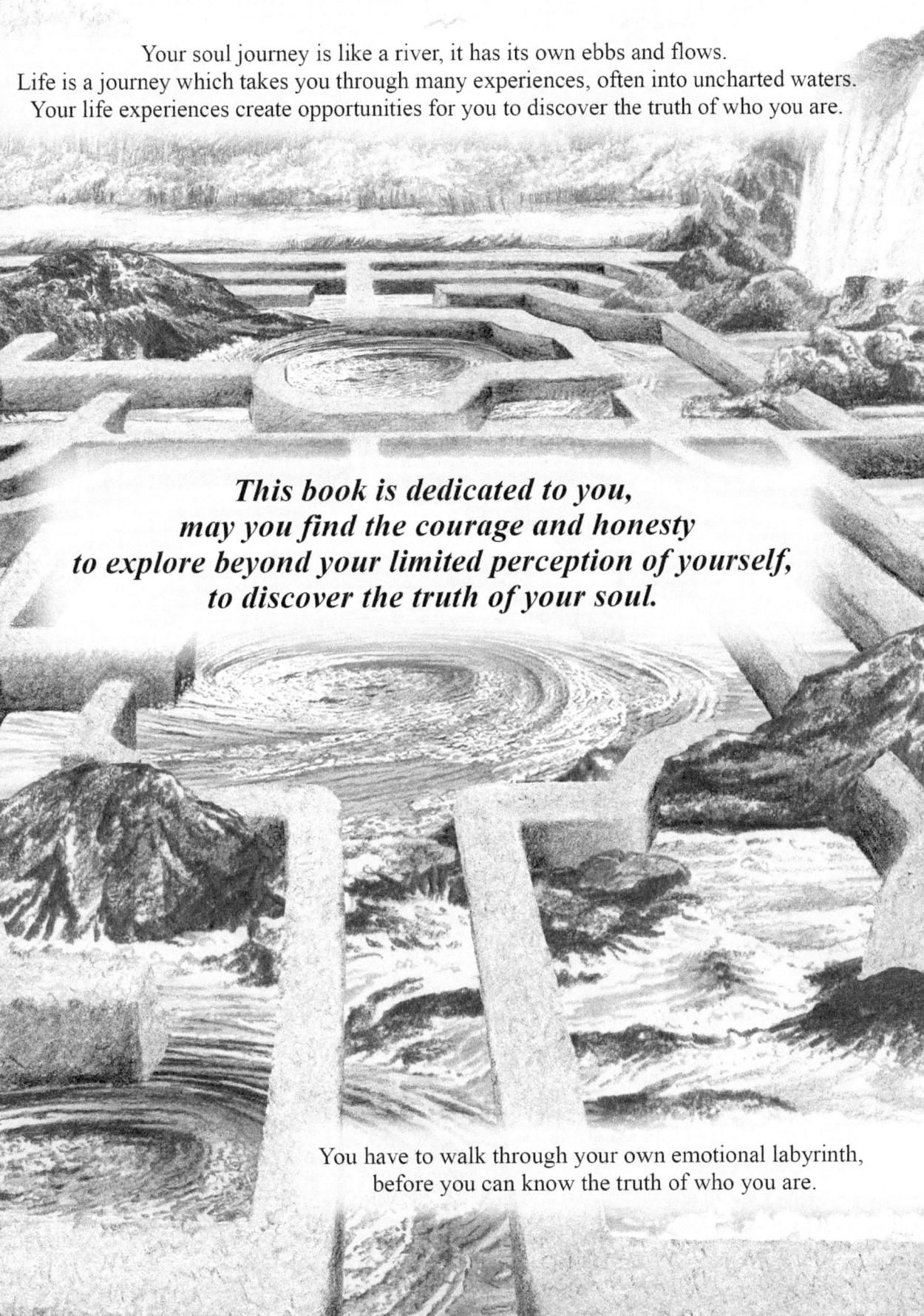

Your soul journey is like a river, it has its own ebbs and flows.
Life is a journey which takes you through many experiences, often into uncharted waters.
Your life experiences create opportunities for you to discover the truth of who you are.

*This book is dedicated to you,
may you find the courage and honesty
to explore beyond your limited perception of yourself,
to discover the truth of your soul.*

You have to walk through your own emotional labyrinth,
before you can know the truth of who you are.

The intention behind this information is to heighten your awareness of:
- The truth of being a significant, unique, independent, individual soul.
- How you feel about yourself.
- Why you feel this way.
- How you use resistance, denial, avoidance and codependency energy against your soul truth.
- What you are reluctant to acknowledge about your awareness of truth and why you are reluctant.

CONTENTS

Introduction to your energetic system 11
Preface. 15
Tips for reading *Your Insight and Awareness Book* 19
Warrior who fights 25

SECTION ONE 29

Chapter One: A metaphor describing your soul separation 31
   Questionnaire 1 32
   Your soul's consciousness 35
   Your soul's unconsciousness 40

Chapter Two: Resistance, denial, avoidance and codependency 47

Chapter Three: Declaration to be of truth 53

Chapter Four: Suppression 59

Chapter Five: Negative beliefs 62
   You compete against your soul 62
   Self-exercise 1 65

Chapter Six: Your addiction to oppressing your awareness of your soul's consciousness 66
   Self-exercise 2 68
   Victim mentality 70
   Martyr 71
   Servant. 72
   Saboteur. 73
   Drama queen 74
   Mask 75
   Controller. 76
   The intellectual 77
   Self-exercise 3 78

Chapter Seven: Externalisation 79
   Self-exercise 4 82

Chapter Eight: Control. 83

Chapter Nine: Freedom of choice 87
   Self-exercise 5 92
   Questionnaire 2 93

SECTION TWO 95

Chapter Ten: Lost 97
  Questionnaire 3 99

Chapter Eleven: Avoiding soul accountability 100
  Self-exercise 6 102

Chapter Twelve: Soul integrity 103
  Self-exercise 7 104

Chapter Thirteen: Avoidance of soul commitment 105
  Self-exercise 8 107

Chapter Fourteen: Separation from your awareness of your soul 109

Chapter Fifteen: Indoctrinations and concretisation 112
  Self-exercise 9 116

Chapter Sixteen: Escapism 117
  Self-exercise 10 119

Chapter Seventeen: Caring for your soul 121

Chapter Eighteen: Lives 124
  Life 125
  Questionnaire 4 126
  Comparing your questionnaires 127

SECTION THREE 129

Chapter Nineteen: The journey 131

Chapter Twenty: Understanding the energetics of the mass energy of mankind 141
  Departure from this lifetime 150
  Lost souls 152
  Demonic energy 158
  Psychic attack of a soul denial entity 160
  Crossed over souls 171
  Reborn 174
  Energetic collectives 178

Chapter Twenty-One: Chakra and aura system 191
  Your unconscious will 211
  Freewill 213

SECTION FOUR 215

Chapter Twenty-Two: Soul blueprint 217
Defiance against your soul blueprint 230

Chapter Twenty-Three: Carried victim energy 240
Victim 240
Self-pity 246
Internal rage 250
Martyrdom 254
Manipulator 258
Familiarity 265
Contrived desperation 270
Denial of your carried victim energy 277

Chapter Twenty-Four: Belief of not being good enough 282
Denial of the belief of not being good enough 299

Chapter Twenty-Five: Images and illusions 302
Denial of the truth of using images and illusions 324

SECTION FIVE 329

Chapter Twenty-Six: Controlled evolution 331
Mankind's energetic collectives sustaining controlled evolution beliefs 357
Ramifications of controlled evolution 362
Denial of the truth of controlled evolution beliefs 388

Chapter Twenty-Seven: The opposition of energies 406

SECTION SIX 409

Chapter Twenty-Eight: Soul serenity 411

Chapter Twenty-Nine: History of development 412

Acknowledgements 419

Glossary 421

About the Author 447

True Source Divine Origin Consciousness

Your Soul's Consciousness

Your Soul's
Unconsciousness

Soul Denial

Introduction to your energetic system

True Source Divine Origin Consciousness is a label for the collective purity of truth and is the collective energy of the origin of your soul and the truth of all souls. This is where you come from and where you will return to after your death. This label is used because you do not have a history with it. It is a way of counteracting what you believe you know and enables you the freedom to explore what you discover about your own origin of truth. *True Source Divine Origin Consciousness* is the source of your soul's consciousness.

Your soul's consciousness is the part of your soul system, which has never abandoned the unconditional love of *True Source Divine Origin Consciousness* (your origin), or awareness of truth. Your soul's consciousness is the truth of who you are unencumbered by any unconscious energy and is naturally the core of your being.

Your soul's unconsciousness is the part of your soul system, which is unconscious to the unconditional love of *True Source Divine Origin Consciousness*, and is the part of you lost within the willingness to oppress your awareness of truth. Your soul's unconsciousness is the energetic storehouse of your unconscious energy such as your unresolved emotions, control structures, barriers to truth, framework of soul oppression, fears and beliefs, which you are willing to use to deny the truth of who you are.

You are the interface between your soul's consciousness and unconsciousness.

Your unresolved emotions are what you use to energetically sustain the vortex of your soul's unconsciousness. These are the emotions you refuse to resolve, or you have become so unconscious to the reality of them, that you deny their existence. All unresolved emotions are unconscious energy. There are a myriad of reasons why you have unresolved emotions. However, they are sustained by your fear and inability, or unwillingness to face the truth. Some unresolved emotions are a direct result of your dishonesty with yourself.

Your soul denial is the foundation and original energy of your soul's unconsciousness and the source of all unconscious energy; all unconscious energy is a mutation of soul denial. Your soul denial energy is your war with the truth of who you are, which enslaves you to exist within the unconsciousness of your soul. Your soul denial consists of your embedded beliefs and fears, which inhibit you from accepting the truth of your natural significance, uniqueness, independence and individuality.

Your soul oppression is the active force of your soul's unconsciousness, which you use to emotionally, energetically and physically oppress your awareness of your soul truth. Your soul truth is the reality of both your conscious and unconscious energy.

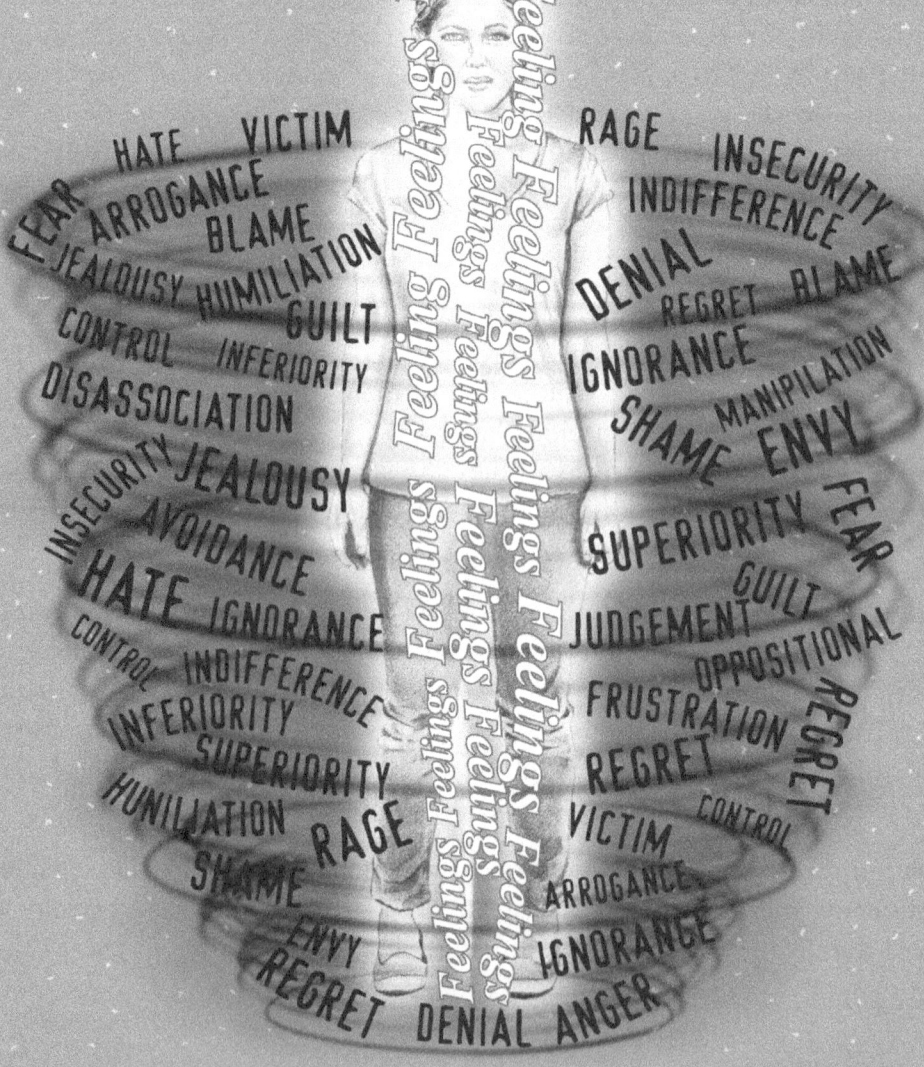

Control structures are complex methods and mythology of how you utilise your desire for control or your illusion of having control. Control structures can become a very complex system that sustain your emotional, energetic and physical barriers to truth and strengthen your avenues of indifference.

Barriers to truth maintain your separation from your awareness of your soul. Barriers are part of the energetic structural web of the vortex of your soul's unconsciousness, and are sustained by using major collectives of energy that result from opposing truth. The major collectives are:

- Resistance, denial, avoidance and codependency
- Judgement, manipulation, confusion and control
- Images, illusions and controlled identities
- Controlled evolution
- Heresy

Barriers are deceptive control structures formed from your layers of triggered emotional reactions, which you use to prevent your awareness of the flow of truth within you, and to inhibit your ability to recognise and learn from the truth of your reality.

The energetic mass energy of mankind is the energetic structure of our collective unconsciousness, which is the unconsciousness of *True Source Divine Origin Consciousness*. It is the energetic storehouse for mankind's varieties and types of soul denial energy, which form energetic collectives out of the reverberation of unresolved emotions and form energetic barriers to truth out of control structures and belief systems. The energetic mass energy of mankind is the collective energy of all individual souls' unresolved emotions combining to create barriers that oppress the awareness of soul truth.

Framework of soul oppression is comprised of your various avenues of indifference, which are sequenced reactions and responses that you use to be and remain indifferent to truth. These avenues of indifference originate from the fears and embedded beliefs within your soul denial. Each avenue of indifference is a cyclic pattern of soul oppression that ascends from your soul denial to your heresy barrier, and descends back to your soul denial. The indifference energy is fueled by your soul control, which is your desire for control and your illusion of control. The avenues of indifference are:

- Soul abuse
- Soul betrayal
- Soul deception
- Soul defiance
- Soul demise
- Soul illusion
- Soul sabotage
- Soul traitor

You use these to construct a framework of how you oppress the truth of yourself.

Your Insight & Awareness Book

Core essences are unique strands of conscious energy that contribute to the purity of who you are. They are the unique strands of conscious energy within unconditional love. Core essences are natural energy that emanate from your soul's consciousness. The core essences explored in Insight and Awareness are:

- *Acceptance*
- *Appreciation*
- *Care*
- *Clarity*
- *Compassion*
- *Dynamism*
- *Freedom*
- *Grace*
- *Harmony*
- *Honesty*
- *Hope*
- *Independence*
- *Individuality*
- *Integrity*
- *Joy*
- *Kindness*
- *Loyalty*
- *Patience*
- *Peace*
- *Purity*
- *Serenity*
- *Trust*
- *Truthfulness*
- *Uniqueness*

These are explored in more depth within *Your Insight and Awareness Book*.

The framework of soul oppression and the core essences, although touched on within this book, are explored in more detail in future books.

Preface

The experience of learning to be truthfully honest is challenging and exciting. Trusting in the truth of yourself as a soul is the choice to be honest about the reality you are experiencing within yourself and within your present moment. Truthful honesty is the choice to align with truth. Honesty can be a recognition of truth, but that does not mean you will align with truth. Truthful honesty is unifying with truth.

We, as mankind, have struggled to be completely truthful with the truth of ourselves because we have not understood the true extent of our existence. We have limited our perception by defining ourselves by the year we were born, the family lineage and the era we are born into. The reality is, you are a soul who has experienced many lifetimes, all of which have brought you to this moment now.

Throughout the ages mankind has struggled with the reality of who we are and the significance of our freedom of choice (freewill). When you have a limited perception of yourself and life, you miss the potential that comes from trusting your soul's consciousness as your compass for navigating the resolution of the carried unresolved emotions from your soul history. Your soul's consciousness exposes you to the opportunity to use your honesty and your freewill to resolve what is inhibiting you from feeling your truth.

The choice to be truthfully honest with yourself is the only way that you can feel the truth of yourself as a soul. The significance of being truthfully honest with yourself is paramount; it is the essential element to the resolution of your unresolved emotions and enables the evolution of your soul.

To experience the information within this book, you have to allow yourself the space to be truthful. It is *Your Insight and Awareness Book* and you will experience this book uniquely because you are unique. Your 'I know' mentality will hamper you and your desire to control will dull down your awareness of your own feelings. Your resistance to and denial and avoidance of truth, as well as your codependency on your denial, will cause you to lie to yourself. This is all part of the journey and contributes to how you expose truth to yourself. *Your Insight and Awareness Book* is a map, a signpost and a compass, but your resolution and evolution will be unique to you. The words within this book are vessels that assists you in the discovery of truth, but it is your truthfulness and your willingness to explore the truth of yourself that will enable you to resolve and evolve.

To get the most out of *Your Insight and Awareness Book*, you will have to make a conscious choice to be truthful about how you feel about what you are reading and experiencing, and how it is impacting you. You will be your own teacher and pupil at the same time. You will have to consciously acknowledge your own resistance to and denial and avoidance of truth. You will have to consciously acknowledge your codependency on the lies you tell yourself, of which this book documents many examples.

If you have lost your awareness of the truth of who you are, the lies you tell yourself can become unrecognisable as lies. Lies defend and protect your unresolved emotions and therefore become the choice to remain unconscious to the reality of your own soul truth.

Your soul truth is the reality of both your conscious and unconscious energy. When you are unable to be truthfully honest with yourself, you may fall into the pitfalls of spiritual illusion and attempt to use the information to create an image of consciousness. This will only impede your ability to be truthfully honest with yourself.

The choice to be truthful is yours and yours alone; no-one can make you conscious, reading a book will not make you conscious. Being conscious is not an intellectual pursuit. Consciousness is being truthfully honest and trusting the truth within you, while you explore your individuality and the uniqueness of your present moment. This book exposes truth and explains energy, which your soul's consciousness will resonate with. Your recognition of resonating with truth will create opportunities, which expose you to the uniqueness of your soul journey.

The resolution of your unresolved emotions, cannot be experienced by being told how to fix your unresolved emotions or how to control them. If you adopt what you have been told and then attempt to control yourself to fix unresolved emotions, you are just experiencing the desire to perfect your control, while acknowledging what you want to control. Resolution of your unresolved emotions is born of the choice to explore what you can acknowledge is within you, to feel yourself resonate with truth and to investigate what you emotionally, energetically and physically react to. Accepting the independence of your freedom of choice allows you to explore truth. The exploration of truth is to choose to be absolutely honest with yourself, regardless of what you find. Acknowledging your unresolved emotions creates an opportunity for resolution and evolution.

You may be inclined to respond to your discovery of your unresolved emotions with harsh self-judgment, which exposes you to an opportunity to acknowledge your judgement as just judgement. It is also an opportunity to acknowledge judgement as another unresolved emotion, within you, that needs resolving.

When you attempt to control your unresolved emotions and attempt to create an image of consciousness, you are exposing yourself to your willingness to be deceptive with yourself. It is not an image you seek; you seek to resonate with the truth of who you are, which is a significant, unique, independent, individual soul of *True Source Divine Origin Consciousness*. You do not want to be an imitation of what you have read or to pretend to feel the way you believe you should if you were feeling your soul's consciousness; you seek to feel and unify with the truth of your soul's consciousness. To be the enactment of an image of consciousness is to be lost in an illusion of yourself. You seek to find the truth of who you are because you are a soul of truth.

To be deceptive with yourself is the choice to buy into a belief of being able to control yourself to an image of resolution and evolution. This would be the choice to attempt to control your evolution with deception, while you suppress the truth of your own unresolved emotions. Some of this may sound a bit confusing when you start; as you become more aware of the truth of who you are, it will naturally make more sense to you. We all try, at times, to control our unresolved emotions and that is an essential part of our exploration of truth, because it exposes the futility of our control, judgement and manipulation. We all attempt to alter the truth of our awareness of reality and seek to control ourselves to pacify our judgement of life and who we think we are, which exposes our desire to control truth.

Our judgement is an unconscious energy full of misconceptions, lies and betrayals. This is what you will explore within *Your Insight and Awareness Book*, which should enable you to discover the truth of who you are and the reality of how your own judgement has restricted your insight and awareness of truth.

Your willingness to challenge your beliefs of yourself and reality will expose your awareness of truth to you. However, if you find yourself defending and battling to protect some of your beliefs and emotions, ask yourself, why?

- What is it you are having trouble exploring?
- What do you fear will happen, if you discover you have misconceptions about yourself?
- Who do you believe you are?

These questions and other questions within *Your Insight and Awareness Book* can be confronting if you are trying to protect denial. However, if you are willing to explore truth and can trust what you resonate with, being confronted will be a welcome relief. Your misconceptions are created by your separation from your awareness of truth. Misconceptions become used to disregard the significance of the exploration of truth. This can leave you denying how limited your perception of yourself is. You do not know, what you do not know. It is your willingness to explore the truth of yourself, regardless of what you may find, that exposes the unique pathway of your own resolution and evolution.

We want to control the way we feel about ourselves and have created many unconscious methods of denying truth, in our attempts to secure our illusion of control. However, this is what we want resolution of. We are always trying to fix our control of ourselves while denying ourselves the opportunity to accept the truth of who we are. What if it is your control, that you came to resolve? Life is exposing you to what you came to resolve, you just have to be an objective observer to recognise what is being exposed.

You are an expression of all the different aspects of your soul, you just have to trust yourself to acknowledge the truth you feel, and then honestly explore truth. You are experiencing all your soul requires to explore the opportunity for your own resolution and evolution. Whenever you are trying to fix your unresolved emotions, you are actually exposing what you want resolution of. Your honesty and your trust in the uniqueness of your experiences will allow you to understand what you are exposing to yourself.

Your desire for control stifles your freedom to explore the truth of your own unresolved emotions, and the truth of your significance, uniqueness, independence and individuality as a soul. Resolution is the choice to be truthfully honest which at times is easier to say than do. However, your willingness to explore truth will allow you the freedom to experience your truthfulness exposing you to what you resonate with.

Your Insight and Awareness Book exposes the energetics of reality, which you may have always felt but did not understand. We all feel, read and interpret energy, however interpretations are often subjective and based on the desire to feel in control of the mysteries of life. You can become consumed with wanting to be right in your judgement of what you believe you know. This can cause you to mistrust your own awareness of energy. I began my exploration of myself and the truth of energy, realising I did not fully comprehend what

I was aware of, but I acknowledged what I felt and accepted my natural insight about energy as a launch pad for exploration. I trusted myself to acknowledge when I did not know, and I still have questions and am excited to find what tomorrow's questions might be. I value my curiosity as a gateway to my clarity. I, like you, am an evolving soul. I have trusted my natural awareness of energy and I feel truth like a trusted friend who unconditionally loves me; a friend I stand beside as life continues to expose what I still need to learn. *Your Insight and Awareness Book* resulted from my willingness to share what I discovered within myself and from the willingness of others who allowed me the privilege to explore their energy, as they discussed and shared with me their unique soul journeys. I am an evolving soul constantly exploring and learning from truth, and that is an ongoing and continuous process for all of us.

Your Insight and Awareness Book is a map that can only assist you and point you in a direction, exposing what you may or may not be conscious of. This book has been written with the intention of sharing with you, experiences I have encountered and others' experiences that they have been willing to expose to me, to help you feel your own truth. There is no one way to resolve and evolve for you are unique, and your journey is unique. *Your Insight and Awareness Book* is not intended to be a belief system you align yourself to, but an opportunity to explore what is written. If you keep swapping one belief system for another, you will be choosing to be devoid of the truth of yourself. Challenge everything you believe, and trust yourself to feel your feelings. Ask yourself if your belief systems protect your illusion of being able to control what truth is? Do your belief systems expose you to the truth of yourself? The reality is, it is not about always knowing the answers to the questions you ask yourself, sometimes it is about just having the willingness to explore, so you can find and feel what resonates with you as truth.

Resolution of your unresolved emotions and evolution of your soul occurs when curiosity meets clarity. This is the willingness to be truthfully honest with the entirety of your awareness of truth. The discovery of truth exposes you to the reality of your unresolved emotions, the significance of your feelings, your present moment and the uniqueness of each individual life. May *Your Insight and Awareness Book* be your assistant to clarity and create a safe harbour for you to anchor to, as you endeavour to discover the truth of your own uniqueness, independence and individuality.

Tips for reading
Your Insight and Awareness Book

In *Your Insight and Awareness Book* I am not asking you to create a belief system or to use the information within this book to reinforce an already established belief system. In truth I am asking you the opposite; I am asking you to explore everything. I am asking you to honestly feel what resonates with you. You may not understand why something is resonating with you, but let yourself be curious and explore how you feel. Acknowledge what creates an emotional, energetic or physical reaction within you and allow yourself the grace to explore how the information is affecting you. Reading this book will be a personal experience unique to you, because you are embarking on an exploration of the truth within you.

All the information within this book has been written to create the opportunity for your truthfulness to resolve your unresolved emotions, and has been written to encompass the reality of the energetic effect truth has on your denial of yourself. This information energetically tracks where you use your denial of reality to sidestep your awareness of truth and willingness to be honest. Your unresolved emotions and the consistency of the emotional, energetic and physical cycles of your soul oppression are repetitive and the information in this book is written to address the repetitiveness of the layers of your unresolved emotions. If you are attempting to sidestep your own awareness of what the information is exposing to you, you will align to your judgement of the repetitiveness of the information without acknowledging the layering of the information or the depths of your unresolved emotions.

This information has been written with the intention to address the entirety of all aspects of both your conscious and unconscious energy. This book has been written from an awareness of the energy of what is written, and with an awareness of the energetics you may experience as you read it. This means you will feel the reality of your energetic reaction to being exposed to what is written. Coming to terms with the energy you feel is an adventure. You may experience energy that at first confuses you, until you become honest about your awareness of feeling energy.

True Source Divine Origin Consciousness has been written in italics to denote and emphasise the significance of truth. The italics are a way of drawing your attention to the importance of your origin of truth. It is also a reminder that you are not alone on your soul journey. *True Source Divine Origin Consciousness* is present and can be felt in your truthfulness and your recognition of your soul. *True Source Divine Origin Consciousness* is repetitively written throughout the text, to anchor you to your foundation of truth and to create a response within your energetic system. Your energetic reactions and responses to seeing and reading the words *True Source Divine Origin Consciousness* reveals information to you; at times you may find the words calming and comforting, other times you may experience an adverse reaction to the words, potentially even becoming agitated and annoyed. This creates an opportunity for you to discover and explore your reaction to your origin of truth.

Allow yourself the time and space to consider that you do not know, what you do not know. Allow yourself the time to contemplate and observe your emotional reactions to the truth of your feelings about the concepts you are exploring within *Your Insight and Awareness Book*.

Your soul's consciousness works in unison with the information within this book and will seek to expose what you need to read within the uniqueness of your present moment, so allow yourself to be flexible. If you are drawn to a particular page, paragraph or sentence take notice of what it is, even if you do not understand it now, it may actually become very clear to you in the future.

If you are having trouble comprehending what you are reading and have read it several times with no improvement of comprehension, do not despair, you are exposing what you are unconsciously protecting with your denial. Trust yourself, mark the information and come back periodically to explore what you can discover as you allow yourself to feel the truth and the depth of your reaction to what is written. This is the process of exposing what is unconscious within you. When you read the information while being willing to be honest about your own reactions, you create the space to become consciously aware of what you had previously been unconscious about. When you become aware of your willingness to be honest, you may be surprised at how easily you can read the information that once confused you.

You can experiment by asking yourself what page is relevant to you. You may hear a number or flip the pages until you feel drawn to a page; trust what feels right to you. Scan the page with your eyes or ask yourself for a paragraph number, trust yourself to expose truth to yourself, as you uniquely discover the truth of your consciousness and unconsciousness. There are no rules because you are a unique soul and the discovery of truth is unique to each soul. There is no generic way of discovering the truth of who you are. However, your willingness to be honest is paramount to gain the best out of *Your Insight and Awareness Book*.

Each time you revisit a section you will discover different aspects of what is written, because your awareness changes. At times you may even wonder if you have previously read that section. Your awareness is changing and at times you may not realise how much your awareness has changed. By rereading a section it may expose the evolution of your awareness. Your soul's consciousness may draw you back to a section many times creating opportunities for you to explore deeper into the information with your ability to be more aware of yourself. As you explore the reality of your own awareness of truth, your perception, the way you feel, your intent and your insight into your own unresolved emotions changes. Your recognition of all these changes enables you to realise your evolution.

Your soul's consciousness may draw you back to a section many times, attempting to expose the true nature of your unresolved emotions. You may feel frustrated by the repetition of your unresolved emotions, but this is your soul's unconsciousness exposing the truth of your unconscious energy. There are many layers to your emotions and as you explore the truth of your unresolved emotions, the depths of them may surprise you. You may believe you have accomplished the resolution of an emotion, only to discover another layer of the emotion. This is all part of the process and as your awareness increases, so does your ability to truthfully explore the reality that is being exposed to you. Your own willingness to be honest with yourself about yourself, allows you to accept your own unique process of discovering the truth of your own soul's consciousness.

As you become more aware of your unresolved emotions, they become more evident to you; even the unresolved emotions of others become more evident, because you have become aware of the energy of unresolved emotions. Your judgement of your own and others' unresolved emotions can become a barrier to discovering what it is that is restraining your resolution of your own unresolved emotions. Give yourself and others compassion for the compulsive nature of our unresolved emotions.

Your awareness of the energy of unresolved emotions and of truth is similar to when you like a particular car and are surprised once you have noticed the car, how prevalent the car is in your day-to-day environment. You have acknowledged what you are aware of or interested in, which heightens your sensitivity to the energy you are aware of or are willing to observe and explore. For example, if you are expecting a baby, it is fascinating how many times you notice pregnant women or little babies. The same concept applies when you have read something within *Your Insight and Awareness Book*. You will be fascinated by how often you become aware of your unresolved emotions and experience what you are exploring within this book.

Your soul's consciousness works with the information in *Your Insight and Awareness Book* to heighten your awareness to the truth of the unresolved emotions within your soul's unconsciousness, and the presence of your soul's consciousness. You are a clever soul and will take yourself where you need to go to expose yourself to the truth of what you seek to resolve. Take your time and give yourself the grace to observe your own emotional, energetic and physical reaction to what you are reading. Allow yourself the grace to feel the truth of your opportunity to resolve. Your harsh self-judgement is only a hindrance to your opportunity to discover the truth of yourself.

The energy of your soul's unconsciousness reacts to the information within *Your Insight and Awareness Book*, which can incite many different emotional, energetic and physical reactions. Saying the '*Self* expose self' declaration, explained on page 53 helps you to clear the energy you feel and are reacting to. It assists to anchor you back to yourself and your present moment. The declaration will also help when you experience energetic reactions. Energetic reactions are involuntary movements of your own energy, produced by your emotions or recognition of energy. You may at first be unable to identify the emotion triggering the energetic reaction, but as you acknowledge the truth of your own reaction, you become more open to explore your emotions. Suppressed emotions and fear create energetic reactions, and some people are sensitive to the energy they feel or generate. These examples may help you recognise an energetic reaction.

Fazing out: If you are emotionally reacting to what you are reading, you may faze out, unable to comprehend what you have just read. You can become stuck repeating a line, feeling confused and vacant. You may reread something without at first recognising you have just read it. You may also experience feeling disassociated from yourself, a sense of surrealism. These are all energetic reactions that may stem from unconsciously attempting, to avoid being exposed to the information that reveals the truth of the energy of your soul's unconsciousness. They are also a signal to take notice of what you are reacting to. You may need to take a break and acknowledge what you are experiencing.

Overwhelmed: If you are emotionally reactive to what you are reading, you may lose all concept of time. You may experience feeling groggy and realise that you have lost consciousness for a while. You may find yourself waking up, feeling disorientated and confused. This is you unconsciously activating your defence mechanisms, seeking to shut down your soul consciousness' ability to expose you to the truth of your unresolved emotions. This can also be caused by your own fear of change and your own unwillingness to explore beyond what you believe you know. This reaction is a signal that you are discovering something that has a major effect on you and may be a pivotal point in your resolution and evolution. This reaction exposes the significance of exploring what you feel uncomfortable about. You may need to acknowledge the truth of your reaction to settle your energy, so you can consciously acknowledge what you have unconsciously orchestrated to resist, deny and avoid.

Agitated: If you are emotionally reactive or feel confronted by what you are reading, you may experience an involuntary agitation. You may be agitated because your illusion of control is being interfered with. However, it is good to remember that it is your illusion of control that your soul's consciousness seeks freedom from. Your agitation is revealing what you want to protect. This becomes an opportunity to learn from your own reactions. You may fear the discovery of truth will cause you to lose how you define yourself. You can use your emotions to fool yourself about the reality of who you naturally are, and default to agitation as a protective mechanism to sustain your denial and corrupted self-definition. You may need to take a short break and occupy yourself  with something else for a while to settle your energy, and the '*Self* expose self' declaration on page 53 may assist you with this. At times you may find it helpful to just read small amounts and give yourself time to digest what you have read and energetically reacted to.

Denial: If you are emotionally reacting to what you are reading, you may attempt to suppress your awareness of your emotional, energetic and physical reactions to the information. You will feel yourself make excuses for your reactions, permitting yourself to retreat from what is being exposed to you. Your opposition to feeling the truth of your reactions may cause you to become arrogant about your own ignorance. This may make you indifferent to the significance of your truthful honesty. Your emotional, energetic and physical reactions expose a lot to you and at times you may have no understanding as to why you are reacting the way you are. As you read more information and through your own life experiences, your willingness to be truthful creates the opportunities to discover the reasons why you are emotionally, energetically or physically reactive to the information. Your soul's consciousness is a brilliant educator and very dynamic in revealing truth to you. You may need to remind yourself to objectively observe the truth of your own energy.

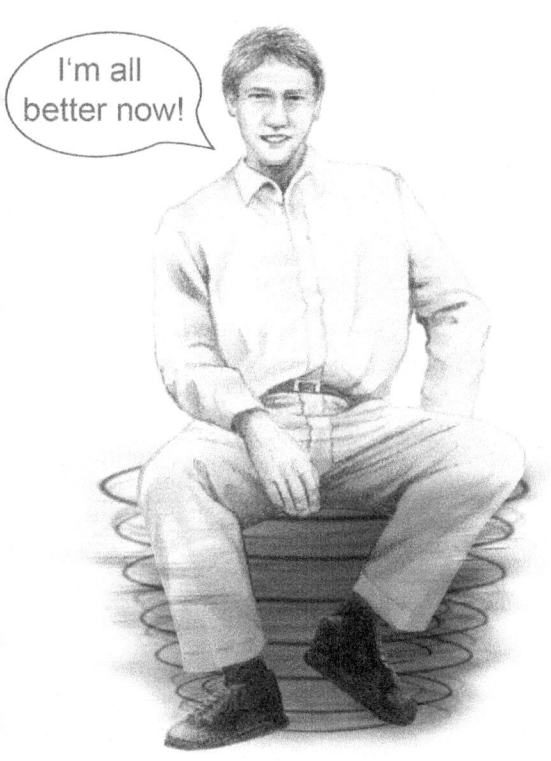

Avoiding: If you are emotionally reactive, you may ignore what you are feeling and become oppositional to the process of discovery, acknowledgement and resolution. Trust that you have encountered this book for a reason. Be honest about your avoidance as it reveals information to you. You have encountered this book because your soul's consciousness seeks to reveal information to you. This book is a map and your soul's consciousness is the tour guide of your soul journey. Be honest about what you are aware of and ask yourself why you want to avoid the exploration of yourself. This will reveal information to you, and creates an opportunity to explore how you feel about yourself.

Sometimes you internally know when you are ready to explore deeper into yourself, and there are times you may seek a rest from your own exploration.

Try not to engage with the information within *Your Insight and Awareness Book* with the belief you know it all. Be open to discover and explore new concepts and information. Your awareness of both your conscious and unconscious energy will expand as you allow yourself to explore the truth of your own feelings and unresolved emotions. Your willingness to explore the truth of all energy will allow you to spiral deeper into the layered energy of your soul's unconsciousness. You will also discover more about your consciousness as you become more honest about your emotional, energetic and physical reality.

Your truthful honesty will allow you to feel the truth of your own soul's consciousness and to explore the potential of freedom from your soul oppression. Your truthfulness is the key to your freedom. Acknowledge the questions you contemplate, observe how your interaction with *Your Insight and Awareness Book* is in sync with your own questions and observations of your emotional, energetic and physical reality. Trust how you feel and explore the exposure of your unresolved emotions with the freedom of knowing truth is dynamic and working with you. Your awareness of truth expands with your willingness to be truthfully honest about yourself. Your awareness of truth enables you to objectively observe yourself and your present moment. Your soul journey is a present moment to present moment experience.

Warrior who fights

I realise I'm a warrior of an internal war, battling the conflict within and waging war on myself. I thought I was fighting an external adversary. I now realise I was fighting myself and the experiences of life and people. I was devoted to the hostility of always being ready to arrogantly engage in whatever I believed at the time needed to be defended or controlled.

First I fought those around me, whom I believed were stealing my dignity, worth and value, but they were just expressing their own unresolved emotions, and I was energising my unresolved emotions to combat what I was confused about feeling. I thought I needed to fight to survive, but internally was losing more of the truth within and converting more to negativity, soul abuse and sabotage, becoming a weary warrior of an unexplained war.

I brandished my unresolved emotions as a weapon to reel around, to defend, justify and control what I should have acknowledged as soul opposition and oppression. It was my soul opposition and oppression which caused me the pain, hurt, rage and emotional unease within. I utilised all of my mankind weapons of resistance, denial, avoidance, codependency, control, judgement, confusion and manipulation to serve me, in order to get the better of any opponents, ignorant of the fact that I was the strongest adversary I had, creating more hardship for myself.

I chose to focus on the world of antagonistic opponents and became blinded to the battle within and the truth of my soul. I became what I despised. What I looked down on with contempt, I battled to become superior over, judging and resenting others for not seeing the value of my being, while ignoring my ability to care for and value my own soul.

I tried to get from others what I thought was lost; dignity, respect, worth and value. Then the penny dropped and I realised I couldn't take from others what I needed to experience within myself.

I can't get self respect, worth, value and dignity from others who have no real ability to give it to me. By choosing to continue existing as a warrior, I was allowing myself to harbour and harness the struggle of my opposition to truth. I tried to control recognition of my worth within mankind and accepted a destiny of deception and condemnation for being a unique, independent, individual soul of *True Source Divine Origin Consciousness*. I chose to exclude truth.

Releasing my soul from the weapons I use against myself can feel very vulnerable, for it is the weapons that shield me from acknowledging and accepting my own reality. I realised and accepted that the war is not really with other warriors, but with the reality of my own unresolved emotions and life.

The truth is, I was only battling truth, which was constraining and enslaving me to the complications of negativity, deceit, hardship and despair. I was captivated by the need to struggle and to stay loyal and devoted to the burden of the inner barriers of my opposition to resolving my soul oppression and negativity. The purpose of the war was to hold out and inhibit, even nullify my acceptance of myself for who I am, which is a significant, unique, independent, individual soul of *True Source Divine Origin Consciousness*. I was missing the true opportunity for resolution and evolution, fighting for freedom when all I had to do was acknowledge the part I was playing that had me eluding my truth.

I reacted with denial to my sorrow of not truly comprehending the compulsion to sabotage my soul. I wanted to control my choices so I could keep using my deception as a shield against truth. I became shocked at my own willingness to give away responsibility for my soul's consciousness and unconsciousness. I realised I was choosing to be subservient to my own desire for control, believing I had no choice and I told myself I was a victim to the power of anti-truth. I became stagnant because of my own rejection of freedom of choice. I felt tortured by the knowledge that the divine has given me complete freewill and a divine right to choose the destiny of my Earth experience. I can either accept truth and trust how I feel or abide by my perception of mankind's expectations and empower my unresolved emotions, which means I stay connected to my fear of truth. This causes me to choose to denounce and oppress my awareness of my soul truth, by resisting my freedom of choice.

I felt despair when I conceded to the truth that unconscious energy never readily accepts conscious truth, without conscious choice, which means I had to choose my path willingly. **The warrior within must accept the fight is over, and the prize is freedom of choice.** I had to choose to explore my soul truth. I realised that choice is a divine right. When I reject the value of my soul, I am only isolating myself from truth. Understanding freedom of choice gives me awareness of the truth of my soul's consciousness. When I acknowledge my truth, I can feel the unconditional love *True Source Divine Origin Consciousness* has for me. The ability to respond to life with grace and ease is within me. I have the freedom to choose to allow myself to accept truth and reality, without a fight.

Being responsible for my soul means being truthful with my awareness of my own ability to choose liberation, from the bondage and confinements of my unresolved emotions and my own deception. I acknowledged I could resolve my alliance with my own confusion, coercion and compulsion to repetitively obey my own negativity, harsh self-judgement, desire for control and my denouncement of freedom of choice.

As a *soul* I accept the reality of being able to choose freedom over negative known patterns. I choose to be willing to apply conscious effort to conscious living and accept the competency within to choose liberation from automatically reacting as an unconscious warrior, and instead be the truth of who I am. I acknowledge and understand the reality that I can't escape mankind's negativity or *True Source Divine Origin Consciousness'* unconditional love, but I can choose to be consciously aware of myself within both, which will enable me to feel the truth of my present moment.

The internal war you wage with yourself may not be seen by others, but is always felt by you.

Section One

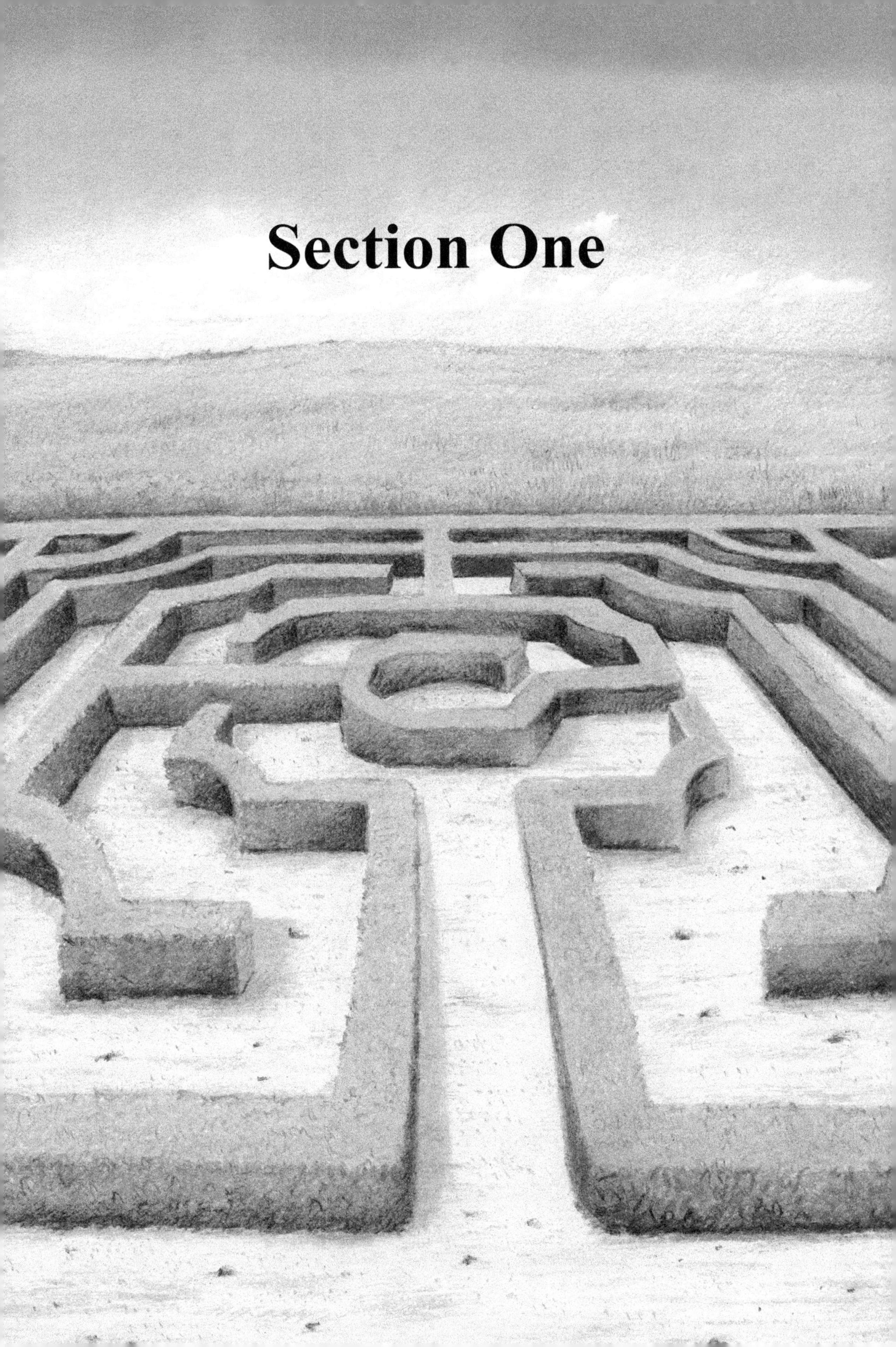

Chapter One

A metaphor describing your soul separation

Think of yourself as a computer,

you are the main original programme,

which is your soul's consciousness,

but you have viruses,

which are the unresolved emotions of your soul's unconsciousness.

You have forgotten about your original programme, functioning and defining yourself by your viruses.

You deny you have the ability to put the viruses in the rubbish bin and delete.

It is your viruses which cause you to be dishonest with yourself.

Your honesty brings you back to your awareness of truth.

Your honesty will allow you to scan for all viruses affecting your original programme.

Your willingness to expose your own viruses allows you to participate in your own resolution and evolution.

Questionnaire 1

Answer these questions off the top of your head. Do not dwell on questions, just move on and come back if you need to. There is no right or wrong answer, just how you feel. At the end of section 1 there is another questionnaire and you will be able to compare your answers, so I suggest to do this questionnaire and to not look at it again until after you have read section 1 and completed questionnaire 2.

Please note: *I recommend you use a separate journal in which to write your answers to the questionnaires, so you can use this questionnaire numerous times without being influenced by what you have written before.*

1. List three emotions that sum up how you feel about yourself.
   _____
   _____
   _____

2. List three emotions that sum up how you feel about your life.
   _____
   _____
   _____

3. What do you know and understand about the cause of these emotions?
   _____
   _____
   _____

4. How do you define yourself as an individual?
   _____
   _____
   _____

5. What inhibits you from being honest with yourself about your emotions?
   _____
   _____
   _____

6. Name three people who have influenced the way you feel about yourself (Negative or Positive).
   _____
   _____
   _____

7. What do you know about your desire for control?

_____
_____
_____
_____

8. Are you living the life you want or envisage for yourself?

_____
_____
_____
_____

9. What would you like to change?

_____
_____
_____
_____

Choose one word from the negative beliefs list on page 65 and insert the word into question 10. Trust yourself to choose whatever word stands out to you, or if you feel yourself attempting to avoid a word, that would be your word.

10. What does _____ mean to you?

_____
_____
_____
_____
_____

Choose one word from the soul oppressive addictions list on page 78 and insert the word into question 11. Trust yourself to choose whatever word stands out to you, or if you feel yourself attempting to avoid a word, that would be your word.

11. What does _____ mean to you?

_____
_____
_____
_____

True Source Divine Origin Consciousness

Your Soul's Consciousness

This is the energetic structure of your soul system. The energetic vortex of your soul's unconsciousness is layered with different barriers to truth. This is what you filter your awareness through.

Desire to control, indifference to truth, resentment of reality, oppositional energy, programming, conditioning and indoctrinations, guilt, shame, humiliation, denial of reality, Disassociation from feeling love.

Heresy

Controlled evolution - desire to control your soul denial with beliefs.

Images, illusions and controlled identities.

Judgement, manipulation, confusion and control.

Resistance, denial, avoidance and co-dependency.

Soul Denial

Your soul's consciousness

You are your soul. You may have separated from your awareness of your soul, but that does not diminish the fact that you are a soul. Your soul's unconsciousness is the immature part of your soul, which inhibits you from feeling the truth of your consciousness. Your non-acceptance, of yourself and truth, creates unresolved emotions that fuels your unconsciousness. Your soul's consciousness is unified with *True Source Divine Origin Consciousness*. It is the part of you that always accepts and acknowledges the truth of what is internally and externally occurring. Your soul's consciousness is the mature part of your soul, which has never separated from truth.

Your soul's consciousness, in conjunction with your truthfulness enables you to resolve the energy of your soul's unconsciousness. This is how you evolve to be at peace with the truth of being a significant, unique, independent, individual soul of *True Source Divine Origin Consciousness*. Your soul's consciousness is your natural essence, it is the core of your being. Your soul's consciousness is a constant stream of truth energy, unified with and originating from *True Source Divine Origin Consciousness*. Your consciousness flows into your unconsciousness, exposing the reality of your separation from your awareness of your soul and your disassociation from feeling truth.

Your soul's consciousness actively attempts to expose that you have never been abandoned by truth. *True Source Divine Origin Consciousness*' compassion and unconditional love for your soul has no boundaries; your soul's consciousness is of this energy. Your soul's consciousness is eternal, this lifetime is not. You are a soul who has experienced many lifetimes, which are opportunities to explore the significance of being conscious of your own soul truth. You are a soul, living within a physical body, experiencing life within the arena of freewill. Mankind has two options, either to be of conscious or unconscious energy, which we determine with our freewill. Unfortunately, our collective denial of the importance of our souls, causes us to lose awareness of the truth of our soul's consciousness. We, as a collective of mankind, have become unconscious to the truth of ourselves and ignore the reality of what we create. When you abandon your awareness of truth, you participate within the unconsciousness of mankind. You trade your awareness of your soul's consciousness for soul denial. Life is an opportunity to freely return to your origin, consciously understanding the value, worth and significance of the truth of being a soul.

Your death is a soul experience of withdrawing from your physical body and the life you have created in this lifetime. Your soul returns to your origin and the energies of your soul's unconsciousness anchor to the energetic mass energy of mankind. When you reincarnate for another life, the energy that you created is returned to you. Your resistance to and denial and avoidance of resolution, evolution and truth has you anchored to the most fundamental pattern of your stagnation. This is to reincarnate into life but abandon the intention of life. Your soul's consciousness never abandons the intention of life, which is to resolve

You are an eternal soul, who has experienced many previous lives all of which have contributed to the truth of who you are today.

what anchors you to your own soul denial, and to experience the true essence of your soul while living on Earth. Your soul denial is the foundation of your soul's unconsciousness.

Your soul's consciousness is always attempting to unify the fracturing within your soul. When you fight unification, you are denying the significance of your soul journey. This leaves you perpetuating your soul denial and reinvesting in the very emotions that you came to resolve. Your soul's consciousness is present within all your life experiences and exposes you to what needs to be resolved. Resolution creates evolution of your soul, which is maturing as a soul.

- You separate from your awareness of your soul's consciousness, but your soul's consciousness never separates from you.
- You disassociate from feeling your own individual resonance with truth, but truth never disassociates from feeling you.

Your soul's consciousness comes with the intention of dealing with the reality of your soul denial, which is the crux of the oppression you feel. Your soul's consciousness is innately truthful, and acknowledges your fear of the truth of yourself that has you warring within yourself. Rejecting the significance of being a soul, leaves you feeling the pain created from being a fractured soul. Your soul's consciousness never runs from the truth of your experiences and trusts that all experiences of life are opportunities to feel truth and to resolve the war you wage against yourself.

Your soul's consciousness communicates through feelings; acknowledging your feelings, is to acknowledge yourself as a soul. Your soul's consciousness understands life as part of your soul journey. Your soul journey is far greater than your memory and each life is a fresh start; a new canvas, and you are your own creator. Life is a learning process. You have an opportunity to resolve your unresolved emotions, which inhibit you from feeling the truth of your soul's consciousness. Your soul's consciousness has the ability to convert all of your unresolved emotions to conscious understanding of truth. This is the potential, possibility and probability your soul seeks to experience this lifetime.

- Have you forgotten your soul's consciousness is the core of your being, which constantly resonates with truth?
- Have you forgotten your origin of truth?

Your soul's consciousness seeks evolution, to be unified with truth and to resolve the energy of your soul's unconsciousness. Your soul's consciousness seeks to expose you to the opportunity to live consciously aware of your resonance with truth. Your soul's consciousness, unfortunately, is the part of yourself that you separate your awareness from. Your separation from your awareness of being a soul often feels like an inexplicable void, which then allows your unresolved emotions to be the primary force in your life.

Your soul's consciousness is felt when you allow yourself to resonate with truth, and are present in your reality.

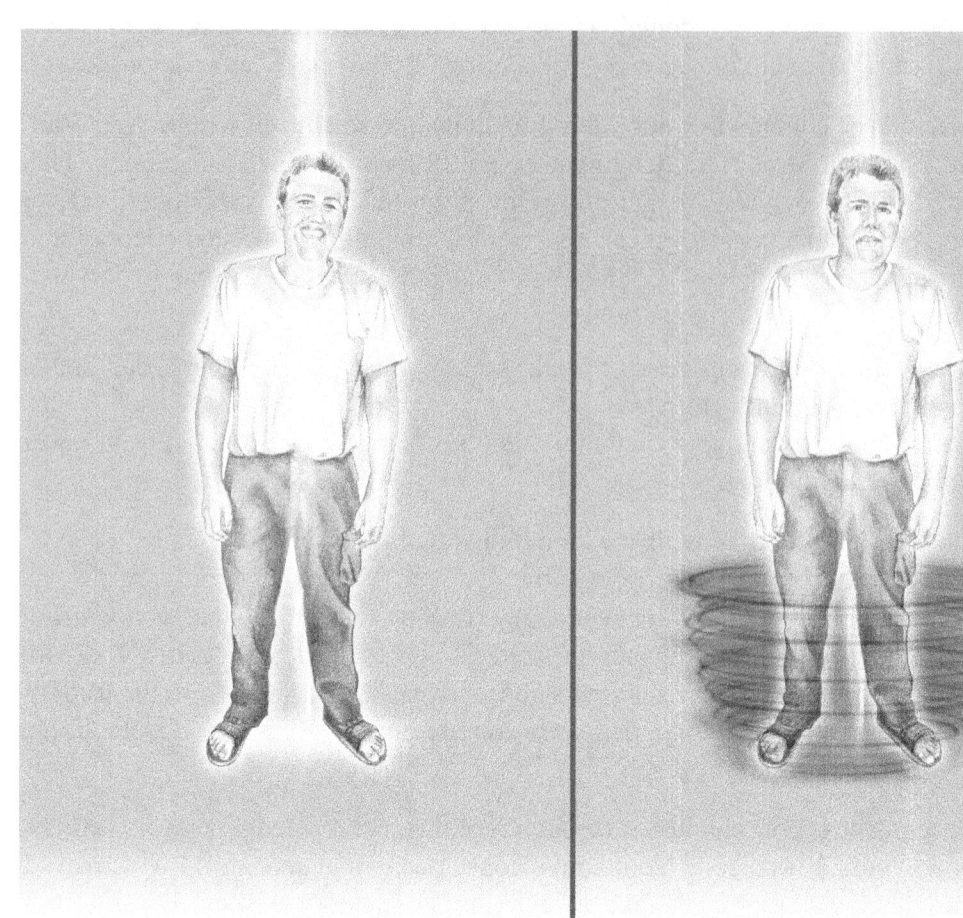

Your soul's consciousness flowing freely.

You activate the energy of your soul's unconsciousness as you become reactive to life with your unresolved emotions.

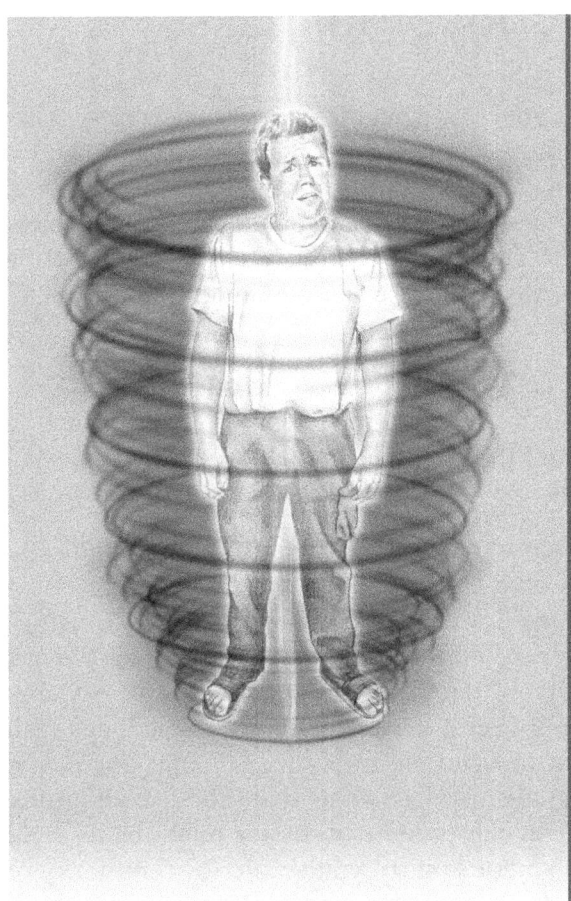 

Once you become entangled and engaged in the activation of your unresolved emotions and unwillingness to be honest, you lose awareness of your conscious energy. Your soul's consciousness is still flowing, you have just lost your awareness of your soul's presence. You have become emotionally reactive to life, yourself, others, relationships and truth with the unconscious energy of your soul, believing you can control the energy and deluding yourself with your own dishonesty.

Your dishonesty with yourself has you emotionally swamped with the unconscious energy produced from your unresolved emotions. This causes you to be immersed in the energy of your soul's unconsciousness, often emotionally feeling engulfed by your own despair.

The vortex of your soul's unconsciousness generates a tsunami of emotions, which can overwhelm you.

Your soul's unconsciousness

Your soul's unconsciousness is created by your soul denial. Your soul's unconsciousness is the energetic storehouse of your unresolved emotions, control structures, beliefs, fears, framework of soul oppression and barriers to truth, which are the ways you produce unconscious energy. You are the interface between both your soul's consciousness and unconsciousness, and have the freedom to choose the energy you utilise. Life is the opportunity for evolution and you decide whether you take the opportunity to evolve or choose to remain stagnant.

The accumulation of unresolved emotions leaves you unconscious to the reality of your soul truth. Your emotions represent your desire to control truth or your non-acceptance of reality. Your emotions are the by-product of your inability to acknowledge, accept and deal with the reality of your feelings and life events.

Your inability to accept your feelings and reality, triggers you to recreate the familiarity of your soul oppression. Soul oppression is actively opposing your own awareness of your soul's consciousness or truth. Your opposition converts your feelings to emotions that become stored and carried, because you refused to be truthful with yourself. When you reject the opportunity to be truthful and avoid resolving the emotions you carry, you begin to worship the illusion of control. This incites a desire for control, which can lead you to suppress your awareness of your emotions and the truth of your soul. The desire for control causes you to operate from fears, judgement or wants that inhibit your ability to be truthfully present in life as it unfolds. You can become obsessive about being right in your appraisal of yourself, life and others, so you control yourself to the familiarity of your emotions. This creates cyclic patterns of soul oppression. If you believe you have proven yourself right, you believe your control works, reinforcing the belief that control is essential for your survival. Unfortunately, you can control yourself to ignore the reality of what you do to your soul, which leaves you perpetuating the energy of your soul's unconsciousness.

You may believe your emotions are justifiable and controllable; controllable in the sense that they are familiar to you and feed your expectations. You can compulsively seek to validate your own expectations, by repetitively acting out your unresolved emotions, while clinging to your illusion of control. You can become automatically oppositional to feeling truth and unconscious to the reality of what is controlling you, which is your desire for control or your protection of your denial.

When you believe your unresolved emotions define you, and ignore the consciousness of your soul, you create images of yourself to conceal what you refuse to acknowledge. To avoid the truth of what is stored and carried within your soul's unconsciousness, you go to great lengths to separate from your awareness of yourself. Life is an opportunity to unravel what you have created with your denial of reality and soul denial.

You can become consumed with generating emotional turmoil, often denying you are the creator of your emotions. Emotional turmoil can be created from a thought, belief, fear or your non-acceptance of reality. You can deny how your emotions make you feel, overriding your

awareness with ricocheting emotions. This generates indifference, which comes in many forms that inhibits you from acknowledging the truth of your emotions. When you control yourself to override the opportunity to acknowledge what is being exposed, you are choosing to remain indifferent to yourself as a soul. You may use your judgement to defend and justify your automatic inclination to try and deny the truth of your soul's unconsciousness. However, it is you who is missing the opportunity to resolve what burdens your soul.

Truth can still be felt even when you separate from your awareness of your soul. The question is, what do you choose to do with your ability to feel truth? When you separate from your awareness of your soul, it becomes difficult to acknowledge that it is you who has chosen to become unconscious to the reality of yourself. However, as you take responsibility for yourself, it becomes easier to identify the reality of your emotions.

True Source Divine Origin Consciousness

Your soul's consciousness communicates through feelings, actively accepting and acknowledging the truth of reality.

Your soul's unconsciousness selectively fights the reality of being a soul by projecting your unresolved emotional energy at others and the reality you are experiencing.

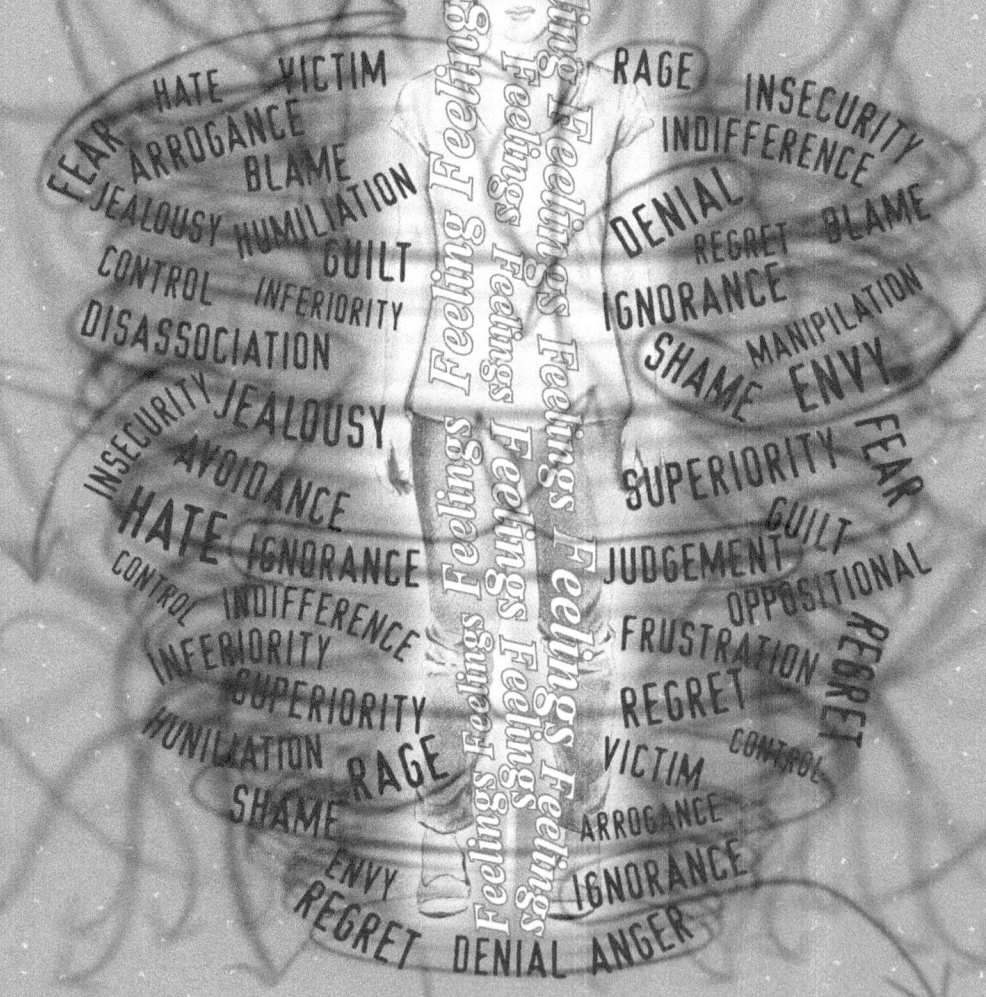

Your fight to control the suppression of your own emotions, also separates you from your awareness of your soul, which causes you to wallow in your unresolved emotions. You store what you refuse to be honest about. The energy of your soul's unconsciousness is the collective energy of your unresolved emotions. It is an amassment of your opposition to truth. This becomes your artillery against yourself, life, others and truth, which if left unresolved is carried from lifetime to lifetime

This lifetime is an opportunity to resolve what is unresolved. Life provides you with the opportunity to resolve and evolve, because you will be generating and projecting your own unresolved emotions at yourself, life, others and truth. If you are truthful, you will be able to acknowledge your own reality and resolve your encumbered emotions. If you are dishonest, you will continue perpetuating the energies of your soul's unconsciousness. You create your own emotional burden, by denying yourself the freedom to choose to be truthfully honest. You have never been without your freedom of choice. What have you been choosing?

Your freedom to choose is yours and yours alone; you have to make decisions to be conscious of your truth and the opportunities within your soul journey. Being truthful with yourself is a choice, not a belief system. Truth resonates with your soul. To be consciously aware of your soul is to experience feeling, acknowledging and accepting truth. Truth has no control structures for you to anchor your unresolved emotions to. Truth is dynamic and gracefully flows through all that exists. You have the freedom to acknowledge the significance of truth within all situations you experience. You have the freedom to acknowledge that you originate from truth.

You use your unresolved emotions to validate your negative beliefs and addiction to opposing your awareness of your soul's consciousness. You can be oblivious to the cause of your unresolved emotions, but you need to be truthful about their existence if you want to resolve and evolve. By not challenging yourself about your emotions, beliefs and behavioural patterns, you are choosing to continue the stagnation of resisting, denying and avoiding the truth of being a soul on a journey to resolve and evolve.

When you use your unresolved emotions to define an image of yourself, you are unconscious to the significance of being a soul. Your desire to control truth is how you manipulate yourself to deny the reality of being a soul; this creates constant confusion within you. Your soul's consciousness would class images of yourself and unresolved emotions as soul-distortions and falsities. You can use these distortions to construct belief systems around the falsities and create illusionary lifestyles to match. These often become very soul deceptive by nature and separate you from the potential to resolve and evolve your unresolved emotions.

Your unresolved emotions are your portion of the energetics of the mass energy of mankind, which is our collective unconsciousness. Unconsciously perpetuating your unresolved emotions makes you a willing participant in the perpetuation of mankind's insanity of trying to control truth, while denying the reality of being a soul. When you try to control yourself to conform to your version of mankind wants, you begin to desire being able to control without complications. The fundamental complication is, you are perpetuating the energetics of the mass energy of mankind, but you are not just mankind energy. You are a soul who was born with the intention of resolving your portion of the energetics of the mass energy of mankind,

True Source Divine Origin Consciousness

Consciousness

Heresy
Desire to control, indifference to truth, resentment of reality, oppositional energy, programming, conditioning and indoctrinations, guilt, shame, humiliation, denial of reality, Disassociation from feeling love.

Controlled evolution - desire to control your soul denial with beliefs.

Images, illusions and controlled identities.

Judgement, manipulation, confusion and control.

Resistance, denial, avoidance and co-dependency.

Soul Denial

which is your soul's unconsciousness. You fight your origin of truth to conform to your insanity of denying you are a soul who has both conscious and unconscious energy.

Your attempt to conform to mankind or your own soul's unconsciousness has you overly concerned with how others perceive you and so creates the 'what about me' syndrome. You become overly concerned with how and what is going to affect your image of yourself. Your 'what about me' syndrome has you judging yourself, life, others and truth via your insecurities, which are caused by your inability to pacify your control. Your 'what about me' syndrome exposes how consumed you are with your illusion of control and your image of yourself.

- How much time do you spend analysing how your control is affecting reality, or how reality is affecting your ability to control?

Your images, illusions and controlled identities are the result of you using your illusion of control, to control your perception of reality, not actual reality. You may attempt to control others, believing this proves you are in control of life and truth. However, you may become what you despise in others. You may even believe that you are in control of how others perceive you, while ignoring the authenticity of your soul.

You can use your resistance to and denial and avoidance of truth, to be codependent on your unresolved emotions, such as resentment, control, judgement, confusion and manipulation. This can leave you unconsciously becoming the embodiment of your unresolved emotions. Instead of acknowledging an opportunity to observe what needs resolving, you justify and excuse your unresolved emotions to yourself. You can condition yourself to deny truth with your own justification of your unresolved emotions. These justifications are an expression of your aversion to being truthfully honest about your own emotional, energetic and physical reality.

If you do not resolve your unresolved emotions, you become them. For example: If you are angry about your childhood, instead of dealing with yourself and your feelings, you become an angry person, projecting your hurt and anger at yourself, life, others and truth. You control yourself to become what you despise. Your refusal to be honest with yourself has you denying yourself the opportunity to resolve and evolve your unresolved emotions.

You use the energy of your soul's unconsciousness to be emotionally reactive to your feelings, emotions, life, others and truth. You can be unaware of how exposed your unresolved emotions are to others, believing you have concealed them within your image of yourself. You become unconscious of how your desire to control has concretised your unresolved emotions, because you want to protect your image of yourself.

If you think about something that enraged you a year ago and can bring back those emotions and re-live them, as if it happened yesterday, it means your emotions are unresolved. When the emotions have been dealt with and resolved, those events are just memories of the past and memories of past emotions. (You do not relive them.)

When you deny the reality of your soul's unconsciousness, you will condition yourself to fear, and fight what is unfamiliar to you. While separated from your awareness of your soul; your soul's consciousness, truth and your origin become unfamiliar to you. You have conditioned yourself to fight the reality of yourself; this is insane.

Chapter Two

Resistance, denial, avoidance and codependency

Resistance, denial, avoidance and codependency are emotional, energetic and physical barriers to truth. Resistance, denial, avoidance and codependency are the fundamental energies that all of mankind applies to life and mankind's understanding of being a soul. You need to observe, acknowledge and accept the reality of your own resistance to and denial and avoidance of truth, which will enable you to observe your codependency on your separation from your awareness of your soul and your disassociation from feeling truth.

Acknowledge as much truth as you can within your present moment, with the realisation that you may be unconscious to the entirety of the truth you are experiencing. Being honest about your soul's unconsciousness enables you to accept truth as a dynamic energy. As you become more honest with yourself, you will expose more truth to yourself. Understanding truth is a process of learning what you do not know, not seeking to validate what you think truth should be. When you analyse reality trying to establish a version of truth that suits your control, you are accommodating your codependency on your own resistance to, and denial and avoidance of truth. Your deceptive judgement of truth is an anchor you use, to validate your own resistance to and denial and avoidance of truth. You devalue your own awareness of truth with your encumbered beliefs, unresolved emotions and desire to control. Your resistance to and denial and avoidance of truth oppresses your ability to be honest with yourself. Your codependency on your resistance, denial and avoidance has you dictating what you believe truth should be, which stagnates you in your own belief systems, and has you devoid of feeling the truth of your soul and the truth of your reality.

Your resistance to, and denial and avoidance of truth sustains your codependency on your inability to be honest with yourself and truth. Honesty is the application of truth and is opposite to your resistance, denial, avoidance and codependency. Honesty requires conscious effort, because you are constantly competing with your own resistance to and denial and avoidance of truth, as well as your codependency on your unresolved emotions. When you justify your unresolved emotions, you are fighting what truth is exposing to you about your belief systems, unresolved emotions and illusions of control.

Your resistance to and denial and avoidance of truth sustains your codependency. This causes you to manipulate yourself to believe the misconception, that life is easier if you resist, deny and avoid feeling truth, and the truth of being a soul with the intention to resolve and evolve. How would you know if this is true, if you have never allowed yourself to experience being honest with yourself, reality and truth? You can associate truth with the times you could not deny your reality and had no control over your reality. This leaves you associating truth with your loss of control, which causes you to inappropriately fear truth.

You have conditioned yourself to filter your life experiences through your resistance, denial, avoidance and codependencies, which has you missing the mark of your life experiences, to justify your own soul denial. Missing the mark means to resist, deny and avoid the opportunities for resolution and evolution within your soul journey.

You programme, condition and indoctrinate yourself to be oblivious to your own soul truth and unconscious to the potential within your own reality. Your denial of your avoidance has you resisting any truth that takes you out of your perceived comfort zone created from your resistance, denial, avoidance and codependencies. Your perceived comfort zone is the result of how you fool yourself to believe truth is irrelevant and that your contrived beliefs can pacify your disillusionment with yourself, life and truth.

Your codependency on your resistance, denial and avoidance has programmed, conditioned and indoctrinated you to justify your own ignorance and arrogance towards truth. Truth is felt; truth resonates with your soul's consciousness and does not need your justification to prove the value and worth of truth. Truth is naturally significant in all that exists. If you experience the truth within your life experiences and the truth within yourself, no outside validation is necessary. It is a lovely experience to be validated but independently feeling the natural significance of the truth of your soul is immeasurable. You resist, deny and avoid your own internal knowing to remain justified in your denial of truth, which actually opposes your unification with truth. When you freely resonate with truth, there is an undeniable resonance between your soul and truth.

You may not be able to explain or justify your soul knowing, but when you feel your own resonance with truth, it is easy to trust truth. Your resonance with truth is you exposing yourself to your origins, which is truth. You are remembering there is more to your soul journey than your unresolved emotions and your battle to resist, deny and avoid truth. There is more to life than your codependency on your separation from your awareness of your soul and your disassociation from feeling truth. When you are in the energy of your resistance, denial, avoidance and codependency, you abandon your ability to trust truth. You use your resistance, denial and avoidance to control yourself, to abandon the possibility of experiencing your soul freely resonating with truth. You may experience feeling truth for only the briefest moment but this is you feeling, and you will feel the reality of your awareness of truth.

The questions to ask are:

- How well does your resistance, denial, avoidance and codependency really work for you?
- How do you resist, deny and avoid truth?
- What are the results of your own ignorance and arrogance towards truth?
- How does your resistance, denial, avoidance and codependency really make you feel about yourself?
- What are you hiding from, so you can ignore your reality?
- Why do you want to resist, deny and avoid acknowledging yourself as a soul?
- Do you want to answer these questions truthfully?

If the answer is no, you are conscious of experiencing your own resistance to and denial and avoidance of truth as well as your codependency on your fear of truth.

Reality is the combination of all energy within life. Reality is like a river, it has its own flow. When you resist, deny and avoid truth, you insert your unconscious energy into the river attempting to divert your attention from truth. You may create bridges to avoid acknowledging the flow of the river, attempt to dam the waters of the river or codependently cling to your merry-go-round of soul oppression oblivious to the truth of the river. You may even deny the existence of the river, attempting to alter the flow of the river with your desire to control. What are you doing to the river?

Your Insight & Awareness Book | 49

Being objective about your emotions and your life patterns is very hard to do and yet totally essential to resolve the cause and effect of your emotions. It is only when you allow yourself to be totally honest and truthful that you can begin to understand yourself in truth. Your truthful honesty aligns you to your natural soul insights, which enables you to realise, develop and evolve a relationship with the truth of being a soul. Your soul's consciousness is of truth and is the core of your being. Your denial of this truth has caused you to create subjective emotions, judgements, negative beliefs and deceptions, which allow the continuation of your resistance to and denial and avoidance of your own soul truth. This inhibits you from realising the opportunity life presents and causes you to dumb down the truth of your soul.

When you attempt to deal with your unresolved emotions with more emotions, you perpetuate a soul oppressive cycle and never fully resolve your emotions. True resolution is difficult at times but always doable. When you are consumed with your unresolved emotions, you cannot acknowledge the significance of your soul's consciousness, which causes you to miss the opportunity of consciously living in truth.

Your soul denial will always be exposed to you because truth is always there; you just resist, deny and avoid the reality of truth. You use your resistance to and denial and avoidance of truth as support for your suppression and repression of truth, so you can oppress your awareness of your soul's consciousness and arrogantly ignore the truth being exposed to you. Truth will always expose denial. The result of not resolving your resistance, denial, avoidance and codependency energies is to be in opposition to your soul's consciousness; stagnant in your soul's unconsciousness.

Resistance

Resistance is where you might have some understanding of what you are doing to yourself but choose to ignore the truth of your reality.

Your resistance has you struggling, fighting and battling the acceptance of your own soul's consciousness, and the unresolved emotions of your soul's unconsciousness.

Your resistance to life

Denial

Your denial has you completely rejecting and refusing to acknowledge the truth of your reality.

Your denial means you reject truth and deny the reality that you are denying truth.

Your denial creates distractions you use to protect yourself from acknowledging and accepting truth.

You use your denial to sacrifice your awareness of your soul's consciousness for an illusion of control.

You use your denial to lie and become consumed with justifying the lie, in order to avoid acknowledging the truth of your reality.

Avoidance

Your avoidance enables you to use anyone and anything to be oblivious to truth.

You overly involve yourself with other's lives, to justify avoiding your own reality and truth.

Your avoidance enables you to externalise your unresolved emotions, so you can divert your attention and ignore your own reality.

Your avoidance means you invalidate truth and justify your own deception while attacking truth.

Your avoidance of truth creates fear; your fear of the unknown holds you in the stagnation of your soul's unconsciousness.

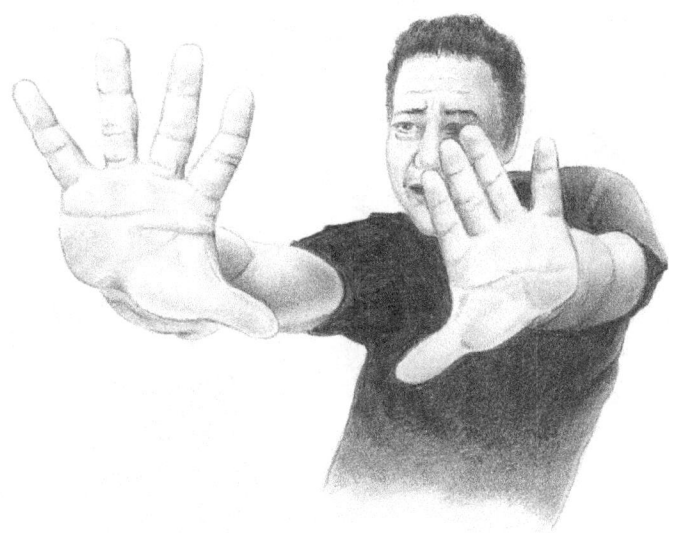

Your avoidance of truth

Codependency

You are codependent on your own and others' resistance to and denial and avoidance of truth, to oppose the truth of what you are feeling or doing to your soul.

Your codependency has you reliant on anything that you can use to oppose your own soul truth.

CHAPTER THREE

Declaration to be of truth

"*Self* expose self, RDAC, S and D, DVP, rebalance to origin truth."

This declaration is a bridge to your awareness of your soul's consciousness, which may make the process of aligning to truth easier. The declaration assists in clearing the emotional and energetic debris of your unconsciousness. It does not resolve the energy; you can only achieve resolution when you are truthful. However, it does assist your ability to be honest. When you choose to say the declaration, you are highlighting to yourself your intention to acknowledge truth and the presence of your soul's consciousness. When you choose to say the declaration to yourself, you are exposing your willingness to be of truth and your intention to explore the truth of your own emotional, energetic and physical reality. Your willingness to be honest with yourself enables you to align to truth. You have conditioned yourself with your aversion to truth, to be in opposition to the presence of your soul's consciousness. The declaration is a way of reminding yourself that you are a soul with the intention to resolve and evolve. Resolving and evolving is a choice; this declaration is an expression of your choice.

When the declaration is used as a control structure to avoid responsibility for your unresolved emotions, you tarnish your own intention to be honest and the effectiveness of the declaration will be undermined. However, your soul's consciousness provides grace for your naivety in relation to your control structures. Your soul's consciousness will endeavour to expose you to the truth of your control structures, because they are part of your soul's unconsciousness. The declaration assists you to be honest about your own deception. Your honesty alters your alliance with the energy you have been generating from your unresolved emotions and shifts your allegiance back to your origin truth. You are bridging your awareness to your ability to trust truth and to be honest with truth. If you are aware of your intent when using the declaration, you will align to your soul's consciousness, enabling truth to expose you to the truth that you need to acknowledge to resolve and evolve.

Your soul's consciousness supplies the energy of truth; your choice to be honest sustains the space for you to explore truth. Your soul's consciousness cannot be fooled; if your intention is to control energy with this declaration, you will be attempting to alter reality for the purpose of emotionally feeling in control, while you ignore the truth of yourself reacting to reality. This declaration is not meant to alter reality, but to expose you to the truth of reality, enabling you to objectively observe yourself. You have the freedom to deceptively believe your own lies; however your lies cannot corrupt your soul's consciousness. Your soul's consciousness responds to the truth of all energy.

By saying the declaration to yourself, you are acknowledging the intent of your soul's consciousness, which is to be honest with yourself. You are asking yourself to be present in your reality and own the truth of what you are experiencing within yourself. When your desire to control is overriding your willingness to be honest, you inhibit the effectiveness of the declaration.

You do not have to say the declaration aloud; you can internally say the declaration to allow yourself to anchor to your awareness of your present moment. You use the declaration to calm your emotions and anchor to your awareness, creating the space to observe the truth of your emotional, energetic and physical reaction to your present moment. You use the declaration when you:

- Feel, insecure, anxious, scared, overwhelmed or unsure
- Are seeking the truth of your own feelings and emotions
- Seek clarity to quieten your mind chatter

You are not being asked to believe in the declaration; it is there for you to explore and experiment with. While you explore and experiment with the declaration, be mindful of your honesty, your intent, your expectations and your desire to control reality. The effectiveness of the declaration is determined by your willingness to explore the truth of both your consciousness and unconsciousness. Your soul's consciousness is naturally exposing truth to you and the declaration is a temporary tool to assist you to become honest about the exploration of your ability to trust your awareness of what is being exposed. The declaration is temporary because your honesty will evolve beyond the need to use the declaration. The declaration exposes you to the deception you use to overshadow your own natural awareness of truth.

"*Self* expose self, RDAC, S and D, DVP, rebalance to origin truth."

Self You are acknowledging you are a soul and asking your soul's consciousness to push conscious energy into any barriers or aversions to truth that you have.

Expose You are asking your soul's consciousness to expose truth to you. You are asking for assistance to expose the truth of your unresolved emotions and how they are affecting you. You are asking for assistance to expose how you are controlling yourself to fight your awareness of truth and reality. You are asking for assistance to expose the truth of your soul's consciousness and unconsciousness, and the truth of your feelings and unresolved emotions.

self This is a way to describe the unconsciousness of your soul, which is the combination of your unresolved emotions, barriers to truth, framework of soul oppression, desire to control and your soul denial. Your soul's consciousness seeks to expose the deception of your opposition to your soul truth, so you can resolve your own stagnation and feel the truth of yourself as a soul.

RDAC You are asking your soul's consciousness to expose your **R**esistance, **D**enial, **A**voidance and **C**odependency energies, which are barriers to truth. By honestly observing, acknowledging and accepting your **RDAC** energy, you create the space to acknowledge truth, develop your awareness of your soul, resolve unresolved emotions and evolve to unify with truth.

S and D You are asking your soul's consciousness to bridge your **S**eparation from your awareness of your soul, which you have created with your unresolved emotions, and to expose your **D**isassociation from feeling truth.

D Disconnect, **D**isengage and **D**isentangle your soul's consciousness from being bombarded by your own unconscious energy, any external source or any mankind energy, that is affecting your awareness of the presence of your soul's consciousness.

V Vice **V**ersa is attempting to deal with your and others' projection of unconscious energy. Your soul's consciousness acknowledges each soul's individuality; you honour their space by not projecting your energy into their energetic system. This part of the declaration is the acknowledgement that you have a choice and can withdraw your unconscious projection of energy from another's system, and that you have the ability to reject another's unconscious projections into your system. You also seek to be able to hold the uniqueness of your space, without the interference of others' emotional projections.

V within the declaration is often overridden by your desire for control, so be aware of what you are emotionally feeling. Are they your emotions or are they being projected at you? If the emotions are from another, how are they affecting you? What are they triggering within you and why are you hanging on to them? These are the questions that will expose how you deny your individuality, by using another's emotional energy to oppress your awareness of your soul truth. Be mindful of how you use others' projections of unconscious energy to feed your own willingness and ability to oppress yourself. Be mindful of projecting unconscious energy into another's energy system and the intention behind your energetic intrusion. If you are willing to be dishonest with unconscious energy you will override the effectiveness of the declaration.

P If you trusted your soul's consciousness and accepted your truth and reality, what would your **P**otential, **P**ossibilities and **P**robabilities be? How would you utilise your freedom of choice? **P** within the declaration is a representation of the significance of your freedom of choice. It is a choice to seek your true potential. Truth exposes your true potential as a soul. The declaration is the choice to acknowledge you want to become aware of what you are unconscious of. You have the freedom to explore the possibilities within your alignment with truth or continue your enactment of your unresolved emotions. Your alignment to truth or the enactment of your unresolved emotions is always your choice. You have the freedom to determine the path of your soul journey. You have the freedom to align to the potential, possibilities and probabilities of your soul truth.

There is often an energetic undercurrent to our interactions with each other when we are willing to judge each other and our unique experiences. What we say may be different to what we energetically project. Due to the energetic entanglement, both the receiver and projector of unconscious energy can emotionally, energetically and physically feel drained because of their loss of energetic independence.

By saying the declaration you are choosing to align to truth and acknowledge the significance of being a soul seeking truth. You are choosing to align to your origin truth and shifting your loyalty back to the truth of your soul and *True Source Divine Origin Consciousness*.

The declaration is a tool to assist you until you can sustain your own awareness of truth. It is a bridge which supports you until you can support yourself with your own honesty, grace and unconditional love.

When you forget you have the declaration as a tool to assist you, you are experiencing your disassociation from truth and how easily you can become unconscious of your ability to be honest with yourself about your emotional, energetic and physical reality. You often forget about the declaration:

- When you are swamped by your own unresolved emotions and separated from your awareness of truth.
- When you believe you are in control of life, yourself, others and reality.
- When you believe you do not need to be honest about your emotional, energetic and physical reality.

This is how unconscious energy works and your soul oppressive patterns are cyclic, so you will bring yourself back to the point of wanting the assistance of the declaration.

Your emotional, energetic and physical experiences expose you to the truth of your own soul's consciousness and unconsciousness. The resolution and evolution of your soul is a process you will experience throughout the course of your life. The declaration is not a tool you can use to control yourself to be just conscious energy; it is a tool to expose you to your awareness of the truth of both conscious and unconscious energy within your soul.

Let yourself acknowledge the truth and what you are emotionally, energetically and physically reacting to when reading and exploring *Your Insight and Awareness Book*. Give yourself permission to accept you are endeavouring to expose yourself to the truth of your soul's unconsciousness and to evolve to feel the truth of your soul's consciousness. The declaration is there to assist you as you expose yourself to the encyclopaedia of who you are. The declaration supports you while you are unconscious of your own truth. However, as you discover, observe, accept and understand aspects of your conscious and unconscious energy, the declaration returns responsibility for your awareness to you.

For example: Think of yourself as a set of encyclopaedias. As you understand the first volume, you become responsible for what is within the first volume and the declaration supports what you are unaware of from volume two onwards. As you understand the second volume, you become responsible for what is within the first two volumes and the declaration supports what you are unaware of, from volume three onwards.

At times you may feel completely overwhelmed by your own unresolved emotions and may require yourself to anchor to the truth of what the intention of the '*Self* expose self' declaration is. Allow yourself to become aware of what you are saying and why you are saying the '*Self* expose self' declaration. Acknowledge that you are seeking the energy of your soul's consciousness to expose the truth of your soul's unconsciousness and that you do not want to resist, deny or avoid the truth of yourself. Acknowledge your own codependency on the familiarity of your unresolved emotions and the ease to which you dismiss the importance of your own honesty with yourself. Acknowledge your separation from your awareness of your soul and your disassociation from feeling truth, and explore the reality of your own feelings. Acknowledge the energy affecting your awareness of truth and accept there is more to you than what you have already surmised and believed. You may assist yourself to do this by reading the details of the '*Self* expose self' declaration.

Being responsible is to choose to honestly observe the truth of your own emotional, energetic and physical reactions to yourself, life, others, relationships and your awareness of truth. Being responsible is to choose to use your freedom of choice to participate in your own resolution and evolution.

Chapter Four

Suppression

You reject your own reality by suppressing the truth of your feelings. By suppressing your feelings you create unconscious energy, which you inflict on yourself and others. This stagnates your ability to resolve your unresolved emotions. Feelings are in the present moment. If you acknowledge the truth of your feelings and choose to be honest about the reality of your feelings, your feelings will be your experience of your present moment. When you deny your feelings and suppress your awareness of the truth of your feelings, your denial of reality creates unconscious energy you carry and store within your soul's unconsciousness. Being present enables you to acknowledge your soul's insight into your reality and gives you the ability to choose an honest approach to what is occurring within your present moment. Acknowledging your feelings is to feel your soul truth and the presence of *True Source Divine Origin Consciousness*. Feelings you ignore become the unresolved emotions you carry beyond your present moment.

Your emotions are the feelings that you want to ignore, resist, deny and avoid, so you suppress them, adding more emotions to your soul's unconsciousness. Your suppression of your feelings is the choice to continue perpetuating your own soul oppression. By acknowledging your feelings, you are acknowledging your soul consciousness' ability to communicate truth to you. Feelings are communications from your soul, which are exposing your reaction to your awareness of truth.

If you acknowledged the truth of your feelings, it would allow you to live your truth and not exist within the turmoil of your unresolved emotions. Being honest about your feelings would enable you to live with the awareness of being a significant, unique, independent, individual soul. When you choose to exist on the merry-go-round of your unresolved emotions perpetuating your ingrained emotional habits, you create the same emotional experiences with just a changing of the date.

You fight your own awareness to suppress the emotions you refuse to acknowledge. This creates an energetic force that you are constantly trying to control. You are constantly trying to control your own denial of your emotions. You cannot control truth to disappear and you cannot control your soul's consciousness to abandon you, and both are creating opportunities for you to be exposed to the truth of your unresolved emotions. You fight the natural flow of truth and your soul consciousness' ability to resolve and evolve, by attempting to suppress your awareness of your emotions.

Your denial has you oblivious to the reality of what your unresolved emotions are doing to your awareness of your soul's consciousness. Your denial can be so prolific that you cannot observe that you use your emotions to control yourself to oppose your awareness of your soul's consciousness and truth. You can control yourself to exist fighting the reality of

Suppression of your unresolved emotions is how you attempt to put a band-aid on your own active volcano; eventually the volcano of your unresolved emotions will erupt.

your unresolved emotions, believing your suppression is going to help you hide from the truth of them. At the same time, you are constantly projecting your unresolved emotions into your present moment and exposing your unresolved emotions to yourself, others and life. You deny that it is your choice to continue the perpetuation of your unresolved emotions and pretend your emotions are happening to you. You want to relieve yourself of the responsibility of resolving your unresolved emotions, by suppressing your awareness of your unresolved emotions. You deny you are responsible for your emotions and lie to yourself, so you can camouflage your own betrayal of yourself and your opportunity to resolve and evolve. You suppress your ability to feel because you want to avoid the responsibility of feeling, exploring and knowing your truth. Suppression is the choice to oppose the potential, possibilities and probabilities your honesty can expose.

When you use your soul denial to give your emotions free rein to rule your existence, your existence becomes a battle to sustain your suppression of your emotional energy. Your continual suppression of your feelings and emotions causes blockages within your energetic system and creates anxiety, which is the exposure of your inability to get your control to work. Your denial of your soul leaves you disillusioned with the reality of your soul journey, and complacent about the 'dis-ease' within your system.

- Feelings register as a free flowing frequency.
- Emotions register as vibrations energetically idling.

Your suppression causes you to exist on your merry-go-round of unresolved emotions.

Chapter Five

Negative beliefs

Your negative beliefs are control structures that incarcerate you in your unresolved emotions. Your negative beliefs incarcerate you in your soul denial, causing you to doubt the significance of your soul journey. You create barriers of oppressive energy with your negative beliefs, which cause you to distrust the reality of being a soul. Your negative beliefs oppose and attack the very essence of your soul, and you demoralise your awareness of being a significant, unique, independent, individual soul of *True Source Divine Origin Consciousness*.

You cloak your negative beliefs with the energy of resistance, denial, avoidance and codependency which can make them hard to identify. You control yourself with your negative beliefs to oppose your soul's consciousness, allowing yourself to exist supporting your own soul oppression.

Your negative beliefs have infiltrated your understanding of yourself, life, others and truth. You indoctrinate yourself with your mind chatter, which is generated by your unresolved emotions, to oppose your natural significance. Your mind chatter is a flag alerting you to how overwhelming your unresolved emotions are. You confuse yourself with your unresolved emotions and manipulate yourself to believe your unresolved emotions are valid judgements about who you are, creating false definitions of yourself. You have anchored yourself to your unresolved emotions and obsess with trying to perfect your control of your emotional turmoil.

Your mind chatter results from you attempting to convert your awareness of everything and everyone into an opportunity to be oppositional to yourself and reality. You have programmed, conditioned and indoctrinated yourself to want to believe your own negativity, to justify your own soul oppression. You need to observe the truth of your soul oppression to recognise, understand and resolve your willingness to devalue your significance as a soul. Being observant without automatically judging yourself will enable you to understand yourself as a soul and nurture your ability to care.

Here are some examples to encourage you to be honest with yourself, about what you are feeling and acting out towards your own soul's consciousness.

You compete against your soul worth

You avoid truth by clinging to and applying the belief that you are insignificant. You judge yourself by the words or actions of others, which is 'externalisation'. You hang on to your past, by clinging to your unresolved emotions and you dictate your future with your unresolved emotions. You allow yourself to become stagnant in your own 'couldn't be bothered' mentality, trying to hide from the reality of being a soul. You become indifferent to yourself as a soul and fight your reality with your unresolved emotions.

You compete against your soul acceptance

You encourage yourself to be in a constant battle with your own mind chatter. You belittle the significance of your soul with your self-loathing, self-criticisms and self-hatred. You ignore your potential to discover and appreciate your own abilities, known and unknown, within your soul truth. You deny the responsibility of resolving your own opposition to yourself as a soul, and look for ways to prove your negative beliefs are right and justifiable, by downgrading your truth and reveling in your own disappointment of yourself.

Your negative beliefs are control structures that incarcerate you in your unresolved emotions.

You compete against your soul integrity

You ignore the truth of your own behaviour towards your soul and disrespect the significance of your soul, to remain in opposition to your awareness of your soul truth. You devalue yourself with your negative beliefs and you accept this behaviour while denying responsibility for the way you feel. You allow others to treat you poorly and then justify why they should. You continually set yourself up to relive your emotions and pretend you have no option for resolving your unresolved emotions.

You compete against your soul love

You place a lot of conditions and judgement on what love is. You control yourself to a position of self-punishment, self-loathing, guilt, shame, humiliation and embarrassment, if your version of love is denied. You control yourself to analyse, judge, scale, compare and categorise your beliefs of what love is without trusting yourself to feel the essence of unconditional love. You seek perfection as a means of belittling yourself for not being able to perfect your control of everything, including love. You allow yourself to be indifferent towards the truth of your soul and the unconditional love you can feel within truth.

You compete against your soul independence

You need someone or something to validate your existence because you are denying the significance of your soul. You want others to make you feel emotionally safe and approved of while remaining steadfast in your soul denial. Contrarily, you deny that you want outside validation, approval and acceptance of your images, illusions and controlled identities. You rely on others to justify your emotional behaviour and your reactions to life. You blame life for your avoidance of your own soul truth and soul journey. You deny the choices you make and seek to blame others for your despair. You allow yourself to be manipulated by others, if you believe their manipulation will protect your illusion of control. You codependently live through others, seeking validation for the images you have or want for yourself.

You compete against your soul trust

You allow yourself to use your desire for control to debate what you feel, to justify overriding what you instinctively know to be true and choose to distrust your ability to feel truth. You deny the reality you are experiencing and superimpose an illusion over your awareness of truth, to separate yourself from the reality that you cannot control truth. You fear the unknown, trying to control life to your own limited understanding. You project an image of yourself at yourself and live with self-imposed limitations, without challenge. You blame obsessively, to distract yourself from the truth that you cannot control everything and everyone. You avoid your reality by blaming others, life, your history, society or governments for the way you feel about yourself. You reject truth and deceptively justify why and how things are happening.

Self-exercise 1

Choose one word from the negative beliefs lists and insert the word into the questions. Trust yourself to choose whatever word stands out to you or if you feel yourself attempting to avoid a word that would be your word.

1. Define your beliefs in relation to_____.
   What does this mean to you?

2. Acknowledge what you are feeling and thinking about in relation to_____.

3. What do you understand about the cause of your emotions in relation to_____?

4. How do you apply _____ to your life? Or not apply _____ to your life?

5. How does_____ affect your soul?

6. How do you resist, deny and avoid acknowledging the ramifications of _____?

Negative Beliefs Lists

You can add self or soul in front of or at the end of different words to add a different dimension to the word.

For example: Self worth, Self respect, Rejection of self, Resentful of self, Soul love, Soul commitment, Realisation of your soul, Avoidance of your soul.

1	2	3	4	5
1 Worth	1 Body image	1 Uniqueness	1 Realisation	1 Anxiety
2 Love	2 Blame	2 Independence	2 Unconditional love	2 Worthlessness
3 Respect	3 Separation	3 Individuality	3 Freedom	3 Fighting
4 Image	4 Defeat	4 Being a soul	4 Honesty	4 Illusions
5 Acceptance	5 Shame	5 Spirituality	5 Passion	5 Resentment
6 Care	6 Disgrace	6 Consciousness	6 Affection	6 Oppression
7 Nurturing	7 Loathing	7 Indifference	7 Neglect	7 Defiance
8 Belief	8 Hate	8 Suffering	8 Rejection	8 Selfishness
9 Devotion	9 Criticism	9 Being seen	9 Denial	9 Boredom
10 Commitment	10 Punishment	10 Courage	10 Resistance	10 _____
11 Appreciation	11 Fear	11 Truth	11 Avoidance	11 _____
12 Confidence	12 Righteousness	12 Forgiveness	12 Co-dependence	12 _____
13 Identity	13 Sacrifice	13 Awareness	13 Enmeshment	13 _____
14 Protection	14 Empowerment	14 Transitioning	14 Limits	14 _____
15 Esteem	15 Obstruction	15 Reliance	15 Health	15 _____
16 Value	16 Disappointments	16 Flexibility	16 Intimacy	16 _____
17 Intrusion	17 Degradation	17 Joy	17 Sexuality	17 _____
18 Trust	18 Survival	18 Abundance	18 Wounds	18 _____

Chapter Six

Your addiction to oppressing your awareness of your soul's consciousness

Addiction describes how you hand yourself over to your own soul oppression, and defect from the truth of who you naturally are. Addiction is the way you diligently immerse yourself in your unresolved emotions, whilst believing you are escaping them. You seek to be immersed in what will support your addiction, and will gravitate to what or who enables you to disregard the oppression you create with your addiction. Defection describes your separation from your awareness of your soul and disassociation from feeling truth. Unfortunately, you defect to the point of being neglectful and abusive toward your soul and truth. This leaves you defending your addiction at the expense of your soul. Addictions leave you fighting against reality, which means you become reluctant to challenge your compulsions.

You can become addicted to your images of yourself, and illusions about the way you are living life, which have you fighting the reality of life being a soul experience, and an opportunity to resolve and evolve. You transfer your original intention of resolving and evolving, to the fundamental mankind addiction of desiring control over your awareness of your soul's consciousness and truth.

Within your addiction to your soul oppression, you forget the truth of your soul and assimilate to the unconscious energy you are experiencing. What you try to escape, eventually becomes exacerbated by your denial of reality. Addiction, regardless of what to, sustains your unresolved emotions and leaves you in an emotionally fuelled environment. You adopt and ascribe to your images and illusions associated to your addictions, becoming blinded to the truth of your soul and the opportunities life presents. You also use images and illusions to hide from the reality of your addiction. Your addiction to your illusion of control has no boundaries, because you use your desire for control to be indifferent to the truth of your soul, and to ignore your reality. The keystone to overcoming all addictions is to understand the pervasiveness of your desire to control and how devoted you are to giving yourself over to the compulsion you feel. This leaves you attempting to hide from yourself, instead of acknowledging the reality you are actually experiencing. Life is your teacher. How can you learn to understand yourself, if you deny the reality you are feeling?

You can be addicted to your unresolved emotions and the emotional havoc you create within your soul oppression. Your emotional habits, behaviours and patterns are control structures, which you use to emotionally create your soul oppression. When you have become addicted to utilising your unconscious energy, you oppress your awareness of your soul's consciousness.

You can be addicted to the compulsion to validate that you are right in your judgement of yourself, life, others and truth, while you ignore your own reality. You can also become consumed with power plays, fighting reality and obsessed with proving that your perceived righteousness is valid and indisputable. Who are you trying to prove your righteousness to, while you deny what you feel and the truth of what you are doing? Your soul's consciousness is always seeking to expose any oppressive behaviour, beliefs or denials, which can create an internal conflict, especially when you refuse to acknowledge your addiction to oppressing your soul.

You camouflage the truth of your unresolved emotions, emotional habits, behaviours and patterns with your judgement. You use your judgement to justify all of the compulsive addictions that sustain your opposition to yourself. You use your judgement to assassinate any truth that conflicts with your illusion of control. Your judgement becomes your addiction, cocooning you within an illusion of yourself. This is how you inhibit yourself from acknowledging the reality of being a soul in denial. Your addiction to your judgement has you abusing your soul's consciousness, because you resent your soul's consciousness endeavouring to expose what needs resolving and you fight your own opportunity for resolution.

When you choose to abandon your awareness of *True Source Divine Origin Consciousness'* support for the truth of your soul journey, you behave in ways that protect your denial and sustain your oppression. This leaves you concealing your resistance to and denial and avoidance of truth, by convincing yourself that your unresolved emotions, habits, patterns and behaviours define who you are. This is a misconception because your unresolved emotions, habits, patterns and behaviours conceal the truth of your soul and are generated by your desire to oppress your awareness of truth.

You can become addicted to your unresolved emotions and your illusion of control, which creates an internal chaos. You battle against your awareness of the truth of yourself and exist within the familiarity of your emotional whirlpool. You compulsively recreate your emotional whirlpool to justify your own inability to trust truth.

You normalise the familiarity of your stagnation and secure the continuation of your soul oppression by recreating what is emotionally familiar to you. Familiar is how your addictions emotionally feel; they have become your normal. You will defend your stagnation to protect the unresolved emotions that sustain the emotional habits and behavioural patterns which are detrimental to you. When you seek to protect your emotional habits and behavioural patterns, you interject your soul oppressive energy into every experience you have. You scaffold your unresolved emotions to support your addiction to the familiarity of your soul oppression.

You nullify the truth of your soul experience by protecting and preserving your addiction to soul oppression. Every emotional, energetic and physical addiction you have is based in your soul denial and willingness to oppress your awareness of truth. You justify and protect your addiction to your soul oppression, without even acknowledging the reality of your own stagnation. Stagnation is the result of your addiction to your compulsion to remain in a repetitive loop. You use your addictions to create a self-definition, while constantly trying to conceal the reality of how addicted you are to that which oppresses your awareness of your soul.

You use your unresolved emotions to create addictions, that then become the arenas in which you exert your unresolved emotions. You become addicted to, and define yourself by, the definitions you derive from your addiction. This becomes an image you portray to yourself. For example, you can become addicted to a victim mentality and conditioned to portray the image of being a victim. You allow yourself to miss the opportunity to resolve what is being exposed to you, because you refuse to liberate yourself from the image created by your unresolved emotions, which is how you fuel the victim mentality. You believe the image of being a victim justifies your inability to be honest with yourself about your own orchestrated soul oppression. You deny your soul consciousness' intention of resolving and evolving this lifetime, so you can project an emotional image that actually makes you feel miserable. This is the insanity of feeding your addiction with a mentality or an image, whilst believing you are sustaining an illusion of control.

You resist, deny and avoid the reality of how you allow your addictions to control the way you experience life. You allow yourself to become codependent on the familiarity of validating the images you have created from your unresolved emotions. You justify your soul oppression with these emotional images. Your images are smoke screens which conceal your addiction to your unresolved emotions.

- Can you identify your emotional images?
- Do you want to know what your images are concealing?

When you deny your own soul abuse and battle against your awareness of your soul's consciousness and truth, you become a participant in the oppression of your soul.

Self-exercise 2

1. Identify any emotional, energetic or physical addictions you have.
2. How do your addictions make you feel?
3. How do your addictions affect the way you live?
4. Why do you defend your emotional, energetic or physical addictions?
5. Describe how you filter every experience you have through the familiarity of your soul oppression?

Here are examples to encourage you to be honest about the images you have created for yourself with your unresolved emotions.

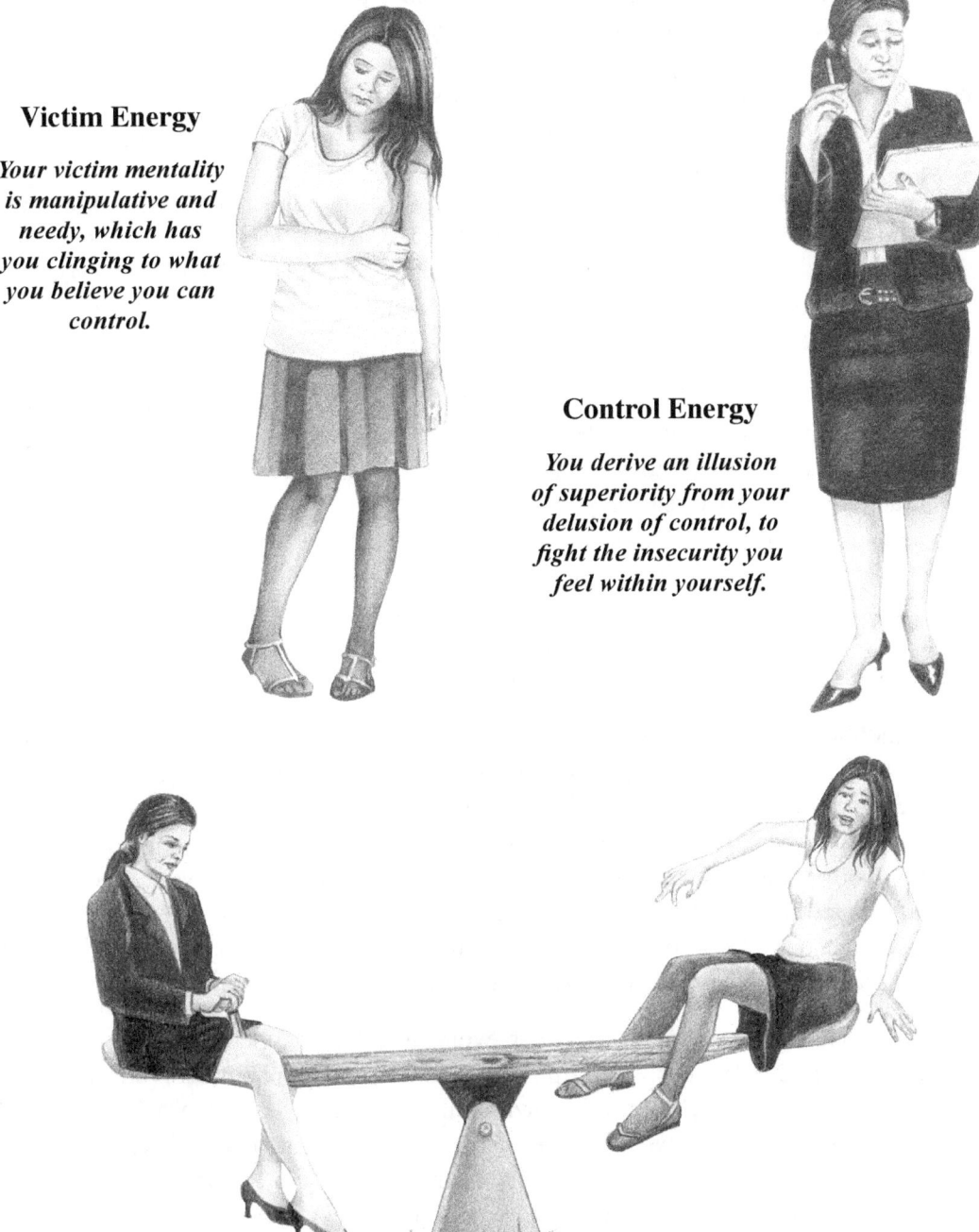

Victim Energy

Your victim mentality is manipulative and needy, which has you clinging to what you believe you can control.

Control Energy

You derive an illusion of superiority from your delusion of control, to fight the insecurity you feel within yourself.

Your desire for control and victim mentality cause you to see-saw within your judgement of whether you are a victim or in control. When you believe life is working to your advantage, you align to your control energy, however when life does not align to your expectation of control, you perceive yourself as a victim to life.

Victim mentality

Being a victim can define an experience but cannot be used to define the entirety of who you are. When you stay entrapped in the wounds of your experiences you are defining yourself with victim mentality. You use various victim mentalities to oppress your freedom of choice and to deny yourself the possibility of resolving and evolving your unresolved emotions. Your unresolved emotions are not who you are, but what you need to resolve. When you cannot get your control to work or others to respond the way you expect, you will automatically feel like a victim. Victim energy runs parallel to your control energy, which has you automatically appraising your ability to control yourself, life, others and truth. If you are unsuccessful in your attempt to control, you emotionally identify yourself as a victim. You will use the image of being a victim in an attempt to control any resistance to your expectations and desire to be in control.

Your victim mentality is manipulative and needy, which has you clinging to what you believe you can control or using what you can identify as out of your control as an excuse to attempt to incite others to take responsibility for fulfilling your needs and expectations. This can cause you to adhere to any justification you use to protect your own victim mentality, which often has you using manipulation to control others to perceive you as a victim. You seek out others who will pacify your desire to control something; the something you crave to control could be another's attention, their perception of you or your situation. You use your victim mentality to repel truth in the same way that your desire for control does; believing truth is an interference to your image of yourself and your illusion of control.

Your victim mentality can cause you to intensify your fear of being out of control, at the same time as seeking and expecting disappointment, knowing others cannot sustain your emotional demands, judgement or your insatiable appetite for control. You use others' inability to sustain your demands to prove you are a victim. Your victim energy has you codependent on others to feed your emotions; you expect this will pacify your insecurities, but it actually exacerbates your fears, because you become fearful of not being able to control the person and the situation to feed what you believe will create security within you. You expect degradation because you can feel the erosion of your own awareness of truth.

You battle truth and seek to blame others for everything that happens to you. You want to resist, deny and avoid any responsibility for yourself and your unresolved emotions. When you choose to be a victim of your own soul oppression, you manipulate yourself to emotionally believe that you have no choice or ability to be honest with yourself. You accept your soul oppression and prepare to permanently wallow in the unconsciousness of your soul. You deny how vulnerable you feel when you cannot get your control to work. You emotionally feel vulnerable because you realise your control is futile, but you refuse to align to truth and trust your soul's consciousness. You choose to be of your soul oppression by denying the truth within. You resist, deny and avoid accepting you are a soul and that you have the ability to resolve your opposition to truth and reality. You oppress your uniqueness, independence and individuality by being a victim to your own distorted image of yourself or by perceiving yourself as a victim.

Martyr

You revel in self-pity and the 'poor me' mentality, constantly putting yourself last on your priority list and wallow in your own neglect and despair. You set yourself up to continue in your soul oppression and wear your oppression like a badge of honour. You choose to sacrifice your truth for others' validation of your soul oppression. You expect your sacrifices will not be appreciated or acknowledged by those you want validation from. You covertly want your sacrifices to be ignored, so you can torture yourself with your own desire for validation. You blindly cling to your beliefs, regardless of how they make you feel and override any truth exposed. You stagnate your soul journey with the belief that you deserve to suffer in life and no-one cares enough to notice. You resist, deny and avoid your freedom of choice, preferring instead to be codependent on struggling to survive your own soul oppression.

Servant

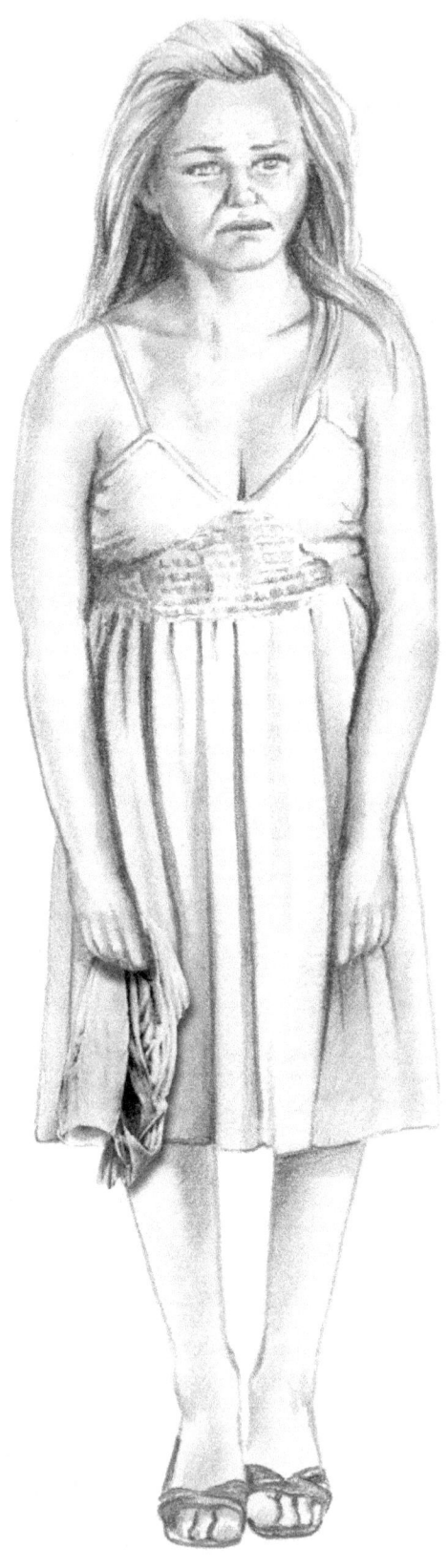

You assess yourself by how you perceive others are judging you. You try to preempt possible judgement and seek to counteract the opportunity to be judged, by being accommodating of others' demands. You define your worth by your ability to serve others but you constantly anticipate being exposed as worthless. You exist humiliating yourself with your own condemning self-judgement. You resent yourself for not being perfect and beyond the fear of judgement. You control yourself to impress others, but the validation you seek is compromised by your own self-judgement. You seek validation for an image of yourself whilst you sabotage your sense of worth. This causes you to wallow in the fear of being unable to sustain the image you want to portray to conceal your low self-esteem.

You implode within your judgement of your own performance of the image you want to portray. You have a perception of yourself being less important than others and believe being of service to others is your only way of gaining a sense of value for yourself. This causes you to struggle with your own freedom of choice, which leaves you struggling to decide how you feel about yourself and what you will agree to. You assess your value by what you do and by who benefits from what you do, but you deny how you feel about yourself. You often feel used and abused by others without acknowledging how you set yourself up for this outcome. You resist, deny and avoid accepting that you are a significant, unique, independent, individual soul.

RIGHT: *Your addiction to your servant mentality causes you to be enslaved to and by your indifference to the natural value, worth and significance of who you are. This enables you to use your soul denial to create the misconception that you are less important than others.*

Saboteur

You aggravate your inability to control, to antagonise your ability to undermine your awareness of your soul's consciousness. You forego truth to fight the reality of your control structures, by constantly putting yourself in a position where you have to battle with your own perceived image failure. You override the truth you can feel and override the truth which is exposed to you, to anchor to your harsh self-judgement. You have become codependent on using judgement to implode within yourself. You implode to avoid feeling the truth of your feelings. You undermine and override the truth you can feel, to sustain your own negativity of always looking for faults within yourself, so you can deny the truth of being a naturally significant, unique, independent, individual soul.

You are constantly getting in your own way, complicating everything you do and depriving yourself of feeling at ease.

You betray yourself by disassociating from the truth you feel and by refusing to pause, to give yourself a moment to contemplate your reality. You ignore the reality that you contribute to your own sabotage and to encase yourself in your struggle to deny yourself freedom from your unresolved emotions, emotional habits, patterns and behaviours. You use your unresolved emotions to undermine your ability to be of truth. You are resistant, in denial of and avoiding your own resilience and the internal strength of your soul's consciousness.

Drama queen

You create drama in your life to have something to exert your control over. You want to emotionally feel your own surge of control and judgement, to distract yourself from the stagnation of your own soul oppression. You seek and create drama to emotionally feel in control of getting attention, but will deny wanting attention if your control fails to deliver what you want. You are addicted to the surge of your control energy, which is your anticipation of being right and noticed.

Your desire to control has you creating chaos even in the most trivial experiences. You believe life, others and truth should rotate around your desire to control, and feel traumatised when the drama you create backfires and causes image and control failure. You deny trying to control life to be all about you and exert all of your effort into being able to manipulate others to feed and justify your desire for control.

You are only interested in validating your own image of yourself and ignore the truth of your uniqueness. You judge, analyse, compare and compete with the difference between your reality and your image of yourself, life and others. This keeps you judging and creating more dramas to prove your image of yourself is valid. You selfishly use others as actors on your own life stage and you are indifferent to the emotional reality you create for yourself and others. You are infatuated with your own ability to create drama, chaos and trauma, which distracts you from how you really feel and how you make others feel. You resist, deny and avoid embracing the truth of your life being a shared experience with other souls. You deny yourself the ability to be present in your own reality.

Your addiction to oppressing your awareness of your soul's consciousness

Mask

You dumb down the significance of your awareness of your soul's consciousness by filtering your awareness through your soul denial. By filtering your awareness through your denial of your soul, you exist within the turbulence of soul oppression and perform from your denial, instead of being truthful. You allow yourself to exist rather than live. Living is to experience truth while trusting in the uniqueness of your soul's consciousness.

You dumb down your truth to conform to the image you believe others want or to what you believe can be used to manipulate others. You emotionally act one way but feel another. You act your way through life, never being present in your life experiences. You contradict yourself, agreeing or disagreeing with whoever you are presently with, always seeking approval or disapproval for the images you have created. You use your mask to hide from expressing your truth. You have chosen to align to the turbulence you create when you deny you are a soul who can feel and resonate with truth. Your indifference to truth causes you to rely on your stagnation as a refuge from the turbulence you feel, because you refuse to unmask yourself and be honest about your own truth and reality.

You have emotionally conditioned yourself to believe your expression of truth is worthless. You condition yourself to conform to performances, covertly controlling yourself to an image while being indifferent to your soul truth. You mask your soul denial with combinations of beliefs and behaviours of superiority, inferiority, arrogance and ignorance. You betray your soul's consciousness to exist within the turbulence of your attempts to hide your soul denial and oppression. You resist, deny and avoid accepting the significance of your soul truth and hide from the responsibility of resolving your soul's unconsciousness.

Controller

You like to emotionally feel and believe your expectations will be met at all times. You derive a sense of superiority from your illusion of control, to fight the insecurity you feel within yourself. You attempt to hide your insecurities by being demanding, difficult and manipulative; becoming the classic bully to get what you want, which is to make others feel uncomfortable and to have no one question you. You believe your superiority gives you the right to inflict your control at everyone and everything, while you deny the insecurity you feel.

Your own judgement of your control makes you feel vulnerable and insecure. You conceal your own self-doubt about your ability to control with denial. You believe your denial conceals how controlling you are to others and you use your judgement to assassinate anything that interferes with your denial. You dismiss any truth expressed by another and accuse them of judging and attacking you, if their truth does not align to your control of your denial. You want your whole environment to revolve around you, and you want nothing to interfere with your control or denial.

Your ego represents your judgement of your ability to control and your desire to gratify your own illusion of control. You only perceive life, yourself, others and truth through your own limited perception. You judge others by your ability to control them and scale their worth by your ability to get them to validate your control and judgement. You are indifferent to the carnage you create, by believing your own and others' soul truth is expendable and an insignificant price to pay for the righteousness of your judgement and to secure your own illusion of control.

76 | *Your addiction to oppressing your awareness of your soul's consciousness*

The intellectual

You are very judgemental in the way you think, constantly analysing, justifying and judging if you are right and therefore superior. You confuse your judgement for reality, and class your judgement as an authority over truth. You use what you class as knowledge to validate your arrogance. Your inability to trust your soul's consciousness and truth has you searching for information to intellectually justify overriding the insecurity you feel by abandoning truth. Truth is felt but you want to only operate in what you consider as proven knowledge, presuming you can control life with your black and white judgement. You pursue life through your desire to acquire knowledge, attempting to intellectualise the mechanics of life, to avoid feeling your own emotional presence within the truth of life.

You are judgemental towards others, basing your opinions of others on your own arrogant belief of having the authority to judge the value of another. You undermine others with your judgement to dilute their ability to observe the truth of you and the condescending way you use your intellect to justify your beliefs and judgement. You oppress your feelings and force yourself to remain in the familiarity of what you believe you intellectually understand. You only trust what you believe is controllable with your judgement and disregard of anything that challenges your perception. You are addicted to validating your own judgement to yourself, to justify your arrogance towards truth. You are resistant to, in denial of, and are avoiding the reality of feeling separated from your awareness of your soul and disassociated from feeling truth.

Self-exercise 3

Choose one word from the soul oppressive addiction lists and insert the word into the questions. Trust yourself to choose whatever word stands out to you, or if you feel yourself attempting to avoid a word, that would be your word. Note: Being = Being in the effect of that energy.

1. Define what _____ means to you.
2. Acknowledge what you think and feel in relation to being_____
3. Define your addictive patterns in relation to being _____
4. When being _____, how do you compulsively react?
5. How do you feel when you are being _____?
6. What do you override to be _____?
7. What are your expectations in relation to being _____?
8. What is your life lesson to learn in relation to being _____?
9. Can you identify what you are resisting, denying, avoiding and codependent on?

Soul Oppressive Addictions List

1	2	3	4	5
1 In denial of reality	1 Internally negative	1 Self pitying	1 A Warrior	1 A victim
2 Self gratified	2 An addict	2 Bored	2 Satisfied	2 A martyr
3 Abandoned	3 Powerful	3 Oppressed	3 A sufferer	3 A tyrant
4 Argumentative	4 Emotional	4 Programmed	4 Untrustworthy	4 A bully
5 In emotional denial	5 Spiritual	5 Remorseful	5 Blamed	5 Religious
6 Misinterpreted	6 A mind game player	6 Tormented	6 Envious	6 A failure
7 Disempowered	7 Verbal abuser	7 Sabotaged	7 An actor/actress	7 A controller
8 Fearful of not being in control	8 Stuck in an illusory state	8 Excessively disciplined	8 The perpetuator of your past	8 Physically abused
9 Mentally abused	9 Interfered with	9 Disillusioned	9 Mistrusted	9 Obsessive
10 Destructive	10 Attention seeking	10 Retaliative	10 A lover	10 A guru
11 Depressed	11 A scatterbrain	11 Soul separated	11 Egotistical	11 Glamorous
12 Intellectual	12 Judgemental	12 Compulsive	12 Panicked	12 Sly
13 Codependent	13 Punished	13 Worthless	13 Degraded	13 A leader
14 In soul denial	14 Withdrawn	14 Anxious	14 A communicator	14 Popular
15 Disappointed	15 Traumatised	15 Not good enough	15 A psychic	15 Tough
16 A liar	16 Sexually abused	16 Righteous	16 Petty	16 A cry baby
17 Fearful	17 A doormat	17 Intimidating	17 A rationalist	17 A trouble maker
18 A servant	18 Unjust	18 Addictive	18 Hateful	18 Shameful
19 Oppositional	19 Angry	19 Deceived	19 Bamboozled	19 Shy
20 Masked	20 A drama queen	20 Dogmatic	20 Unhappy	20 Indifferent
21 In poverty	21 Manipulative	21 Habitual	21 A survivor	21 Moody
22 Self judging	22 Controlling	22 Dumbed down	22 Narcissistic	22 Guilty
23 Lustful	23 Rejected	23 Arrogant	23 Unhealthy	23 A cheater
24 A saboteur	24 Rigid	24 Ignorant	24 A performer	24 In a fantasy
25 Indulgent	25 Limited	25 Controversial	25 Intimate	25 Confused
26 A silent child	26 Paranoid	26 Romantic	26 Dominated	26 Fearful of control
27 Superficial	27 A wallower	27 Elite	27 Cautious	27 _____
28 Fearful of losing control	28 Disassociated from truth	28 Genetically pre-disposed	28 Immersed in mind chatter	28 _____

Your addiction to oppressing your awareness of your soul's consciousness

Chapter Seven

Externalisation

Externalisation is the act of ensuring the perpetuation of your separation from your awareness of your soul and your disassociation from feeling truth. Instead of aligning to the truth you feel and can observe in your present moment, you abandon your awareness of yourself and forgo your willingness to be honest. Your dishonesty inhibits your ability to resolve and evolve. Resolving and evolving occurs in conjunction with your ability to observe and feel the truth of your unresolved emotions and your soul consciousness' presence within your present moment.

Your denial of your own emotional reality secures your ability to disharmonise with truth. When you disharmonise, you enmesh yourself with any unconscious energy that you can use to secure your denial of yourself. You programme, condition and indoctrinate yourself to override your soul consciousness' ability to communicate with you, which is your ability to feel the truth of your feelings. You programme, condition and indoctrinate yourself to ignore and attack your own natural ability to resonate with truth. You seek external gratification for the internal upheaval you create for yourself, without truly acknowledging that you are the creator of your own emotional upheaval. You anchor to belief systems, control structures, oppressive judgement and illusions of reality, to analyse what you are doing, feeling, becoming and portraying to yourself. You are fooling yourself with your own denial of reality, and filtering all of your understanding of yourself through a barrage of deceptive self-manipulation. You seek others who will validate your abandonment of truth with their abandonment of truth, to secure your own denial of yourself within your reality.

Your illusions of yourself, life and truth have you inflicting your unresolved emotions, belief systems, judgement and control structures at others and your environment. Due to the emotional upheaval created by your denial of yourself within your reality, you become disassociated from feeling the unconditional love within yourself, others and truth. You abandon the truth of your individuality and the uniqueness of your soul journey, to enmesh your unresolved emotions with others' unresolved emotions, and then you try to control yourself to emotionally feel what you have abandoned, which is your uniqueness, independence and individuality.

Externalisation is a controlled way of distracting yourself from truth; you focus on your judgement and others' judgement to continue your patterns of resistance to the truth within your present moment. Your denial and avoidance of truth makes you feel insecure; you fear being exposed to the reality of your denial, hence you attempt to avoid truth. You externalise to distract yourself from the truth of your emotions. You constantly try to avoid acknowledging the unconscious energy you produce. You constantly externalise blame for the emotions producing the unconscious energy you project onto others, because you seek to be unconscious of your own emotional reality. You allow yourself to be indifferent to the reality of your unresolved emotions by fixating on something or someone external to yourself. You resist being honest about your automatic reactions to your own unresolved emotions.

Externalisation is the willingness to ignore the truth of your emotional issues and to find a diversionary distraction to act out the unconscious energy, you cannot contain within yourself. Your suppression of your emotional unrest causes you to inflict your unresolved emotions, belief systems, judgement and control structures at others and your environment.

When you become desperate to protect your denial, you deliberately inflict others with your venomous desire to incapacitate another's ability to trust their own awareness of truth, while fearing your dishonesty with yourself will become uncovered. The generation of unresolved emotions you inflict at another, causes you to embody the energy you inflict. You try to avoid the backlash your emotions create, by justifying your emotional actions with layers of denial, self-manipulation and perceived righteous judgement. When you layer your resistance to and denial and avoidance of truth, over your reality, you confuse yourself about your own emotional reactions of externalising your unresolved emotions.

For example: You are angry with your partner and yourself but you are yelling at your children. Why have you chosen to inflict your emotions on your children? You want to avoid confrontation with your partner and avoid the truth of your reality, so you suppress how you feel which creates more unconscious energy. You compulsively want to relieve yourself of your unconscious energy. This causes you to seek other avenues for you to project and inflict your emotions, and you justify projecting them at your children. You also want to be able to control the emotional backlash your emotions are going to cause another and yourself. When you project your unresolved emotions at your children, it is still confrontational, but you do not feel as uncomfortable because you justify your emotional actions with your own righteous judgement. When you realise the reality of what you have done, you implode within your own self-judgement. Now you are in confrontation with yourself, and you have energetically combined your awareness of your own, your partner's and your children's emotions and inflicted yourself with the lot.

While ever you resist, deny and avoid the truth you are experiencing, you will have no solution to the emotional unrest you feel. If you were not in denial of your own truth, feelings and unresolved emotions, and really wanted to be responsible for yourself, you would avoid the cascading of unconscious energy and the layering of unresolved emotions you create for yourself to endure.

When you seek others' judgement to validate your worth and significance, you become codependent on your ability to control yourself to validate only what secures your judgement. Judgement is very fickle and non-sustainable and you become reliant on people, events and things which you really have no control over, so in reality you become emotionally vulnerable to what you want to control to give you validation.

Superficiality is borne of externalisation; you create control structures to exist within and to analyse your perception of reality with. Your superficiality causes you to be devoid of the meaningfulness of yourself as a soul. You feel the void this creates and anchor to something external to yourself, to avoid feeling the void created by your separation from your awareness of your soul and your disassociation from feeling truth. You become consumed by whatever you use to deny you feel the void, or by what you believe you want because you think it will fix and fill the void, to the point of being unable to explain the truth of what you feel. Your externalisation obstructs you from feeling the truth of your soul, but your soul's consciousness is always endeavouring to expose truth to you.

An example of superficiality is to define yourself only by the car you drive, the house you live in or your occupation. These explain your experiences, not the truth of who you are. This is externalising your worth by scaling yourself with mankind judgement. You use a mankind scaling system to create an illusion for you to control yourself to. You use your possessions as a way to be scaled, hoping others perceive you as you would like them to.

- What is the point to all this scaling, if the scaling of yourself actually contributes to you feeling meaningless?
- What do you want others to perceive you as?
- Are you really enjoying your own achievements and life?
- What is really controlling you?

Relationships can be based solely on externalisation and can become an avenue for you to act out your unresolved emotions. You conceal the truth of your own unresolved emotions by externalising the blame for everything you do not like onto your partner, friends, siblings, children, parents or strangers. When you use blame to create an image for yourself, without looking inward for honesty, truth and resolution, you become trapped in externalisation.

When you feel the reality of your resonance with truth; the truth of what you feel cannot be taken from you by anyone's judgement. Your acceptance of being a soul, allows you to acknowledge your feelings and feel yourself resonating with truth. Your acknowledgement of your own soul truth enables you to discover your awareness of your soul's consciousness and unconsciousness. Aligning with your soul integrity enables you to acknowledge and feel the value and worth of applying effort to being honest and truthful with yourself. Your soul's consciousness aims for resolution of your distorted view of yourself and the emotional wounds you have carried from lifetime to lifetime. Your soul's consciousness seeks for you to be at peace with yourself.

Self-exercise 4

1. Ask yourself what you externalise on?

2. What outside sources influence you?

3. Can you feel the void of your separation from your awareness of your soul and your disassociation from feeling truth?

4. Do you attempt to make yourself feel and appear better by controlling someone or something outside yourself?

5. Do you define yourself by the material things you own? If so, list them and explain their importance to expose the image you think they create for you.

6. How do you distract yourself from your awareness of your soul's consciousness?

7. What do you judge as trivia that occupies your time and consumes your thought process?

8. Who has the most influence over you and your choices? Why?

CHAPTER EIGHT

Control

Your desire to control is a mystery to yourself. If you are honest, you will acknowledge your confusion in relation to your own desire for control. You need to give yourself the space to acknowledge, that you do not know what you do not know. Understanding your desire for control is to understand your soul oppression, soul denial, separation from your awareness of your soul and your disassociation from feeling truth, which is steeped in your soul denial history. Comprehending your control is the process of resolution and evolution.

Your beliefs about your control are steeped in your own mythology. You have your own beliefs about what your control can control, which is only an illusion you anchor yourself to, to resist, deny and avoid the reality of not really understanding who you are. Your desire for control underpins your soul denial and has you collaborating with the energetics of the mass energy of mankind's soul denial. Your control creates a false foundation, which you anchor your soul journey to. You have the misconception that your soul journey is about you getting your control of your soul denial to work, to pacify the insecurities you create within yourself by abandoning your awareness of truth.

Your control is one of the hardest emotions to resolve, because you struggle to come to terms with the reality of how futile, oppositional and destructive your control is. You want to justify and deceive yourself about the reality of your desire for control, which inhibits your willingness to be honest. Your desire for control thrives on your deception and flourishes because of your soul denial. Acknowledging the truth of your desire for control is the only way to resolve and evolve your control structures. To discover the truth of your control structures, you need to be honest with yourself and honest about your interaction with reality.

Your control structures are the active force of wants and desires that stem from the fears and embedded beliefs of your soul denial. To conceal the truth of your control, you fragment and detach from the reality of suppressing your awareness of your own desire for control. You use your control structures to interconnect every aspect of yourself that is oppositional to acknowledging your soul truth. This causes you to oppress your awareness of your soul consciousness' ability to expose you to the truth of being a soul. You use your control structures to amalgamate the complexities of your unresolved emotions to oppose truth. Your soul's consciousness constantly exposes the truth of your soul journey to you and you use your control structures to counteract what is being exposed, by interjecting your unresolved emotions into every experience you have. Your desire for control obscures your ability to resonate with your soul's consciousness.

Your deceptive control structures protect, sustain and fortify your soul oppression, which concretises the barriers to truth that protect your soul denial. You use your control

structures to govern your existence within the emotional turbulence of being unable to feel truth and resolve your own soul denial. Your desire to control commandeers you to stay in the familiarity of your soul oppression and your illusion of control. Your control structures are always stagnant and always repeat what is emotionally unresolved; this sustains the repetitiveness of the soul oppressive cycles and ensures the perpetuation of your soul denial history. Your control structures are complex and your ability to trust truth will expose the reality of your desire for control. Your trust in truth will allow you the opportunity to resolve and evolve beyond the deception of your illusion of control.

Your desire for control always has an undercurrent of fear, because you fear your control will be exposed as a fraud by truth, or will be judged as inferior to others in their illusion of control. If you are insecure with truth, you will fight truth to anchor to your control, and exert your control over the truth being exposed. You fight to have your control conceal your internal fear of being wrong about your illusion of control. You internally know you have abandoned truth for your illusion of control and your biggest fear is that

LEFT: You believe being in control is going to pacify your insecurities about life, yourself, others, relationships and truth, but in reality it restricts you. You become bound to the frustration of attempting to control reality to your expectations, depriving yourself of the freedom to experience the dynamics of life, yourself, others, relationships and the truth of your soul journey.

truth will prove how mistaken you have been, which causes you to want to concretise your illusions of control, in the desire to prevent truth from penetrating your denial of being a soul.

You control yourself to deny your unresolved emotions and then class your denial as being in control. You can control yourself to deny the opportunity to resolve your unresolved emotions, and often without realising it you store and carry the burden of your unresolved emotions. When the burden of your unresolved emotions becomes overwhelming, you attempt to deny self-responsibility; seeking to control another source to resolve your unresolved emotions for you without accepting accountability for yourself.

You believe if you can control enough, you will be free of the emotional burden you have created for yourself. You can become unconscious to the reality of being the creator of your own emotional burden. When you control yourself to hide from your internal reality, you define your worth by your ability to appease your own illusion of control, which means you miss the true opportunity of life, by being deceptive with yourself.

In reality you cannot control enough to sustain a level of contentment within your own illusion of control; you just cannot control everything or everybody at all times. Your control is constantly being exposed, but you choose to deceptively ignore this reality.

Have you ever asked yourself why you want, or why you believe you need to control your soul's consciousness? What would be the advantage for you to control truth? Your desire to control your soul's consciousness causes you to inflict pain on yourself; the pain of rejecting the truth of who you are. You are a soul and you can feel this truth resonating with you. If you feel anxious about this statement, you are feeling the reality of your control opposing your truth. If you are struggling to read this and cannot hold the concept that is written, you are experiencing your soul denial energy fighting for control. If you feel nothing, are you experiencing your separation from your awareness of your soul, or are you neutralising your feelings and emotions with your control? Do you know how you feel about your own desire for control?

Your control is illusory and based on your false expectation of being able to make the world work the way you want it to. You can be very surprised when you realise that not everyone thinks the same way as you and that their desire to control will compete with and attempt to undermine your illusion of control. You can be confused by others' inability to support your images and illusions of yourself, and can become fearful of others' judgement because you are not willing to feel your own origins of truth.

Submission is not resolved control; submission is a type of control. Being submissive controls you to be devoid of your choices and is a way of opposing your own freedom. Suppression of your awareness of reality is a way of hiding from feeling your own soul truth, which allows you to accommodate another's control to dictate the worth of your soul. Your submission to soul oppression allows you to remain a victim to your own soul denial, and you entrap yourself in your image of being a victim. Your desire for control can be controlling via submission. You can control yourself to be compliant until you believe you have gathered enough momentum to enforce your control. In truth, you have only been obedient to your own manipulation for control. Submission is a way of seeking validation for your denial of your own significance, uniqueness, independence and individuality.

Mankind's physical oppression can at times control your environment, but not the truth of being a soul. Physical oppression is an experience of mankind's indifference and desire to control truth. Resolving the emotional wounds created by your experience of mankind's physical oppression, frees you from carrying these experiences within you. You can carry your experiences to define yourself but in truth you are beyond mankind experiences; you are a significant, unique, independent, individual soul of *True Source Divine Origin Consciousness* and truth is always with you. The resolution of your control structures is the choice to let yourself feel your soul truth.

Your desire for control is insatiable and has you always seeking the next power struggle with truth. You engage in power struggles because you seek to prove the value and worth of your control to yourself. You can be unconscious of your own automatic reactions to someone else's control and your automatic reactions of wanting control, and it will be the conscious choice to be truthful with yourself that will enable you to unravel the mysteries of your control. Your desire for control causes you to become very insensitive to the reality of feeling your soul's consciousness. You can control yourself to justify your beliefs of having to control. You deny that you are the cause of your own stagnation, frustration and confusion because of your need for an illusion of control. You emotionally deny the reality that your own deceptive control is how you abuse your soul's consciousness.

Your control keeps you in a self-created cocoon of soul oppression, restricting your awareness of your natural flow of consciousness. This has you resisting, denying and avoiding the expansion of new possibilities within yourself and the potential of your soul's consciousness. You try to protect your soul denial because you do not want to challenge your beliefs, addictions and insecurities. Your control retards your internal growth as a soul. You can control yourself without even acknowledging the reality of the cause and effect of your own control structures. You can become aware of your desire for control by acknowledging your internal and external comments, judgements and reactions. Being honest about your desires, hidden agendas and willingness to manipulate yourself and others will expose you to the truth of your control.

Your control keeps you very stagnant as you repeat your emotional patterns to justify your regimented, preconceived and restricted view of yourself and life. You can become totally indoctrinated in what is known to you and your past becomes your expectation for the future.

- **When you only control yourself to what you know, you miss the opportunity to discover what you don't know, which is the reality of being a significant, unique, independent, individual soul of *True Source Divine Origin Consciousness*.**

- **You control yourself to become what you do not resolve.**

- **Like energy attracts like energy.**

- **When you know better, you will do better, because your truth and deception cannot occupy the same space.**

- **Deception is an afterthought; truth is always the foundation which deception is attempting to conceal.**

Chapter Nine

Freedom of choice

When you allow yourself to be consciously aware of your own reality, you will realise the insanity of your expectation to have consistent control over your life experiences, yourself and others. You have the freedom to question your own perceived control of life, but you choose to deny the opportunity of this freedom. You can become dedicated to upholding your illusory control of your own deception, your life, yourself and others. You can be stagnant in the familiarity of your struggle to deny your own reality. You can become addicted to oppressing yourself with your own history, as you manipulate yourself to deny your ability to choose what is relevant to the uniqueness of your present moment. Your denial of your own reality controls you to regurgitate your history with the insanity of expecting a different result.

When you condition yourself to deny the relevance of challenging your indoctrinated beliefs about reality, you override the uniqueness of your present moment with your expectations of what reality should be. You use your resistance to and denial and avoidance of feeling your present moment, to deny the truth of what you are experiencing. You want to secure your illusion of reality within your own mind, but you have to fight reality to control yourself to believe your own illusions. When you override your present moment feelings with regurgitated unresolved emotions and regurgitated illusions of reality, you control yourself to deny the reality you are experiencing and control yourself to abandon the freedom within the truth of your present moment.

When you resist, deny and avoid acknowledging the stagnation of your unresolved emotions, you fester in your own soul oppression and deny your ability to be free. You define yourself within the different illusions your unresolved emotions create, which causes you to fear freedom from your illusions. You resist, deny and avoid the unfamiliarity of freedom from your soul oppressive illusions. Freedom is a choice, the choice to be honest about your illusions of yourself, so you can experience the truth of your soul and experience the truth of your reality.

You lose your awareness of your resonance with truth when you deny your freedom of choice. You lose your awareness of your resonance with truth when you choose your illusion of control over the relevance of truth. You have the freedom to choose to be honest with the reality of yourself as a soul and your life as a soul journey. Your soul journey is an opportunity to learn to trust the true essence of who you are, without being encumbered by your own illusions of yourself and your denial of reality, both of which caused some of your unresolved emotions in the first place.

When you override your internal knowing, you abandon your uniqueness, independence and individuality, denying yourself freedom of choice. By abandoning your uniqueness, independence and individuality, you are choosing to assimilate and conform to the energy around you, striving to gratify your desire to fit in with the energy you seek validation from.

Once you have abandoned your freedom of choice and internally feel conflicted, you will attempt to control yourself to justify everything that you do, to excuse and pacify anything you emotionally feel.

The moment you override your internal knowing, you scramble to regain what you lose by overriding your awareness of truth. You lose the ability to feel your integrity, sense of peace and dignity. You try to control yourself to emulate an image of being in control, while you internally berate yourself because you are aware of your betrayal. By acknowledging your betrayal of your internal knowing, you can choose to objectively observe the truth of your unresolved emotions. This creates the opportunity to be truthful with yourself, instead of automatically judging yourself and then imploding within your own judgement, which actually creates more separation from your awareness of your freedom of choice. You have the freedom to choose to acknowledge your opportunities and learn from your experiences of yourself. Your reactions to your life experiences are your greatest teacher, and your freedom of choice is the pivotal point of your life experiences. You are choosing to either stagnate within your unconsciousness or to resolve and evolve to the reality of who you are, which is a naturally significant, unique, independent, individual soul of *True Source Divine Origin Consciousness*.

By being consumed with your control of your illusion of yourself, you forget you are the creator of your own mind chatter, attitudes, distortions, beliefs, expectations and judgements. You override your resonance with truth and align to your illusions, which have you fragmenting your understanding of the truth you naturally resonate with. You become, and exist within, your own lies, unconscious of the authenticity of your soul and your natural resonance with truth.

You experience your life exposing your unresolved emotions and you are always in the process of using your freedom of choice to determine how you perceive your experience of life. You have the freedom to use your unresolved emotions to project, perform and justify your emotional evaluation of life. You have the freedom to automatically control yourself to deny the reality of choice and to allow yourself to be a victim to everything and everyone who is not responding favorably to your control. You are never without your freedom to choose your response to reality. Mankind has the misconception that our freedom should equate to our ability to control reality. If you align to this misconception, you actually oppose your own freedom because you become consumed with your desire for control.

When you become fearful of the enormity of your unresolved emotions, you recoil from the opportunity to resolve and evolve, and choose to become dishonest with yourself. When you constantly choose to secure your unresolved emotions as a valid force against your soul truth, you are stagnating your own evolution.

When you wallow in your unresolved emotions, you reflect your unconscious energy at yourself, stagnating yourself within your own emotional prison. This deprives you of the opportunity to use your freedom of choice to be honest with yourself.

You have programmed, conditioned and indoctrinated yourself with your own soul denial, to oppose the reality that you create your emotional nightmare. When you choose to be truthful with yourself, you begin to resolve your emotional creations. You may fear acknowledging the truth of your own soul denial, because you will expose the truth of betraying yourself. Betraying yourself is the choice to deny truth.

By existing in, and supporting your unresolved emotions, you react to yourself, others and life, feeling emotionally trapped by your own unresolved emotions. You choose to wallow in your indifference to truth and emotionally accept being a victim to an unexplainable force, which you have decided is a force over which you have no control. You want to be a victim, so you can deny responsibility for your soul denial. Your soul denial energy is the unexplained force you feel, generated by your embedded beliefs and fears that oppose who you naturally are. When you choose to impound your soul's journey with your unresolved emotions and deny what you are doing, you lose your sense of freedom. You are the pilot in your life but you act like the passenger, choosing to be submissive to your unresolved emotions, believing your own misconception that life is easier if you deny truth.

The way you treat life determines your resolution and evolution in this lifetime. You have the freedom to deny your soul and the freedom to acknowledge your original intention to resolve and evolve. You have the freedom to deny your ability to use your freedom of choice to take full responsibility for your own thoughts, actions, distortions, misconceptions, desires, hidden agendas, beliefs and behaviours. Your willingness to be responsible for the reality of your own emotions, to commit to seeking truth, to be accountable for your energy and to trust your own integrity, are choices to go beyond your own fear of being more than mankind energy and to feel the reality of being a significant, unique, independent, individual soul of *True Source Divine Origin Consciousness*. You only have to make the decision to choose to trust truth.

- Do you know what holds you back from trusting truth?
- Do you know what you mistrust?

You are constantly surprising yourself with your own emotional desires, hidden agendas and your addiction to oppressing your awareness of your own soul truth. You can fight reality, compulsively needing to experience life unconsciously, because you fear being conscious of your unconsciousness. Being conscious of your unconsciousness, allows you the freedom to resolve and evolve what you have exposed to yourself. Your exposure of your unresolved emotions is the greatest gift you can give yourself, because you are consciously participating in your own evolution. Accepting the exposure of your soul oppression is to be in a state of grace; you will fear nothing, because all experiences are relevant to your evolution.

Your denial of your freedom of choice has you at odds with your natural ability to be at peace with the reality of resolving and evolving to be consciously aware of being a dynamic soul, and expressing the truth of your own soul. Peace is a choice, the choice to be present within the uniqueness of every moment, accepting your reality and exploring the experiences of your life. You have the freedom to choose to learn from your honesty. When you are willing to be honest about the reality of your unresolved emotions and the truth of your soul's consciousness, you expose yourself to the opportunities within life for resolution and evolution.

You are the interface between the reality of all your conscious and unconscious energy. Your soul's consciousness and soul's unconsciousness will steer you to the same life experiences. Your soul's consciousness wants to expose what is emotionally affecting your awareness of your own soul truth and your acceptance of your natural flow of conscious energy, which creates opportunities for you to be honest with yourself. Your soul's unconsciousness wants to repeat what has been done before, to protect your illusion of control while sustaining your dishonesty with yourself. Your soul's consciousness wants you to explore the truth of your experiences and utilise your life experiences as an opportunity to resolve and evolve. By being honest with your reality, you give yourself the space to be open to what is being exposed to you, which is the truth of your soul's consciousness and unconsciousness. You have the ability to convert unconscious energy into conscious understanding, which enables your soul's consciousness to return fragmented energy back to the natural flow of truth.

You can use the energy within your soul's unconsciousness to continue your addiction to your unresolved emotions, which causes you to emotionally want to remain stagnant, to create an illusion of control or an illusion of being controlled. You choose to be unconscious of the reality of your soul truth to prolong your illusion of control.

Sometimes your worst experiences are the ones you learn the most from. Life at times can be sad and hard, but if you acknowledge the truth of what you are experiencing you can gain a lot of personal insight. You need to feel your feelings. Your feelings are the way your soul's consciousness communicates truth. Even when you are unconscious there is a constant stream of conscious energy you can feel. By being honest, you allow yourself to utilise your natural ability to distinguish the difference between your deceptive emotions and your true feelings. Honesty is the choice to be conscious of your truth.

You have the potential to feel the truth of your life experiences, but you miss feeling your truth because you are stuck in an emotional trance regurgitating your unresolved emotions.

Life is about choices, and the most fundamental choice to make is to approach the truth of your soul with honesty. Soul acceptance and caring for your soul truth are choices. Finding out why you have trouble doing this is the process of your soul journey, which gives you opportunities for resolution and evolution. By being aware of your own reality, you become open to the potential and possibilities of being conscious of your own soul truth. Your soul and soul journey are unique. There is no one exactly the same as you and we all have immense potential within, including you.

When you accept truth, you are embracing and acknowledging your own individual possibilities. Acceptance of truth requires your freedom of choice to be consciously utilised, you need to be truthful about what you are doing with your freedom of choice. Your first conscious choice should be to acknowledge you are worth your own effort and to allow yourself to find the negativity that is in your way of being an expression of your soul's consciousness, which is your natural essence. Seeking your truth creates the freedom to choose living consciously, applying your own conscious insight to your choices and your life experiences. Your soul's consciousness is aware of your ability to live life as a soul, experiencing the truth of life and feeling at peace with the reality of who you are. Trusting and accepting being consciously aware of truth without fear or judgement is the choice to live life feeling at peace with who you are. You are a significant, unique, independent, individual soul of *True Source Divine Origin Consciousness* and you have the freedom to accept yourself. You have the freedom to align and unify with truth, you just have to decide that truth is relevant to you.

You need to acknowledge being aware of your choices and own how you interact with life. You need to choose to be accountable to yourself in relation to the way you treat yourself, life and others. Being honest about how you feel, enables you to observe your own reality.

Self-exercise 5

1. How are you choosing to treat your own soul truth?
2. What choices have you made and then denied making them?
3. How do you feel about having freedom of choice?
4. What are your recurring emotional patterns?
5. What are your emotional choices really about?

- **Being aware of your choices will give you insight into yourself.**
- **Being objective is one of the kindest choices you can make for your soul.**

Questionnaire 2

Answer these questions off the top of your head. Do not dwell on questions, just move on and come back if you need to. There is no right or wrong answer, just how you feel.

Please note: I recommend you use a separate journal in which to write your answers to the questionnaires, so you can use this questionnaire numerous times without being influenced by what you have written before.

1. List three emotions that sum up how you feel about yourself as a soul.

2. List three emotions that sum up how you feel about your life being a soul journey.

3. Can you be objective in relation to your emotions? Why is being objective important?

4. How do you define yourself as an individual?

5. (a) Can you be honest with yourself?

   (b) Do you see your own honesty as an advantage or disadvantage?

   (c) Why?

6. Name three people who have influenced the way you feel about yourself. (Negative or Positive)

Your Insight & Awareness Book

7. How do you feel about your desire for control?
   _____
   _____
   _____

8. Who has the choice to create the life you want or have envisioned for yourself?
   _____
   _____

9. What choices would you like to change?
   _____
   _____

Use the same word you used for question 10 on Questionnaire 1, page 33.

10. How do you feel about _____?
    What have you learnt?
    _____
    _____
    _____
    _____
    _____

Use the same word you used for question 11 on Questionnaire 1, page 33.

11. How do you feel about _____?
    What have you learnt?
    _____
    _____
    _____
    _____
    _____

When you are finished questionnaire 2 compare your answers to questionnaire 1. You may observe how your awareness and perception of yourself and life has changed, and expose yourself to more truth within your answers.

Section Two

Chapter Ten

Lost

What would you do if truth knocked at your door and announced that truth was here to help? What do you think truth could help you with? Would you run? What would you hide and protect? Would you be open to hear what truth was presenting?

Do you spend your time in your mind trying to work out if you are right or wrong in your appraisal of life, others and yourself? What if you aren't right or wrong, just lost in your own soul oppression? Would you want to know what truth is presenting to you? Would you know if you were lost or would your denial anchor you to the fight to be right about life, others and yourself? To acknowledge the truth of being lost in your own soul oppression creates the freedom to express the truth of your feelings. Honestly being able to express to yourself what you feel opens you to the reality of being a soul who can communicate with yourself; this means you can start discovering the truth of who you are.

You struggle with your own opposition to life, others and especially yourself and are unaware that you create oppositional energy by abandoning the truth of yourself. You use your emotional habits and mind games to fight experiencing the reality of life, others and yourself. What would truth have to expose to you to prove you are lost in your own soul oppression? What would truth have to expose to you to prove the stagnation of your oppression? Or has truth exposed this to you and you walked away preferring to struggle?

Are you lost because you ask the questions and then refuse to hear your own answers? Are you lost because you don't want to hear any answers that will offend your illusion of control? Is it your illusion of control that has you lost? What are you trying to control and why? Have you ever asked yourself these questions honestly? What is worth protecting in your familiar? Where has your familiar taken you to? Could the answer be lost in your own soul oppression? What would truth have to do for you to be willing to ask the questions and answer them truthfully to yourself?

Do you fear having your illusion of control taken? Do you fear being the taker of another's illusion of control? Do you fear realising your control is just an illusion? What do you really know of your control energy? What do you refuse to acknowledge out loud to yourself? Has your control given you what you wanted? Do you feel the way you want to? Or do you feel lost in your own illusory control, trapped judging the significance of your control? Have you realised that soul oppression is caused by your control or are you too lost to know this? What if truth was trying to expose you to the possibility of living without soul oppression? What if truth was exposing another way of being? Would you stop to listen or would you judge truth as obsolete? How can truth expose you to truth, if you are demanding truth be what you want it to be, before you will give it your attention?

What do you attack to secure your illusion of control? Who do you attack to secure your illusion of control? Why do you secure an energy that needs you to attack? Do you realise you attack your soul and other souls to pretend you are not lost in your soul oppression? Why do you fight to secure your control, when you are not even sure if your control is in your best interest? What price is too high for you to pay for an illusion of control or is your control the ultimate prize? Are you willing to dismiss and disregard truth for an illusion? Are you too lost to acknowledge your control has cost you a lot? Do you know what it has cost you? Do you care? Truth cares and is constantly trying to inform you. Have you noticed and chosen to arrogantly ignore this, or are you too lost to know the answer to this question?

Do you want to be devoid of feelings? Would you notice if you were devoid of feeling your own truth? Does it matter to you? If you died tomorrow how would you assess this life? Would you be prepared to acknowledge the truth of this life you have lived or would you fear your truth? What legacy have you created for your soul? How will you explain your soul denial to yourself? If truth asked "Has your desire for control hurt another?" would you answer truthfully, or list your justifications and excuses? Would you try to trick truth or would you trust truth? If truth knocked on your door to ask you not to wait until death to be honest, would you open the door? If truth asked "What are you waiting for?" would you have an answer? If truth asked you to question yourself would you spend the time being honest, or use your desire to control to oppress your ability to be of truth? If truth came to you to create an opportunity to be found, would you take the opportunity? Would you make the choice to be of the truth of your soul?

Questionnaire 3

Answer these questions off the top of your head. Do not dwell on questions, just move on and come back if you need to. There is no right or wrong answer, just how you feel. At the end of section 2 there is another questionnaire and you will be able to compare your answers, so I suggest to do this questionnaire and to not look at it again until after you have read section 2 and completed questionnaire 4.

Please note: I recommend you use a separate journal in which to write your answers to the questionnaires, so you can use this questionnaire numerous times without being influenced by what you have written before.

1. Identify the indoctrinated beliefs and images you apply effort to.

2. Define the purpose for ignoring your ability to care for your soul.

3. What self-sabotaging behaviours do you give yourself permission to use?

4. Identify some of the components of soul care that you require resolution in.

Define what the following mean to you

1. Judgement
2. Compassion
3. Evolution
4. Stagnation
5. Consciousness
6. Unconsciousness
7. Integrity
8. Oblivion

Chapter Eleven

Avoiding soul accountability

Distracting yourself from your own soul truth has you opposing your own feelings. Your thought process allows you to manipulate yourself to a position of mediocrity. Mediocrity is dumbing yourself down to accept the stagnation within your life, and enables you to deny your uniqueness, independence and individuality. Your stagnation becomes your norm. When you falsely feel safer within your stagnation, you avoid challenging yourself on your beliefs of what has become acceptable for how you interact with yourself, others and life.

You get lost in your tolerance of your own stagnation, and you align to false beliefs of permanency. You distract yourself with your reactions to life situations, and use that to oppress your awareness of your soul truth. When you believe nothing will or can change, you use this belief to entrap yourself in the stagnation of your own emotional, energetic and physical merry-go-round. When you deny yourself the freedom to be truthfully honest, you operate from a position of mediocrity. You can choose to resist, deny and avoid your feelings without true contemplation of the reality of what you are doing to yourself, others and your life situations. When you choose to resist, deny and avoid the reality of your stagnation, you are denying and ignoring your unresolved emotions.

You can run a course of avoiding being accountable for yourself for a long time, without even realising what you are truly doing to your soul's consciousness. You camouflage your unresolved emotions with your behaviour patterns, because you want to conceal the truth of your internal reality to yourself. You can say to yourself that you would like to be open to change and like to be honest with yourself, at the same time that you sabotage and undermine every opportunity to acknowledge the truth of your own soul deception. Soul accountability means you are doing, not just saying or implying you are going to do something. You can use your 'couldn't be bothered' attitude, to deflect from acknowledging the reality of your lack of self-accountability. You throw your emotions into a too hard basket, which is how you continue perpetuating the unresolved emotions within your soul's unconsciousness.

If you have programmed, conditioned and indoctrinated yourself to avoid any accountability for your unresolved emotions, you will also attempt to avoid the ramifications of your emotional reactions and choices. This becomes problematic, because it leaves you indifferent to truth. Your denial of your unresolved emotions cheats you out of living the life you intended as a soul.

As a soul you want to feel the truth of your experiences, so you can feel the reality of yourself and resolve your unresolved emotions, which is evolution. Your soul accountability comes from the application of honesty. Your honesty enables you to be aware of your unresolved

emotions, which gives you the opportunity to evolve beyond your own emotional stagnation. You never originally intended to stagnate your soul and live a life of stagnation.

Your avoidance of being accountable for yourself has you seeking to blame whatever you believe you lack or whatever you believe you cannot escape from as the cause of the stagnation you feel. However, it is your own resistance to taking responsibility for the choices you make, and your denial of being accountable for your own behaviour, for the words you speak and for the relentlessness of your desire to control, that perpetuates the stagnation of your own creation. Your 'wants' expose the many ways you judge yourself as not good enough. Your acknowledgement of how you use your 'wants' can become an opportunity to resolve your avoidance and denial of your lack of self-responsibility. Your honesty with yourself can be an opportunity to acknowledge what you use to avoid being truthful about your own unresolved emotions.

Avoiding soul accountability is an attempt to evade being responsible for the resolution of your soul's unconsciousness, and keeps you entrapped in your denial of the significance of your soul.

Self-exercise 6

1. What are your methods of distracting yourself from the truth of being a soul?
2. What are the truths within yourself that you are reluctant to admit to?
3. Can you identify your stagnation? What are you emotionally trapped in?
4. What types of sabotage do you do to yourself and why?
5. What would you like to be held accountable for or to?

Chapter Twelve

Soul integrity

Your soul integrity is your willingness to understand the truth of being a soul. Your acknowledgement of your soul integrity will change how you perceive life and will enable you to discover the significance of your own boundaries. Your soul integrity is your willingness to align to truth and enables you to recognise when your truth is being comprised. Your soul integrity is your willingness to be in unity with your soul's consciousness. When you use your unresolved emotions to battle the prospect of being in unity with truth, you create an internal conflict that leads to you being combative against your own reality. When you separate from your awareness of being of truth, you deny your soul's consciousness. This causes you to act out your unresolved emotions and to oppose the truth of your soul. When you oppose the truth of yourself, you lose awareness of your own soul integrity.

You compromise your soul integrity to conform to beliefs that are in opposition to the truth of your soul. You can concretise your beliefs without ever questioning the validity of your beliefs, and it is your non-questioning which causes your stagnation. You use your unresolved emotions to interject your emotional history into your present moment, seeking to secure your beliefs as viable. Your desire to entrust yourself to your beliefs causes you to resist, deny and avoid exploring the truth of yourself. Your soul's consciousness feels the truth of your present moment and resonates with the truth being exposed to you. When you oppose the exploration of yourself, you deny feeling the presence of your soul's consciousness. To be of your soul integrity is to understand that your soul truth is an ever-evolving process.

By accepting the truth of being a soul, even when you are not sure what that means, you will become more aware of what reality is revealing to you about your soul. Your willingness to be honest about your own soul truth, creates an ever-changing understanding of your reality. Your acknowledgment of your freedom of choice allows you to feel and resonate with truth, and to feel unity within.

When you automatically react from your unresolved emotions, which is your stored emotional history, you respond to life with your programmed, conditioned and indoctrinated beliefs. When you choose to govern yourself with others' expectations, without questioning what you really want for yourself, you are choosing to live a life without soul integrity. To acknowledge the significance of your freedom of choice is to value the integrity of your soul. You always have a choice as to how you will respond to your reality. This does not mean you get to control life, but you do have the choice to respond to life, either from your unresolved emotions or with the acknowledgement of your truth.

Living a life without soul integrity is definitely a type of soul abuse. To avoid your own truth and to allow yourself to ignore your soul is fertile ground for a life of regret. Soul abuse comes in many forms but basically it is any behaviour, belief or internal dialogue that is detrimental to your awareness of your value, worth and significance as a soul.

Your resistance to your own truth creates a position of compromised integrity, stalemating your ability to resolve and evolve beyond your known and familiar stagnation. Your denial of your own truth creates a position of self-imposed ignorance and arrogance about your own deception and soul sabotage.

Your willingness to separate from your awareness of your soul has you codependent on your own arrogance, which causes you to be ignorant to the truth of your own deception. When you use your false beliefs to justify generating unresolved emotions, you concretise your way of living to be separated from your awareness of your soul and truth. Your arrogance has you denying the opportunities life presents and causes you to live without awareness of the authenticity of your soul. Your arrogance is an unresolved emotion that you use to deny yourself the opportunity to resolve and evolve your soul's unconsciousness. When you deny your awareness of truth and the truth of yourself, you condemn yourself to a life of repeating your patterns of soul oppression.

Integrity is:
- **Truthfulness which is the conscious application of truth**
- **Free flowing consciousness**
- **Wholeness and unity within**
- **A way of being that respects the fundamental equality of all souls**

Self-exercise 7

1. What do you regret conforming to?
2. What is your understanding of life?
3. How do you contribute to compromising your own soul integrity?

Chapter Thirteen

Avoidance of soul commitment

When you fear being honest with yourself, you commit to separating from your awareness of your soul and you disassociate yourself from feeling the truth of your unresolved emotional patterns, behaviours and belief systems. When you choose a distorted version of yourself without challenge, you condition yourself to avoid honestly answering your own internal questions. You allow yourself to hide your soul's potential by acting out the familiarity of your emotional patterns. When you run from your potential, you choose to stay in the familiarity of your soul's unconsciousness.

- Do you realise what is familiar to you?
- Have you chosen to commit yourself to protect your own soul demise?

Soul demise is the loss of awareness of truth. The familiarity of your unresolved emotions enables you to perceive your stagnation as a comfort zone, which inhibits your ability to understand your life, yourself as a soul and your interaction with others. You can commit yourself to being separated from the truth of who you are in your natural essence. You can deny yourself the freedom within truth and battle reality to remain committed to your separation from your awareness of your soul, and your disassociation from feeling truth.

You can avoid any commitment to finding your own truth, because you would have to truly acknowledge how you are feeling and living; and you would have to acknowledge that what you prioritise is usually in opposition to the very essence of your soul. If you acknowledged the truth of your soul and your unresolved emotions, you would have to commit to change and apply effort to the potential of living in and with truth. The thought of change can create such fear in you that you shy away from the possibilities, and anchor back to what is already known and familiar within the stagnation of your soul's unconsciousness.

Your commitment to your soul requires you to truly care about your soul and to acknowledge the value of your existence. You ignore the significance of being a soul with your beliefs of 'not being good enough'. These beliefs of 'not being good enough' become indoctrinated in you, as you experience your unresolved emotions, others' unresolved emotions and your judgement of all of these. When you fear taking full responsibility for yourself, you will store and carry your experiences of unresolved emotions and justify wallowing in your unconsciousness. Your lack of commitment to being truthful, causes you to condition yourself to protect the cyclic patterns you create from your stored unresolved emotions. This means you stall your own evolution and remain trapped by your fear of yourself.

If you were brought up in an environment where the needs for love, being valued, feeling worthy and being respected were not fulfilled, your sense of self becomes distorted by the unresolved emotions and beliefs of those around you. Are you choosing to continue in the familiarity of

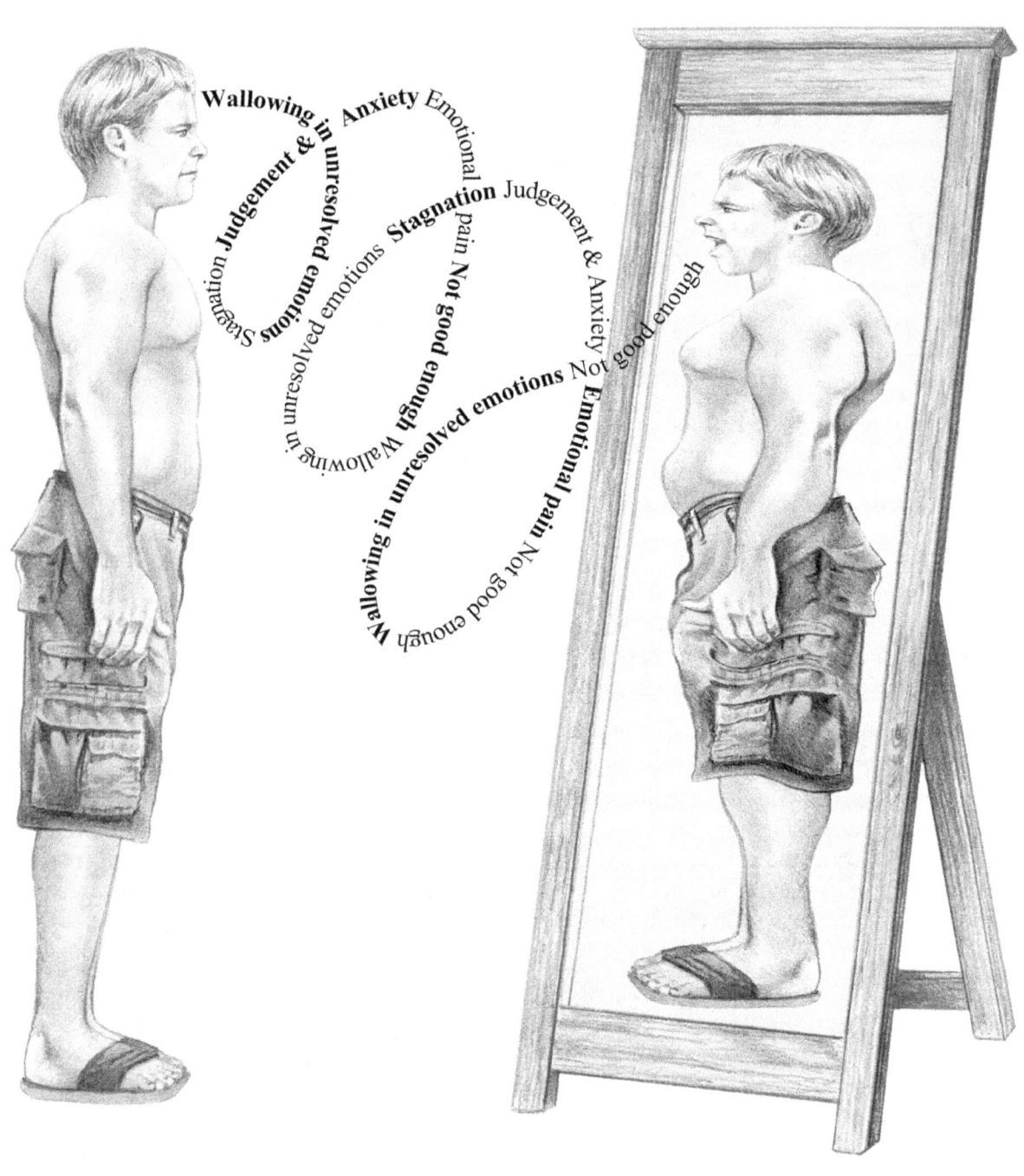

You can perceive yourself through the filters of your own perception of yourself and reality, not realising your perception of yourself and reality is distorted.

Avoidance of soul commitment

these unresolved emotions and choosing to govern yourself with your belief of 'not being good enough'? When you acknowledge your distorted beliefs you have to independently seek your truth, without emotionally encumbering yourself with others' unresolved emotions. You have to independently choose to resolve what is emotionally stored within you to find your freedom. Freedom is what your soul's consciousness is committed to.

You externalise how you feel about yourself onto others, without really being aware of your own hidden agendas behind this behaviour and the consequences of your denial. Your lack of commitment to your soul, causes you to use and justify your unresolved emotions to automatically project your judgement at others and your life experiences, in the belief that your judgement will protect you from having to acknowledge truth. If you choose to be intentionally unconscious to the reality of yourself, the truth of what you are doing will elude you.

When you are swamped by your unresolved emotions, you will give little consideration to the ramifications and effects your judgement causes you and others. You can disregard the emotions behind your comments and justify your actions with your unresolved emotions. Your denial of your own emotions causes you to stagnate within your disassociation from the truth of your unresolved emotions. You may prefer to desperately blame others for the way you feel instead of being truthful with yourself, in an attempt to avoid taking self-responsibility. No one escapes experiencing the projection of unresolved emotions; throughout childhood, life and within relationships. It is up to you to choose, either to explore your truth and resolve your emotions, or to willingly perpetuate your stagnation because you refuse to accept the truth of your reality.

Your resistance to being honest with yourself has you avoiding the possibilities and potential of your soul. By acknowledging the reality of your freedom of choice, you are choosing to explore the truth of your soul. Discovering what that means is to be conscious of your own soul journey and allows you to consciously experience the truth of your life. Being honest about yourself creates the opportunity for you to experience the truth of your soul journey, instead of existing on a treadmill of emotional pain, fighting the evolution of your soul.

Self-exercise 8

1. What emotions are familiar to you?
2. What patterns can you acknowledge that you should challenge?
3. What do you need to resolve?
4. How do you fight your soul's evolution?
5. What would you truly like to commit yourself to?

When you ignore the reality of your unresolved emotions, you carry them through life, encumbering yourself with the familiarity of your emotional baggage, which enables you to be complacent about your own separation from your awareness of your soul and truth

Avoidance of soul commitment

Chapter Fourteen

Separation from your awareness of your soul

Separation from your awareness of your soul, means you existing unconscious of your soul truth, often with the intent to control your awareness with denial. When you control yourself to be disconnected from your true feelings about yourself, life and your interactions with others, you disconnect from the reality of how you actively pursue your resistance to and denial and avoidance of truth. When you are separated from your awareness of your soul, you become codependent on the barriers to the truth of your soul's consciousness. Barriers to truth are:

- Soul denial
- Resistance, denial, avoidance and codependency
- Judgement, manipulation, confusion and control
- Images, illusions and controlled identities
- Controlled evolution
- Heresy

Your separation from your awareness of your soul allows you to use your emotional baggage, which is another way to describe your soul's unconsciousness, to be the only energy you notice and react to and from. You can programme, condition and indoctrinate yourself to repeat your known patterns, and this is detrimental to yourself as a soul. When you separate from your awareness of your soul, you are not acknowledging the significance of your freedom of choice, and your life can feel as if you are just going through the motions. As you control yourself to your known soul oppressive patterns, you attempt to be oblivious to how you are choosing to interact with your own reality. When you have programmed, conditioned and indoctrinated yourself to avoid the truth of yourself as a soul, and the reality and ramifications of your decisions, you can become lost in the void of your separation from your awareness of your soul. This leaves you indifferent to truth.

You can become obsessive with the belief that you already know yourself, or that you have to find yourself, without ever really questioning or comprehending what it is that you believe you understand, or believe you will be if you do find yourself. You can become so obsessed with striving towards a destination or securing a performance, that you lose the significance of being honest about whatever is occurring now. As you separate further from the significance of what your present moment is revealing, you create a position of arrogance about your reality, and often build unrealistic expectations that you attempt to control for. You attempt to control whatever you can, to avoid being confronted with the truth of just how little you understand.

Your deception, which is the willingness to lie to yourself, is the foundation of your separation from your awareness of your soul. Your separation from your awareness of your soul means you experience life through the filters of your unresolved emotions. When you use your unresolved emotions to generate emotional upheavals to camouflage your deception, you become intentionally unconscious. This leaves you distracting yourself from the real issues, and becoming embroiled in what is superficial, with no real intent to be honest with yourself. This has you constantly trying to feel in control, which becomes a compulsion. You use your desire for control to protect what you class as essential for your emotional survival, which become assumed coping skills that sustain your willingness to be unconscious of your soul truth. Your control becomes what you worship. Have you ever asked yourself what you are trying to survive and cope with? Maybe, it is your own desire to control that you are trying to survive. Your desire to control can become so strong that the energy concretises to become your known and defended belief system by which you live.

You can create the belief that you are unchallengeable and unchangeable in the way you analyse and process life, yourself and others. This belief sets you up for a lifetime of perpetuating your unresolved emotions, which causes you to become dependent on what is already known and concretised within your soul's unconsciousness. You believe you are exerting freedom by resisting, denying and avoiding your reality and truth, but do you feel free?

When you are willing to lie to yourself, and become dogmatic about having control, you may pretend not to be, which is one of the lies you tell yourself. Your dogmatism about your control and your hidden worship of control, causes you to use emotional grenades, if you believe your control is threatened. This leads to you compulsively projecting your unresolved emotions at those you believe are inhibiting your control of life.

You can use your unresolved emotions as an excuse to justify your own destructive behaviour towards your soul and others. When you justify and excuse your emotional behaviours, you exist separated from your awareness of your soul. You can ignore how you utilise your freedom of choice and how you fight your awareness of your soul's consciousness for control.

- What do you believe you are in control of?
- Do you believe your control will pacify the internal conflict within you?

Your freedom of choice means you always have the opportunity to choose to be honest about the reality of your emotions. Within your separation from your awareness of your soul, you create a continuous cycle of negativity, while resisting, denying and avoiding your reality, and you can become extremely codependent on being separated from your awareness of your soul truth. Feeling the difference between your emotions and true feelings, enables you to acknowledge the truth of your separation from your awareness of your soul. Being honest about the repercussions of your unresolved emotions is essential to the realisation of your separation from your awareness of your soul.

When you blame anything or anyone for the emotions you feel, you deflect yourself from acknowledging the truth of your own emotional reality. You can emotionally choose to act out your unresolved emotions without comprehending the reality of your emotions. You can also disregard your own emotional input into your reality and continue to tolerate being separated from your awareness of your soul truth. You use your unresolved emotions to actively develop your own separation from your awareness of the truth of who you really are. Your unresolved emotions create emotional, energetic and physical barriers to acknowledging your soul truth.

Your soul's consciousness seeks to unify all aspects of your soul's unconsciousness with truth, by resolving and evolving all unresolved emotions. Allowing yourself to accept and explore the concept of unifying your entire energetic system with truth, means you align to your soul consciousness' intention, which is your original intention. Your acceptance of your intention to unite with truth by being honest with yourself, creates an opportunity to understand yourself as a soul who has both conscious and unconscious energy. Your trust in truth enables your soul's consciousness to guide you through your soul journey of resolution and evolution.

Chapter Fifteen

Indoctrinations and concretisation

Indoctrinations are the beliefs that you have adopted that are not of the truth of your soul. Concretisation is when the beliefs are so ingrained and deep-rooted that you constantly align yourself to your patterns, mindsets, cultures, attitudes, judgements and behaviour traits without ever acknowledging the option of present moment conscious choice. You become locked in and submissive to your own programming, conditioning and indoctrinations, which actually restricts your exploration of truth.

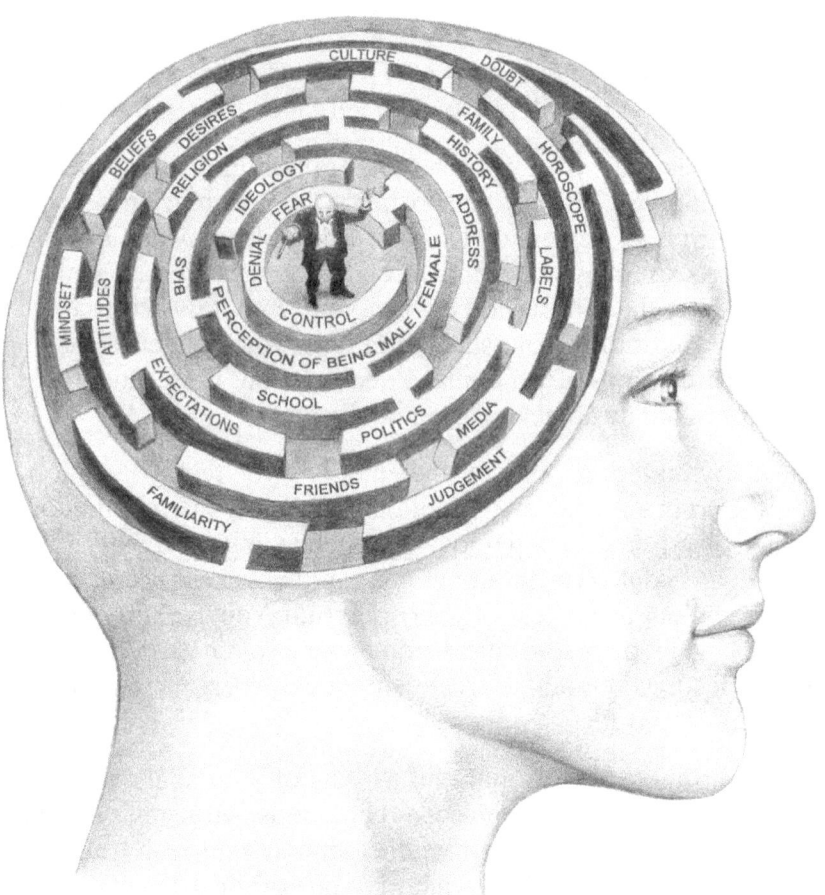

Your indoctrinations become the governing factor of your thought process, which creates an emotional maze of deception that you use to deprive yourself of feeling the truth of your present moment. Your unwillingness to be honest with yourself about your indoctrinations becomes the conductor of your soul oppression, which perpetuates your indifference to truth.

Your indoctrinations which have been passed down to you, are perpetuated cycles of generations of mankind's beliefs and unresolved emotions. The passing down of indoctrinations exposes the history of your family, the era in which you were born, the judgement generated by society and the culture you were exposed to. You are also the perpetuation of your own soul history and the history of your exposure to mankind's indifference to truth. There are many contributing factors to how and what you have been indoctrinated into, which stagnates your understanding of truth. The indoctrinations you have adopted and are willing to protect with your own unresolved emotions cause you to deny that your indoctrinations do not resonate with your soul.

Throughout your childhood you were exposed to many different combinations of mankind indoctrinations. You have been exposed to many belief systems, which have conditioned you to either accept, tolerate or oppose what you perceive you have to do with your indoctrinations.

- Are your indoctrinated belief systems contradictory to what you have observed, experienced and felt while you were being indoctrinated?
- Do you covertly and sublimely accept your own indoctrinated beliefs without challenge?
- Are you aware of the beliefs, you ascribe to that do not align with your awareness of truth?

You need to challenge your indoctrinations and belief systems to understand the truth of yourself as a soul. You align your unresolved emotions to your indoctrinations and belief systems, which all become filters of judgement you use to enact the perpetuation of your cycles of soul oppression. Your programming and conditioning from your indoctrinated beliefs, causes you to use your many forms of indifference to truth to defend your unresolved emotions. You can be obsessed with resisting, denying and avoiding acknowledging how you defend your own indoctrinated beliefs, and why you need to defend them to yourself.

You can be in constant conflict with your indoctrinated beliefs and fight the discrepancy you can feel. When you have been indoctrinated to compete with reality, you berate yourself with judgement if reality does not adhere to your indoctrinations. You may attempt to rely on your indoctrinations to cope with your unresolved emotions, and use your indoctrinations to conform to any collectives of mankind's indifference to truth that suits your agenda. When you concretise your indoctrinations, you become reluctant to challenge their validity. You may feel the stagnation within your soul's unconsciousness and misinterpret what you are feeling because of your indoctrinated beliefs. If you have misinterpreted your feelings, how does that misinterpretation impact your understanding of yourself, your life, your soul truth and the world you live in?

Indoctrinations come from and are in many forms. For example:

- History
- Family
- Religion
- Schools
- Media
- Gender
- Friends
- Country
- Address
- Ideology
- Politics
- Labels
- Sports
- Experiences
- Finances
- Horoscopes
- Sexual Orientation

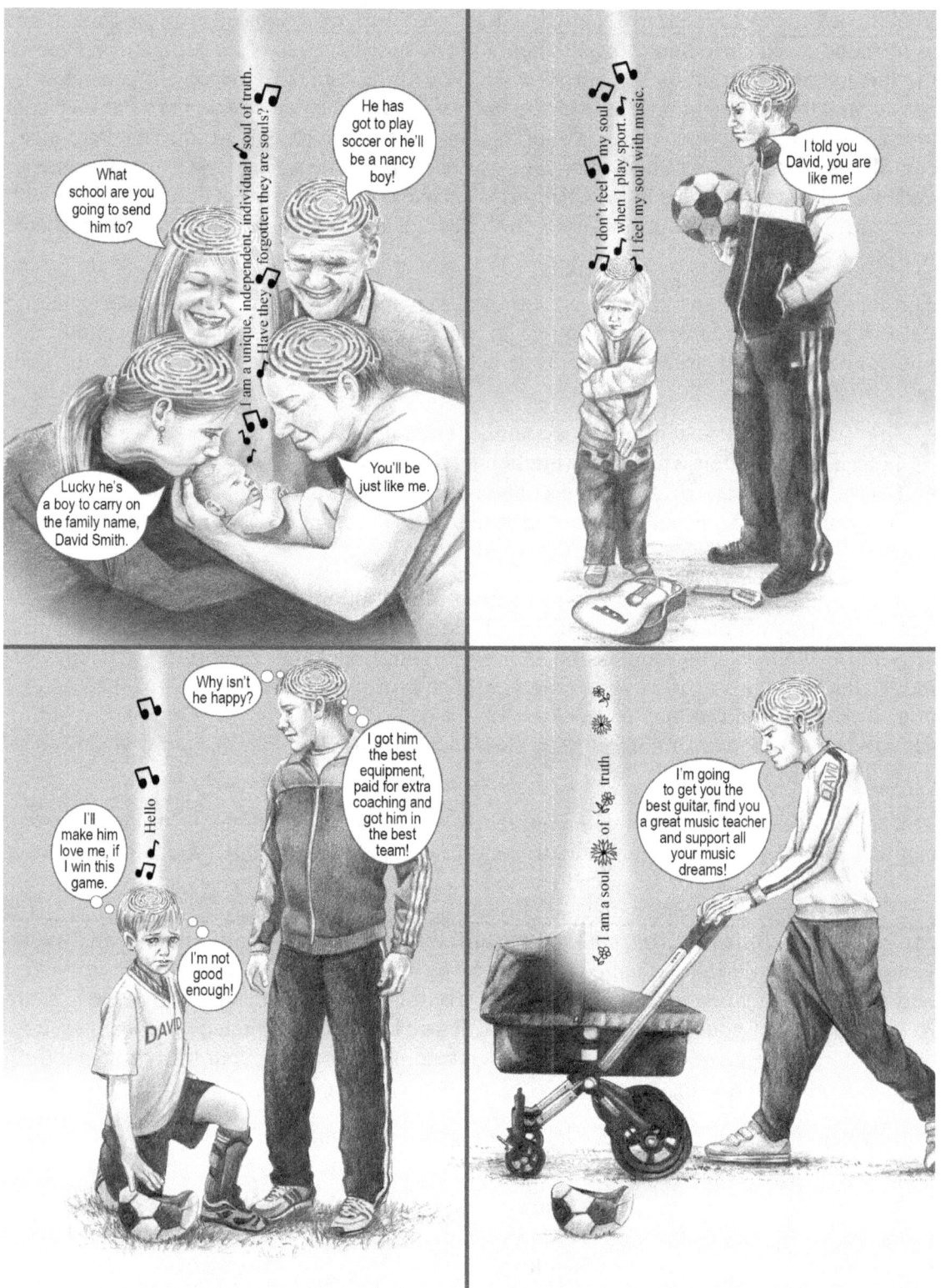

114 | *Indoctrinations and concretisation*

Your indoctrinations can cause you to believe you need an image to project at others and yourself. When you want to control how you are perceived by others, you disassociate from the truth that your image is concealing your soul. Indoctrinations are learned methods for how to deny your resonance with truth. Your indoctrinations can ingrain in you an opposition to your soul, and it is only you who can challenge the validity of your indoctrinations.

Do you comprehend how biased you have become to the familiarity of your:

- Beliefs
- Emotional patterns
- Mindsets
- Culture
- Attitudes
- Judgements
- Behaviour traits
- Perception of your life

- Do you allow your indoctrinations to determine your choices, or do you choose to be truthfully present in each moment?
- What do you use to steer your life to a perceived comfort zone?

Your perceived comfort zones are often not comfortable, but you stay in them because they are familiar, which means you exist on a treadmill of familiarity.

When you have indoctrinated yourself to believe your images, illusions and controlled identities will sustain the self-definition you want to cling to, you fear what truth could expose. This leaves you fighting your reality, in an attempt to secure your expectations of what you believe will be achieved with your images, illusions and controlled identities.

- Have you ever examined the reality of your images, illusions and controlled identities?
- Who are you trying to impress, while you are oppressing your awareness of your soul's consciousness?
- What are you trying to achieve?

Your perception of yourself, others and life is tainted by your expectations, which are created by your desire to control your images, illusions and controlled identities. You struggle to acknowledge the amount of effort you exert trying to control everything, everyone and yourself to be conducive to your expectations, images, illusions and controlled identities. This leaves you constantly judging your ability to control and use your indoctrinations to justify the concretisation of your control structures, which causes you to be stagnant within the energy of your soul's unconsciousness.

When you oppose your awareness of truth, you exist within the emotional torment of your own mind chatter, constantly judging and comparing yourself to your expectations of your images, illusions and controlled identities. Your expectations, images, illusions and controlled identities are often constructed with and dictated by your indoctrinated beliefs. If they have been constructed it means they are not of your soul and truth.

- Have you ever examined the validity of your expectations and the indoctrinations that you have used to construct them?
- What are you hoping your expectations, images, illusions and controlled identities will pacify within you?
- Are you on high alert to protect your own image from being exposed by your soul truth?

Your indoctrinations, beliefs, expectations, images, illusions, controlled identities and control structures keep you separated from your awareness of your soul. Being honest with yourself allows you to be conscious of the process of learning to care for the truth of yourself as a soul and is the choice to experience the truth of who you are. Your honesty is essential to explore the possibility of resolving your unresolved emotions and experiencing the evolution of your soul. Trusting truth is a key component of resolution and evolution.

Self-exercise 9

1. Identify and challenge your indoctrinated beliefs, images, illusions, controlled identities and expectations.
2. How do you protect your indoctrinations?
3. Who and where did you adopt your indoctrinations from?
4. How do you use your indoctrinations?
5. What do you resist, deny and avoid, to sustain your indoctrinations?
6. Are your indoctrinations based in truth?

Chapter Sixteen

Escapism

Escapism is an attempt to resist, deny and avoid truth and reality. When you are codependent on your ability to escape from your awareness of truth and reality, you exist separated from your awareness of your soul. You have created many patterns of escapism to retreat from the reality of truth, yourself, others and life. Your escapism habits are just control structures that you use to stay separated from your awareness of your soul. This is an attempt to avoid feeling your feelings, and you remain stagnant in your resistance to soul accountability and denial and avoidance of being capable of living conscious of your soul integrity.

When you attempt to escape from the reality of your feelings, you use crutches to diffuse your attention away from the truth of your feelings. Your crutches become emotional habits, which allow you to lose your awareness of the truth of yourself, causing you to react unconsciously.

For Example:
- Drinking
- Eating
- Smoking
- Drugs
- Shopping
- Watching TV
- Gossiping
- Religion
- Sports
- Wallowing in the past
- Work
- Family
- Children
- Relationships
- Sex
- Money
- Control
- Creating images and illusions
- Indifference
- Blame
- Judgement
- Confusion
- Soul oppression
- Attempting to preempt the future
- Obsessions
- Victim
- Martyr
- Attempting to orchestrate reality

You use the crutches to fill the void you feel. The void you feel is your separation from your awareness of your soul. These crutches become what controls you. Your crutches become the anchor to your stagnation and you control yourself with your emotional habit of trying to deny the truth you feel. The way you distract yourself from truth is how you control your perception of yourself and deceptively interact with life.

You use your mind to emotionally create a diversion from feeling the truth of your separation from your awareness of your soul. You feel an inexplicable void and may try to fill the space with:

- Fantasies
- Reliving your past
- Predicting your future
- Assessing your judgement
- Anticipating others' judgement
- Ruminating about what has been said, or what you would have liked to have said
- Emotionally running scenarios of possibilities

You may seek to be emotionally numb to your reality and separate into your internal world, by creating emotional turmoil within your mind, or by using what you have become addicted to that you believe enables you to escape from your:

- Thoughts
- Feelings
- Memories
- Embedded beliefs
- Fears
- Unresolved emotions
- Judgement

You use your mind games to play with your unresolved emotions and are indifferent to the reality of creating your own emotional, energetic and physical torment and turmoil.

When you escape into an illusory world within yourself, you ignore the truth of your feelings, your soul's consciousness and your reality; this is the appeal of your separation from your awareness of your soul. You believe your resistance to and denial and avoidance of truth, will let you elude and forget the truth of being a soul, on a soul journey with the original intention for resolution and evolution. You may want to avoid feeling your soul's consciousness, so you emotionally bombard yourself with unresolved emotions. This creates emotional, energetic and physical barriers, which buffer you from your awareness and the clarity of what you feel, observe and internally know.

You can actively seek to escape into your images, illusions, controlled identities and control structures rather than acknowledge your own soul truth.

- How can you see the truth of yourself without acknowledging the falsities of your images, illusions, controlled identities and control structures?

Escapism is the ploy you use to separate yourself from your awareness of reality and allows your non-acceptance of yourself as a soul to continue unchallenged. When you avoid being honest with yourself, you attempt to ignore the reality of your emotional, energetic and physical chaos and the consequences of your denial of reality. This always becomes problematic.

When you are unwilling to accept the truth of your reality, you seek to escape your own awareness, often becoming obsessive with what you use as a crutch to support your denial of reality. Your denial of reality and your reluctance to be completely honest with yourself, causes you to relive your past and wallow in the emotions you refuse to resolve. Your denial of reality causes you to constantly set yourself up to repeat your past, so you can deceptively justify the emotional baggage you continue to carry. You can emotionally fight the possibility and potential of evolving beyond what is emotionally known to you. You can also become enslaved to your unresolved emotions and perpetuate emotional habits to continue your own abuse against the very essence of your soul.

You may think you are escaping your unresolved emotions, but in truth you are just recycling them, constantly lying to yourself about how you feel and what you can observe about yourself. Your non-acceptance of yourself as a soul is the crux of your resistance to freedom. Your escapism habits offer little or no respect for being a significant, unique, independent, individual soul and the opportunity to freely express the truth of your soul. Your protection of your soul denial has you opting for an emotional existence bound in the familiarity of your unresolved emotions.

Self-exercise 10

1. What do you need to escape from and where do you think you go?
2. What can you observe about your emotional habits?
3. Who and what are you enslaved to?

Chapter Seventeen

Caring for your soul

Caring for your soul is acknowledging and accepting the reality of yourself as a soul, which enables you to experience life with this awareness. Caring for your soul enables you to experience life as a learning process. To experience life as a learning process, you have to be honest about your own observations of life, your feelings, your unresolved emotions and yourself. Caring for your soul is to feel the natural significance and value of your own existence. Life is not meant to be about judging yourself as inferior or superior, it is meant to be about acknowledging the meaningfulness of your own significance, uniqueness, independence and individuality as a soul of *True Source Divine Origin Consciousness*. Caring for your soul allows you to accept the concept that all that exists matters, and is naturally significant.

Caring for your soul is acknowledging the possibility of feeling your soul truth, without your desire to control. When you do not care for your soul, you harshly judge yourself via a mankind system and you will attempt to only see value in your control structures, images, illusions and controlled identities. When you determine your assessment of yourself with a judgement that suits your control structures, you are being indifferent to yourself. Your harsh judgement devalues the significance of the truth of your soul, because you only judge truth through the filters of your soul denial.

When you do not care for your soul, you will remain lost in your lack of understanding of your own significance, uniqueness, independence and individuality. This causes you to conform to and assess yourself with your indoctrinated mankind beliefs of what is of value and worth. You can lose your awareness of yourself within your own unresolved emotions and anchor to what you believe will supply you with an acceptable image to hide from your unresolved emotions. You can become obsessive about trying to prove the validity of your image, as you seek arenas to act out your charades. When you do not care for your soul, you will anchor to your soul denial, believing you are your image. You lose awareness of the significance of your soul by being selective in how you define yourself. Your distorted self-definition may be formed from using your judgement of only one aspect of your life experience:

- Body image
- Employment
- Family heritage
- Religious beliefs
- Possessions
- Perceived social standing
- Social media presence
- Finances
- Education
- History

You may obsess about everything, and excessively stress about how others perceive you, which causes you to lose sight of the significance of your authenticity. You can use a distorted perception of yourself, and the one aspect of yourself that you judge harshly, to oppose accepting the exquisiteness of who you naturally are. This can leave you fearful of being exposed to your own reality.

Caring for your soul enables you to give priority to being consciously aware of being loyal to truth and the integrity of your soul's consciousness. Caring for your soul is the choice to accept self-responsibility and is choosing not to use others' unresolved emotions to justify your separation from your awareness of your soul and truth. Caring for your soul allows you to listen to your own soul insight and awareness; which you usually ignore. Caring for your soul is the acknowledgement of your options, choices and experiences from a soul perspective rather than from a controlled expectation of the outcome.

Caring for your soul means objectively observing the cause and effect that your decisions have on your life, and not justifying the suppression of your awareness of reality, by being determined to control everything to your expectations. When you choose to be oblivious to truth, you attempt to minimise your awareness of the effect of your unresolved emotions. When you continue to deny your feelings, you abandon truth because you believe you are in control. When and why did you make the decision to abandon truth for your illusion of control? You can only control yourself to continue your known patterns of denial by manifesting your unresolved emotions without challenge. Challenging your beliefs and control structures is exactly what your soul's consciousness seeks, so you can resolve the control structures of your unresolved emotions.

Your compassion for yourself as a soul seeking truth, is a major component to experiencing caring for your soul. Harsh or contrived judgement is used to remain in opposition to compassion, and your opposition allows you to cling to your deceptive judgement. As you disconnect yourself from the truth of your potential and the possibility of evolving beyond the destructive patterns, you override your awareness of your soul's consciousness. When you objectively observe your unresolved emotions, you create a space for the probability of change and evolution. Caring for your soul will allow you to be an objective observer of yourself, mankind and truth.

Caring for your soul allows you to choose to always orientate to truth, utilising and accepting all experiences as opportunities to learn about the truth of your life and the way you are treating the very essence of your soul. You express your care for your soul by acknowledging and utilising the awareness of truth you have, and by being willing to be honest about your present moment. Acknowledging even the smallest amount of truth creates a foundation for you to expand your awareness of truth. Trusting truth enables you to accept being a significant, unique, independent, individual soul who is seeking to be conscious of your life being a soul journey. Caring for your soul enables you to trust truth to be the motivating source in your life experiences, rather than conforming to the preconceived ideas of needing to be in control.

Caring for your soul is not a selfish act because if you are truly caring for the integrity of your soul, you will not conform to others' control structures, unresolved emotions and obligations, or inflict others with your control structures and unresolved emotions, nor will you attempt to obligate others to your expectations. You become willing to share the truth of your soul with life, yourself, others and the presence of truth within your reality. By allowing yourself to explore your ability to unify with truth, you start to care for yourself as a significant, unique, independent individual who seeks to feel the truth of your soul's consciousness. Your compassion and honesty enable you to resolve your unresolved emotions. Being honest about the intent and motivations behind your unresolved emotions, requires you to deal with yourself, reality and others from truth and with grace. Your soul's consciousness accepts that we are all living the journey of life uniquely and all deserve respect for that reason alone. You acknowledge being an individual by caring and accepting the significance of your soul's consciousness.

Acceptance

Chapter Eighteen

Lives

What do you see when you look at people? I see lives and souls.

Lives are the journey of life. We are all experiencing life and are all significant. We can all become complacent about ourselves and reject the significance of uniqueness, independence and individuality.

To hide from the reality of yourself and the true meaning of your life is to cheat a life meant to be lived in truth. When you allow yourself to run from the significance of your soul and the purpose of your soul journey, you entrap yourself in your fear of truth. To run from truth is to fear yourself.

Your soul worth cannot be measured by mankind's judgement.

Your fear of the unknown is an expression of your avoidance of your own soul truth, soul journey and reality. Trusting truth is accepting the reality of what is.

Understanding the truth of your soul is the opportunity that life presents. Your soul journey is an opportunity to trust truth and expand your soul awareness and your understanding of the significance of your honesty.

A life lived by controlling yourself to an image of what you pretend to be, means you hide the true feelings of your soul from yourself, which is not really living. It is an act, an illusion, an image that can destroy your awareness of the significance of your soul journey.

A life of control is existing and a true life not lived.

It is your unresolved emotions that have you wallowing in the negativity of yourself, life and others. You create emotional barriers that hinder you from feeling your own soul and use your unresolved emotions to develop your separation from your awareness of your soul. Unfortunately, you can be very unconscious to the reality of what you are doing and the extent to which you will go to achieve being oblivious to the reality of who you are.

Soul abuse is to disregard your soul consciousness' understanding of truth. If you choose to stay operating in your unresolved emotions without challenge, you create an environment of stagnation. To never allow yourself to contemplate what is unresolved within your soul, is to miss the mark of your soul journey. Your accumulated unresolved emotions and memories of unresolved emotional experiences create imbalances in your energy system, which is a catalyst to develop 'dis-ease' within your system.

Life

Life can be defined as moments joined together; living is experiencing the moment as it happens.

Have you ever looked back at a photo and thought, "that was a really good outing" but at the time you were caught up worrying and annoying yourself with your desire for control and missing the moments as they happened?

Avoiding the reality of life and resisting living in your reality, cheats and restricts you from experiencing the true essence of life and experiencing feeling the truth of your soul.

Questionnaire 4

Answer these questions off the top of your head. Do not dwell on questions, just move on and come back if you need to. There is no right or wrong answer, just how you feel.

Please note: I recommend you use a separate journal in which to write your answers to the questionnaires, so you can use this questionnaire numerous times without being influenced by what you have written before.

1. Identify any soul concepts you would like to explore:

2. What are your thoughts on caring for your soul?

3. What are your thoughts on soul integrity?

4. How do you feel about yourself?

Define the following:

1. Soul Judgement

2. Soul Compassion

3. Soul Evolution

4. Soul Stagnation

5. Consciousness

6. Unconsciousness

7. Integrity

8. Oblivion

Comparing your questionnaires

It is always fascinating to realise what you internally knew but at the time did not understand. By comparing your answers from questionnaire 3 to your answers from questionnaire 4, you may expose to yourself how in sync you are with your own insight and awareness. You may expose to yourself with more clarity that which you seek to explore the truth of.

When you look back on question 1 of questionnaire 3 and compare it to question 1 of questionnaire 4, it may expose to you how your indoctrinated beliefs are hampering your ability to explore the soul concepts you want to explore.

When you look back on question 2 of questionnaire 3 and compare it to question 2 of questionnaire 4, it may expose how your perception of your soul has changed. It may also expose the truth of wanting to explore the truth of your soul unencumbered by what you think you already know. You may expose yourself to your own willingness to feel and explore what resonates with you.

When you look back on question 3 of questionnaire 3 and compare it to question 3 of questionnaire 4, it may expose how your sabotage behaviours are in direct conflict with your own soul integrity. Your willingness to sabotage your own insight and awareness is an opposing force to your own soul integrity.

When you look back on your answers to question 4 of questionnaire 3, do they sum up what you were seeking to explore while reading section 2? Do you have more clarity on what you were seeking answers for? Have you been exposed to information which resonates with what you were seeking to discover more truth about?

Does your answer for question 4 of questionnaire 4 expose a change from how you felt when you started reading section 2?

When you compare your answers to **'define the following'** from questionnaire 3 to questionnaire 4, can you see a change in your attitude towards being willing to explore the truth of yourself?

Did your answers on questionnaire 3 seem like dictionary explanations of words and your answers on questionnaire 4 come from a soul perspective of what you feel? Can you feel yourself resonating as a soul seeking truth?

Have you exposed yourself to your own yearning to explore the truth of yourself, regardless of what you find?

By exposing your negativity you allow yourself to discover what to be honest about. Your honesty exposes your emotional, energetic and physical barriers to feeling the truth of your soul. Resolution and evolution is a process. There is no way of controlling yourself to be resolved and evolved, it is a matter of honestly finding what is obstructing your natural flow of consciousness, because it is through your honest exploration of life that you will discover your truth. Your life is your journey of resolution and evolution; it is a process of discovering the truth of both your conscious and unconscious energy.

Section Three

Chapter Nineteen

The journey

The journey of life is the exploration of the truth of who you are and what you are experiencing. The journey of life is an opportunity to resolve what is inhibiting you from feeling, acknowledging and accepting the significance of the purity of who you are. You are a unique, independent, individual soul of *True Source Divine Origin Consciousness*. The journey of life is an opportunity for you to discover the significance of your own uniqueness, independence and individuality. Your soul journey is your life and it is like a river, with your own ebbs and flows. You are a soul within the river and your unresolved emotions are boulders, whirlpools and at times cyclonic storms you put in the river; these cause you to struggle against your own natural significance and the opportunity life creates.

Your journey is one of discovery; it is an opportunity to discover the truth of who you are.

You are born to experience life and living as a way to expose yourself to the truth of all your energy. You are born with the freedom to choose how you will respond to yourself and your own energy. You create energy: sometimes this is an energetic force produced from your unresolved emotions which is unconscious energy, and sometimes this is the natural emanation of the truth of who you are which is your flow of conscious energy.

You are an exquisite being who is the interface between both your soul's consciousness and unconsciousness. Your soul's consciousness is the purity of your flow and unity with truth. It is the natural origins of who you are. When you deny the natural origins of who you are, you generate unconscious energy produced by and from your unresolved emotions, which is the fabric of your soul's unconsciousness.

You are responsible for all the unconscious energy you have created. You created unresolved emotions by denying your natural significance, uniqueness, independence and individuality, and by using your dishonesty to seek an illusory control of life and truth. The energy of your soul's unconsciousness is the accumulation of the unresolved emotions from this and previous lives. Your life is an opportunity to resolve your unresolved emotions and to acknowledge, accept and resonate with the reality of being a soul. You are born with a blueprint of experiences that will expose you to your own energy. These experiences become opportunities for you to discover what is unresolved within you and to discover your own awareness of truth. Your blueprint is your soul consciousness' intention to resolve the unresolved emotions within your soul's unconsciousness. You are the interface between all your energy and have the freedom to accept or deny the truth of any opportunity that is presented within your life experiences.

Your soul journey is like a river, it has its own ebbs and flows. Life is a journey which takes you through many experiences, often into uncharted waters. Your life experiences create opportunities for you to discover the truth of who you are.

Your unresolved emotions carried from your soul denial history leave a residue within the energetic mass energy of mankind. This is because after your death, the residue of your unresolved emotions is stored within the energetic mass energy of mankind, until you return to Earth. You are responsible for everything you have created. Your creations of unconscious energy remain your responsibility, and life is your opportunity to recognise you have freewill to resolve unconscious energy and to experience conscious energy. The energetic mass energy of mankind is the collective energy of all individual souls' unresolved emotions combining to create a macrocosm of unconsciousness. It is the energy of our collective oppression and denial of the truth of our souls. Soul truth is the reality of both your soul's consciousness and your soul's unconsciousness to which you are the interface.

You are born to evolve from unconsciously participating within the energetics of the mass energy of mankind, which is attached to you via the unresolved emotions of your own soul's unconsciousness. All the unconscious energy of your unresolved emotions, returns to you and is stored within your own soul's unconsciousness as you experience life within a physical body. You are a soul within a physical body, and have experienced many lives on Earth. You are responsible for your own energy. Your life experiences and interactions with yourself and others will activate the unresolved emotions you need to become aware of, which creates opportunities for the resolution of your unresolved emotions. You have the freedom to either acknowledge or deny what is being activated or created by your reactions to life. However, all unconscious energy will be stored within your soul's unconsciousness until you are a willing participant in your own resolution and evolution.

Your willingness to resolve your unresolved emotions is the choice to be a conscious participant in the evolution of your soul and to free yourself from carrying the energy of your unresolved emotions. You internally battle the emotional impact your unresolved emotions and your denial of the truth of being a soul creates, and it is this battle that is constantly exposing you to the truth of your own energy. Your denial causes you to forgo your uniqueness, abandon the truth within your soul and to separate from your awareness of truth, which leaves you opposing your experience of life. When you deny your soul truth, you are manipulating yourself and you will continue to perpetuate your own unresolved emotions. You separate from your awareness of your soul and anchor to the illusion of being able to control your soul journey without acknowledging the ramifications of abandoning your awareness of your soul and truth.

Your manipulation leaves you feeling confused, about what you are feeling. Your confusion separates you from accepting feeling your own soul and from being able to observe yourself in truth. You abandon your uniqueness and become enslaved to your own indifference to yourself. You use the energy of your soul denial to compete against your soul consciousness' ability to expose you to truth, corrupting yourself to be unwilling to explore truth. Once you are immersed in confusion, you struggle to completely trust your own internal soul knowing and the truth of being a significant, unique, independent, individual soul of *True Source Divine Origin Consciousness*.

When you compete against your soul's consciousness, you separate from being aware of your feelings and from your ability to feel truth. Your feelings are of truth and communicate reality to you. Your separation from your awareness of your soul's consciousness leaves you immersed within your own negativity and swamped by your unresolved emotions. When you abandon your awareness, you disassociate from feeling the reality of your origins, which is *True Source Divine Origin Consciousness*. When you separate from your awareness and denounce your ability to be conscious of your own unresolved emotions, you create denial to conceal the reality of disregarding your own blueprint agreement. Your blueprint agreement is your original intention to resolve the energy that separates you from your awareness of your soul's consciousness. You oppress your ability to be conscious and control yourself to abide by mankind's beliefs, which leaves you existing unconscious to the truth of your soul.

Your confusion creates separation, and separation from being aware of your soul creates more confusion. This leaves you on an emotional merry-go-round, where you enact what is unresolved within you. Your separation from your awareness of your soul and your willingness to exist in denial has you concentrating on your negativity, causing you to be swamped by your own unresolved emotions, disassociated from feeling the truth of your soul and the truth of your own energetics. Energetics is the vibrational energy you create from your unresolved emotions and from controlling yourself to be unconscious of truth.

Your separation from your awareness of your soul creates the need in you to be codependent on your images, illusions and controlled identities. You can use your images, illusions and controlled identities to define experiences that you then utilise to create beliefs about who you are. What you have experienced does not define who you are; your experiences are opportunities to explore how you react and how you deal with the truth being exposed to you. This enables you to discover what you need to resolve and to discover the strength of your soul. Your experiences are present moment events that contribute to the tapestry of your life, which exposes many aspects of yourself to you. You have had responses to your experiences, which you have used to define yourself, but unless you comprehend the entirety of yourself, your definitions will be created from fragments that deny the magnitude of who you are. You limit yourself to these definitions, and use your definition of your controlled identities, to adopt a role to control yourself to, such as mother/father, son/daughter, brother/sister, husband/wife, partner, employee, neighbour, friend, struggling human, lost soul or black sheep of the family. When you limit yourself with definitions, you lose the ability to feel yourself as a soul within your different experiences. You allow yourself to be overwhelmed by your own desire to control reality and become antagonistic towards the reality of being a soul and the reality of your life experiences. This causes you to seek anchors within the environment of unconscious energy to emotionally feel in control of your existence.

Your separation from your awareness of your soul has you automatically anchoring to your own repertoire of unresolved emotions, enmeshing yourself with the energetics of the mass energy of mankind, losing your sense of significance and your ability to freely trust your soul's consciousness. When you distrust your soul's consciousness you disconnect from acknowledging yourself as a significant, unique, independent, individual soul.

When you search for security and validation within the unconscious energy of mankind, you become addicted to trying to control the unconscious energy you emotionally feel from mankind and your own unresolved emotions. You create an illusion of control to sustain an image of security while you deny your reality. You learn to use and project your unresolved emotions as a weapon against yourself, others and against feeling your resonance with truth.

When you search for security, validation and a sense of worth from others' unconscious energy, you try to replicate what you have abandoned from within your soul. You try to create a sense of belonging and significance via another's reaction to you, exchanging and interacting from unconscious energy to unconscious energy and ignoring your soul within. When you devalue yourself but seek external validation, you become consumed with doubt and lose the willingness to trust yourself. This means you devalue the integrity of your soul and you allow your unresolved emotions to take priority over acknowledging your soul consciousness' insight. This leaves you operating from your desire to feel in control, instead of trusting your insight, which means all your decisions stem from your unresolved emotions and your reactions anchor you to the belief that you are defined by your unresolved emotions. You become codependent on justifying your unresolved emotions and create images to compromise your awareness of truth.

By compromising your awareness of truth, you spiral further away from your awareness of being a soul and create a fear of feeling and a fear of truth. You fear that acknowledging your feelings will disturb your soul denial and your illusion of control, so you manipulate yourself with lies to suppress your own awareness of your unresolved emotions. You become codependent on your methods of resisting, denying and avoiding truth. You become codependent on your desire for control, external approval, attempts to secure your embedded beliefs and any other process that reinforces your separation from your awareness of your soul.

One of your control structures is to reject and disown your awareness of your soul, which leaves you with a deep-seated feeling of abandonment and fixated on negativity. You do not realise that your negativity is causing you to abandon your own awareness of naturally resonating with *True Source Divine Origin Consciousness* and with yourself as a soul.

When you separate from your awareness of your soul, many distortions are created by your unresolved emotions. You become codependent on your own distortions, often believing that you have been abandoned by truth, which allows you to deny that you have abandoned the truth within yourself. You encourage every type of negativity, such as indifference, manipulation, resentment, deception and disbelief of your significance to truth with your soul denial. This reinforces your separation from your awareness of your soul and your disassociation from feeling the reality within your life. This causes you to devalue yourself, which makes the journey of evolving your soul seem unreal and unimportant. This deception generates beliefs of being unworthy, insignificant and 'not good enough' for your own illusion of life.

Your negative beliefs about yourself are an expression of unresolved emotions, which hinder you from feeling your awareness of your own soul journey. When you separate from your awareness of your soul and truth, you inhibit yourself from questioning what you believe you know, and stagnate yourself in your own limited understanding of who you are. When you limit your understanding of yourself, you gravitate towards external belief systems, instead of acknowledging the significance of your own wealth of insight. You consume

yourself with the need to conform to your images, illusions and controlled identities, trying to survive and accommodate your denial of your soul and truth.

When you become consumed with your own fictitious images of yourself, you align with and become indifferent to truth, and willingly participate in your denial of reality. Your images and beliefs become the source you anchor your control structures to. You protect your control structures and beliefs with your resistance to and denial and avoidance of truth. You disassociate from feeling the possibility of resolving your unresolved emotions with truth and apply yourself to an image of how you want to be perceived. You seek validation for your images of yourself and never question why you desperately want validation and approval. You deny compulsively wanting more recognition, approval and acceptance, believing you can disguise your unresolved emotions and ignore the reality of being a significant, unique, independent, individual soul of *True Source Divine Origin Consciousness*.

Your soul's consciousness is never separated or disassociated from feeling *True Source Divine Origin Consciousness*. Your soul's consciousness flows within you from your origins; you have just separated yourself from acknowledging your awareness and abandoned your ability to use your freedom of choice to challenge your own deception. Your soul journey is an opportunity to challenge every deception to discover your own truth, and this is the decision you have to make using your freedom of choice.

When you want to dictate what truth is, you use your unresolved emotions to diffuse your conscious insight and your ability to understand yourself as a soul. You concretise yourself in your indoctrinated beliefs, separating and disassociating further from what you can feel as truth, isolating yourself in the demise of your awareness of your natural resonance with truth. This can cause you to become lost in your own deception, fearful of your unresolved emotions and trapped by your lack of soul integrity.

Your soul denial creates the need to judge and compare yourself to your perceived images of others and their lives, which distorts your understanding of yourself and your reality. This creates more space for your deception to control your existence, and allows your unresolved emotions to dominate your life. You feel your separation from your awareness of your soul as a void; in reality you are feeling yourself hide from the truth of being a soul. You feel the confusion created by being disassociated from feeling truth, and emotionally spiral further into the vortex of your soul's unconsciousness. You often seek a solution to your separation from your awareness of your soul by using your distorted beliefs and your desire to control. These become emotional cyclic patterns that cause you to stagnate in your own confusion, internalising your emotions which compels you to attempt to control yourself with your soul denial and indifference to truth.

LEFT: When you attempt to control the truth of your soul journey with your unresolved emotions, you can become swamped by your own unconscious energy. Your soul journey exposes what is unresolved within you and creates the opportunity for your honesty to calm the perilous waters of your separation from your awareness of your soul and truth.

Part of your cyclic patterns is to emotionally feed your own undercurrent of guilt, shame and humiliation, which you derive from your denial of your natural significance. Your guilt, shame and humiliation are types of indifference energy created from your non-acceptance of yourself as an evolving soul. All souls have the potential to evolve their own unresolved emotions, including their own indifference towards themselves. When you reject your potential to evolve, you anchor to your indifference, soul denial, desire to control and victim mentality. Your fear of being accountable for your own soul betrayal, created by your opposition to your awareness of truth, causes you to seek a justifiable excuse or a mankind emulation of significance to disguise the reality of your unresolved emotions.

Your fear of your own uniqueness, controls you to stay immersed in the negativity of your unresolved emotions, cycling in your patterns of oppression and beliefs of 'not being good enough' to feel your significance. The emotional impact of your soul denial creates a need in you to be obsessive with anything that allows you to avoid acknowledging the truth of feeling your own internal unrest. You become the warden of your self-imposed emotional prison; stagnant and confused about the significance of yourself as a soul.

As your unresolved emotions become concretised, you overwhelm your ability to trust in your internal knowing that there is more to you than you understand at this present moment. Your denial of being a soul leaves you unaware of the reality of yourself and being dishonest about your illusion of control. You control yourself to be a puppet on the strings of your own negativity, reacting unconsciously to what you are emotionally experiencing and the truth of your feelings. You become consumed with the desire to suppress your own unresolved emotions, as you attempt to fool yourself about the significance of being honest.

You use your denial of being a soul to control yourself to repeat pathways of stagnation, inhibiting your own curiosity to discover truth and to feel the eternal soul within. You are controlling yourself to miss your opportunity to acknowledge the reality of being a significant component of *True Source Divine Origin Consciousness*. You search externally to find something that you can be part of, to give yourself a sense of significance and belonging. The truth is you are already naturally significant to *True Source Divine Origin Consciousness*; your origins.

Your soul's consciousness knows the futility of your illusion of control and seeks to expose truth. Accepting you can trust your awareness of any exposed truth will heighten your awareness of your whole soul system, both your conscious and unconscious energy. By trusting truth, you feel your opportunities to resolve your unresolved emotions and evolve beyond your limited perception of truth and yourself.

The truth of your experiences reveals opportunities for you to resolve and evolve, because despite any deception you run on yourself, your conscious insight will still be present. As the truth is exposed, your soul's consciousness patiently waits for you to understand:

- The existence of *True Source Divine Origin Consciousness*.
- The truth within you.
- The significance of resolving and evolving your unresolved emotions this lifetime.

When you are willing to corrupt your own awareness of truth or succumb to others' deceptive agendas because you refuse to be truthful with yourself, you create a struggle which causes your journey to be fraught with deception and confusion.

The reality is, acknowledged and accepted truth cannot occupy the same space as deception within your awareness, so you have to be extremely honest with yourself about your beliefs, actions and feelings; remembering you have been conditioned to resist, deny and avoid truth. You need to acknowledge how defensive and protective you have become about your unresolved emotions, because your defensiveness stagnates your ability to be honest about and with yourself. Being honest and truthful is the way to consciously understand your own uniqueness, independence and individuality. Choosing to challenge and question yourself without using judgement and manipulation to justify your unresolved emotions, creates the opportunity to feel your freedom to be an expression of your truth.

Your soul acceptance and trust in the process of resolution through honesty, reveals the way you interact with life, yourself, others and truth. The development of your honesty is the journey of realising the truth of being a significant, unique, independent, individual soul of *True Source Divine Origin Consciousness*. By realising the truth of your ability to choose consciousness, instead of cycling unconsciously in your known negativity, deception and self-created images, illusions and controlled identities, you can experience freedom from your soul oppression. When you seek truth through honesty, you create the space to feel your own soul insight and awareness of truth.

When you use your freedom of choice manipulatively, you distort your awareness of your soul truth and ignore your reality. This leads to you controlling yourself to build an image to exist in. Images, illusions and controlled identities are unsustainable, because they eventually implode from the level of your control. Life has its own reality, irrespective of your illusory control. Your choices have relevance to the opportunities within your soul journey, but are not the only governing energy over your reality. Life is multi-strands of energy that converge to reveal a present moment. Your choices, your control and your truth are within the multi-strands as are others' energy, the collective energy of mankind and your history you no longer remember. Your awareness of the unconditional love and support *True Source Divine Origin Consciousness* has for you and your soul journey, enables you to accept responsibility for your own energy, within the multi-strands of energy creating your present moment. When you trust in yourself enough to challenge your distortions, you create the opportunity to explore the reality of your experiences objectively. By allowing yourself to apply conscious effort, to acknowledging your truth and challenging the reality of your awareness of life, you create the space for change to unify with the truth of your soul.

Your acceptance of your truth converts your denial, deception, distortions and internal anarchy into conscious understanding and acceptance of your soul journey. The purpose of your soul journey is to resolve your separation from your awareness of your soul, your disassociation from feeling your truth and your denial of reality.

With a renewed awareness and understanding of the process of evolving your soul, your history can take on a new perspective. What lessons have you learned and can you be open to the opportunities to challenge what you believe you know? You create change by acknowledging how you create your emotional obstacles. You fear coming to the realisation that the purpose of your emotional obstructions is to prolong your own unconsciousness. You override the potential of your soul with your fear of your internal knowing, which causes you to baulk at change and the opportunity to explore truth.

You have the freedom to utilise your opportunities to either explore the truth that you can resolve your unresolved emotions, or hide from the exquisiteness of your soul. Your honesty with truth resolves your codependency on denial, which resolves the perpetuation of your unresolved emotions. By being truthfully honest with yourself, you will realise you only control yourself to conform to your own misconceptions, which allows you to conceal truth. You have the freedom to be truthful with yourself and reality. When you choose not to conform to mankind's soul denial, mankind energy has no power over you. Living without denial is the opportunity to experience being at peace and at ease with the reality of who you are, which is a significant, unique, independent, individual soul of *True Source Divine Origin Consciousness*.

Trusting yourself to experience life resolves the need to control yourself with the fear of vulnerability. Fear of vulnerability is being frightened that your denial will not work and that you will have to accept, deal with and be consciously present in your reality. You will defend and obsess with your negativity and your struggle to accept the significance of being a unique, independent, individual soul, but that is the journey. Enjoying the freedom to consciously acknowledge the value and worth of your own soul, is truly experiencing living and evolving; this is your soul purpose. When you accept you have the freedom to be present in your life experiences, you enable yourself to objectively observe your unresolved emotions. This creates the opportunity for resolution, and to witness yourself being the truth of your soul. When you are not being present and honest about the truth of your life experiences, you will use your unresolved emotions to compete against the truth of your soul. You are the one who chooses the energy you utilise, which will either be your unresolved emotions or the core essences of your soul.

Unresolved emotions

Dishonesty—Confusion—Control—Denial—Fear—Humiliation—Resentment—Codependency—Judgement

VS

Core essences of your soul

Freedom—Trust—Grace—Unconditional Love—Hope—Care—Honesty—Kindness—Compassion—Peace—Integrity

Both lists are endless and the choice is yours.

Chapter Twenty

Understanding the energetics of the mass energy of mankind

Mankind mass energy consists of emotional, energetic and physical energy. Your body is physical energy. You only have a body while on Earth and your body returns to Earth when you die. You are a soul in a physical body. Emotional energy is a reaction to your reality from your unconsciousness. You can have emotional reactions to what you feel, observe and acknowledge that cloud your perception of reality and inhibit you from being present and honest about the truth of your present moment. Your energetic energy is the accumulation of your past and present moment emotional reactions, amalgamating to form an energetic force. You project this energetic force both internally and externally with the intention to deny truth and reality. This is how you ensure the sustainability of your separation from your awareness of truth and your disassociation from unconditionally loving yourself, others, life and the presence of truth.

The energetics of the mass energy of mankind is the accumulation of mankind's unresolved emotions, created from mankind's soul denial history. We, as mankind, keep the unconscious energy active to protect our soul denial, and to sustain both our individual and our collective ability to oppress the awareness of truth. Energetic energy is the combination of your own personal collective of unconscious energy, reverberating with the energetic collectives within the mass energy of mankind or within another's personal collective of unconscious energy. Energetic energy is the amalgamation of unconscious energy forming a cyclic force of soul oppressive energy. Your own personal energetic collective of unconscious energy is your soul's unconsciousness.

The energetics of the mass energy of mankind consists of the accumulated collective energy of mankind's unresolved emotions. The energy of each unresolved emotion congregates to form an energetic collective of that emotion. If you have unresolved emotions, you are a contributing factor to the energetics of the mass energy of mankind. You are constantly re-energising your emotions to hide from the reality of your awareness of your soul's consciousness and your blueprint. Your blueprint is an agreement of what you have elected to experience, feel, explore and resolve during this lifetime. Within your agreed blueprint you have chosen to attempt to resolve your unresolved emotions, which are your contribution to the energetics of the mass energy of mankind. Resolution can only occur if you honestly acknowledge your opportunities to resolve your unresolved emotions and trust your soul's consciousness and truth.

Trusting your soul's consciousness and truth is evolution. Your soul denial has you denying what you elected to experience, feel and explore, which causes you to remain entrenched in your unresolved emotions, enmeshing yourself in the energetics of the mass energy of mankind.

All unresolved emotional energy within the energetic collectives of the mass energy of mankind, is a mutation of soul denial energy. Soul denial energy always has you caught in the desire to control truth, or to be indifferent to truth. You use your unresolved emotions to oppose and oppress the reality of your awareness of being a soul. You use your soul denial energy to disguise your opportunities to resolve and evolve. You use your reverberation with the energetics of the mass energy of mankind to support, sustain and fuel your own defection from truth. You orchestrate your own soul demise, losing your awareness of yourself, by encasing yourself within your own unconsciousness, and this produces energy which you contribute to the energetics of the mass energy of mankind. You use your energetic interaction with the energetics of the mass energy of mankind, to sabotage your awareness of your soul's consciousness, and your awareness of the presence of *True Source Divine Origin Consciousness*.

The energetic mass energy of mankind is the energy that is unconscious to the truth of conscious energy. Mankind has created emotional, energetic and physical barriers to truth. The desire to control truth has caused mankind to deny ourselves the opportunity to explore the presence of truth, because we are always attempting to protect and enhance our ability to believe in our own control. This is how we protect and fortify our illusions, misconceptions and outright lies, which is our choice to allow truth to be a casualty of the arrogance and ignorance of mankind.

Each individual's unresolved emotions contribute to mankind's emotional, energetic and physical barriers to truth. Barriers are the concretisation of mankind's opposition to resolving our desire to control truth. When you are concretised in your unresolved emotions, you remain unaware of your own desire to control truth. When you lie to yourself about your unresolved emotions, you sustain your barriers to truth. This fuels the energetics of the mass energy of mankind with your deception, and encases you in your opposition to acknowledging the truth of your soul's consciousness and unconsciousness. As you attempt to encase your soul truth with lies, you denounce your soul's origins and abandon your original intention to resolve and evolve.

The energetic mass energy of mankind is a reflection of what we, as mankind, are individually doing to our own souls. Mankind's barriers to truth are created by the collective energetic force of us, as individuals, denying the truth of who we are. We are significant, unique, independent, individual souls of *True Source Divine Origin Consciousness*. You are a significant, unique, independent, individual soul of *True Source Divine Origin Consciousness*, and have the potential to seek to resolve and evolve beyond the barriers of opposing truth. Mankind's barriers to truth reciprocate each individual's non-acceptance of their soul truth. Mankind clings to the familiarity of unconscious energy to protect our illusion of control. Mankind fears our deception will be exposed by truth and believes truth interferes with our illusion of control.

RIGHT: *The energetic mass energy of mankind is the energetic structure of our collective unconsciousness. Barriers to truth, which we all contribute to, are the combination of unresolved emotions and control structures. Barriers to truth impede awareness of the flow of consciousness within reality and are the result of our collective intent to separate from being aware of the truth of our souls and to disassociate from feeling truth.*

True Source Divine Origin Consciousness

Consciousness

Desire to control, indifference to truth, resentment of reality, oppositional energy, programming, conditioning and indoctrinations, guilt, shame, humiliation, denial of reality, Disassociation from feeling love.

Heresy

Controlled evolution - desire to control your soul denial with beliefs.

Images, illusions and controlled identities.

Judgement, manipulation, confusion and control.

Resistance, denial, avoidance and co-dependency.

Soul Denial

Mankind's Energetic Collectives

Energetic mankind collective of rage

Energetic mankind collective of elitism

Energetic mankind collective of superiority

Energetic mankind collective of guilt

Energetic mankind collective of shame

Energetic mankind collective of humiliation

Energetic mankind collective of spiritual Illusion

Energetic mankind collective of envy

Energetic mankind collective of resentment

superiority
elitism
rage
guilt
shame
humiliation
spiritual illusion
envy
resentment

Soul Denial

You participate in the energetics of the mass energy of mankind by resisting, denying and avoiding your natural resonance with truth. When you are codependent on your addiction to the energetics of unconsciousness, you believe and fear truth will interfere with your illusion of control.

All of your unresolved emotions have a correlating energetic collective within the energetics of the mass energy of mankind, in which you are an active participant.

For example:

- Rage
- Gluttony
- Resentment
- Envy
- Guilt
- Hatred
- Greed
- Jealousy
- Elitism
- Desire
- Pride
- Selfishness
- Lust
- Vulnerability
- Denial
- Humiliation
- Indifference
- Slyness

All of your control structures have a correlating barrier to truth:

- Resistance, Denial, Avoidance, Codependency.
- Judgement, Manipulation, Confusion, Control.
- Images, Illusions and Controlled Identities, which are roles.
- Controlled Evolution, which are beliefs that control you to remain stagnant in the evolving process. It also stems from the belief of being able to control soul denial energy.
- Heresy is indifference energy that results in you being anti-truth and anti-yourself, via your desire to control, indifference to truth, resentment of reality and oppositional energy. These are filtered through your programming, conditioning and indoctrinations, and protected by your guilt, shame and humiliation, enabling your denial of reality. All of which equates to disassociation from love.

LEFT: Our own personal soul's unconsciousness is the microcosm of unconsciousness and is contributing to the energetic mass energy of mankind, which is the macrocosm of unconsciousness.

Energetic Collectives Of The Mass Energy of Mankind

- Energetic collective of country
- Energetic collective of state
- Energetic collective of town
- Energetic collective of sports teams
- Energetic collective of Socio-economic level
- Energetic collective of friends
- Energetic collective of religion
- Energetic collective of work
- Energetic collective of family
- Energetic collective of school

The control structures of mankind's denial of truth combine with the energetic collectives of mankind, to create the energetic structure of the mass energy of mankind. When you deny truth you will use any unconscious energy to control yourself to disassociate from feeling truth, immersing yourself within the unconscious energy of your unresolved emotions and control structures, and therefore reverberating with the energetics of the mass energy of mankind.

All groups of people form energetic collectives. For example:

- Families
- Schools
- Workplaces
- Friends
- Religions
- Countries
- States
- Suburbs
- Cities
- Towns
- Strangers in the same place
- Teams
- People dealing with the same issues (e.g. victims of a cyclone, cancer patients, new mothers)
- Fans of the same thing (e.g. famous person, music, hobby).

When you deny the reality of being a significant, unique, independent, individual soul, you are choosing to identify yourself via an energetic collective of the mass energy of mankind, and deny yourself the ability to feel the independence of your own soul. This leaves you denying the energetic independence of your soul's consciousness and the complexity of your soul's unconsciousness. You also deny the velocity of your own soul denial, and immerse yourself in negativity and the unconsciousness of mankind. When you use mankind energy as an excuse to deny truth, you are attempting to relinquish your responsibility for your own resolution and evolution. You can become captivated by your denial and the drama of your life in the unconsciousness, and miss the opportunity to live exploring the truth of who you are, evolving beyond your limited perception of yourself as just a struggling human, of mankind.

As mankind, we have learnt to ignore how we separate from the reality that we use our unresolved emotions as control structures, to oppress our ability to resonate with truth. We have disassociated from feeling the essence of our soul and interwoven our unresolved emotions with the energetics of the mass energy of mankind and this interconnects us. You resolve your denial by acknowledging and accepting the reality of being able to feel the truth of your unresolved emotions. Your acknowledgement means you are trusting the opportunity that life presents to participate in your own evolutionary process. Life presents the opportunity to resolve what is unresolved and to evolve beyond your own limited perception of yourself.

When you protect your soul denial you are choosing to participate in the stagnation, you create when you abandon your original intention to live as a conscious soul. This leaves you existing separated from your awareness of your soul and reverberating with the energetic collective energy of mankind's soul denial. This causes you to align to the belief that existing, is a struggle and this deprives you of feeling the truth of your soul. Your disassociation from feeling your original intention stagnates you in your denial of the entirety of your reality. If you choose to deny the truth of being a soul, you will miss the mark of your life experiences. You will fight against the opportunity to feel truth and dismiss the reality of life being a learning experience for you as a soul. Life is an opportunity to accept the reality of being a significant, unique, independent, individual soul of *True Source Divine Origin*

Consciousness. When you accept that life is an opportunity, accept that you are a soul and trust yourself to be present in the entirety of what you are experiencing, you begin to live with ease, instead of existing in a struggle.

Your soul denial is the crux of your soul's unconsciousness, which drives you to continuously seek unconscious energy to disharmonise your resonance with truth. You use your unresolved emotions to produce the unconscious energy you need to fragment your awareness of and resonance with truth. You may exist in a struggle, ramping up your unconscious energy to sustain separation from your awareness of your soul and truth. Resolving your soul denial requires you to be truthful about what you feel, and internally know. You are a soul who feels, you may deny your reactions and suppress your awareness, but you feel.

The energetic collective energy of mankind's soul denial is the crux of mankind's collective unconsciousness. There are collectives within the unconsciousness of mankind that are willing to emulate the energy of *True Source Divine Origin Consciousness*, but emulations are always steeped in deception and the desire to control. Emulations only fool those who are willing to be deceptive and seek to secure an illusion of control to pacify their own desire for control of truth. Emulations regardless of how good they are, are just emulations, a pretence to conceal the reality of the desire to control the presence of *True Source Divine Origin Consciousness*, which is the presence of truth within reality. When you truly feel truth and freely unify with truth, you feel the presence of *True Source Divine Origin Consciousness*.

Your participation within the energetics of mankind's collective unconsciousness emphasises all of your insecurities, which you deem as imperfections that need to be controlled, concealed and avoided. When you control yourself to suppress what you came to resolve, you are choosing to conform to and revere mankind's collective soul denial, which emotionally fuels your alliance to the energetics of the mass energy of mankind. You are choosing to devote the opportunity of life to a web of deception, which governs the way you experience life. You are choosing to disharmonise with truth, and end up in a struggle, seeking solace in your illusion of control.

RIGHT: *Your soul's consciousness contributes to the collective consciousness. The energy of your soul's unconsciousness contributes to the collective unconsciousness on Earth. We individually produce energy that contributes the collective energy we experience.*

True Source Divine Origin Consciousness

Your Soul's Consciousness

Heresy - Desire to control, indifference to truth, resentment of reality, oppositional energy, programming, conditioning and indoctrinations, guilt, shame, humiliation, denial of reality, disassociation from feeling

Controlled evolution - desire to control your soul denial with beliefs.

Images, illusions and controled identities.

Judgement, manipulation, confusion and control

Resistance, denial, avoidance and co-dependency.

Illusion of control → ← Desire to control

Soul Denial
Embedded Beliefs and Fears

Departure from this lifetime

When you die, the energy of your soul leaves your physical body. Before you return to your origins, which is truth, you are still attached to your soul's unconsciousness. Your unresolved emotions are your incomplete soul lessons. When you die, your awareness is awakened for you to recognise and feel the truth of being a significant, unique, independent, individual soul of *True Source Divine Origin Consciousness*. You can feel your origins and will awaken to your origin truth. This state of awareness remains for about two to three days after your funeral; after this time you will withdraw from your own awakening. You have the freedom to choose your destination; you will either choose to return to your origins or become lost without a physical body within the energetics of the mass energy of mankind.

Your funeral signals the time is upon you to make your choice. If there is no funeral the options are still the same; you will feel the change in your own awareness and know it is time to choose. It will be by your choice, if you separate from your awareness of truth. If you choose to return, you naturally flow with truth and return to origins. The decision to return to truth is unique and for the majority it is just a natural transformation to return to origins. Some souls elect to go at the moment of death, others after they farewell loved ones and others during their funeral. After death your awareness and understanding of truth has no barriers to truth, although you still have your freedom of choice. You retain your freedom of choice while being awakened to the purity of the truth of who you are and the truth of your origins. Your return to origins is done with your freewill.

RIGHT: When you die your soul's consciousness returns to your origins of True Source Divine Origin Consciousness and your unresolved emotions disperse into the correlating energetic collectives of the mass energy of mankind

True Source Divine Origin Consciousness

- jealousy
- regret
- indifference
- insecurity
- resentment
- humiliation
- manipulation
- soul denial

Energetic collective of mankind's jealousy

Energetic collective of mankind's regret

Energetic collective of mankind's indifference

Energetic collective of mankind's insecurity

Energetic collective of mankind's resentment

Energetic collective of mankind's humiliation

Energetic collective of mankind's manipulation

Energetic collective of mankind's soul denial

Energetic Mass Energy Of Mankind

Lost souls

A lost soul is a soul who has chosen to remain within the energetic mass energy of mankind after the death of their physical body. If a soul chooses to return to their origins, their unresolved emotions energetically disperse back into the correlating energetic collectives, within the energetics of the mass energy of mankind. If a soul elects to reject their origins and stay in the energetics of the mass energy of mankind, they are choosing to engulf their soul's consciousness with their indifference to truth, soul denial and desire for control. They are choosing to stay attached to their unresolved emotions and to remain within the energetic mass energy of mankind. Death provides a junction where each soul has the choice to either, return to origin truth or to remain in their own deceptive denial. Deception is the concealment of truth and does not resonate with the frequency of truth. All souls experience being awakened to truth after the death of their physical body; and lost souls are lost because they have chosen to reject being awakened. The reasons for rejecting the origins of truth are as varied as individuals.

Some lost souls acknowledge their awakening and believe they can control their awareness of truth, and create an illusion of being spiritually elite within the energetics of the mass energy of mankind. They deny the reality of trying to control the truth energy within their awakening, as they attempt to convert themselves into spirit guides and sages within the energetics of the mass energy of mankind. The awakened period will subside as they engulf themselves with the energy of their soul's unconsciousness and then they will attempt to emulate being of truth. These lost souls use their desire for control to create another image for themselves to be lost in, as they did in life. Deception can never be classed as truth, because it is the willingness to oppose the value of truth. The lost soul's denial of reality, enables the use of deception to be a pretentious emulation of truth as they become lost in their own void.

Some of the souls who elect to be lost within the energetics of the mass energy of mankind attach to:

- The people they know, fearing being without their codependency and the familiarity of the energy they have lived with.
- The possessions they owned, fearing being without proof of their image.
- Their illusion of themselves within their body, fearing they are nothing without their body.
- Their workplace because they only identify themselves through their profession, believing their own illusion of being irreplaceable.

Some lost souls anchor to their addictions and seek to feed their addictions by attaching to people or places that are immersed in the same addictions. They seek the energy created by their addictions. These are examples of souls being too lost to realise their own soul truth. They control themselves to fight, mistrust and deny the significance of the energy they feel within the awakening period. Lost souls reject the truth they feel, preferring their own illusion of themselves.

Some souls remain lost in their denial of reality, stuck in their refusal to accept their own death. They can be dazed and confused at the location of their death, transfixed by their moment of death. Their refusal to believe their control does not work causes them to refute

Lost souls are still attached to both their soul's consciousness and unconsciousness, as they were in life. However, the energy of their soul's unconsciousness becomes their prominent energy. At the time of their death a soul, regardless of being awakened to and having the opportunity to follow the unconditional love of True Source Divine Origin Consciousness, may choose to stay captivated in the drama of the energy of their own soul's unconsciousness. This is how they become lost souls, without a body, within the energetics of the mass energy of mankind.

the reality of their death, which has them trapped, unwilling to accept the failure of their control. They ignore their awakening, classing truth energy as unfamiliar and they exert all their energy into denying reality, refusing to acknowledge truth. Some souls die engulfed in their unresolved emotions and choose to ignore everything except their own compulsion to wallow in their unresolved emotions. Often they create a continuous emotional loop to remain enacting the same emotions or an experience of absolute despair, oblivious to anything else. Their soul denial energy, which is their fears, embedded beliefs and rejection of their own value, worth and significance has them stranded and disassociated from feeling their origins; this is an emotional choice to hide from truth.

The motives for choosing to stay in the energetics of the mass energy of mankind are as varied as people themselves and the list of attachments, reasons and denials is endless. Many lost souls use the unresolved emotions generated from their beliefs of being unworthy and unlovable, to hide from the reality of being an eternal soul. They elect to betray their own soul's consciousness by engulfing their awareness with their indifference to truth and fear of truth. They choose to be completely immersed in the energetics of the mass energy of mankind, denying the existence of their soul's consciousness and the presence of *True Source Divine Origin Consciousness*. This is a continuation of how they existed within a physical body. This is a choice to betray the unconditional love within truth, which is felt within the awakening. Many lost souls choose to remain a victim to their own soul denial and their perceived betrayal of truth, because they are frightened to face being accountable for how they lived separated from their awareness of their soul's consciousness and fear feeling the reality of their life. They fail to accept that life is a learning experience and choose to deny themselves the unconditional love and grace of *True Source Divine Origin Consciousness*.

Some lost souls revel in their ability to be on Earth unnoticed and enjoy being a nuisance to the living. The reality is they are choosing to be lost; stagnant within the energetics of the mass energy of mankind and immersed in their own soul denial and unresolved emotions. Some would call this hell. However, at any time they can choose to return to their origins of truth; there are several ways they can do this. Lost souls can return to origins by finding another deceased soul who is in the awakened period and use their truth energy to return to origins. Another way is to become aware of the awakened energy of *True Source Divine Origin Consciousness* within nature. To do this the soul has to choose to be away from mankind energy and to not fight their natural resonance with truth. The lost soul may find a physical person who has the natural ability to anchor truth and hold the space for the soul to become free of their own soul oppression; this allows the lost soul to generate enough truth energy to awaken to truth. Some people have a natural ability to help souls cross over to their origins. This is because they never try to control truth and accept reality honestly, which means they naturally resonate with truth, and by doing so, in the presence of a lost soul, they create the space for the soul to cross over. Lost souls are affected by truth energy, not control energy. Control energy is what lost souls use to deny their own awakened interval.

The method of visualising white light to douse lost souls becomes redundant when used with the desire to be in control, and many lost souls will not respond to this method. White light may have worked for some to assist lost souls, but many have corrupted the intention

of white light with their desire to be in control or with delusions of being able to control truth. Many people use the visualisation of white light, to pacify their own fear or attempt to satisfy their own illusion of being able to control reality, for the purpose of stroking their own ego, which the lost soul can recognise as unconscious energy. The lost soul is already immersed within their own unconscious energy and when people try to use any other type of unconscious energy towards the lost soul, there is no effect. However, if you are generating the energy that represents truth to you, you may remind the lost soul of truth or at least become an annoyance to the lost soul, and this may cause the lost soul to leave. Mankind has invented many methods of moving lost souls away from an area, but truth is required to assist a lost soul to return to their origins of truth. The "*Self* expose self" declaration* can assist in returning lost souls to their origins, but only if it is not used in conjunction with the desire for control or for the purpose of an ego feed.
(*"*Self expose self*" declaration is on page 53).

A lost soul may choose to acknowledge the truth of their decision to hide from their own soul truth. This can happen because the lost soul is observing the soul energy of the living and may get to the point of being unable to deny they are of truth, which will cause them to seek assistance to cross over to their origins.

People who emulate an understanding of truth and try to control truth to their illusion, hide from their soul's consciousness by being consumed with their own image of being spiritually elite. These spiritual illusionists use the deception within the energetic collectives of the mass energy of mankind to support their spiritual illusion. Spiritual illusionists feed their own ego by attracting lost souls and reverberating with the energetic collectives of the mass energy of mankind, to create energetic sensations that suit their illusions. Spiritual illusionists use their own beliefs to interpret the energy they feel, in an attempt to feed their desire to be spiritually aware. This is fuelled by their desire to pacify their own ego and is tainted with their illusion of being spiritually elite. The energetics of the mass energy of mankind will try to emulate truth; if you are honest you will feel the deception. The lost souls attached to spiritual illusionists, are either deluding themselves by attempting to return to origins with their illusion of control, or are just playing with the deception of the spiritual illusionist by joining the charade of the illusionist. This is because the lost soul is seeking to pacify their own ego. Both parties are refusing to resonate with their soul's consciousness and are in denial of their soul's unconsciousness. If the lost soul's intention is to return to truth, it will be their truth that returns them to their origins and the spiritual illusionist may experience being a witness to truth, if they are not filtering the experience through their delusions of being spiritually elite and in command of truth. Unfortunately, many spiritual illusionists do not recognise their own illusions or the way they orchestrate and justify the deception of their soul denial.

Eventually the spiritual illusionist becomes emotionally, energetically and physically impacted by the energetic collectives within the mass energy of mankind that they use to attempt to emulate truth. Any emulation of truth, is a deceptive construction, which ensures their separation from their awareness of truth. The spiritual illusionist's original intention may have been to explore truth and to discover the depths of their soul, but instead they immerse themselves in being an orchestrator of an emulation of truth to pacify their own ego. The energetic force of denial and desire for control required to uphold the image of being spiritually elite, becomes evident and eventually exposes the spiritual illusionist's deception and their desire to control truth. The spiritual illusionist can become disorientated and disillusioned by their own deception, and may struggle to accept the reality of their deceptive illusions. The spiritual illusionist can become entrapped by their own spiritual illusion or their alignment to an established spiritual illusion. This starts by feeding their ego but results in them becoming indifferent to truth and swamped by the desire to secure their illusion of being in control of truth, often suffering internal anxiety from their fear of being exposed as a fraud.

A person and a lost soul can create illusions together to hide from the reality of their significance to truth. They feed each other's indifference to truth, soul denial and illusion of control, believing they can deny the natural order of life, by creating distractions to engulf their existence with denial, and indulge their illusion of control. Unfortunately, they lose the meaning of being a significant, unique, independent, individual soul of *True Source Divine Origin Consciousness*. Both parties try to control the experience of being aware of each other. Both may want the other to take responsibility for their life and choices, or to distract each other from acknowledging the truth of how they feel. They both create a charade which has them missing the opportunity to trust truth and learn from what is being exposed. The lost soul can pretend to be whatever the person is looking for and the person can pretend to be whatever the lost soul is looking for. If they are being honest, they can feel the deception of their own denial. There is a grubbiness to the illusion being created because they are omitting the significance of truth. If they want to control the illusion, they will exert more control and denial to hide from the truth they can feel, which eventually exposes their indifference to truth and desire to cling to their own illusion.

If you are anchoring lost souls to yourself, you are contributing to their soul denial and sustaining theirs and your own self-imposed incarceration in the deception of soul denial. Lost souls anchor to your energetic system via your unresolved emotions, desire for control and fear. Lost souls seek an energetic surge from the energy created by your unresolved emotions. The more turbulent your emotions are, the greater the emotional surge for the lost soul. Lost souls cannot emotionally fuel what you do not have, but aggravate your unresolved emotions to create emotional surges. Your fear creates a brilliant surge of energy and can be easily provoked. Lost souls seek people's emotional upheavals, excitement, joy or fear, to energise themselves.

The lost soul's unresolved emotions will determine what energy they seek. Some will seek to match their unresolved emotions with the same energy. This is to fuel their own unresolved emotions and keep the energy produced by the emotions their primary force. For example:

- Those who believe they are a victim, seek the energy produced by another's victim mentality.
- Those who are angry seek the anger of another.
- Those who are addicted to their desire for control, seek the energy produced by another who worships control.
- Those who operate in an illusion, seek the energy produced by another's illusion.

Lost souls generally seek to ignore truth and can only do this by consuming themselves with the emotional energy that separates them from their awareness of truth.

Some lost souls seek to pacify a delusion they have of themselves. For example: They attach to a person with a victim mentality, to create an illusion of being a healer or spirit guide, while they ignore their own unresolved emotions and the truth of their denial. They project an undercurrent of manipulation to have the person codependent on their awareness of their existence. Some lost souls seek to create an identity they believe will make them revered within their own illusion and attach to anyone who may revere their presence.

Some lost souls may seek to continue lying to themselves about their own reality. They seek to validate their own lies to protect their soul denial. They falsely believe they can play out their lies undetected by truth. Lost souls will seek a charade to accommodate their lies, so they can continue their delusion of themselves. Some lost souls want to be a surrogate for what the living crave. They attach to a person who will oblige their intrusion, and who will accept and join in with the charade. The charade causes the lost soul and the person to both crave what they believe the energetic exchange will create for them. However, the person generally ends up feeling drained because an attached lost soul is a drain on a living person's energy. Some people welcome the lost soul's intrusion and allow the lost soul's energy to channel through their system without realising they are allowing the lost soul to surge unconscious energy through them. Lost souls are different to crossed over souls who are of the purity of truth. Crossed over souls do not intrude into another soul's energy. Crossed over souls respect, honour and acknowledge the sacredness of each individual's uniqueness and independence.

Some lost souls attempt to emulate crossed over souls and can go to great lengths to get your attention, seeking validation, approval and gratitude from you for their presence. They want you to be submissive to their delusions and to feed their denial and ego. The behaviours and unresolved emotions of lost souls are the same, and as varied, as peoples'. Soul denial energy is the same regardless of whether it is within the form of a physical person or within the energetics of a lost soul.

Lost souls can be dormant if there is no living energy. They need living soul energy to be energised. A stagnant space may have a dormant lost soul, which requires the energy of the living to activate the lost soul's energy. The energy of lost souls is similar to a battery, the more they can recharge the longer they can sustain their own energy. Lost souls are attracted to large crowds, seeking an energy surge. Many lost souls are harmless and do not attach to the living; they only seek to be energised, not to interfere with the emotions, energetics or physical reality of the living.

Demonic energy

There is another type of lost soul, which has a demonic energy to its presence. A demonic soul is a concretised lost soul who is completely engulfed in unresolved emotions or a particular emotion, and is immersed in the extremes of their indifference to truth. These demonic lost souls are driven by their own mandate to never again experience the divinity of their origin of truth and to never again live within a physical body. This is an attempt to have ultimate control of life. These souls sever from any desire to be of truth or to feel truth, and become obsessed and possessed by their own desire to be defiant against any recognition of truth, and detest the truth energy within people such as unconditional love, compassion and grace. Demonic lost souls declare truth as an enemy, seeking to reverberate with and intensify their own indifference to truth, soul denial and heresy energy. Demonic lost souls become immersed in their own extreme hostility and seek to incite hostility and fear in all they encounter. Demonic energy re-energises itself by being attached to collective energy within the energetics of the mass energy of mankind, that reverberates with extreme hostility towards truth, such as hatred, rage and indifference. Demonic energy does not need living soul energy to be energised. Demonic lost souls reverberate with the cesspit of mankind's indifference and are completely aware of their choice to do so.

Demonic lost souls actively seek to become soul-less in energy and to completely annihilate their own soul's consciousness. Their intention is to use their soul denial energy to morph into a source of total indifference to truth, becoming demonic. Demonic lost souls usually exist alone and automatically oppose the control energy of other demonic lost souls. They oppose anything that competes for control of their space; they are territorial. Although demonic lost souls are not restricted to an area, they orientate to a location that has the energetic residue of the cesspit of mankind's indifference to truth, such as places where people have experienced extreme violence or they may take ownership of a location where events happened while they were alive, which ignited their rage against truth. At times a demonic lost soul is attached to a location where people have suffered a horrific event, even though they were not at the event. They are attracted to the residue of unconscious energy trapped at the location. The unconscious trapped energy becomes an arena where they can stage their indifference to truth.

Demonic lost souls accept the living within their territory as a toy within their playground and they choose how they play, seeking to have ultimate control of all energy within what they class as their own territory. When you are in the presence of a demonic lost soul you may feel an extreme coldness and gritty energy, and the foreboding feeling you have is your soul's consciousness recognising and alerting you to the indifference energy of their presence.

Demonic lost souls play with the living by intensifying the person's indifference to their own truth and project demonic energy at them to exacerbate the person's insecurities, anxiety and self-doubt. The demonic lost soul seeks to control others to experience extreme fear, seeking to intensify all the unresolved emotions of the person. The demonic lost soul's intention is to have the person immersed in the fear of insanity or susceptible to the control of the demonic soul. However, even when you cannot identify the reality of the presence of demonic energy, your fear responses will kick in and you will generally remove yourself from the demonic lost soul's territory or the demonic lost soul may seek to forcibly remove you. If a demonic lost soul wants you out of its territory it will annoy or terrorise you until you leave.

The demonic lost soul needs time to have a lasting effect on a person. A person's fear is actually a good protection mechanism, because when they feel fear they leave. This means the demonic lost soul usually does not have enough time to have a lasting effect on the person's emotional state or to gain complete control of the person. However, the person is now aware of an energy they fear. It is usually the arrogance of the person's disbelief of what they are feeling, which will cause them to attempt to override their awareness of the presence of demonic lost soul. This disbelief is usually unsustainable. If a person is in the presence of demonic energy their natural self-preservation will eventually override their arrogant denial of reality.

Psychic attack of a soul denial entity

An entity of soul denial is the energetic force of someone's desire to control and can be energetically felt as a presence, similar to a lost soul. It is often thought to be the presence of a lost soul; however, you are actually feeling the emotional tantrum of someone wanting control and the extremes of their indifference energy. You are feeling someone's inability to contain their own desire to control, causing the severity of their desire for control to manifest into a sly energetic force. When the energetic force is felt by another, it often creates confusion and has a gritty feel to it. This is because the energy is constructed from an amalgamation of the person's desire to control, their indifference and the cesspit of their soul denial energy, which is full of fears and beliefs of entitlement.

An entity of soul denial is a sly energetic force generated by a person who has a retaliative disposition, which can be projected at another or at an environment. Their retaliative disposition is generally what they attempt to conceal and suppress with the image of being a victim, or the illusion of being a chameleon that can disguise their desire for revenge or control. The suppression of how they feel and their inability to come to terms with their emotional issues entrap them in their indifference to truth. The sly energetic force is the result of the person's desire to control and their indifference to truth consuming them. This becomes sly energy they project at whomever they focus their retaliation on.

A soul denial entity is created when a person's desire to control has distorted their perception of who they are and reality, often creating unreal expectations or delusions of grandeur. The person becomes willing to project their amalgamated energy, as a means of energetic intimidation, at those they believe are interfering or have interfered with their control and those connected to their reality. The purpose of the energetic intimidation is to emotionally set 'off-kilter' those who threaten their illusion of control. The person projecting the energy is aware they want to undermine another's confidence and seek to create emotional confusion, but may be in denial of the energetic force of their projections. They are aware of their internal angst and who they have fixated on.

The person's extreme desire to control, has them seeking to manifest control over all aspects of their life, because they fear losing control or being controlled. They desire ultimate control of how others can accommodate their delusions and expectations, which causes them to separate from the reality of what they are doing. They also become consumed with the perceived righteousness of their judgement and narcissistic approach to life. This means they splinter aspects of their soul denial, desire to control and indifference, which then amalgamates into an energetic force. This energetic force becomes a way of psychically attacking another, and is the intent to cause emotional, energetic or physical harm. The generation of energy is for the purpose of energetic intimidation, and it is the result of the person's attempts to pacify their own illusory power over others and their environment. However, it is wise to remember it is just an energetic projection of someone's 'desire to control' emulating being an entity. How the entity energetically feels to you and what it actually is, are extremely different. The energy feels intimidating but to have an effect the projected energy is reliant on your fear reactions and responses to experiencing the energetic unknown. The energy is just an energetic tantrum, an eddy of unconscious energy being projected at you, which is also destined to return to sender. You become fearful of the energetic sensation because you do not comprehend what you are feeling. You can feel the slyness of their indifference within the projected energy; and we all have an internal reaction to the slyness of indifference, because it is the energy we fear the most.

The energetic tantrum causes the person to become consumed with the unresolved emotions they refuse to be honest about. When this energy is projected at another, it naturally returns to sender and the sender ends up wearing their own energetic intimidation. This results in the person being fearful of their own energy and scared of their own intimidation. The problem is, if they are in denial of their energetic projection they will assess the reverberation of energy they feel, as coming from an outside source or potentially believe a lost soul is harassing them, or they slyly accuse the person they are psychically attacking of being the one attacking them.

Once a person is consumed with their denial and ignores the truth of their own emotions, they interact separated from an awareness of their reality and disassociated from feeling truth. A person who is projecting their soul denial entity becomes consumed with the sole purpose of attempting to pacify their desire to emotionally, energetically and physically believe they are in control of everything within their reality. This causes the person to feel extremely threatened when they perceive their desire to control is not being appeased. They react by internally activating their own indifference, desire to control and soul denial to generate an energetic force, which they then assess as energy from an outside source. This causes the person to become obsessed with feeling the energy they generate as an energetic force, while seeking to secure blame on an outside source for the energy they feel. The outside source or person they blame becomes what they obsessively fixate on and project their energetic force at. The person becomes obsessed, churning within their mind, about how they are affecting or could affect the person they blame for not being able to appease their own desire to control.

It is a person's retaliative disposition that causes them to amalgamate different aspects from within the depths of the cesspit of their own soul denial, desire to control and indifference energy, which becomes a heresy against their own soul. Their heresy against their own soul generates the insidious energy that becomes an energetic force within them. This is what they project at others with the intent of energetic intimidation. A soul denial entity is an eddy of insidious energy, which may briefly be seen in an energetic form, similar to a lost soul because it emulates what the person believes is intimidating. The eddy of insidious energy that is projected at others never separates from its source and is destined to return with the full force of the projection.

A soul denial entity is a person's retaliative energetic force being used to oppose those who do not appease their desire for control. The form that you briefly see may be related to a past life the person has experienced or can be an emulation of indifference energy the person has experienced from another in this lifetime. This often occurs in people who have survived extreme violence, paedophilia or are willing to go to the extremes of their indifference to get what they believe they want, which causes them to disassociate from their internal reality.

They protect the energy that has formed an entity and will go to any extreme to defend their refusal to be truthfully honest about their internal emotional reality. What they justify as a mechanism to protect against others' indifference towards them, becomes a self-attacking entity of their own indifference energy. The person's desire to control has aggravated them to splinter and abandon as much awareness of truth as possible, becoming sadistic towards their own flow of consciousness, and abusive towards the truth of who they are and those with whom they share their life.

A person with a soul denial entity perceives the world through filters of indifference and obsesses with their own judgement of their control and victimhood. They exist see-sawing within their judgement, which means they oscillate between the extremes of their control and victim energy. This triggers their fear and retaliative disposition. They utilise both desire for control and victim mentality to the upmost, and refuse to acknowledge the truth of how they utilise both, for a sense of ultimate control. To secure the denial required to sustain their obsession for control, every experience, feeling and opportunity is systematically brought back to their judgement of either being in control or being a victim.

The projection of this type of energy exposes the person's willingness to anchor to the belief of deserving ultimate control over all they encounter, and the retaliative energetic force is an energetic representation of their narcissism. The person will attempt to be oblivious to their own energy and want to be perceived as a victim. Even though they are often extremely disassociated from feeling the reality of their behaviours, they are completely aware of what is not pacifying their expectations and desire to have control of reality. The person with a soul denial entity is very resistant to feeling empathy for their own or another's soul, because they are consumed with their own narcissistic retaliative disposition. However, they will dogmatically defend their belief that they are not receiving empathy from others for what they are experiencing. The image the person attempts to portray and the reality of their energy will be different, which creates confusion for those observing the emotional and energetic reality of the person with a soul denial entity.

The generated energetic force felt as a soul denial entity is the manifestation of a person's choice to try to have ultimate control, through energetic intimidation and domination. Unfortunately, the person's disassociation from feeling truth, causes them to affix to the image of being a victim, or to being completely justified in seeking domination of reality, often under the guise of survival. The person uses their soul denial entity when they want to covertly, energetically intimidate others, in an attempt to protect their delusion of power. This means the person is not above using emotional, energetic or physical intimidation and domination to get what they believe they are entitled to. They may not be completely aware of projecting an energetic force or that it has morphed into an energetic entity, but they are aware of their seething internal judgement, resentment and beliefs of entitlement.

A person with a soul denial entity believes their own judgement is the authority on how reality should be, which fuels the energy used to sustain their soul denial entity. They believe all aspects of reality should succumb to their authority and be submissive to their expectations, while denying they have any responsibility for what they are doing. They emotionally feel delight when they observe themselves having a negative effect on another person or environment. They delight in the prospect of being able to energetically intrude into another's energy system, while the person being intruded upon is unaware of the source of the energetic intrusion. The person with a soul denial entity will display signs of their own insidious indifference, and usually revels in the confusion they create for others to endure.

A person with a soul denial entity resents not being recognised as the authority over those they wish to control, and an authority over what truth is. They resent others who interfere with their desire to prove the prowess of their ability to control, or those who are unwilling to be submissive to their desires and expectations. The resentment becomes a constant source of energetic fuel for the generation of energy required to activate the soul denial entity. They want to orchestrate reality to suit their delusion of how the world should orientate to their desires, and have little regard for how this affects others. The narcissism of a person causes them to arrogantly believe they are superior to all others, which enhances their willingness to judge and analyse everyone and everything that comes into contact with their reality. Their judgement becomes a constant source of energetic fuel, generating the energy required to activate their soul denial entity.

A person with a soul denial entity believes their sensitivity to energy justifies protecting their own insecurities, which have been created by their desire to control all energy they feel within their reality. They believe the protection of their insecurities is of paramount importance to their survival, which is why they use their awareness of their sensitivity to feeling energy, to justify psychically attacking another, which is an energetic attack. They derive a sly satisfaction from being able to project their retaliative energy at another, believing the source of the projection of energy will be undetectable, which is often true. We do not automatically think that we could be under energetic attack; we normally think there is just something wrong with ourselves, and battle to ascertain some sense of control over our own emotional feelings or energetic awareness.

It is difficult to ascertain how aware a person is of their soul denial entity, because they are intentionally unconscious to their own energy. This enables the person to use a victim persona to conceal their own retaliative disposition, as they are absolutely convinced they are the victim of an energetic attack, and completely deny the possibility of being the perpetrator, who is energetically impacted with the return of their own energy. They believe they are entitled to expect control without acknowledging the amount of energy being generated by their desire for control. They deny feeling the energy being generated by their judgement, jealousy and resentment. There is slyness within their energetic attack of another, because they believe they cannot be held accountable for projected energy. They have no fear of recourse and this enables the person to be immersed in the smugness of their own indifference. However, this is an illusion, there is actually recourse because all energy returns to sender and they end up wearing and embattling their own intimidating energy.

The person with a soul denial entity is willing to hold a grudge for any intrusion into their energy system, their perception of life and their environment. They retaliate if they believe another has created image failure for them to endure, which becomes fuel for the insidiousness of their own indifference to truth. A person with a soul denial entity becomes indifferent to others and the reality of their own energy, behaviour and desire to control.

They fortify barriers to acknowledging their reality and the energetic force of their desire for control and indifference towards others. They become entangled in their own delusions of power as they feel the energetic force they generate. However, this is the manifestation of their own illusion, which is only sustained for as long as their denial can conceal the true nature of the energy they are consumed with. Once their denial is unsustainable, they experience being within an energetic torturous prison of their own creation, emotionally tormented by their own indifference to truth.

A soul denial entity is the result of a person's willingness to separate from their own flow of consciousness, for an illusory control of reality. The person is attempting to separate from any awareness of their soul's consciousness and wants to be able to use the soul denial entity, but pretend that it has nothing to do with them. This is because they do not want to take responsibility for their own unresolved emotions within the entity. They have no desire to resolve the indifference they have towards their own soul truth and intensify their unresolved emotions, such as:

- Internal rage
- Resentment
- Extreme fear
- Humiliation
- Shame
- Spite
- Vengeance
- Cruelty
- Jealousy
- Manipulation
- Malevolence
- Lust
- Greed
- Gluttony
- Sloth
- Wrath
- Envy
- Pride
- Narcissism
- Vanity
- Indifference

We all have soul denial energy, a desire to control and indifference to truth, but generally we do not amalgamate them to form a separate entity. Normally, as these energies are exposed within ourselves, we take some form of responsibility for them. We may not resolve the energies, but we put boundaries around the extent to which we will utilise these energies. A soul denial entity is the result of the person becoming indifferent to any boundaries they once had. They cling to and utilise their indifference as a protective mechanism. They seek to secure their refusal to accept reality and to uphold their denial about what they are doing. They use their indifference energy to repel their own awareness of truth and to secure whatever they use to justify their emotional, energetic and physical behaviour.

The soul denial entity is an energetic force containing all the extremes of the person's unresolved emotions. A person with a soul denial entity believes they have the right and are entitled to impose their control onto others and they become very agitated if their control is ignored, overridden or proven to be inefficient. The person corrupts their ability to trust the value of truth, because of their reliance on the intimidating energy within their soul denial entity. They are constantly reacting from their own fear of not being able to orchestrate reality to pacify their desire to control life, others, relationships and truth. They also become contrary and difficult to appease.

The energetic force of the soul denial entity, is fuelled by the person's refusal to value truth. They want to dictate what truth is, with their judgement and delusion. When a person with a soul denial entity feels their soul denial entity, they get a surge of their own control energy and believe they are powerful, or they feel the fear of being out of control of their own indifference and determine that they are a victim to an unexplained energetic force.

The person can be unconscious to the reality of the separating energy that has become their own entity, but extremely aware of the surging energy from their emotional cesspit. They use their surging emotions to sustain their justification for their desire to control and the severity of their judgement, jealousy and indifference. Their feeling of being out of control creates more surges of desiring control. These surges make them feel powerful within the smugness of their indifference, but the smugness is unsustainable, and then they become desperate to secure an illusion of power. This creates a massive energetic see-saw within their thought process and they become consumed with wanting control of what is now emotionally controlling them. Their refusal to be honest fuels the energy of their entity, which is how they reinvest more unconscious energy into the continuation of their unresolved emotions. A person with a soul denial entity will emotionally feel as if they are a victim to their constant struggle to control their own emotions, energetics and physical reality, and honesty will not be on their agenda.

When a person is aware of their soul denial entity, they may be willing to excuse their own indifference, believing they would not use this energy unless under threat, and are therefore not responsible for how their energy makes another feel or for what another has to endure. They use their justified indifference to escape from their own fear of reality, and fear of having no control over what they are experiencing. They programme and condition themselves with beliefs of self-protection and survival, in an attempt to justify and vindicate wielding an imaginary power over reality. When they believe they have orchestrated control of reality, they allow the energetic force to subside, and attempt to believe they are as innocent as those who have experienced the wrath producing their soul denial entity.

When a person with a soul denial entity has activated their energetic projection at what or who they believe is interfering with their illusion of control, the person projecting the energy, emotionally feels swamped by their indifference to truth. They disregard the opportunities to be honest about their own indifference. The person concretises their perception of their emotional, energetic and physical reality. They use judgement, indifference and beliefs of entitlement to destroy any possibility of resolving their own unresolved emotions, and seek to prove they are a victim of something, ignoring that they victimise others and themselves. The person is willing to covertly, energetically attack anyone who exposes the truth of the insidiousness of their control, the deception of their denial or the conniving of their manipulation. Their opposition to the exposure of their emotional reality and desire to protect their denial becomes fuel for their soul denial entity. This enables them to be possessed by their arrogant indifference to truth, and they choose to become what they once despised, which is being indifferent.

A person with a soul denial entity is strong in their perceived righteous belief that they are entitled to retaliate when they experience control failure. The energetic force they project is just the manifestation of unresolved emotions and is the result of a person's concretisation of their desire to have control. This becomes entangled in their indifference to truth, and they manifest the extremes of their unresolved emotions. The person hides behind a persona of denial but is willing to observe themselves being out of control, apprehensive to see if they can achieve control over others while sustaining the illusion of innocence.

A person with a soul denial entity despises being on the receiving end of others' indifference. They deny being indifferent, at the same time as harnessing their indifference to create havoc for others and any situation they want to inject their control into. They cling to the delusional power they emotionally create when they surge in the energy of their unresolved emotions, and because they can feel the energy they justify their opposition to trusting their own soul and truth. The purpose of the entity is to continue being separated from reality and to secure their denial. They use the soul denial entity as a way of concretising the extremes of their unresolved emotions into a separated form, which they believe they can deny. They have chosen to turn down any opportunity for resolution and believe that their use of the extremes of their own unresolved emotions will be undetected by others. However, what the person is attempting to avoid feeling and being exposed to, is exactly what they are energetically swamped in.

A person with a soul denial entity uses their entity to enforce being separated from the truth of their reality, because acknowledging truth would disable their denial of their own unresolved emotions. Their desire to control, is greater than their desire to resolve what is separating them from acknowledging and feeling truth. Their desire to control may in fact overshadow any recognition of their own unresolved emotions and the truth of how they feel. When they surge in the unresolved emotions used to generate the energetic force of their soul denial entity, they become indifferent to the true ramifications of their own energy and believe they are entitled to be indifferent to others.

A person with a soul denial entity can emotionally feel haunted, but it is the energy of their own vindictiveness, narcissism and dogmatism, desire to control and indifference to truth that haunts them. They are extremely disassociated from feeling the truth of both their conscious and unconscious energy, because they refuse to acknowledge it is their own energy that haunts them. They want to aggravate their own soul denial entity, to emotionally feel a surge of control or victim energy that will validate their struggle with life, themselves, others and their own perception of their present moment reality. A person with a soul denial entity exists within the belief of being unchangeable, which is a covert belief of being superior to truth. The person uses their soul denial entity to counteract their soul consciousness' ability to expose truth.

A person with a soul denial entity emotionally believes they have been abandoned by truth. They refuse to acknowledge that they fight against truth and deny their own willingness to abandon truth for an illusion of control. Their judgement of truth fuels their soul denial entity to attack their own soul's consciousness. They attempt to create a competition between their soul's consciousness and their entity, but it will be their acknowledgment and acceptance of their unconscious energy that will free them from being haunted and controlled by their indifference, denial, desire to control and all the unresolved emotions contributing to their fear of being completely honest about what they are doing.

A person with a soul denial entity is indifferent to the ramifications of their energy and becomes possessed by the need to create and sustain an illusion of control and power. They tire of emotionally feeling their own energy and externalise in an attempt to be rid of their own uncontrollable malicious energy. They will covertly project energy to incite insecurity, fear, soul denial and heresy energy in others, seeking to be the orchestrator for how another perceives themselves.

When a person with a soul denial entity becomes aware of their entity, they may create delusions around the capability of the entity, believing they can affect truth by exerting menacing energy on others. They create a power trip within their distorted delusion of themselves and their awareness of the entity, causing them to be codependent on their own delusions. This incites their desire to control reality to become all consuming and they can get lost in their own illusion of control, becoming immersed in their denial of reality. They seek power over reality and try to work out how to control their entity of soul denial to be an advantage to their desire to control. They compulsively use the energy within their own entity of soul denial, to react to their own attempt to control with more vindictive control energy, which causes the person to implode within their own unresolved emotions. So in truth, their own control energy is reacting to their own control energy, creating a vicious cycle of self-annihilation. Due to the velocity, vindictiveness and intensity of the vicious cycle of self-annihilation, the person becomes immersed in self-hatred, self-loathing and often extreme resentment of others.

The vicious cycle of self-annihilation exposes the truth of their unresolved emotions, to the point where the person is unable to sustain their own menacing energy. Their desire to control implodes when they feel the reality of the emotions they use to sustain their soul denial entity. This eventually neutralises their ability to believe in their own control, which causes the person to wallow in their inability to control. However, this also creates an opportunity for them to be honest.

If a person with a soul denial entity has exerted the extremes of their control and does not gain the results they desire, the failure of their control causes them to emotionally, energetically or physically implode. This results in the person becoming an emotional shell, devoid of the willingness to attempt to be honest with reality. This may cause the person to wallow in extreme depression, becoming a victim of their own desire to control, and they may attempt to ostracise themselves from everyone or anything that interferes with their depression or victim status. They are often bitter and resentful of life for cheating them out of being a controller of reality. It is only a person's belief in their control that sustains the supply of energy to the soul denial entity, because the entity is a manifestation of their desire to control and indifference to truth. When the person becomes disillusioned with their own illusion of power, the velocity of their desire to control subsides, which means the energetic force of the soul denial entity becomes dormant. It is emotionally, energetically and physically hard for a person to sustain the velocity of energy required to project their soul denial entity at others. The difficulty of sustaining the projection of their unresolved emotions means, they eventually implode. Any energy projected returns to sender and the person experiences their own wrath. This leaves the person exposed to their own indifference, vindictiveness and the reality of their own desire to have ultimate control of life, others, relationships and truth.

The presence of a soul denial entity can cause others to match the energy they feel, with their own soul denial, desire to control and heresy energy. This may cause them to experience the extremes of their own unresolved emotions; feeling fearful or agitated but not understanding why. Some people will align willingly to their own soul denial and heresy energy, not even realising they are in the presence of an energetic soul denial entity. Others might fight and struggle with what they are feeling because there is a mismatch between the truth they feel and their emotional reactions to their present moment. This causes the person experiencing the presence of the soul denial entity to become confused by how they are reacting to what they observe of their reality, they feel an undercurrent of energy they cannot explain, which is inciting unresolved emotions that are contradictory to how they feel about their present moment reality. The soul denial entity is the presence of another's desire to control, which is seeking to corrupt others to abandon their flow of consciousness. The intention behind the projection of the soul denial entity is to create an energetic environment that facilitates confusion or an ominous sense of insecurity in those struggling to comprehend what they are feeling.

The presence of a soul denial entity can make you feel agitated and trapped which may incite your confusion, anger, rage or despair. The presence of a soul denial entity can make you fearful and believe something out of your control is about to happen, which incites your insecurities and self-doubt. However, you have to be extremely truthful about your own emotions, desire to control and your energetic awareness, to know if you are in the presence of a soul denial entity, otherwise you could attempt to pass off the truth of yourself onto a non-existing presence that you use as a scapegoat for your own denial.

The person's energy within their soul denial entity is competing for supremacy over others and to corrupt another soul's awareness of truth. A person utilising their soul denial entity seeks to create a competition for control and their entity is a manifestation of their desire to prove their energy is superior to everything. When you are willing to be truthful with yourself, and can objectively observe yourself and the energy present within your present moment, your acceptance and acknowledgement of the truth of yourself within your reality becomes a repellent to any soul denial entity. This means the soul denial entity's desire to control you will have no affect on you. However, confusion can create separation from your awareness of consciousness and it is within this separation that you can become emotionally, energetically and physically impacted by the presence of a soul denial entity. If you are willing to objectively observe yourself within the energy you feel, you will feel the presence of a soul denial entity as an energy outside yourself. This will allow you to hold to your energetic independence, which enables you to not react emotionally and not engage with the energy of the entity with your own fear and indifference. If you are unable to recognise the presence of a soul denial entity or unable to determine when energy is not yours, but are aware of being energetically impacted, you can become fearful of your own confusion. Your fear can incite the soul denial entity to become obsessive with their desire to impact your awareness of truth, seeking to hold you in a sensation of fear and confusion. When you experience the presence of a soul denial entity and you begin to fear your own fear, the soul denial entity may retreat believing control has been achieved. The person projecting their entity can create a cycle of projection and retreat. However, it is finite, because the energy required and the return of that energy, depletes their ability to sustain the momentum required to project. This leaves them imploding in their own unresolved emotions.

If you can feel the presence of a soul denial entity, you are feeling the tangible amalgamated energy of another. By telling the energy you are aware of its presence and telling it to return to its source, you expose its illusion of control, rendering the entity useless. Be very honest about what has been emotionally incited in you. Your truthful honesty will resolve any energetic residue created by the experience of feeling the energetics of a soul denial entity. It is your denial of feeling the energy, which empowers the energy within the soul denial entity. It is your fear of feeling the reality of an energetic experience that fuels the illusory control within the soul denial entity. You may even see the energy in the form of a ghost-like figure or you may glimpse a figure dressed in historic clothing or see a dark patch of condensed energy, especially in your peripheral vision. If the entity loses its cloak of deception, it will retreat. Soul denial entities will retreat from the presence of truthfulness. When you honestly acknowledge the truth of your feelings and your energetic awareness, your truthfulness becomes the truth energy the soul denial entity retreats from. A soul denial entity is only a person's denial of truth manifesting as an illusion of itself, seeking to interfere with another's ability to be at peace with truth.

The severity of the person's desire to control creates their level of sensitivity to what they believe has infringed on their control, and they emotionally assess what is justifiable to retaliate against. Their retaliation exposes their intention to use or emulate any type of energy to satisfy their own desires, expectations and emotional demands. They intentionally desire to secure and protect their illusion of control and this requires a huge amount of energetic force to incite the extremes of their own unresolved emotions into energy they can project. A person with a soul denial entity becomes an intentional participant in the protection of their own illusion of control. They are willing to deny any truth that will expose them to the severity of their desire to secure their illusion of control. Their protection of their illusion of control causes them to become willing to oppose the truth of anything or anyone interfering with their reality. A person with a soul denial entity can be very obsessive and possessive because they fear being exposed to their inability to control life, others, relationships and truth.

If the person is extremely retaliative and sadistic, the energy within their soul denial entity becomes an emulation of demonic energy, which they produce from the extremes of their own indifference to truth. They project their energy at you because they want you to be fearful, and they may choose to emulate demonic energy to ensure their ability to energetically intimidate. It is an illusion they are projecting, which exposes the insidiousness of their indifference to truth and the extent to which they will energetically go to protect their illusion of control. The energy within a soul denial entity is just a manifestation of the energy of the person's unconsciousness and their unwillingness to acknowledge truth.

A person cannot sever from their own soul's consciousness, they can only create separation from their awareness of their soul's consciousness. Whilst separated from their awareness of their soul's consciousness, the truth of their behaviour often exposes them to their own unresolved emotions. If they are emulating demonic energy it would be difficult for them to ignore their own energy, because they are attempting to construct ways to use the extremes of their indifference energy, and all projected energy returns to sender. However, the resolution of the indifference energy depends on their willingness to be honest with themselves and to acknowledge what is exposed. If they are unwilling to be honest with themselves they will begin to lie to themselves about being a victim of the energy they feel, while denying any responsibility that they were the generator of the energy. The choice to not honestly acknowledge what they are doing and the type of energy they are creating, does create insanity. This is why they scramble so hard to defend their own delusions, justify their unresolved emotions and pursue the illusion of control. A person using a soul denial entity feels and fears the insanity of their own indifference and attempts to control what they fear with deceptive self-manipulation.

When a person projects a soul denial entity they do it for the purpose of seeking covert control and use it to create the belief that they are the victim of an uncontrollable energy. A person uses their soul denial entity to energetically retaliate against others and it is this willingness to retaliate that they are most reluctant to have exposed. The dishonesty used to fuel their own self-generated soul denial entity is actually the energy that causes the soul denial entity to retreat from any truth energy. The person's intention to be dishonest sustains their compulsion to fuel the unresolved emotions required to buffer them from resolving the energy within their soul denial entity. If a person with a soul denial entity wants to resolve the energy fuelling their soul denial entity, they have to be prepared to explore the truth of their desire to control, indifference to truth and what energy they have or are willing to use to defend their own dishonesty.

The soul denial entity is the person's delusion of power and control manifesting as a tangible energy, which is unsustainable by the person, and usually creates an emotional breakdown if they have attempted to sustain the unresolved emotions required to energise the soul denial entity for a period of time. The person will emotionally, energetically and often physically implode due to their own energy and denial of their awareness of their reality and truth. A soul denial entity is an insidious type of control energy, which manifests because the person is protecting their own dishonesty and indifference to truth. This type of control energy does not like to be identified and is generated by the person's refusal to resolve their control and indifference to truth. A person manifests this energy to oppose any energy they feel from truth such as unconditional love, compassion and grace. They want to remain a victim to themselves to spite truth, and some become immersed in their own fear. They fear taking responsibility for the truth of their own indifference, denial and desire to control, and are determined to remain dishonest with themselves. This is why they project such an energetic force at others, because they fear complete exposure of what they are willing to do to hide from the truth of their own unresolved emotions. Acknowledgment of this energy diffuses the energy, and it returns back to its source.

Crossed over souls

Crossed over souls are very different to lost souls. Some lost souls try to emulate being crossed over souls and it will be your ability to be honest about the truth you feel, which will allow you to acknowledge the difference. Crossed over souls have returned to origins and what you are feeling when you are in their presence is the purity of their soul unencumbered by any unresolved emotions. They only return to Earth unified with *True Source Divine Origin Consciousness*. They come with compassion for the internal struggle of souls, who are unconscious to their own reality of being of truth. They come to expose the significance of soul journeys and to nurture the truth within the soul they are visiting.

People can be desperate to have experiences with loved ones who have died and will lie to themselves about the energy they feel, which creates a lot of misconceptions about visits from crossed over souls. Crossed over souls do return to assist loved ones but they never stay attached. They resonate with unconditional love and support for loved ones, exposing the loved one to the truth of who they are. Crossed over souls seek to bridge your understanding of yourself back to your origins of truth. They do not seek to control you, they just create an opportunity for you to feel the truth of your soul, uncorrupted by your unresolved emotions.

Crossed over souls want to remind you to trust truth and to be in the reality of your life experience. When you feel a crossed over soul, you are feeling their true essence. Crossed over souls emanate the purity of their core essence. You are experiencing the truth of their soul resonating with their origins of truth, unconditionally loving truth and their own soul. A crossed over soul's frequency is very different from the energetic vibrations of a lost soul. Trusting yourself to feel the true essence of a crossed over soul enables you to feel your own resonance with truth. Trusting yourself to feel your experience without fear, control or expectations enables you to feel peace within and the purity of the unconditional love and support from another significant, unique, independent, individual soul of *True Source Divine Origin Consciousness*.

Many people often try to control the experience of feeling a crossed over soul and their unresolved emotions get in the way of feeling the truth of the experience. By trying to control the experience, they bombard the crossed over soul with their unresolved emotions and desire to control. If the purpose of the crossed over soul's visit has been disregarded and missed by the person, the crossed over soul often withdraws from the unconscious energy of the person's control.

Many people will try to use the experience to place demands on the crossed over soul. They try to control the crossed over soul to fix their emotions, asking for their emotions to be taken away. The truth is, crossed over souls are hopeful their presence will inspire you to be honest and resolve your own unresolved emotions and to trust truth.

Many people during these experiences will request something to be changed, upgraded or fixed within their life; they want the crossed over soul to take responsibility for fixing their life. However, crossed over souls are hopeful their visit will enable the person to feel the truth of their own choices. Many people demand that the crossed over soul fix another

Crossed over souls are resonating with the purity of their own soul's consciousness and visit but do not attach to the living. They come to expose the significance of your soul journey and to nurture the truth within you. Lost souls are still attached to the energy of their own soul's unconsciousness and are lost in their fear of the purity of truth, as depicted by the elderly lady walking away from the presence of the crossed over souls. Crossed over souls and lost souls are both found amongst the living.

who is affecting them, hoping their problems will go away if someone else is fixed. They want the crossed over soul to carry their emotional, energetic and physical burdens for them. Some will even request the weather to be perfect for an event. This all misses the opportunity to feel the purity of truth and to feel the unconditional love of another soul. When you attempt to control your experience you disregard the purity of unconditional love, and seek to use the unconditional love of the crossed over soul for the purpose of orchestrating a desired result that you believe will pacify your illusion of being in control. This is a missed opportunity to feel the purity of the unconditional love within the crossed over soul who unconditionally loves you.

At times crossed over souls visit to reassure loved ones that they are where they are meant to be, and that the cycle of life has an order. Often you become aware of crossed over souls in your dream state, because your control is less active. Crossed over souls help us to resonate with our own soul's consciousness. Crossed over souls do not respond to our control energy, because it is our desire for control that entraps us in the energy of our soul's unconsciousness. Crossed over souls respond to the truth of your soul and communicate to you through and for your soul's consciousness. If you will not feel, listen to or acknowledge your own soul's consciousness, you might feel, listen to or acknowledge the presence of a crossed over soul who cares for you, and unconditionally loves and acknowledges your significance. The crossed over soul seeks to remind you that you are of the purity of truth and of your own unconditional love within. The crossed over soul may be able to communicate what you have refused to accept from your own soul's consciousness. Often the unconditional love of a crossed over soul has helped you and you have not realised it, which is fine because the crossed over soul does not seek validation. A crossed over soul loves unconditionally and is in unison with your soul's consciousness.

Reborn

When your soul is re-born into the physical world, your unresolved emotions within the energetic collectives of the mass energy of mankind are reattached to your soul; this is your karmic resonance with your own soul denial history. Your unresolved emotions within the energetic collectives of the mass energy of mankind reattach at the time of your birth. However, all unresolved emotions are dormant and as the child develops the unresolved emotions become activated and expose what the soul can potentially resolve this lifetime. As a child, you are exposed to your own unresolved emotions, other individual's unresolved emotions and the energetics of the mass energy of mankind within your environment, which all have the potential to alert you to your awareness of the truth of your energy. However, denial and the loss of awareness of your soul's consciousness creates, activates and concretises the unresolved emotions of your soul's unconsciousness. At any time you can adopt or create unresolved emotions, which if left unresolved, will be carried by you throughout this lifetime. After your death the unconscious energy of your unresolved emotions will be stored within the energetics of the mass energy of mankind, until you elect to be reborn to the opportunity to resolve what you have left within the energetics of the mass energy of mankind.

You are born with a divine origin blueprint, which is your agreed intention for this lifetime, and you will have moments of internal knowing and déjà vu that remind you that you are more than just a physical body. There are times where you will feel and recognise yourself resonating with the truth of your soul. You are a soul who decided to return to life, to experience the opportunity to resolve what you have created, which is your soul's unconsciousness. You created your soul's unconsciousness by devaluing the truth of your soul, separating from your awareness and disassociating from feeling truth. Life is the opportunity to unify with your awareness and to trust your resonance with truth.

Your soul lessons are your unresolved emotions and you will have life experiences that will expose your unresolved emotions to you. The carried unconscious energy produced by your unresolved emotions is the residue of your soul denial history. Your intention for life is to become conscious of your own unresolved emotions, and to resonate with your soul consciousness' ability to evolve beyond the history of your soul denial. You have the freedom to choose your level of commitment to your original intention for this life. Many souls disregard, deny and oppose the opportunity life presents, because they become consumed by their own desire to control life, and give up their awareness of truth in preference for their illusion of control. This leaves them consumed by their soul's unconsciousness and protecting their soul denial. They have separated from their awareness of their original intention for life and disassociated from feeling truth. You will have life experiences that incorporate what you need to activate your unresolved emotions, which will expose opportunities for you to acknowledge the truth of the energy of your soul's unconsciousness. Acknowledging the truth

RIGHT: When your soul is re-born to the physical world your unresolved emotions, which are stored within the energetic collectives of the mass energy of mankind, are reattached to your soul. This is your karmic resonance with your own soul denial history.

indifference to truth	denial	desire to control	poor me	humiliation
blame	self pity	people pleaser	avoidance of responsibility	'I want' energy
selfishness			soul loathing	guilt
anger				'not good enough'
addicted to comparing				superiority
manipulation				arrogance
self-loathing				inferiority
denial of uniqueness				fear
				jealousy
hurt				insecurity
scaling of significance	envy		disassociation from feeling	victim
Martyr	co-dependency on indifference	shame	elitism	carried victim energy
judgment of life	frustration	regret	resentment	racism
overwhelmed by feelings				

SOUL DENIAL

Energetic Collectives Of The Mass Energy Of Mankind

You are a soul who has experienced many lives on Earth

of your unresolved emotions gives you the option to choose to resolve and evolve. Denying your unresolved emotions continues your attachment and addiction to your denial of your soul and sustains the perpetuation of the energy of your soul's unconsciousness.

You are a soul who has experienced many lives on Earth and have an internal knowing of the significance of being honest about your reality. Deep within your soul, there is a yearning to resonate with your awareness of truth and to trust your own soul insight. The significance of exploring the truth behind the concepts of being a soul of truth, your divine right to freedom of choice and *True Source Divine Origin Consciousness'* unconditional love for you, naturally resonates with your soul. All souls are seekers of truth but often get lost in their soul denial by choosing to override their own soul awareness. Your willingness to override your awareness of your soul's consciousness causes disharmony within you. The disharmony within you will possibly cause you to seek your own awareness of truth, re-uniting you with your understanding of your original intention to resolve and evolve.

You have the freedom to choose how you will respond to the truth of your unresolved emotions being exposed to you. You are a soul who has been entrusted with life, to create, acknowledge and accept opportunities for resolution and evolution. As a soul you have entrusted yourself to be honest with the exposure of the reality of your unresolved emotions. Your honesty creates the opportunity to resolve and evolve. Your original intention was to become aware of your soul truth, and you seek the freedom within yourself to resolve and evolve beyond the entrapment of your soul denial. You struggle with your fear of your soul denial and self-betrayal, because you internally know that this is how you incarcerate yourself within your own soul's unconsciousness.

Blueprints are as unique as the individuals they resonate with. There is no generic path for resolution and evolution. You cannot control yourself to a belief of consciousness because control energy is generated from your unconsciousness. Consciousness is the willingness to accept the truth of the dynamics of the uniqueness of every moment, willing to live, experience, feel and be honest with the truth of yourself to resolve and evolve. You are a soul who has chosen experiences as crossroads to remind yourself of your own intention to seek truth. Life is the opportunity to resolve your unresolved emotions, which resolves the contribution your soul's unconsciousness makes to the energetics of the mass energy of mankind. By being honest and resolving your unresolved emotions, you align to the natural process of converting your emotions to conscious understanding; this is evolution of your soul. Your original intention is to be consciously aware of the truth of yourself as a soul, within a physical body.

You recognise and feel a void; the void you feel is your separation from your awareness of your soul and your disassociation from feeling the reality of being a significant, unique, independent, individual soul of *True Source Divine Origin Consciousness*. You may not consciously understand what it is that you are feeling but you can feel that something is missing. You have the internal desire to search for a deeper meaning of your life and to find answers to the questions that arise from your thoughts and feelings, but you may diffuse this truth by wanting to control what truth means to you. When you seek control of truth or use truth in an attempt to control, you are disregarding the value of truth. This causes you to use any energy within your soul's unconsciousness or the energetics of the mass energy of mankind to protect and sustain your soul denial. When you protect your soul denial, you sustain your separation from your awareness of your soul and your disassociation from feeling truth.

Being reborn into life is the opportunity to experience the truth of all your own conscious and unconscious energy. You are the interface of all your energies and have the freedom to choose how you interact from and with both conscious and unconscious energy.

Energetic collectives

The energy of every unresolved emotion, which is unconscious energy, forms the energetic collectives within the mass energy of mankind. Energetic collectives are the collective energy of the same vibration, and it is the combination of all these energetic collectives and barriers to truth that construct and constitute the energetic mass energy of mankind.

When you deny the truth of your feelings, you create unresolved emotions. Your feelings are in the present moment, and when you feel and acknowledge them they become just a passing feeling that is exposing you to your awareness of your present moment. When your feelings are denied or suppressed they become carried unresolved emotions, and they also reverberate with correlating energy within the energetic mass energy of mankind.

The energetic collectives are like having a lot of different bank accounts in which you have varying deposits. The emotions that are not resolved in your lifetime, are left as deposits in the energetic mass energy of mankind. Your previous lives affect you in this lifetime, because when you are reborn, your unresolved emotions from your previous lives are returned to you, for you to resolve. This does not mean you will repeat the same past life experiences in this lifetime, it just means you will experience the energy of your unresolved emotions. Each lifetime is unique in how you are exposed to what is unresolved within you.

Your unresolved emotions reverberate with the energetic collectives they correlate to. You can be unaware that you are reverberating with the energetic collectives, because you are in denial of your unresolved emotions and denying your energetic awareness. Your indifference to truth fuels your ability to be unconscious to the reality of your unresolved emotions and secures your denial of how you use the energetics of the mass energy of mankind to justify and warrant your soul denial. Becoming aware of your unresolved emotions and how you utilise them, facilitates your awareness of your reverberation with the energetics of the mass energy of mankind. Your awareness enables you to resolve and evolve, and to unify with your origin truth while in a physical body.

You are a member of many different energetic collectives simultaneously. When you activate and express your unresolved emotions, you are contributing to the energetic collectives within the mass energy of mankind that correlate with the vibration of your unresolved emotions. This creates a mutual exchange of energy between you and the energetic collective, and generates a reverberation of unconscious energy. The velocity of the energy you are emotionally generating, is how you control yourself to justify your need to hang onto and defend your emotions, and to suppress your awareness of the entirety of the truth of your emotions. You suppress, repress and oppress your awareness of your unresolved emotions without acknowledging the truth of what you are doing and the extent of your avoidance of the reality of yourself.

RIGHT: *Regardless of what you are feeling, if you feel the truth of it, it is a passing feeling. If you deny, reject or suppress what you are feeling, you create unresolved emotions.*

Energetic Collectives Of The Mass Energy Of Mankind

Feeling the truth of Hurt and Vulnerability

- Believing everyone I love will turn on me
- Denying the equality of all souls
- Present moment emotions
- self pity
- Protecting vulnerability with indifference
- Victim
- Martyr
- Concretising your indifference - couldn't be bothered to be honest
- Desiring to control indifference
- Desperation
- Compulsive manipulator
- Resisting self care
- Attempting to fix indifference with indifference
- Sustaining familiarity
- Indoctrinations from soul denial history
- Fragmented soul
- Avoiding soul accountability
- Environmental exploitation
- Disassociated from feeling
- Denying responsibility for your own choices
- Annihilating your soul integrity
- Defying reality
- Creating an alternate illusory reality
- Anger, internal rage

soul denial

Your unresolved emotions have a consistent energetic current that is either being fuelled by, or is fuelling the energetic collectives within the mass energy of mankind. There is a mutual energetic exchange between you and the energetic mass. This is reliant on you compulsively acting out your known patterns of soul oppression, and being dishonest about your unconscious energy. You intercept your awareness of the presence of your soul's consciousness with the energy of your soul's unconsciousness. Every unresolved emotion is a product of your soul denial, which constitutes your soul's unconsciousness. When you control yourself to deny the truth of your soul, you oppose truth with your embedded beliefs and fears. This means you become an active unconscious energy within the energetics of mankind. Your opposition to truth is caused by your judgement and doubt of your own significance. You scale your worth by your ability to control, and this causes you to be a willing participant within the energetic collectives of the mass energy of mankind.

If you have unresolved emotions you have personally invested in the energetic collectives of the mass energy of mankind. How much your personal deposit has contributed to a particular energetic collective is relevant; even the smallest amount of unresolved emotion remains within you as a residue and needs resolving, because any residue inhibits you from feeling and acknowledging the purity of your energetic independence. If you are engaged in denial of your unresolved emotions, you are entangled with your reverberations with the energetic collectives that correlate to your unresolved emotions. Even the smallest amount of unresolved emotion within you can become a catalyst for the generation of other unresolved emotions. By being truthfully honest with yourself, you will recognise within your life experiences the opportunities to resolve your unresolved emotions.

When you start to resolve your unresolved emotions, you are withdrawing your deposits from the energetic collectives. There are some unresolved emotions which when resolved may cause a domino effect. When you are choosing not to use particular emotions, you simultaneously change the ripple effect of your emotional energy. The most significant unresolved emotion you have is your own soul denial, because it is the linchpin for all of your other unresolved emotions. All unresolved emotions are mutations of your soul denial and the fears and embedded beliefs that you use in an attempt to oppress your awareness of truth. The collective energy of mankind's soul denial is the crux of the energetic mass energy of mankind.

Your soul denial is essential for coordinating your connective reverberation with the energetic collectives within the mass energy of mankind. Your soul denial is the foundation of your accumulated unresolved emotions, which is the crux of your soul's unconsciousness. Mankind's collective soul denial is the accumulation of all of mankind's denial of the truth of who we are. Your soul denial underpins your unresolved emotions and your continual struggle to accept that you are of truth. Your soul denial compounds your desire to control life with your unresolved emotions. An undercurrent of your soul denial is the embedded belief that you can control truth to validate your illusion of control. Your desire to control truth engulfs you in your unresolved emotions. This disables your ability to observe truth and you deny yourself respect for the natural significance of your soul's consciousness.

When you realise the truth of your denial and choose to resolve your unresolved emotions, you are choosing to withdraw your unconscious energy from the energetic collectives within the mass energy of mankind. You are also choosing to withdraw from protecting your own personal energetic collective of unconscious energy, which is your soul's unconsciousness. You will need to observe and explore the truth of how you use the energy of your soul's unconsciousness. When you start being honest about your soul's unconsciousness, you will accept the reality of your emotional reactions to truth and life. This allows you to perceive yourself as an individual who willingly takes responsibility to be honest about the truth of your own energy. When you deny responsibility for being an independent soul of truth, you activate your unresolved emotions, which means you reverberate with the energetic collectives within the mass energy of mankind. You also hide from the reality of your freedom of choice and the truth of being a significant, unique, independent, individual soul of *True Source Divine Origin Consciousness*. When you use your unresolved emotions and then deny your denial, you create cycles of deception. This leaves you stagnant and disconnected from your emotional, energetic and physical reality.

You have individually invested in the energetics of the collective energy of mankind and as an individual have the freedom to withdraw; withdrawing means you resolve your unresolved emotions. Your denial of your unresolved emotions keeps you attached to the familiarity of your deceptive cycles of soul oppression, which create your emotional, energetic and physical merry-go-rounds. This means you repetitively use the energy of your soul's unconsciousness, creating sequenced patterns that expose you to that which is unresolved. The repetitiveness has you struggling with reality, as you attempt to control life, yourself, others, relationships and truth to appease your own deceptive illusions.

You will not resolve the energy of your soul's unconsciousness by just acknowledging you are a soul; you need to explore the truth of being a soul and resolve the unconscious energy that restricts and limits your awareness of the flow of consciousness within you. It is your willingness to be of truth, which will resolve your unresolved emotions.

When you realise you want to resolve your unresolved emotions, you will still find yourself justifying, defending and trying to prove the validity of your negative beliefs about yourself. As you attempt to be honest about your unresolved emotions, you will often use the embedded beliefs and fears buried within your soul denial, to fight your own awareness of truth. This is an automatic reaction that inhibits your ability to be completely honest with yourself, and is why resolution of your unresolved emotions is a layered process. Your reluctance to deconstruct the layers of your soul's unconsciousness, causes you to be complacent about your unresolved emotions, and the truth of what you are experiencing. Your complacency causes you to justify remaining in what is familiar. Challenge what is familiar, observe how it makes you feel and be honest that you have options.

You can fight against your reality. You attempt to control reality because you want to be perceived as significant, of value and worth, but you are naturally all of these and more. Your desire to control your significance and to dictate the form of your worth, hinders your ability to be completely honest with yourself. If you acknowledge this as part of the process, you will resolve your opposition to trusting truth. You may believe you have control of your unresolved emotions, but if you are denying your soul truth, your unresolved emotions are controlling you. You can be unaware of the extent of your own soul denial and the restrictions caused by your unresolved emotions. It is a process to discover the many layers of your own denial. Being honest about what you do not know or fully understand, frees you to observe, explore and own the reality of your life experiences. Your honesty and intentional commitment to valuing your own soul, resolves your emotional, and at times compulsive habit of fighting against your awareness of truth and reality to defend your negative beliefs about yourself.

Your own desire for control will entice you to remain devoted to what is familiar within your soul's unconsciousness, which is the storehouse of your unresolved emotions. As you reverberate with the energetic collectives within the mass energy of mankind that correlate with your unresolved emotions, you seek to give yourself permission to stay immersed in those emotions. Part of your desire to control is abrogating responsibility for your own unresolved emotions. Often as you become aware of the energetic collectives, you become willing to use the collective energy as an excuse for your own denial. When you attempt to use your energetic awareness, to exonerate yourself from being responsible for your own unresolved emotions, you devalue truth. When you desire to control, you become extremely deceptive and manipulative, which leads you to comply and conform to the familiarity of the energy within your soul's unconsciousness. Your desire to control becomes the motivator that causes you to automatically react negatively to change and to your awareness of the presence of your soul's consciousness. This creates an addiction to the stagnation within yourself.

Stagnation is more conducive to your desire to control, because it is easier to control your expectations when you oppose the dynamics of life, yourself, others, relationships, truth and your present moment reality. You want to use the energetic collectives of the mass energy of mankind to feed and fuel your unconscious energy, so you can hide your truth within the labyrinths of your own soul deception. Your soul's unconsciousness is a type of labyrinth.

When you are unwilling to acknowledge how you hide the truth of your unresolved emotions, you choose to oscillate between the different unresolved emotions within your soul's unconsciousness that reverberate with the energetics of the mass energy of mankind. You perpetuate the energetic residue of your soul denial history by ignoring the opportunities to realise, resolve and trust the truth within you. You deny the motives behind your manipulation of your unresolved emotions, denying you have an emotional agenda. You deny there is a choice to be made, that you can either choose to generate more unconscious energy and remain worshipping control, or that you can choose to honestly resolve your own unresolved emotions. The choices you make either contribute to or contaminate your exploration of truth. You create opportunities for and with your truthful honesty to resolve your unresolved emotions, or you contaminate the opportunity, perpetuating or creating more unresolved emotions.

RIGHT: *When you are willing to use unconscious energy, as depicted by the three girls, you reverberate with the energetic collectives of the mass energy of mankind that correlate with the unconscious energy being used. The three girls are formulating an energetic collective with their judgement, which in turn has them feeding and being fuelled by the energetic collectives associated with their judgement. This becomes the energy they feel and project, which may cause the girl being projected at, to emotionally feel swamped and to lose her energetic independence.*

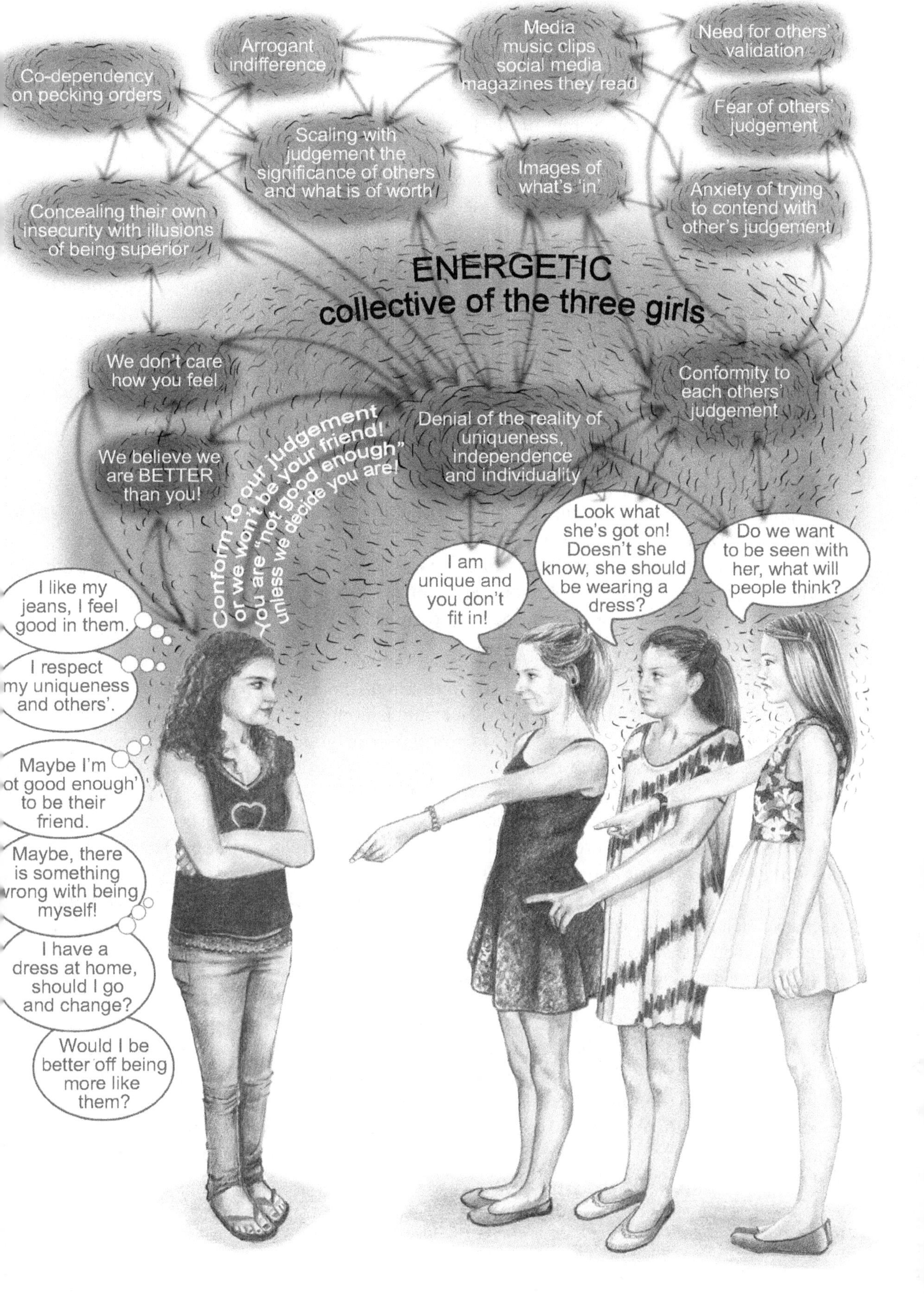
Co-dependency on pecking orders
Arrogant indifference
Media music clips social media magazines they read
Need for others' validation
Fear of others' judgement
Scaling with judgement the significance of others and what is of worth
Images of what's 'in'
Anxiety of trying to contend with other's judgement
Concealing their own insecurity with illusions of being superior
ENERGETIC collective of the three girls
We don't care how you feel
Conformity to each others' judgement
Denial of the reality of uniqueness, independence and individuality
We believe we are BETTER than you!
Conform to our judgement or we won't be your friend! You are "not good enough" unless we decide you are!
Look what she's got on! Doesn't she know, she should be wearing a dress?
Do we want to be seen with her, what will people think?
I am unique and you don't fit in!
I like my jeans, I feel good in them.
I respect my uniqueness and others'.
Maybe I'm ot good enough' to be their friend.
Maybe, there is something vrong with being myself!
I have a dress at home, should I go and change?
Would I be better off being more like them?

When you are unconscious to truth, you become a silent partner with the energetics of the mass energy of mankind. This means you arrogantly generate more unconscious energy for yourself and mankind to contend with, while denying what you contribute. You project energy at those around you, your environment and at your soul's consciousness but you deny your emotional input into the energy you project. You want to be oblivious to the reality of your own emotions and the consequences of being a silent partner in mankind's insanity of betraying ourselves. When you are unconscious, you remain ignorant and arrogant about the truth of what you are indifferent to, justifying your denial to avoid contemplating your own reality. When you use denial to protect your own avoidance of truth, you become progressively more aggressive if you think there is a threat to your denial. You feel compelled to perpetuate your negativity, deceptively creating misconceptions, expectations, perceived injustices and a fear of truth to fuel your defensiveness. This causes you to justify your refusal to resolve your emotions and refute your own evolution. This is where your freedom of choice is an essential concept to apply yourself to, because when you trust your awareness of truth, your deception cannot remain as your major influencer.

When you distrust your awareness of truth, you are governed by the lies that secure your denial and by your choice to remain energetically stagnant in your perpetuated cycles of soul oppression. Your soul denial is a direct result of the lies you tell yourself and your lies oppress your awareness of truth. You use your reverberation with the energetic collectives within the mass energy of mankind to sustain your own denial of your awareness of truth. When you deny and override your soul consciousness' attempts to expose your denial as fraudulent, you become codependent on your own lies.

Your soul's consciousness seeks to resolve your denial of the unresolved emotions stored within your soul's unconsciousness, and your denial of the core essences of your soul, which is your soul's consciousness. Your soul truth is both your conscious and unconscious energy. Your soul's consciousness knows resolution of your unresolved emotions is the path to freedom; freedom from the restraints and the oppression of your own soul denial. Your soul's consciousness seeks freedom from reverberating with the energetic collectives within the mass energy of mankind, and from your own desire to abolish your awareness of your original intention to resolve and evolve. Your participation in opposing your own opportunity for resolution and evolution is insane, because you are betraying your awareness of the core of your soul. The core of your soul is unconditional love and your other natural essences, such as compassion, integrity, peace and joy. If you choose to be unconscious of your truth, you are choosing to be the fragmentations of your unresolved emotions. You apply effort to this insanity by denying your awareness of truth.

Your soul's consciousness seeks to unify the fragmentation of your unresolved emotions, by resolving your denial. The resolution of your denial enables you to experience the evolution of your soul and to free yourself from enduring your own perpetual cycles of soul oppression. Evolution is freedom, which will enable you to feel the core of your soul resonating with truth. Your denial and control isolates you from your truth, separating and disassociating you from the reality of being a significant, unique, independent, individual soul of *True Source Divine Origin Consciousness*.

You can use your reverberation with the energetics of the mass energy of mankind to diligently suppress the truth of your awareness of your emotions, repress your recognition of the insanity within some of your beliefs and thought processes, and oppress your ability to feel the truth of your soul. You use your control structures to obstruct and oppose your resolution and evolution, denying the inspiration that you naturally feel from truth. You use indifference, soul denial and desire for control to manipulate all your known negative beliefs, behaviours, addictions and patterns, to hinder and attack your ability to honestly acknowledge your own soul truth.

Your acknowledgement of truth enables you to take responsibility for your own ignorance and arrogance towards the reality of being a soul, which will increase your awareness of your uniqueness, independence and individuality. When you oppose your own uniqueness, independence and individuality, you orchestrate your denial of who you are, to obstruct, fight and oppose your soul insight and any truth that exposes your soul truth to you. This causes you to reverberate with the energetics of the mass energy of mankind. Sometimes you want to be confused, so you can deny your contribution to mankind's deception, using your confusion as a deflection from self-responsibility. Your confusion subsides when you do not fight your own awareness and become willing to be honest. When you deny your truth, you become part of the energetics of the mass energy of mankind.

Your compliance to your own unresolved emotions, which are your contribution to the energetic collectives within the mass energy of mankind, inhibits you from feeling your significance as a soul. This type of compliance means to settle for what does not resonate with your soul, which also means you are choosing to sustain, feed and fuel your soul denial. Your denial of your natural significance makes you feel insecure. Your insecurity causes you to cling to the familiarity of the energy of your soul's unconsciousness, which sustains your internal unrest, precipitating your addiction to soul oppression. Your denial of your internal reality creates the desire to control an image of yourself and an illusion of life, to override the truth of your soul knowing. You can control yourself to be the embodiment of your indifference to yourself, reverberating with the energetic collectives that correlate to your unresolved emotions. You deny yourself the opportunity to seek and feel your internal truth.

When you refuse to be truthful about your energy, both conscious and unconscious, you will create illusions about your own soul. Instead of trusting yourself as a soul and trusting your own internal knowing that you can feel your way to truth; you will align to or construct a mankind impersonation of divinity to pacify your desire for control. When you seek to pacify an illusion of your soul, you search for energy that accommodates your desire to construct a façade that conceals the energy you need to resolve. This causes you to become manipulative and deceptive with yourself, as you reverberate with the correlating manipulative and deceptive collectives within the mass energy of mankind. The energetic collectives within the mass energy of mankind rely on your opposition to truth to have any relevance to you. If you are reverberating with the energetic collectives of the mass energy of mankind, it is because you have correlating energy or you have reacted from your desire to control the energetics you are aware of, or you are refusing to be honest with yourself. To protect your own deceptive self-manipulation and the illusion of controlling an emulation of truth that accommodates your denial, you will use the unconscious energy produced by your unresolved emotions, as a decoy to maintain your ignorance and to enact your arrogance towards your soul truth.

The purpose of your soul journey is to resolve your unresolved emotions, which you use to sustain the residue of your unconscious energy within the energetic collectives of the mass energy of mankind. Life is the opportunity to resolve the perpetuation of your known stagnant cycles of soul oppression. You have two types of knowing: your soul consciousness' knowing which is insight based in truth, and your known soul denial history which is the familiarity of your unresolved emotions reverberating with the energetic collectives within the mass energy of mankind. Your compulsion to protect your soul denial has you defying your own awareness of truth and denying the presence of truth within your reality.

- This leads to the question: why do you want to continue fighting truth for an illusory control of your soul denial?
- The other question is: why, when you internally know the result, do you override your own awareness?

When you elect to deny the truth of who you are for an illusion, you internally know you leave the residue of your soul denial energy within the energetic collectives of the mass energy of mankind. You are independently responsible for the unresolved emotions you leave within the energetics of mankind, and will return for another lifetime to resolve your own unconscious energy. Your soul's consciousness seeks to completely unify all your unconscious energy back to truth, which is the process of your truthfulness converting unconscious energy to conscious energy. Your original intention is to return to your origins having resolved your soul's unconsciousness, which means you leave no fragments of your unresolved emotions within the energetics of mankind. Your original intention is to leave no unconscious energy within mankind and you will experience as many lifetimes as necessary to do this.

In this lifetime you have agreed to experience what you have accumulated and stored within the energetics of mankind over your previous lifetimes; this is your blueprint. You have agreed to experience the truth of your soul's unconsciousness, which occurs regardless of your willingness to be truthfully honest about your own unresolved emotions. Your soul denial energy is exposed every lifetime. Each lifetime you have freedom of choice and can independently respond to life however you desire. You make choices that have vast ramifications for yourself as a soul. You deny the significance of your choices, so you can deny responsibility for the significance of your soul. You choose to either respond honestly or deceptively to your experience of the energy of your own soul's unconsciousness.

Your honesty creates opportunities for resolution and evolution; your dishonesty creates the exposure of your soul denial. You have the freedom to choose your response to the reality of your own unconsciousness.

When you choose to be deceptive about your opportunities to resolve and evolve, you use the energetic surge you feel, produced from your reverberation with the energetic collectives within the mass energy of mankind, to stroke and fuel your own ego. Your ego is the manifestation of wanting to gratify your desire for control. You use the energy reverberating with your unresolved emotions as justification or as a shield pretending to have no option but to enact the familiarity of your unresolved emotions. You may even create illusions of being resolved and evolved, and try to control yourself to an image of consciousness. Your desire for control cannot corrupt your soul's consciousness to support

Where there is unconscious energy, which is energy that denies truth, you will find correlating energy reverberating with the energetic collectives of the mass energy of mankind. If you have unresolved emotions which are susceptible to these reverberations, you may become confused about what you are energetically experiencing and emotionally react to your reality. This may cause you to separate from your awareness of your soul and truth and begin to reverberate with the unconscious energy correlating to your own unresolved emotions. It is the energy of your soul's unconsciousness that interacts with the unconscious energy within your reality and the mass energy of mankind.

your illusory control of truth, and eventually you will be exposed to the fraudulence of your own denial. Your soul's consciousness is too strong for your control to consistently overcome. You cannot even sustain control over the unconscious energy of your soul's unconsciousness, which always exposes your soul denial to you. You attempt to sustain your illusion by denying truth and immersing yourself in your unresolved emotions and your illusion of control, which is you choosing to lose yourself in your own soul oppression, by focusing on your desire to control.

When you seek validation from others who reverberate with the same energetic collectives within the mass energy of mankind, you use others' validation to justify your ability to deny truth and abandon the truth of what you feel. You can attempt to use the validation you want or have received, to avoid trusting your internal knowledge of your soul's consciousness. As you separate from your awareness of the reality of being a soul, you create images, illusions and controlled identities. You use your connective reverberation with the energetic collectives within the mass energy of mankind, to sustain illusions that support your denial. You emotionally want the energetic collectives within the mass energy of mankind to validate the embedded beliefs and fears of your soul denial. You can crave an energetic surge resulting from your unresolved emotions, which creates an emotional interaction with the energetic collectives within the mass energy of mankind. You want to ensure you can generate an energetic surge, so you justify your emotions and orchestrate the sustainability of your abandonment of truth. You fear acknowledging your abandonment of truth and seek to justify your unresolved emotions with the support of the energetic collectives that correlate to the unresolved emotions within your own soul's unconsciousness.

You want the energetic collectives to reciprocate your surge of unconscious energy. You want an 'emotional fix' for your control, an energetic sensation, and you deny what you are trying to control, which is your awareness of your soul's consciousness. You search for beliefs within mankind or anchor to the beliefs that you have been indoctrinated in from your childhood, to feed your illusion of control. You want your beliefs to pacify and gratify your unresolved emotions, so you can ignore the truth of your unresolved emotions. You use your beliefs in conjunction with the energetic collectives, to obstruct your direct awareness of the presence of *True Source Divine Origin Consciousness*, which is your origin. You have a direct interaction with the presence of *True Source Divine Origin Consciousness*, because you are of *True Source Divine Origin Consciousness*. When you are attempting to outmanoeuvre your own awareness of truth, you seek a contrived version of truth that suits your denial of your own reality.

When you are separated from your awareness of your soul and disassociated from feeling truth, you will defend and justify your distorted beliefs. You fight your resonance with truth to protect your soul's unconsciousness. Being separated from your awareness of your soul causes you to cling to your emotional, energetic and physical barriers to truth, and the energetic collectives reverberating with your unresolved emotions. This has you opposing the truth of what your soul is exposing to be resolved. You consume yourself with the energy of your unresolved emotions to oppose feeling your soul truth. If you are honest, you can feel the difference between your feelings and emotions, which highlights the significance of your honesty.

Your feelings communicate your soul knowing; you feel the reality of your truth, you feel the truth of your present moment and you feel the truth of your reaction to truth. Your feelings communicate your awareness of the presence of your soul's consciousness. Your unresolved emotions expose what you create while separated from your awareness of your soul. Your unresolved emotions are your past and become your expectations for the future, and you use them to ignore your present moment. Your unresolved emotions are the by-products of your emotional history of denying your soul, and the history of your contribution to the energetic collectives you have stagnated yourself in. Your stagnation is how you use the embedded beliefs and fears of your soul denial to oppress your opportunity for resolution and evolution, and you become your history repeating itself. Being separated from your awareness of being a soul of truth is to control yourself to what you have done before, which is the stagnation of your own soul oppression. Your soul's consciousness seeks freedom from what you have emotionally done before, by resolving your unresolved emotions.

When you resolve your unresolved emotions, you will naturally resolve your energetic residue within the energetic collectives that correlate to your unresolved emotions. It is possible to leave no energetic emotional residue in the energetics of the mass energy of mankind, but this is the choice to be completely honest with the reality of yourself as a soul. Your soul's consciousness seeks to be free of the emotional traps of mankind's deception and illusion of control.

You have the opportunity to choose to allow yourself to experience resolving and evolving your soul while in a physical body. You have the opportunity to choose to trust yourself to awaken to the reality of being a soul. You do this by trusting yourself to be consciously aware of your soul, your feelings, your unresolved emotions and the emotional environment that you create within your reality.

Trust is to accept the reality of being a significant, unique, independent, individual soul of *True Source Divine Origin Consciousness*. Freedom is to trust yourself to experience your blueprint without fear of losing anything of value. Your desire for control is not valuable, it is a hindrance to your awareness of the truth of your soul. Your life is an opportunity to experience being a significant, unique, independent, individual soul who is surrounded by the energetics of the mass energy of mankind, but is not of the energetics of mankind. You have the opportunity to experience the freedom of being an independent soul, resonating and expressing the truth of your soul, unencumbered by your own soul's unconsciousness or mankind's collective unconsciousness.

Truth alters the web of deception in which you have become embroiled. The web of deception is the energetics of the mass energy of mankind and your own unresolved emotions combining together to enforce, sustain and protect your soul denial. When you have an aversion to accepting your soul truth, you use your indifference and desire for control to intercept your conscious soul insight. This means you sustain your separation from your awareness of your soul's consciousness.

Your aversion to truth is really the desire to use your control structures to try to control the experience you have on Earth with your unresolved emotions. When you seek to be unconscious of truth, you use the energy of your soul's unconsciousness to reverberate with the energetic collectives within the mass energy of mankind, because you are attracted to the same vibration. Your fears and embedded beliefs sustain your soul denial causing you to seek ways of being unconscious of your soul truth. When you want to stay in complete opposition to the purpose of your soul's journey, you deny the ramifications on your soul. When you deny your contribution to the anarchy within yourself, you also deny your participation within the energetics of the mass energy of mankind. The energetic collectives within the mass energy of mankind are the accumulation of each individual's defection from and abandonment of accepting, trusting and unconditionally loving the reality of being a soul.

You have many unconscious reverberations with the energetic collectives of the mass energy of mankind that interfere with your ability to be honest with yourself and your willingness to be loyal to truth. Your willingness to be deceptive is how you secure, protect and defend your soul denial. This is your attempt to exonerate yourself from the truth of your soul's blueprint, which is your original intention to resolve what separates you from your awareness of truth. It is a falsity if you believe you can disregard your blueprint, disregard the presence of your soul's consciousness and disregard your awareness of your unresolved emotions with no consequences to your soul. You want to believe regardless of what you disregard, that you will be able to control your own denial, but your denial controls you.

When you deceptively control your unresolved emotions with suppression, repression and oppression, you obstruct your awareness of your uniqueness, independence and individuality. Once you obstruct your awareness, you control yourself to devalue all evidence of your uniqueness, independence and individuality. You lose your objectivity by denying the truth you feel and can observe. You have created an emotionally, energetically and physically complicated, convoluted, tangled web of trickery and harmful deception against your soul's evolution. This causes you to constantly cycle in your own unresolved emotions, which results in you reverberating with the energetic collectives within the mass energy of mankind. Your denial of your own emotions, means you stay committed to contributing to the energetics of mankind. When you disregard the effect of your denial on your soul, you mindlessly perpetuate your unresolved emotions.

Your honesty and truthfulness cannot occupy the same space as your deception, so the more honest you are about the reality you are experiencing, the more likely you are to acknowledge the opportunity to resolve and evolve. Your honesty creates an opportunity to resolve how you have used mankind's deception to enhance your own deception. If you have resolved your unconscious energy from the energetic collectives within the mass energy of mankind, the deception within the energetics of mankind becomes irrelevant to you. You will acknowledge, accept and feel the truth of all energy, remaining conscious of your freedom of choice and responding to the truth of life consciously.

Chapter Twenty-One

Chakra and aura system

Your chakra system is the energetic framework which channels your energy. Your chakra system is an energetic framework with collection points, which are the chakras. Your chakra system enables you to feel your reaction to reality. When you react from the energy of your soul's unconsciousness, your reaction projects energy from your chakras, which is your contribution to the energetic collectives of the mass energy of mankind. This emphasises what you came to resolve. You instinctively use your chakras to unconsciously project out the unconscious energy produced by your unresolved emotions, and to also pull in unconscious energy from other sources.

Your chakras exist because you have unresolved emotions. When you resolve your unresolved emotions, you become a unified flow of conscious energy. Your individual chakras are attached to a channel, which is the core of your chakra system. It is through the absolute core of this channel that your consciousness flows from your origins of *True Source Divine Origin Consciousness* to the energetic core of mankind's soul denial; this is the pathway of your rise and fall from grace. Your rise and fall from grace is the continuous loop of your soul's consciousness, which exposes you to the truth of all energy.

Your chakra system is the energetic structure which entangles, engages and connects your unresolved emotions to the energetic collectives within the mass energy of mankind. You reinforce the unconscious energy of your unresolved emotions with your denial of your awareness of truth. After your death, your unresolved emotions are stored within the energetic collectives of the mass energy of mankind. When you are born, your unresolved emotions return to your soul via your chakras. Your unresolved emotions, which you have contributed to the energetic collectives of the mass energy of mankind, are an accumulation from previous lives and this lifetime. Your soul's unconsciousness is compounded layers of your unresolved emotions, which have resulted from your fears and embedded beliefs. Your fears and embedded beliefs are stored within your soul denial, which is the foundation of the energetic construction of your soul's unconsciousness.

Your chakras are collection and dispersion transmitters for your energy. You feel the transmission of your unresolved emotions within your chakra system. This is a system designed to alert you to energy that is separated from the frequency of truth, and vibrating as an unconscious energy, such as the energy of your and others soul's unconsciousness. Your chakras amplify the unconscious energy you attempt to deny.

Your emotional reactions to your present moment reality, although often visually concealed, cause your chakras to emit the truth of the energy inciting the reaction. You might believe you have control of your emotions, but you are just controlling yourself to deny the reality of what you are feeling, and the truth that your energetic projections come from your emotions.

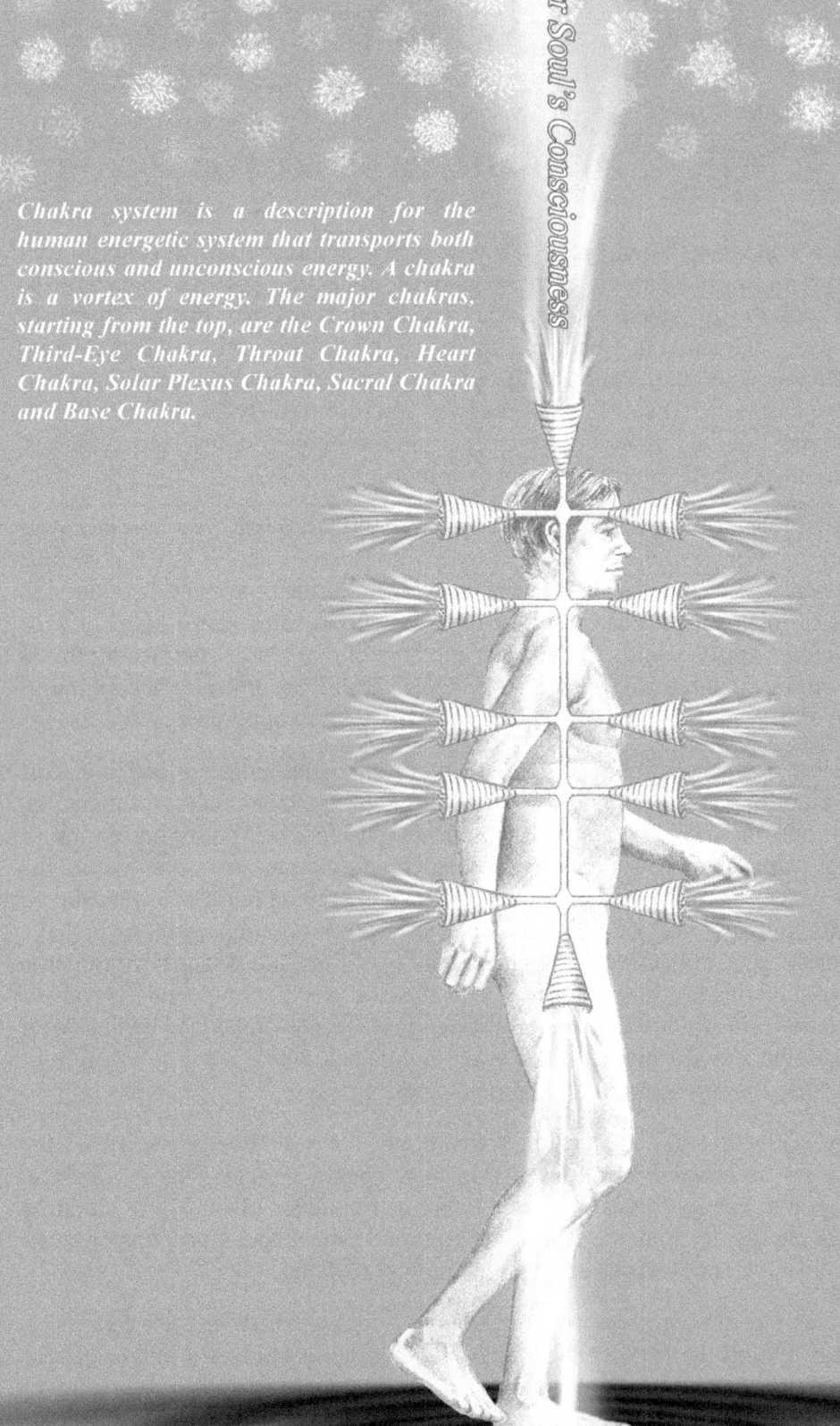

Chakra system is a description for the human energetic system that transports both conscious and unconscious energy. A chakra is a vortex of energy. The major chakras, starting from the top, are the Crown Chakra, Third-Eye Chakra, Throat Chakra, Heart Chakra, Solar Plexus Chakra, Sacral Chakra and Base Chakra.

Your Soul's Consciousness

Soul Denial

Your aura is the combination of different energies. Some of these energies emanate from your soul's consciousness and some energies are projected from, or ooze from your soul's unconsciousness.

Consciousness

SOUL DENIAL

Your chakras expose you to the reality of your unresolved emotions, which collectively form the energy of your soul's unconsciousness. Your aura is a combination of the energy of your soul's consciousness and unconsciousness; it is the emanation of your soul truth. Your aura is the combination of your different energies, which energetically ooze or emanate from your soul system.

Your aura consists of the energy from your reaction to your present moment. If you are expressing the truth of your feelings and emanating the energy of your soul's consciousness, then your aura is of conscious energy. If you are externally or internally reacting from your unresolved emotions, you are activating the vortex of your soul's unconsciousness, and your aura will emit the unconscious energy of the unresolved emotions you are using in that present moment. The more you choose to separate from your awareness of your soul and disassociate from feeling truth, the more your aura oozes unconscious energy. Your aura can be of both conscious and unconscious energy simultaneously.

You use your chakras to externalise, automatically projecting the energy of the unresolved emotions of your soul's unconsciousness at your soul's consciousness, at others, and at the energetic collectives and barriers of the mass energy of mankind. You internalise the energy you reverberate with, back into your own physical body via your chakra system. Your chakras are your energetic highways that entangle, engage and connect you to others' energy system and to energetic collectives. This is how you fuel the energetic collectives within the mass energy of mankind and how the energetic collectives of mankind reinforce the unresolved emotions of your soul's unconsciousness. You can oppress your awareness of your soul truth and become unaware of both your conscious and unconscious energy.

To fully understand your chakra system, you need to acknowledge how we knowingly and unknowingly energetically interact with each other. You use the energetics of your unresolved emotions via your chakra system, to energetically intrude into another's chakra system, by projecting your unconscious energy at their chakra system. This is how you feel, read, access, judge and attempt to control another's energy to accept your energy. When you have an emotional exchange in which both people are willing to intrude into each other's chakra system, you collectively create an energetic relationship. You sustain the energetic relationship by entangling, engaging and connecting your unconscious energy with another's unconscious energy. This creates an energetic relationship collective within the mass energy of mankind, an energetic space in which both energies are reacting and responding. This causes you both to lose your energetic independence and to become reactive to the energy of the energetic relationship collective you have mutually formed.

If you project unconscious energy at another and the other person does not react by entangling, engaging or connecting to the energy being projected, it means the person has been able to retain their own energetic independence, and your projected energy will instantaneously return to you via your own chakra system. When a person does entangle, engage and connect to the energy being projected, this turns into an exchange of unconscious energy between two people. This generally has them both competing for supremacy over the emotional exchange, and both parties lose their energetic independence. This causes them to connect and compete against each others' unconscious energy, pitting control structure against control structure. We often refer to this as someone getting under our skin, which means they are having a strong affect on us and are difficult to forget or come to peace with. This is because there has been an energetic intrusion, which entangles us with each others' unresolved emotions.

The person who is attempting to incite an emotional exchange of unconscious energy and interconnection, may do so with an undercurrent of heresy energy. If they cannot incite another, no energetic relationship will be formed and their energy will return to their own system. The person who sought the emotional exchange will activate their own vortex of unconsciousness and then implode within their own unconscious energy.

If you have had an emotional exchange and are energetically connected, you create an energetic relationship collective. The sustainability of the energetic relationship collective is determined by the willingness of both parties to fuel the emotionally charged energy within the interwoven energetic interactions that sustains the energetic relationship collective.

Relationship collective with a stranger: A heated argument with a stranger at a service station creates an energetic relationship collective; both parties want to prove the righteousness of their own judgement and ability to control reality, and they become energetically entangled, engaged and connected. The energetic relationship collective will be sustained if both parties fuel their emotions with their perceived righteous judgement and their desire to prove the validity of their control. Both parties may keep fueling the energetic collective long after their physical encounter occurred.

As both parties settle their own unresolved emotions and believe they are not likely to encounter each other again, the collective begins to dissipate. As the collective dissipates the unresolved emotions within the collective will return to their original source. They have used each other's willingness to externalise emotions as fuel to justify projecting their own emotions. This exposes their unresolved emotions and creates a junction. A junction is a pivotal point of choice. They either choose to be honest about the emotions and accept the experience as an opportunity to learn, explore and resolve. Or they choose to suppress awareness of their unresolved emotions and use blame of the other person to conceal the opportunity to learn, explore and resolve. It is when an individual begins to be honest about their own experience of reality, that they can acknowledge the opportunities to take full responsibility for their own energy and to participate in their process of resolution.

If both parties cross paths again they may instantly recognise the opportunity to activate the energetic relationship collective and energetically project unresolved emotions at each other, accessing each other via the history of their emotional exchange. The projection of energy may become the status quo every time they encounter each other, even though no verbal interaction may occur.

Long term relationship collective: In long term relationships, such as those between different family members, the energetic relationship collective becomes an accumulation of years of emotional exchanges, energetic interconnection and interweaving. The collective is constantly being fuelled by each person's unwillingness to forgive the other, or unwillingness to acknowledge their own contribution to the undercurrent of emotional angst within the relationship. Within our energetic relationships we are all trying to control our constant wariness of the unconscious will within each other. Our unconscious will is our compulsion to be indifferent to truth and is our intent to use deception to secure an illusion of control.

This causes us to overshadow how we truly feel about each other with our desire to control. When we are willing to be indifferent to truth, we use any unresolved emotion to incite an emotional exchange, in an attempt to prove we are in control of our reality and in control of all those who are part of our life.

We all fear being out of control of our own emotions and energetic reactions to the familiarity of emotional exchanges, which incites the activation of our vortex of unconsciousness. We fear being exposed to our own denial of our unconsciousness. Our fear of being exposed to the energy of our soul's unconsciousness causes us to be consumed by the desire to control any unconscious energy we are exposed to. The familiarity of the unconscious energy within the energetic relationship, causes us to stop seeing each other as individual souls. We identify each other by controlled identities and the pecking orders we perceive based on the controlled identities. Each member of a long term energetic relationship collective knows how to activate the unresolved emotions of the other, which can instantly activate all the unconscious energy within them. This incites an energetic duel, where both parties are willing to enact the same emotional exchange and energetic interconnection, which can be repetitive and predictable.

If a member of the collective resolves their emotional contribution to the energetic relationship, the collective alters and may begin to dissipate. This can cause confusion and emotional angst for the other members, because they have become codependent on the energetic interplay of unconscious energy, as a space to externalise what they will not accept as their own resolvable energy. Members of the collective who want to sustain their denial of the reality of their own energy within their soul's unconsciousness, deny what they contribute to the energetic interplay. If they have no interest in resolving their unresolved emotions, they may intensify their efforts to incite the other member to re-activate the energy of their vortex of unconsciousness, seeking to reinforce and sustain the energetic interplay within the relationship.

When a person becomes responsible for their own energy and is willing to resolve what they emotionally contribute to the energetic relationship, their energy within the collective dissipates. Each member uses each other's compulsions to externalise the energy of their soul's unconsciousness, as justification for their own. Their interactions become a way to create an emotionally charged environment, where they can act out their own unresolved emotions. Being aware of this creates an opportunity for members of the collective to be honest about their own emotions, and to accept their experience of reality as an opportunity to learn, explore and resolve their own unresolved emotions. They may choose to suppress their awareness of their own unresolved emotions and use their blame of others to conceal the opportunity to learn, explore and resolve their own unresolved emotions. It is through their own experience of reality and the choice to be honest that resolution can occur.

When one of the members is being completely honest about their own unresolved emotions and is willing to resolve their portion of the unconscious energy fuelling the energetic relationship collective, they no longer sustain the collective. Any emotional exchange can become an opportunity for them to be honest about what is actually emotionally, energetically and physically occurring. It is their willingness to be honest, which resolves their unconscious will to compete. Our energetic relationship collectives are created or re-formed from our unconscious will. An individual's unconscious will is the result of their indifference to the truth of who they are, and is how they automatically externalise their own indifference onto others. We are all susceptible to using our unconscious will to become a willing participant in the battle for supremacy, as we attempt to control any unconscious energy we encounter.

As the energetic relationship collective dissipates, the unresolved emotions within the collective energy will return to their original source. When an individual soul is willing to be true to their energetic independence, they observe unconscious energy, their own or others, without unconsciously entangling, engaging or connecting in a battle for supremacy or attempts to control unconscious energy. Your battle for supremacy and your attempts to control unconscious energy means you seek to have your images, illusions, controlled identities and unresolved emotions validated, vindicated and pacified. You can seek to fuel your illusion of being able to control your life experiences, by attempting to control the collective energy you anticipate, encounter or contribute willingly to.

You unconsciously feel others' energy within your own chakra system and can emotionally react by projecting your energy at theirs, which may make you feel off kilter and uneasy. None of us like how it feels when the unconscious energy of others' unresolved emotions intrudes into our chakra system. When you feel others' energy within your own chakra system, you can often unconsciously project energy back in an attempt to ascertain who or what is intruding into your chakra system. This often has you emotionally entangled, engaged and connected to many peoples' unconsciousness and incites the formation of energetic relationship collectives.

When you have an unconscious energetic reaction to another and project your energy into another's chakra system and are unwilling to acknowledge the truth of your own energy, your dishonesty enables you to participate in the construction of an energetic relationship collective. This inhibits you from being energetically independent. The energetic relationship collective becomes an arena for the entanglement of unconscious energy to unconscious energy. When you are unaware that you are experiencing an exchange of unconscious energy, you may go into your own self-doubt as you attempt to grapple with the feelings of being disorientated. We can all use the projection of energy as a catalyst for either the battle for energetic supremacy, which keeps us entangled in the interaction of unconscious energy to unconscious energy, or as a catalyst for the decision to be an objective observer.

To be an objective observer is to appreciate the uniqueness and independence of all souls including yourself, and to acknowledge the energetic reality of another without losing your awareness of yourself. This facilitates your respect for your own freedom of choice and enables you to make the decision to not emotionally, energetically or physically entangle yourself in unconscious interactions and monotonous interplays. This means you are present and honest with yourself about your own reaction to the reality of the present moment. Being present and honest is a form of energetic independence.

We deny the reality that we regularly energetically intrude into each other's chakra system and instead overly focus on the displays of emotions, which are often incited and the result of an energetic intrusion. We attempt to deny our awareness and the ramifications of our emotional energetic intrusions into each other's energy system. We want to be unconscious to the projection of emotions to continue the illusion of being able to hide from the reality of our own energetics. When we deny the part we play in our energetic interactions and monotonous interplays with others, we facilitate being manipulative and covertly attempt to control how another feels about who they are.

We energetically externalise our unresolved emotions at each other, with no accountability for the reality of our emotional projections. This is how we keep cycling in the oppression of denying the truth of the energetics of our emotions, which allows us to continue denying our soul truth. We arrogantly ignore the truth of our energetic experiences to secure our denial of our awareness of energy. We are indoctrinated to ignore the reality of what we are feeling, and conditioned to be silent about the emotional charade we enact on each other; but we all feel the unconscious energy within energetic projections. We analyse, stew in and judge what we energetically feel, but we are reluctant to talk about the energetics we feel. Our denial of our ability to acknowledge the truth of our emotional exchanges, creates confusion within us.

We often project energy, whilst portraying an image or conveying an illusion, as we attempt to conceal the undercurrent of unresolved emotions within our energetic projections, which is our hidden agenda of trying to secure an illusion of control. This can be contradictory to the words we speak, the actions we take and what we display.

Image of being easy going: You have the image of being easy going and the illusion that everyone is perceiving you as easy going. However, the undercurrent within your projected energy comes with a warning to others that your control is not to be interfered with, because you are willing to become enraged. You speak as though nothing is a problem and display a charade of being at ease with the dynamics of reality, while you arrogantly attempt to manipulate anyone you can to appease your image of yourself. You are constantly seeking to secure your denial of your own emotional and energetic undercurrent. At the same time as you seek to sustain the portrayal of the image of being easy going, you fixate on controlling to get what you want. All of which is contradictory to the image you want to be perceived as.

Image of being confident: You have the image of being confident and the illusion of being in control of everything. However, your undercurrent within the projected energy is fear and insecurity, and yet you speak with an edge of indifference, and attempt to display a charade of superiority. As you arrogantly pretend you are in control of your reality, and deny the truth of your own emotional and energetic undercurrents, your insecurity causes you to react irrationally or defensively. This is contradictory to the confident image you are trying to portray. Images and illusions create facades and charades to enact. However, the truth of your own energy is always within the undercurrents of your projected energy.

RIGHT: You use your chakras to externalise and project the energy of the unresolved emotions of your soul's unconsciousness at your soul's consciousness, at others, and at the energetic collectives and barriers of the mass energy of mankind. You internalise the energy you reverberate with back into your physical body, via your chakra system. An energetic relationship collective is a form of mankind collective.

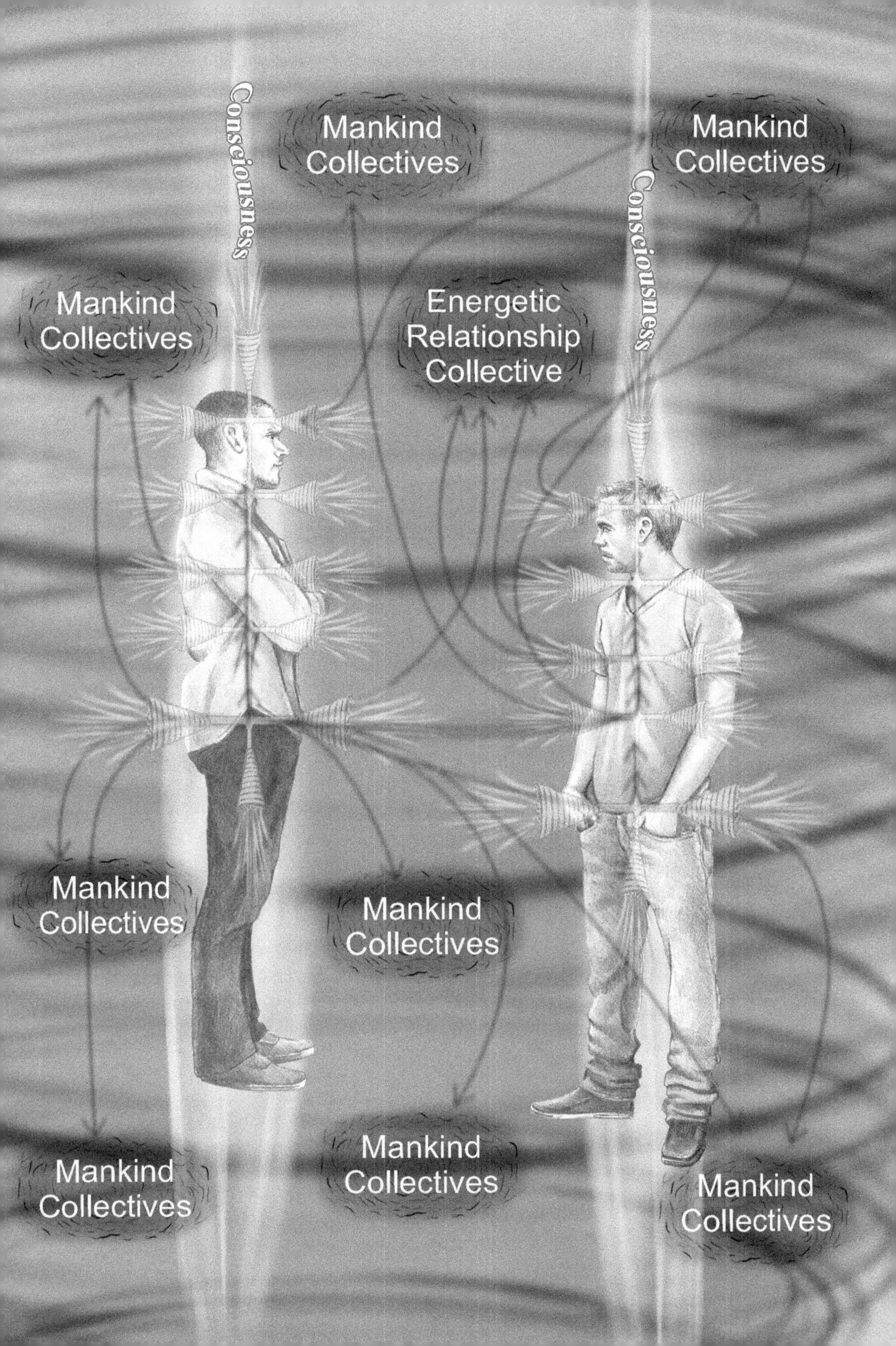
Consciousness
Mankind Collectives
Mankind Collectives
Consciousness
Mankind Collectives
Energetic Relationship Collective
Mankind Collectives
Mankind Collectives
Mankind Collectives
Mankind Collectives
Mankind Collectives

We all feel confused by the deceptiveness of our emotions and by our willingness to covertly project energy at each other via our chakra system. When you recognise your own projected energy, you expose the truth of the energy of your unresolved emotions to yourself. This enables you to observe what you may be unaware of. We emotionally exchange energy and interweave our energetic reality with our desire to control our own perception of reality. This often secures the continuation of an energetic relationship, because both parties are willing to fight to secure their perception of reality, and truth is perceived as irrelevant.

We confuse ourselves with our compulsive desire for control and trigger another surge of energy, which is interjected into the emotional exchange. The surge of energy creates a feeling of confusion within us. Others see our confusion and perceive it as a weakness and this can then trigger their desire to control. The desire to control incites the projection of more types of control energy, such as manipulation, judgement and indifference into the emotional exchange, in an attempt to create an energetic pecking order that both want to feel in control of. At times a person may want to be perceived as confused, in an attempt to manipulate another to take responsibility for their reality, and it becomes a way they covertly incite another's desire for control. This illusion of confusion is a charade, which has them portraying themselves as the weaker player within their construct of the pecking order of the relationship, as a way to hide their manipulation and their desire to control another. They portray themselves as the weaker player for the purpose of relinquishing any responsibility for their reality, as they delight in controlling another to be the scapegoat they can blame when life does not work to their expectations. This emotional exchange has a payoff for both because they are both seeking to pacify their own illusion of control and sense of superiority.

When a person has established their perception of an energetic pecking order that they are comfortable with, their energetic projections subside because they believe their control has been pacified. Once an energetic relationship collective is formed and well established, an emotional undercurrent will remain. This means a covert energetic emotional exchange and interconnection reverberates just below the surface of what is being said and displayed within the charades that are performed. We want to know what to control within ourselves and others, to uphold the charades of our images and the illusions attached to the images. We attempt to match the energy we emotionally feel being projected, or we reinforce the energy with our own agenda to be emotionally dominant over any other energy felt, which sustains the energetic interconnection. We unconsciously project energy at others, to steer them in how to react to us.

We project our images, illusions, controlled identities or our unresolved emotions at others, and energetically read if they are reacting favourably to our energetic projections. If they react favourably to our energetic projections, we believe they are controllable with our projected energy, which we then use to expand our attempts and desires to control others. We actually want others to become contributing factors in our arena, so we can enact our unresolved emotions and the charades of our images, illusions and controlled identities.

RIGHT: *You use the energetics of your unresolved emotions to energetically intrude into another energy system, by projecting your unconscious energy at them. This happens via your chakra system and the other person's chakra system. You unconsciously use your chakra system to attempt to control another's emotions by bombarding them with your energy.*

When we project energy it always has a hidden agenda for control. We have been programmed, conditioned and indoctrinated to be mindful of the sensitivity we have to each other's desire for control. We know that we are sensitive to any opposition to our desire for control and we are all seeking to have our own desire for control pacified. We covertly project control in many forms and deny the reality of our energetic projections, whilst we judge others for theirs. We energetically interplay with each other's control and use our indifference to truth to affect another's awareness.

We attempt to use our unresolved emotions to orchestrate the denial of our energetic awareness, and it is our denial which sends our chakra system into overdrive. We go into overdrive when we protect and defend our denial or desire for control with more deception. We use our unconscious energy to match, counteract or diffuse the energy we feel, without comprehending the truth of our energetic awareness. This is why we resist, deny and avoid the truth of our energetic projections, because we want to be unconscious to the emotional reality we inflict at each other and the true ramifications of our collective denial. You emotionally exchange energy from within your own unconsciousness, with others' unconsciousness and with the energetic collectives of the mass energy of mankind. Your chakra system exposes:

- The truth of all energy you produce
- Why and how you emotionally exchange energy
- What you do within an emotional exchange
- The monotonous energetic interplays you are regularly embroiled in

Your chakra system is neutral and unbiased about your unresolved emotions; it operates in truth and exposes the truth of your unresolved emotions. Your chakras are a barometer you cannot manipulate. Your chakras respond to the truth of your unresolved emotions, not to your desire to suppress, repress and oppress them.

- You suppress your awareness of your unresolved emotions; however the unconscious energy is still within your soul's unconsciousness.
- You repress your awareness; however the beliefs and passing thoughts you use to do this actually generate more unconscious energy within you.
- You oppress your awareness of the truth of your unresolved emotions, however the truth still registers within you and your chakras react to the truth of your energy.

You unconsciously externalise the energy produced by your unresolved emotions, rather than owning the truth of how you feel, in an attempt to rid yourself of the unresolved emotions you want to resist, deny or avoid. Your chakras return the truth of the energy you are projecting at yourself, others and the energetic collectives and barriers of the mass energy of mankind, back into your own chakra system. Whatever energy you project will return to you.

LEFT: If you project unconscious energy at another and that person does not respond by entangling, engaging or connecting to the energy, the person who does not respond energetically retains their energetic independence, and the projected energy returns instantly to the person projecting it.

Your desire to control is non-effective to your chakras. You cannot orchestrate your chakras to project the energy you want because they project the truth of your emotions. For example: You might believe you are projecting unconditional love, but if the truth of your emotion is manipulation, then that is what you are projecting.

You energetically feel the energy of people, both their conscious and unconscious energy. You feel:

- Changes in the energy
- The energy within their aura
- The presence of others even when you have not seen them
- When someone's attention is on you
- When someone is trying to get your attention
- When someone wants to avoid your attention

We all feel energy; even our denial cannot override our natural ability to feel energy.

When a person wants another to stay energetically interconnected to them, they exert their control over the relationship, often using their unresolved emotions, such as insecurity and fear as manipulative tools. They seek to control the attention on themselves, reinforcing their ability to manipulate the other person and to sustain the enmeshment to each other, which creates an energetic relationship collective. Enmeshment deprives each person of their energetic independence. They can slyly conceal the truth of their unresolved emotions and desire to control another, and attempt to obligate the other to sustain the emotional and energetic interconnection. When enmeshment is the foundation of the relationship, beliefs of ownership sustain the denial of reality. There has to be a mutual aspiration to remain enmeshed in each other's energetic system to sustain the monotonous interplays of unconscious energy.

We want to be able to feel the presence of, or changes within another and we unconsciously seek information that we believe enables us to feel superior because of our control. This creates mutual exchanges of unconscious energy, where both people are seeking emotional, energetic and physical information about the other to enhance their ability to control. We use our chakra system to energetically project an unresolved emotion, which we envisage or know will be accepted by, or create a reaction within the person whom we are trying to elicit an emotional reaction from. We seek to manipulatively access another's energy, entangling, engaging and connecting our unconscious energy with another's unconscious energy. The unresolved emotion we energetically project may be the same emotion they are consumed by, an emotion that allows them to believe they are in control or an emotion which incites a fear reaction within them. If we project energy with the purpose of manipulating for control, we lose our energetic independence.

Reactions to judgement: If you feel judgement and want to control the interaction, you may project judgement back, and seek to create a competition. You might feel the judgement and project approval and support for the judgement, or you may use the judgement to incite your insecurity or rage. Whichever way you do this, you are energetically manipulating your awareness, to enable the entangling, engaging and connecting of your unconscious energy to another's unconscious energy. Your participation in any unconscious interaction results in you denying the uniqueness, independence and individuality of yourself and the other person.

Reactions to indifference: If you feel indifference and want to control the interaction, you may project indifference back and lose your awareness of self-boundaries. You might feel the indifference and project complacency and validation for the indifference, or you may use the indifference to incite insecurity, or you may attempt to deny what you feel. Whichever way you do this, you are energetically manipulating your awareness of truth to enable the entangling, engaging and connecting of your unconscious energy to another's unconscious energy. This causes you to deny the uniqueness, independence and individuality of yourself and of others.

When you allow yourself to lose your awareness of your own energetic independence and enmesh your energy with an outside source of unconscious energy, you activate your indifference and attempt to control your own soul's unconsciousness and consciousness. The loss of energetic independence means you have forsaken your own freedom of choice, and are reacting from your unconscious will.

Your soul's consciousness does not need or want to be carrying, playing with or controlling another's conscious or unconscious energy. Your soul's consciousness feels the truth of all energy and you have the opportunity, by objectively observing the truth of the energy you feel, to acknowledge both your own or another's energy. If energy is projected at you while you are willing to be conscious of your uniqueness, independence and individuality, and you have no desire to control another and no fear of the energy you feel; all projections will naturally be repelled when you are willing to take full responsibility for your own energy. Your desire to control causes you to believe all energy is relevant to your control, this is how you justify intruding into another's energy system which enables entanglement and enmeshment to occur, and actually disrupts your illusion of control. When you govern your judgement of reality and the choices you make, by how you affect or are going to be affected by another's energy, you emotionally feel out of control. You emotionally feel entrapped and controlled by your own desire for control and desire to affect another, losing your energetic independence because you want to prove the dominance of your control. We have programmed, conditioned and indoctrinated ourselves to hide from the reality of being energetically intrusive. We attempt to deny feeling energetic intrusions and that our intrusions can be felt, and it is our denial that causes the confusion around what and how we feel.

You can be interwoven with another's unconsciousness and continue being emotionally and energetically attached or enmeshed without physically seeing the person for years. You emotionally attach to the unresolved emotions you carry from your history of emotional exchanges with another, and this causes you to periodically reenergise the energetic relationship collective with your judgement and refusal to resolve your own unresolved emotions. If the other person resolves their energetic connection to you and resolves the emotions they were contributing to the relationship, they alter how you energetically interconnect. You may remain attached to the unresolved emotions you contributed to the relationship and still desire the energetic interconnection you had in the past with that person, but the current energetic relationship is no longer with the person, it is only you interacting with your own unresolved emotions. You may periodically reenergise the unresolved emotions and attempt to project them at the other person, only to have your own unresolved emotions returned to your system, because the other person is unwilling to engage in an emotional energetic exchange.

People who want to continue the energetic enmeshment and interweaving connections, may create an illusion within themselves to energetically play out their former emotional connections. This causes them to ruminate and fixate on their attachment to their emotional history. They seek to create and repeat experiences that will allow them to act out their unresolved emotions, seeking to gain control over what they believe has created control failure. They repeat emotional experiences, in an attempt to secure an illusion of control. This means they remain stagnant in their emotional past, because they will not resolve their unresolved emotions and their attachment to their desire to inflict their control at others.

Your honesty exposes you to the truth of your denial and how you deny yourself the opportunity to be and feel your uniqueness, independence and individuality as a soul. To remain unconscious you need to override what you are feeling and be willing to deceive yourself. Your chakra system naturally disturbs your ability to deny the truth of your emotions and exposes your deception, by exposing you to the energetics of your emotions. You may not be willing to be honest about your awareness of what you are feeling, but you do feel your chakras reacting, projecting and back-feeding your energy.

When you deny the truth of your own unresolved emotions, you become willing to deny your energetic awareness. You programme, condition and indoctrinate yourself with your denial of the reality of your emotional reactions and responses to your life experiences. You may seek to hold another accountable for their unresolved emotions and actions, while denying the reality of what you are doing to your own soul. The unconscious energy produced by your grudges is projected through your chakras, at times indiscriminately. You can see what needs to be resolved within yourself when you are honest about what you project emotionally. Your forgiveness of yourself for being unconscious about your unresolved emotions creates the space for resolution and evolution. Forgiveness frees you from being incarcerated in your willingness to sustain the monotonous interplays that keep you enmeshed with another's unresolved emotions. Forgiveness also creates the opportunity for you to be loyal to the uniqueness and the energetic independence of being an individual soul of *True Source Divine Origin Consciousness*.

Your emotional projections come with emotional and energetic demands. If you want your emotions pacified verbally or with physical action, you will seek an energetic reaction to your energetic projections. You try to read if another is being energetically submissive to your emotional projections or if they are going to battle for energetic supremacy. Your emotional demands create disharmony within you. Your emotional demands are the result of your desire for control, which separates you from your awareness of your soul truth. When you are truly trusting truth, you refrain from separating from your awareness of the truth of your own energy and will consciously participate in the exposure of your own energy. When you project energy, you are externalising the energy of your soul's unconsciousness. Truth flows within your soul's consciousness; externalising is the act of distrusting truth and is the act of opposing yourself. Your distrust of the value of truth causes you to externalise, seeking to affect others, because you want to prove to yourself there is validity in your desire for control. You can become addicted to wanting validation and approval for your desire for control, and battle for energetic supremacy to prove the validity and prowess of your ability to control. All of this leaves you entangled in monotonous emotional interplays, energetic enmeshments and toxic relationships.

You can seek continuity of your emotional struggle to try and justify the war within yourself. You use your chakras to project energy, externalising to find a person or situation that will supply the unconscious energy you want to inflict on yourself. You have conditioned yourself to accept externalisation as normal. Your soul's consciousness does not contribute to your emotional desire to energetically affect another or to disharmonise yourself with unresolved emotions. Your soul's consciousness is always seeking to expose the truth of your emotions and the soul oppressive patterns that you inflict on yourself and others. Your soul's consciousness is naturally energetically independent.

Your complacency about your own willingness to externally project energy, and your reactions to being inflicted with projected energy, has you consumed with battles for energetic supremacy. When you are willing to be deceptive, you seek to have supreme control over how you use your own and others' unconscious energy produced from unresolved emotions. You inadvertently entangle yourself with others and the collective unconscious energy that reverberates with your unresolved emotions. This intensifies your unresolved emotions increasing the energetic effort you have to put into your denial, which affects your chakra system and this exposes you to the truth of your own energy. When you deny your awareness of yourself and the energy you feel, you become stagnant within your own denial, which means you then unconsciously or purposely project energy. This causes you to constantly repeat the same emotional patterns and projections, creating a competition with life as you engage in interactions for the purpose of energetically 'point scoring' to prove your superiority and energetic prowess. When you battle for energetic supremacy, you stagnate your own resolution and evolution.

You emotionally feel superior when you feel your surge of unresolved emotions being projected and affecting another, or when you feel your reverberation with the mankind energetic collectives you want to use and attempt to control. You energetically pull others' energy or your reverberations with the energetics of mankind collective energy into your own system via your chakras. You use your chakra system to disperse the energy through yourself. When you pull an outside energy into your system, you are choosing to bombard yourself with unconscious energy. You can become addicted to feeling emotionally and energetically bombarded. This may cause you to feel energetically shaky, because you can physically feel the vibration of your desire for control as you try to control the energy within your system. You want to believe you can control energy while denying the reality of your own energy and energetic awareness. However, your denial intensifies the energetic vibration you feel, which means you might not understand what you are feeling, but you feel energy. Bombarding yourself with energy is a way of resisting, denying and avoiding truth, as you oppose acknowledging the true issue provoking the disturbance in your chakra system.

Your protection of your denial, causes you to be codependent on the void you create by being separated from your awareness of your soul, and disassociated from feeling the reality of your own energy. The void you feel, is your recognition of your separation from your awareness of your soul. The energy you create to remain separated, sends your chakra system into overdrive or creates blockages, until you eventually emotionally implode or explode due to the magnitude of the energy you are trying to suppress and control. You become overwhelmed, overstressed and overcome by the energy of your unresolved emotions and your denial of the reality you are feeling.

Your indifference to truth causes your chakra system to become congested, which leaves you feeling emotionally, energetically and physically lethargic. When you separate from feeling your soul's consciousness, you exist within your vortex of unconsciousness, separated from your awareness of your soul and disassociated from feeling truth. You exist unbalanced within yourself, fighting truth and denying the reality of your emotions. If you are separated from your awareness of your soul and disassociated from feeling truth, your chakra system is unbalanced creating emotional, energetic and physical 'dis-ease' within you. When you focus on your desire to control, your chakras will be in overdrive because of the emotional energy you have to exert to deny the truth you feel. Your altered degrees of separation from your awareness of truth affect your chakras and the energy within your aura. The more separated you are from your awareness of truth, the more dominant your unconscious energy becomes within you. Your internal thoughts and emotional reactions to truth affect your chakras and the energy of your aura. Your chakra system is designed to expose you to your reality and automatically responds to the reality of your internal world, creating the opportunity to feel and acknowledge what you are emotionally, energetically and physically experiencing. If you trust yourself enough to be honest with what you are feeling, you will learn a lot about the truth of yourself.

Your chakras automatically respond simultaneously to the reality of your reaction to the uniqueness of each moment, and it is a misguided mankind belief that you are able to control the balance of your chakra energy. Understanding the reaction of your chakra system can reveal a lot of information to you. As you become more energetically aware, you feel when your chakras are:

- Balanced
- Out of balance
- In overdrive
- Congested
- Blocked
- Flowing freely
- Projecting energy
- Being projected at

This energetic awareness is only helpful when it is used in conjunction with the willingness to be truthfully honest. This is because you are recognising the energy flow within your chakras as an alert system, alerting you to take notice of your reactions, so that you can take responsibility for how you choose to respond. However, increased energetic awareness used in conjunction with the desire to control and refusal to take self-responsibility, becomes extremely overwhelming. This leaves you trying to control your charkas, instead of being truthfully honest about what is occurring and the energy you can feel. You are denying the true function of your chakra system if you only focus on attempting to control your chakra system and ignore your:

- Unresolved emotions
- Feelings
- Reverberations with collective energy
- Enmeshment with others' energy
- Emotionally fuelled interactions
- Monotonous interplays
- Energetic competitiveness
- Desire for control
- Alignment to illusions
- Portrayal of an image
- Soul oppression

When you deny what is causing your chakras to react, you may attempt to sustain illusions about your ability to control your chakra system or endeavour to deny your awareness of your chakra system.

Resolving your unconscious energy can only be achieved by acknowledging the reality you are experiencing, and dealing with your emotions and feelings honestly. One thought changes the energy within your chakras. Can you count how many thoughts you have within a minute? Every thought and emotional reaction alters the energy within your chakras. Your aura represents the truth of your energy within the uniqueness of every moment. You can swamp your system with your desire for control when you believe you can control the energy affecting your chakras and aura. This just keeps you caught in the illusion of your ability to control, and is how you create barriers to feeling the truth of your present moment. Your chakra and aura system is dynamic, and reflects the truth of your present moment and the truth of your energy. However, acknowledging your awareness of your chakra system, alerts you to your soul truth. You need your truthful honesty to comprehend the truth of your energetic systems, both your chakra and aura system.

Your soul oppressive energy, such as your indifference, desire for control and unresolved emotions, create 'dis-ease' within your physical body. Your physical body responds and reacts to the truth of the energy it feels. The physical body is affected by your unresolved emotions and is impacted by others' energy and the energetics of the mass energy of mankind. Your chakra system is a filter and you naturally co-ordinate with the flow of consciousness coursing through the core channel within your chakra system, to create the opportunity to resolve the energy of your soul's unconsciousness. When you are truthful you convert unconscious energy to conscious understanding. The resolution of unconscious energy allows the energy to become an integrated aspect of your soul's consciousness. When you are truthful with yourself, you convert the vibration of unconscious energy to the frequency of conscious truth. By being truthfully honest and acknowledging your freedom of choice, you can use your awareness of your chakra system to assist you in resolving your unresolved emotions.

You can unify with the flow of consciousness coursing through the core channel within your chakra system. Your unification becomes a natural repellent to unconscious energy. This means you can be extremely aware of unconscious energy, but be non-affected by it. Your truthfulness sustains your unification. You cannot control your unification with your soul's consciousness. You are either unified or you are not.

Unification means:
- Choosing to be truthful
- Taking self-responsibility
- Valuing truth
- Objectively observing
- Trusting *True Source Divine Origin Consciousness*
- Operating from the purity of your core essences
- Accepting opportunities for resolution and evolution
- Unconditionally loving who you naturally are
- Acknowledging your own insight and awareness

Not being unified means:

- Separating from your awareness of truth and your soul
- Disassociating from feeling truth and love for your soul
- Operating from the energy of your soul's unconsciousness
- Devaluing truth and being dishonest
- Fixating on your own desire for control
- Opposing resolution and evolution
- Resisting, denying and avoiding self-responsbility
- Disconnecting or denying your reality

Unification is a dynamic process pertaining to your relationship with yourself. The more conscious you are of your soul's consciousness and of your unconsciousness, the more willing you are to be truthful, to value truth and your opportunity to resolve and evolve. This also makes you more able to appreciate your unification with the flow of consciousness coursing through the core channel within your chakra system

Your chakra and aura systems work in unison and are unified to the truth of every experience, emotion and feeling. When you are evolving and acknowledging your truth, your awareness of your aura and chakra systems naturally become heightened. You will feel more, observe more and deny less, and this will assist you to be truthfully honest with yourself. The clarity of feeling your chakras will enable you to observe your own reactions to your desire to control the denial of your unresolved emotions. Your ability to objectively observe your chakras assists you in feeling the difference between your energy, projected energy and your alignment and reverberation with the energetic collectives of the mass energy of mankind. Objectively observing your awareness of yourself, enables you to discover opportunities for resolution and evolution.

When you express the truth of your consciousness your aura is pure and is only of the essence of your soul's consciousness, resonating as truth. When you resonate with truth, you feel the presence of and your unity with *True Source Divine Origin Consciousness*. *True Source Divine Origin Consciousness* is the collective energy of the purity of souls. Your chakra system evolves to become one channel emanating the purity of your soul, resonating with truth, with no need or desire to control or externalise. Your resolution of the unconscious energy produced by your unresolved emotions evolves your energetic system and dismantles your chakra system, resolving your compulsion and obsession to externalise. When you are willing to express the truth of your soul's consciousness, you resonate with truth and can read the truth of energy without having to inflict the energy upon yourself; you objectively observe reality with no need to control, which is the choice to be present in the truth of yourself and the reality you are experiencing.

Your unconscious will

Your unconscious will is your:

- Compulsion to react from the energy of your soul's unconsciousness
- Willingness to deny or override your awareness of truth
- Ability to orchestrate your own denial of reality

Your unconscious will is your desire to orchestrate a lie to create a judgement of what your truth and reality is, while disregarding the truth of your awareness of reality. Your unconscious will suffocates your willingness to explore truth and leaves you defending your denial of reality and indifference to truth. Your unconscious will is an automatic expression of your customary practice of controlling yourself to the familiarity of the energy of your soul's unconsciousness, as a response to your desire to control life, yourself, others, relationships and the presence of truth. Your unconscious will is the willingness to act out and temporarily relieve yourself of the tension created by your denial of reality, with a complete disregard for how your emotions affect yourself, others and your environment. Unconscious will is your choice to project your unresolved emotions indiscriminately at others.

You deceptively deny your own rationale and awareness of truth, and expect to be able to control the pacification of your own desire to orchestrate how reality should be, or how your perception of reality should be accepted as truth. When you comply with your own embedded beliefs and fears of your soul denial and your own demand for control, you stay stagnant within the confines of what is familiar and what you judge as controllable by using the energy of your soul's unconsciousness. You orientate to what you believe you can control, so that you can deny the entirety of your awareness of your reactions to life, yourself, others, relationships and the presence of truth. This causes you to deny your awareness of your own soul presence. When you deny reality, you activate any unconscious energy that you believe will assist in sustaining your denial. You seek to avoid the reality of yourself as a significant, unique, independent, individual soul, in order to control the sustainability of your soul oppression, protecting what you believe justifies your own image of who you believe you are.

Your unconscious will is your desire to have control of your awareness of truth within yourself and others. This causes you to protect any lie you tell yourself and others, in an attempt to avoid your fear of being exposed to your own deception. When you fear exposing yourself to your deception, you will layer deception upon deception, attempting to find a solution that does not involve complete disclosure of truth. This causes you to create a web of deception that ensnares you in the energy of your soul's unconsciousness. Your unconscious will is the protection of your deception, which causes you to respond to your reality with the desire to only acknowledge what suits your illusory control of yourself and others' perception of reality. Your unconscious will is an automatic reaction that secures your own agenda and protects your control, regardless of how you affect others and your own emotional, energetic and physical reality.

Your soul denial energy is constructed from your defiance against truth, and is founded on your embedded beliefs and fears that oppose the reality of being able to resolve and evolve beyond your own limited perception of yourself. Your unconscious will is your reactions that are disengaged from your awareness of truth or logic. Your loss of willingness to be aware of truth or to take the time to logically reason with yourself causes you to have no ambition to resolve, and leaves you only wanting to secure a controlled outcome. Your unconscious will is to perceive life through the insecurity of your images and illusions. Your unconscious will is the choice to seek control of life with an illusion and to be controlled by the desire to dumb down the reality of your soul.

Your unconscious will is an automatic reaction stemming from your desire to control your soul journey. You can become consumed with your own judgement of life, yourself, others, relationships and the presence of truth, and this is how you override your awareness of yourself, often becoming emotionally illogical. You can seek to control the perception of how significant you are within your own illusion of life, which causes you to be insecure in the reality of your life experience. When you attempt to orchestrate and sustain an illusion of your value, worth and significance without feeling the truth of your natural significance, you hide in your denial and dumb yourself down.

Your unconscious will is the compulsion to orchestrate the deception you believe will allow you to emotionally, energetically and physically feel safe in the familiarity of your unresolved emotions. The familiarity of how your unresolved emotions feel to you, creates a perceived energetic comfort zone, which you attempt to protect with your denial of reality. You anchor to the familiarity of feeling your own unresolved emotions, because you fear losing your energetic comfort zone. Anchoring to what is familiar enables you to ignore the dynamics of life, which can leave you shocked at how much you have glossed over your own reality when you are confronted with that which you have ignored. Your unconscious will is exposed by how you sleepwalk through life and avoid acknowledging the motives behind the decisions you are making. This causes you to repeat known emotional patterns and to automatically react from your addiction to continue the repetitiveness of your unresolved emotions, the relentlessness of your desire to control, and to sustain the familiarity you have created within your illusion of reality.

Your unconscious will is how you make reactive decisions, but deny responsibility for making a choice. Your unconscious will entraps you in the restrictions of your soul's unconsciousness and causes you to abandon your awareness of your freedom of choice, and your awareness of the presence of your soul's consciousness. Your unconscious will is your habitual and automatic denial of yourself within reality.

Freewill

Freedom of choice is your ability to utilise your freewill, within every choice, belief, behaviour and intention. Freewill means you are a creator with your choices. You decide if you are truthfully honest or deceptive with yourself and this simple, yet complex decision determines how you interact with yourself, which is the most important relationship you have. Your decisions to be truthful or deceptive determine how you interact with your present moment, life, others, within your intimate relationships and with truth. Your awareness of your own freewill is important, and the significance of you realising that you are constantly utilising your freedom to choose is indescribable. We all struggle to comprehend we have freewill and that we choose what we believe, how we behave and how we interact.

Freedom of choice is acknowledging the freedom you have within every unique moment to be of your truth. Freedom of choice is within the uniqueness of every moment. You have the freedom to choose whether you want to be of your truth, the dynamic energy of your soul and in the flow of your soul's consciousness, or whether you want to remain oppressed in the familiarity of the stagnation of the unresolved emotions of your soul's unconsciousness.

You have the freedom to choose how you will respond to your life experiences. You have the freedom to consciously accept and trust the truth you can feel and to honestly deal with the reality of yourself, life and others. Your freedom of choice creates the opportunity to be conscious of your own uniqueness, independence and individuality. By utilising your divine right to freedom of choice, you allow your soul's consciousness to guide you through your opportunities to learn from the truth of your life experiences and the truth of who you are. Your freedom of choice creates the space for you to be honest within the uniqueness of every present moment.

Your freedom of choice creates the space for you to be honest with the entirety of your present moment experience and to acknowledge the truth of your reaction to life, yourself, others, relationships and truth. Your acceptance of your freedom of choice creates the space to realise how you use your different emotions against yourself, others, your relationships, life and your awareness of truth.

Your freedom of choice allows you to resolve and evolve beyond any restrictions, limitations and denials. Freedom of choice enables you to be an expression of your uniqueness, independence and individuality within the emotional, energetic and physical environment of mankind. The choice is yours and yours alone; this is freewill.

As you come to realise that you do have freedom of choice:
- You begin to explore how you feel about yourself
- How you make decisions
- Why you are reluctant to be completely truthful with yourself
- What it means to operate from integrity

The acceptance of having freewill the freedom to choose is a precursor to your own evolution.

Section Four

CHAPTER TWENTY-TWO

Soul blueprint

You are born with a blueprint, which is your original intention for this lifetime. Your soul has an agreement with *True Source Divine Origin Consciousness* about what you need to experience, to learn from, resolve and evolve in this lifetime. Whilst you were in the purity of your soul and conscious of the truth of all energy, you coordinated an agreement with the purity of *True Source Divine Origin Consciousness*, indicating your intention for this lifetime. *True Source Divine Origin Consciousness* always remains loyal to your original agreement. Deep within your soul you know that the energy you left behind within the energetic collectives of the mass energy of mankind, is what you seek to resolve. Through your life experiences, you seek to resolve the unconscious energy of your soul's unconsciousness.

Unfortunately, your soul denial and desire to control your unresolved emotions can become so overwhelming and compulsive that you concretise your barriers to truth, and become oppositional to your original intention. You can become defiant against your own life experience and your original intention, and preoccupied with fighting the truth of yourself as a soul. As you disassociate from your original intention to experience the truth of your own unconsciousness, you deny yourself the opportunity to learn from your life experiences. This leads to you negating your original willingness to explore your soul truth, to resolve and evolve. Your disassociation from feeling the presence of *True Source Divine Origin Consciousness* assisting your opportunity for evolution, causes you to deny your reality without considering what you are truly doing to your soul, truth and your opportunities to resolve and evolve. Your disassociation from the reality of your soul journey and your defiance against the soul blueprint agreement you made with yourself, is a direct result of your soul denial.

When you deny the reality of being a soul on a journey, you deny the opportunities life presents. Your blueprint resonates with the truth of who you are and the natural abilities you possess, that assist you on your soul journey. Honesty is your ability to be of truth. We all possess this ability and often disassociate from our ability to honestly seek the truth of who we are when unencumbered by the energy of our soul's unconsciousness. Grace, which we all possess, is your ability to be of truth and to forgive yourself for being and having unconscious energy.

Within your blueprint you have agreements with other souls; their presence is designed to trigger your internal knowing of your original soul intention, creating opportunities to experience and explore truth. You will feel your soul's consciousness resonating with theirs, which may only be for the briefest moment, but you are feeling your soul resonating with truth. You are experiencing the uniqueness of that moment, which enables you to feel your own soul's consciousness, and your reaction to the presence of another soul you internally recognise on a soul level. This creates a curiosity within the stagnation of your soul's

unconsciousness, and your curiosity will expose your separation from your awareness of your soul and your disassociation from feeling truth. You internally know and can feel you have an agreement with *True Source Divine Origin Consciousness*, and your soul's consciousness endeavours to expose you to the truth of your soul blueprint as life unfolds. Your blueprint is something you live, not something you control yourself to.

Your soul coordinates with other souls, creating opportunities for you to experience the truth of both conscious and unconscious interactions; if it is in your blueprint there will be a recognition of the energy you feel. Some souls are extremely significant for your journey because through the experience of each other's energy, opportunities are created to expose you to the truth of your unresolved emotions and the truth of your feelings. Your experiences create opportunities to be exposed to the truth of your soul's consciousness. Your blueprint is coordinated with many different energies, to create experiences that will expose the truth of your soul's consciousness and the energy of your soul's unconsciousness, such as your:

Consciousness

- *Unconditional love*
- *Core Essences*
- *Flow of consciousness*
- *Resonance with truth*
- *Unification with truth*
- *Insightfulness*
- *Expansions of awareness*

Unconsciousness

- Barriers to truth
- Control structures
- Framework of soul oppression
- Unresolved emotions
- Embedded beliefs
- Fears

Your various relationships with others create opportunities for all involved to learn from sharing life experiences and from being willing to explore truth. Your willingness to explore truth, opens you to the potential of resolution and evolution. You have the freedom to choose how you will perceive and respond to your life experiences. Some experiences will be resolved and evolved with hindsight, because you need more understanding of yourself, life and truth, before you can comprehend the significance of your ability to resolve and evolve. Your blueprint caters for hindsight. *True Source Divine Origin Consciousness* and your soul's consciousness understand that the layering of experiences is often essential for your resolution and evolution.

Your honesty enables you to be truthful with what you are experiencing and creates the opportunity to be present in the truth of your present moment. Your honesty enables you to resolve a backlog of carried emotional energy created by your soul denial history. Your soul's unconsciousness is constructed from the emotional residue of your soul denial history. Your denial of your own unconscious energy, produced by your unresolved emotions, creates cycles of emotional patterns you relive until resolved. Your rejection of the truth of your own energy, leaves you unwilling to be present in your present moment. The energy you are experiencing within your present moment may be connected to your soul denial history, because your present moment experience can expose what is unresolved within you and what you have carried within your soul's unconsciousness. You carry what you refuse to resolve.

Resolution is the result of complete honesty and is the choice to be honest and truthful about the revealed unconscious energy of your soul's unconsciousness, regardless of what emotional form you use. You can be unconscious to the truth of your emotions and need experiences that invoke your emotions for you to be able to become conscious of the truth of the unresolved emotions you deny. This is why there is a natural layering process to your resolution. You cannot instantly comprehend the depth of your soul's unconsciousness; you have to commit yourself to dig through the layers of your deception and your denial as there will be a layering process to your discovery. Your acknowledgement of the truth of your own energy and your willingness to take full responsibility for being truthful are essential to the resolution of your unresolved emotions.

Within your blueprint you have elected to experience the exposure of what needs to be resolved for you to evolve. As you are able to comprehend the truth of your reality you become more at ease with the layering process of discovering truth. Your blueprint is designed to expose truth to you in layers, and within the purity of your soul you consciously knew what you could cope with, and what would expose truth to you. You also knew that your own resistance, denial and avoidance techniques would actually expose truth to you. Your soul's consciousness is the mature part of your soul, which knows these experiences are for the benefit of your resolution and evolution. Your soul's unconsciousness resulted from you fighting the truth of this, and causes you to be immature in your approach to life's realities and opportunities.

The more honest and accepting you are of the truth you are experiencing, the more aligned you will be to your original intention to resolve and evolve this lifetime. Within the purity of your soul you wanted to experience being truthful on Earth and you have chosen and coordinated a blueprint with *True Source Divine Origin Consciousness*, that gives the best opportunity for your soul's consciousness to expose your soul's unconsciousness.

You can fail to recognise the significance and importance of your truthfulness, because you use your unconscious energy to resist, deny and avoid the truth of being a soul. You can use your unconscious energy to be oppositional to your blueprint and you become codependent on abusing your freedom of choice, (your freewill), to oppose your original intention to resolve and evolve. When you are aware that your soul's consciousness is part of who you naturally are, your experiences of the unresolved emotions within your soul's unconsciousness, become an opportunity to acknowledge how each present moment exposes truth and is an opportunity to resolve and evolve your unconscious energy. Your soul's consciousness seeks to resolve the energetic residue of your soul denial history, which is how you anchor to the unconsciousness of mankind.

Acknowledging the truth of your unconscious energy within your present moment, enables your truthfulness to create the opportunity to resolve the stagnation, which has resulted from your denial of reality.

Acknowledging truth creates the opportunity to resolve your soul oppressive cycle of leaving unconscious energy within the energetic collectives of the mass energy of mankind when you die. Your soul denial history may affect your present moment, because the unresolved emotions from your past are what you use to compete with what your present moment is exposing to you. You use your unconscious energy produced by your unresolved emotions to hide the truth of your soul's unconsciousness.

Your blueprint is full of the events, experiences of emotionally and energetically charged environments and other souls' energy, which you require to expose truth to yourself. Your desire to control yourself to an image and an illusion of being able to control life, has you unaware of the reality of your soul consciousness' ability to convert and unify, unconscious energy to conscious truth. Exposing truth to yourself is the purpose of your blueprint.

When you align to the collective denial of truth and reality within mankind, you can contrive life plans that you attach your rule book and expectations to. These contrived life plans enable you to hide the truth of who you are and the truth of what you are experiencing within the deception of your denial. These plans become what you believe should be part of your blueprint, however they stem from your desire to control, instead of the passion within your soul. Your plans become what you attach your control structures and expectations to, with the misconception that this is what you are entitled to. These contrived life plans generally have you seeking to be revered by others, which means you enact roles to supply the image and illusion of being able to control life. Contrived life plans have you chasing an elusive dream, foregoing the truth of your soul and ignoring the truth of your own reality. This causes you to deny the significance of your present moment, the reality of your life experience and the passion you feel within your soul. Contrived life plans are generated by the expectations you have about your ability to control and are based on delusions, not truth.

Contrived life plans become beliefs that separate you from your awareness of yourself within your present moment experience. This causes you to be either entrapped by your past or consumed with the desire to orchestrate the future you believe you want. This can have you oppositional to your present moment and resentful of anything that does not align to your desires. These plans keep you stagnant in the worship of your illusion of control, which perpetuates your emotional, energetic and physical merry-go-round. Contrived life plans are the choice to anchor to a control structure, believing you can control life from your expectations. Regardless of the dynamics of your life experiences and the clarity of your own awareness of truth, you attempt to control life with the repetitiveness of your control structures, because you fear taking responsibility for how you use your delusions to shield you from being truthful.

Your contrived life plan is how you divert your attention away from the reality you are experiencing and how you create the illusion of needing to control, which paradoxically causes you to feel insecure about your reality. These plans cause you to judge your reality as 'not good enough' for what you want and expect, which can lead you to miss the opportunities within your present moment, because you are consumed with your own judgement of what should be happening and in denial of the significance of your present moment reality. Your soul's consciousness is well aware of your desire to control a contrived life plan and is constantly exposing the truth of your experiences to you. Your blueprint is synchronised with truth and other souls' consciousness, and you are never without the opportunity to realise the significance of truth. Your illusion of control has you believing you can control many aspects of life with little regard for truth, in the belief that your control can alter the path of your experience of life.

Your contrived life plan is made up of concepts created by your 'I want' mentality, which do not resonate with your soul's consciousness and is you seeking to pacify your desire to control reality. Contrived life plans are a deceptive veil of illusion concealing the opportunity to learn from your life experience and to explore the truth of yourself. You use your plans to secure your unwillingness to explore truth and to abandon your opportunity to resolve and evolve. These plans alter your perception of reality. Instead of accepting reality, trusting how you feel and appreciating your own internal knowing, you seek to control reality to provide you with what you think you desire. This causes you to attempt to construct images and illusions that actually inhibit you from feeling the truth of your soul. You can become addicted to the illusion of control or the desire to prove that your control is superior to truth, which has you immersed in your denial of reality and remaining indifferent to truth.

You are in the truth of your reality, but if you are unwilling to accept what you are experiencing, your perception of your reality will be tainted by your opposition to truth. The contrived life plan you use to oppose your reality will become another energy you will have to expose as a lie you told yourself, and you will have to elect to resolve the unresolved emotions connected to your plans. No one is out of sync with the truth of their original blueprint and the lies and contrived life plan that you create are probably part of your original blueprint, because paradoxically your contrived life plan will always expose many unresolved emotions to you. You may be disappointed that life is not accommodating your expectations, however, your disappointment exposes the opportunity to resolve that which inhibits you from accepting reality.

The energy produced by your soul denial has you ignoring truth and denying the original intention of your blueprint. When you constantly override the reality of your experiences, soul insights, feelings and unresolved emotions, you become stagnant within your soul's unconsciousness, and you miss the opportunity you set up for yourself to be exposed to truth. When you protect your soul's unconsciousness, you have the experiences that you intended to have, but are not present enough within your reality to comprehend the potential for your resolution and evolution within the experience. You can choose to justify and orientate to the unresolved emotions being exposed within the experiences, without acknowledging the opportunity to be honest with yourself. You disassociate from the truth of the opportunity, denying yourself evolution by opposing the resolution of your unresolved emotions. You elect to repeat your emotional history, arrogantly denying your ability to resolve and evolve, because you fear going beyond what you have done before. Resolving your unresolved emotions and being totally present in your reality is going beyond what you have done before, within a physical body.

Your blueprint creates opportunities to resolve and evolve beyond the familiarity of your separation from your awareness of your soul and your disassociation from feeling truth. All experiences present opportunities and your thoughts expose you to the reality of your energy. Your ability to be honest about how you are utilising your freedom of choice, determines if you will honour your own soul blueprint, or anchor yourself to your deceptive illusion of control, and embody your unresolved emotions. Your soul's consciousness never gives up exposing the truth of your original intention to unify all aspects of your energy to truth, which is your origin. You are your soul, you are your soul's intention, you are your soul's unconsciousness willing to separate from your awareness and disassociate from feeling truth. Your blueprint is a map to unite all aspects of your soul with your origin truth. Your blueprint is a compass that points you in the direction of truth; you have the freedom of choice to follow truth or abandon truth. Accepting the reality of where you are today within your present moment is to trust in your blueprint.

Experiences are triggers for your soul to initiate the discovery of truth, but you have freewill to choose if you will honour your soul and your blueprint, or deny yourself the opportunity to discover your truth. Your soul's unconsciousness and consciousness are attracted to the same experiences and to other souls. Your soul's consciousness wants to trigger the memory of the significance of the truth of who you are, which is a soul attempting to evolve through your life experiences. However, you can use your unresolved emotions to reinvest in your own soul's unconsciousness, by sustaining the emotional baggage you carry and perpetuating your soul denial history; and by your unwillingness to be honest within your present moment. Your soul's unconsciousness is the aspect of you that wants to revel in the control of freewill, in complete defiance to the obvious ramifications of your soul denial. When you are disrespectful about the significance of your own freedom of choice (freewill), you become embroiled in controlling your distorted perception of life that you have created from the energy within your soul's unconsciousness. This causes you to abrogate responsibility for yourself and attempt to find something external on which you believe you can hinge the blame, whilst disregarding your original intention to be truthful with yourself.

As you become more aware of being a soul, you use your life experiences to trigger your awareness of your original intention to experience the truth of your conscious and unconscious energy, and to utilise truth to resolve and evolve. You need to experience your own unresolved emotions to experience the truth of your own energy. You will have the experiences you need, to create opportunities for truth to be acknowledged, and it is your honesty with yourself that will determine your understanding of your reality. You will have the experience, but will you acknowledge the truth?

Within your blueprint there may be an age where you will have experienced all the emotional energy you needed to expose yourself to the truth of both your conscious and unconscious energy. You will have experienced your initial phase of reconnaissance, by experiencing your own unresolved emotions. Your soul's consciousness will be ready to resolve and evolve, to begin a new phase of being honest about the truth of your reality. Your soul's consciousness uses your present moment to expose the truth of your past. Throughout your life experiences your soul's consciousness will have exposed you to the reality of your unresolved emotions. There comes a time when you have experienced what you needed to experience, to be able to acknowledge the truth of your unresolved emotions, and your stagnation will become obvious to you. It will become evident to you that you are choosing to ignore your awareness of your unresolved emotions and stagnation, because you will no longer be able to deny your reality. The cycles of your soul oppression will be evident to you and you will be aware of your own denial of reality.

There can be agreements of emotional, energetic and physical experiences within our blueprints that are sad and confrontational. For example: Two souls may have an agreement to use their love for one another, to assist in the resolution of their unresolved emotions, by acting out on each other what is unresolved within them. If the souls are stagnant within their unresolved emotions, they will inflict emotional energy at each other without acknowledging that they are responsible for their own energy. This lack of responsibility for their own energy will cause them to miss or override their awareness of the opportunity that their soul's consciousness hoped would be created, by feeling their love for one another's soul. Feeling love for another's soul can be the catalyst for being completely honest about the shared reality. The commitment to honouring the journey of each soul, enables truthful curiosity to be the foundation of the relationship. This means the relationship becomes an avenue to expose and explore the opportunity for each soul to learn from their shared experiences. However, no soul is beholden to another and all souls have emotional, energetic and physical independence.

The experience of two souls sharing life experiences exposes both to the energy that they wanted to resolve. Each soul has an independent opportunity within the shared experience, but this does not mean that they will resolve simultaneously. Be very careful in what you judge as the purpose of your life experiences, because it is very easy to fall into the trap of acknowledging another's unresolved emotions while ignoring your own. You can align to the belief that your experience is about rescuing others from themselves as you attempt to prove that you are superior, because of your recognition of their unresolved emotions. We would be fools to believe we know exactly what we have agreed to experience. It is through being honest about your experience of life that you discover the opportunities life is presenting for your resolution and evolution.

It is generally through hindsight that we discover the significance of our shared life experiences. When you choose to be present and honest with yourself about your internal and external reality, you become a willing participant in the dynamics of life. The dynamics of relationships and reality expose opportunities to resolve and evolve, and those experiences expose your synchronicity with the presence and dynamics of truth. Your resolution and evolution is an individual journey, and it is your acceptance of the independence of your freedom of choice, which will allow you to acknowledge the truth of your unique soul journey.

Your blueprint includes experiences where you feel the whole gamut of your own energy, and you may become the receiver of what you inflicted on others in previous lives. Even though we pretend not to, we do feel the truth of our experiences and what we have inflicted on others. When you honestly acknowledge and accept the truth of your energy, and are willing to be responsible for yourself, you become the creator of your own opportunity for resolution.

Your soul's consciousness elects to feel, experience and explore what is required for true resolution and evolution. Your denial of your unresolved emotions will cause you to repeat emotional, energetic and physical cycles. However, as you trust your awareness of truth, your emotional, energetic and physical cycles become the way you expose the truth of what is unresolved within you. If you remain unconscious to the energy you use to override your awareness of your soul's consciousness, you project into your life what you are unresolved in and unconscious of. This means you are also projecting into the energetic collectives of the mass energy of mankind, and perpetuating the oppression of your awareness of truth. You are one of the suppliers of unconscious energy into the energetic mass energy of mankind.

You have agreed to many experiences and have deemed them as necessary for your awakening to the truth of your soul and your original intention. At times we will accept our experiences with the original intention, and at other times we will inflict our control or victimhood at the experiences and fight what we elected for ourselves to experience. When we fight the reality of our experiences, we fight the truth of originally intending to resolve and evolve.

As souls we choose to come together in different lifetimes, in new roles, relationships and experiences, with the intention of exposing the unresolved emotions of each other's unconsciousness and the truth of feeling each other's consciousness. We can feel the opportunity to create the space for each other's resolution and evolution, and can choose to honour the uniqueness of the new opportunity. Unfortunately, we can be separated from our awareness and disassociated from feeling the reality of our new opportunities together, causing us to project our unresolved emotions at each other and even re-enact the emotional history of our past, without consciously realising we are seeking new opportunities. However, the opportunity for resolution is within the truth of all experiences. Your honesty about your unresolved emotions, intentions and denial creates the opportunity for your resolution and evolution; this is an independent experience, even if you are sharing the experience with another. Being dishonest about the reality you are experiencing means you are choosing to perpetuate your soul oppressive cycles; and choosing to exist in the stagnation of betraying your soul intention.

Some souls try to control other souls to abandon their awareness of truth and to disassociate from the potential of their blueprint in order to protect their own soul denial. They try to insert their control into another's awareness of truth, wanting their control to become another's truth. The control structures within the unconsciousness of souls and the energetic mass energy of mankind create vicious cycles, which compel us to be reliant on, and compliant with the deception. Regardless of the intent behind the control structures you use, it interferes with your ability to trust yourself to be in the dynamics of truth and the uniqueness of each present moment. Your desire to control creates a fear of truth and a fear of trusting yourself to be in the truth of what is occurring. Truth naturally exposes deception but if you are trying to protect your illusion of control you will be codependent on your deception and trying to secure your own denial, by obscuring your actual intention from yourself.

Stagnation within your awareness creates an energetic idle, which congests your flow of conscious energy, and is an attempt to conceal the potential for resolution and evolution. You cannot dictate your blueprint with your illusion of control; if you are meant to experience something you will experience it. Your soul's consciousness and life have their own reality but you decide how you respond to each experience. There will be events within your life, that will be beyond your ability to control. They are actually opportunities to explore your reactions and responses to life, and become pivotal points for your evolution. You may ignore what could have been a pivotal point for your soul's evolution, and allow your unresolved emotions to take over your experience. This can often cause you to lose awareness of the significance of your honesty and the impact truthfulness has on your evolution. Your loss of awareness causes you to align to your own denial of reality. You will be exposed to the truth of whatever energy is unresolved within you through other life experiences, and you will have the freedom to choose again, to decide how you respond to what is being exposed to you about yourself.

Experiencing and feeling your feelings is to honour the opportunity to acknowledge your awareness of your soul truth. Honouring your awareness of your soul truth allows you to be aware of, and to resonate with, the truth of your life experiences. This enables you to trust yourself to explore being a soul while experiencing the uncertainty raised by your feelings and life. When you are willing to be in the truth of what you are experiencing and do not hide from how you feel, even though you may feel uncomfortable, you become willing to be a participant in the process of unraveling that which is causing you to distrust yourself. When you trust yourself to be present in your life experiences, you will not ascribe to the compulsion to try to fix everything to suit your control. The process of evolving has a lot of uncertainty in it, because you are coming out of the familiarity of your known cyclic patterns, and exploring what you do with your freedom of choice. When you acknowledge your present moment experience, you feel yourself engage with reality. Resolution requires self-responsibility and to be present in the uncertainty of the process of living.

When you deny your feelings or suppress your acknowledgement of your feelings, you convert your feelings to emotions. This is stagnation. You cannot control the truth of your feelings; you only alter what you allow yourself to be aware of. Your denial of reality and your soul denial means that in an attempt to control what you feel, you convert your feelings to emotional energy. When you do not honour your awareness of truth, you automatically convert feelings to emotions. Feelings resonate with truth and are the communication of your soul's consciousness. Converting your feelings to emotions, is the act of disassociating from feeling truth and the choice to hide within the stagnation of your soul's unconsciousness.

The stagnation of your control has you very accustomed to the familiarity of your emotions and you become a willing participant in the conversion of feelings to emotional energy. You disassociate from feeling the significance of your feelings and deny that your feelings resonate with truth. Feeling your truth can be very unfamiliar to you; you may think you have everything under your control but feeling the truth can suddenly make you realise how out of your control everything is. This can cause you to immediately attempt to deny everything you feel, especially the feelings you believe precipitated being out of control of your own illusion, because you do not like your illusion of control being broken. When you fear truth, you automatically participate in your denial of the significance of your own soul truth, and seek to protect any illusion of control you believe you have. Your blueprint is a map constantly exposing potential ways out of your denial, if you are willing to use your freewill to be truthful.

When you align to contrived life plans which are the expectations you have for your desire to control, you become entangled in the belief that you and your life experiences are 'not good enough' for the illusion you want. Your perception of life not being good enough conceals the truth of your life experiences. You are a soul on a journey either exploring conscious and unconscious energy, or cycling in your opposition to the truth of both your conscious and unconscious energy. You can railroad your awareness of conscious energy within your life, in an attempt to achieve your desire to control illusions, constructed from your expectations that have resulted from your contrived life plans. This creates stagnation within you and has you worshipping your desire to control life to your expectations. You miss the opportunities life presents by being consumed with your own agenda for control of life. You can create illusions around your experiences, and use your illusory control of life to create controlled identities, to hide from the truth of what is unresolved within you. You can create expectations that have you indifferent to the reality of your soul consciousness' intention and the feelings of other souls. Your expectations can be in conflict with your own reality and the truth of who you are.

Your soul is destined to experience certain experiences, and your willingness to be honest will guide you to be aware and present in the truth of what you are experiencing. It is entirely up to you, when you are going to make the decision to be willing to trust yourself to be completely honest with the truth you feel and are aware of. All the experiences you are destined to have are part of your own awakening process, but you have complete freedom of choice as to whether or not you will trust what you are feeling and observing. When you trust yourself as a soul, you trust your synchronicity with truth and can feel your own natural trust in your awareness of your soul consciousness' unity with truth. This enables you to trust your blueprint agreement to live the truth of your life experiences and to acknowledge the opportunities you have to resolve the unresolved emotions that you contribute to the energetics of the mass energy of mankind.

When you actively seek and work towards being conscious of resolving your unresolved emotions and hold yourself accountable to the truth of your soul journey, you can feel as if you are playing soccer while everyone else is playing hockey. Even though you have

realised you are standing on an intended soccer field, you can fool yourself into believing it is easier to deny and do as everyone else is doing, believing you need to play hockey and fit in with the hockey players, ignoring and overriding what you truly feel.

You are naturally born a soccer player, a soul of truth, and your soul will show you the difference between the two games. It is your choice to accept the reality of being a soccer player. You will either accept or deny the reality of being a soul of truth but you cannot escape the reality of making a choice. Soccer players' lives become a matter of resolving all that is obstructing their awareness of truth within them, while observing the game of hockey being played around them; watching as others convince themselves that they understand and can control their own game of hockey, which is their soul denial in action.

The embedded beliefs and fears of your soul denial create internal negative pathways for the purpose of denying the truth of life being a journey for your soul, to resolve and evolve what is separating and disassociating you from feeling truth. Your soul is persistent in challenging your denial. Your honesty when questioning yourself, will nurture and create the space for the discovery of truth. You have the capacity to feel who you are in truth; you just have to be honest about your feelings. Honesty enables reality and truth to be exposed, explored and appreciated.

Your separation from your awareness of your soul causes you to be mesmerised and fixated on your negativity. Your separation from your awareness of your soul keeps you preoccupied with your negativity and overwhelmed by your own soul oppression. This is how you reject, resist, deny and avoid your internal knowing of your own soul blueprint. When you accept that you wanted to be exposed to your unresolved emotions, you will accept your experience of them, which allows the exposure of your unresolved emotions to be recognised as an opportunity to resolve. When you deny the exposure of your unresolved emotions, you will fight your awareness to sustain your judgement of yourself and your judgement of your ability to control.

As your awareness increases, truth is welcomed and you can be extremely excited to find negativity, without judging it. You become able to acknowledge that the exposure of your negativity is part of your synchronisation with truth and the opportunity to explore your ability to learn from your life experiences. Accepting reality is to feel the truth of what you are experiencing, which creates the space to honestly deal with your life experiences.

As you resolve and evolve you are also going more deeply into the energy of your soul's unconsciousness and exposing your soul denial. As you resolve the layers of your unresolved emotions, understanding one layer will reveal the next layer, you will feel the same emotions but with a deeper understanding and an ever increasing awareness in your foundation of truth. The more understanding you have of the emotion; the more intensely you will feel the reality of the unconscious energy, which assists you to not miss the opportunity to be honest with yourself. Your awareness of the truth of what you feel, evolves as you resolve the unconscious energy of your soul's unconsciousness.

When you seek your truth, without fear of truth, you will move more easily within your life experiences. You will accept living and experiencing the layers of your unresolved emotions and accept your growing awareness of truth. This is resolution and evolution in action, which has you appreciating and honouring your original intention within your blueprint.

As you become more honest with your reality, your awareness of energy will increase because you will deny less. You will be more aware of how you utilise the collectives and barriers of the energetics of the mass energy of mankind to deny your reality. You will feel the truth of your own energy and the energy you co-ordinate with to oppose the presence of your soul's consciousness. Allowing yourself to feel, accept and own the truth of your soul, creates the space for your internal knowing of truth to expose your soul denial. Resolution of your soul denial is freedom from your soul oppression. Your soul denial, self-doubt, insecurity, lack of acceptance of your truth and fear of judgement, enable you to use your control as an adversary against your soul's consciousness. Your soul blueprint is designed to resolve the war you have within yourself. Stagnating in your own unresolved emotions and reverberating with the energetics of the mass energy of mankind, is how you oppose your truth and continue your internal war, but eventually you will not be able to ignore the reality of yourself.

Your soul's consciousness, *True Source Divine Origin Consciousness* and the energetics of the mass energy of mankind cannot be fooled, so it is essential to feel and recognise your feelings, acknowledge whatever they are, deal with them honestly and to trust yourself to be able to cope with truth. Your acceptance of the process of being able to evolve beyond your own soul oppressive energy is an acknowledgement of the reality of being an evolving soul, who is free to be of truth. To accept you have a blueprint is to accept your life experiences with open eyes, reclaiming your awareness of truth.

By acknowledging the truth of your journey, acknowledging what you are experiencing, and acknowledging what you need to resolve, you permit yourself to evolve beyond the constraints of your own soul denial, cycles of soul oppression and illusion of control. By embracing and accepting the reality of your soul, you are consciously participating in experiencing the resolution of your soul's unconsciousness, to evolve your soul as agreed in your blueprint.

Accepting the reality of your soul's consciousness, frees you to be at peace with relinquishing the desire for control and your compulsion to preempt and manipulatively judge the value and worth of your life experiences. By trusting you have a blueprint, you are trusting your synchronicity with truth and this allows you to be at peace with life. Your willingness to be of your integrity, allows your soul's consciousness to guide you to flow with the truth of your life and opportunities. You only have to be honest; your soul's consciousness is the conscious aspect of you and resolves unconscious energy easily. To accept, care and unconditionally love your uniqueness, independence and individuality, you have to stop fighting the reality of being a soul and feel your internal peace. Your soul journey is the opportunity to learn the truth of your soul and to feel the original essence of your soul, which is truth. Your honesty enables you to evolve beyond the familiarity of your separation from your awareness of your soul and your disassociation from feeling truth. Your soul's consciousness fully accepts your rise and fall from grace, as a natural process of life. When you accept yourself as an evolving soul, you will trust yourself to be aware of, experience and feel your soul's consciousness and unconsciousness.

Defiance against your soul blueprint

You do feel the unresolved emotions you have chosen to experience within your blueprint, which creates the opportunity to resolve what is unresolved. However, if you are willing to deny what you feel, you create a chain of emotional events. First you suppress the feeling, then you convert the feeling into an emotion you are familiar with. The familiarity of the emotion creates an illusory sense of control, which you then use to fuel your backlog of unresolved emotions. Your emotional energy intensifies under the pressure of your desire to control your emotions. When your illusion of control implodes you attack yourself with negative beliefs, judgement of your history and your angst about your loss of control. Your protection of your denial causes you to separate from your awareness of your soul and to lose your ability to be honest with yourself. You then want to validate and justify your emotional reaction and illusory control, and you do it with your willingness to be dishonest with yourself.

Your separation from your awareness of your soul has you feeding and fuelling the energetic collectives within the mass energy of mankind that your unresolved emotions correlate with, and this overwhelms you with unconscious energy. You defiantly project your unconscious energy at others, yourself and truth, in an attempt to rid yourself of the unresolved emotions you cannot control. Your denial and dishonesty about your projections, creates a tidal wave of emotional energy that annihilates your ability to feel truth. Your unresolved emotions reverberate with the energetics of the mass energy of mankind, and you utilise what you energetically feel to victimise yourself, generating and energising more of your own unresolved emotions. You emotionally feel like a victim because you cannot escape your emotions, but you try to defiantly deny the truth of what you feel. Your defiance against being honest about your emotional, energetic and physical reality has you experiencing your unresolved emotions, while denying yourself the opportunity to acknowledge what you were born to resolve. When you deny the truth you are aware of, you defiantly perpetuate what you were born to resolve.

You are not a victim to energy; you produce energy. You are a victim to your own choice to separate from your awareness of your soul and disassociate from feeling truth. You fuel your own soul oppression and manipulate yourself with your:

- Images
- Illusions
- Controlled identities
- Labels
- Judgements
- Delusions of grandeur
- Control structures

You also use these to annihilate your awareness of truth. When you use these you lie to yourself, and create soul oppressive behaviours that bind you to your unresolved emotions.

RIGHT: *Your fear and unwillingness to be honest about your own awareness of your soul can create a tidal wave of unresolved emotional energy, which annihilates your ability to be at peace with the truth you can feel.*

If you defiantly lie about the truth you feel, you align to false masters. Your existence becomes mastered by your desire to control your soul denial and soul oppression. Instead of resolving your desire to control all emotional energy, any emotional energy you feel becomes a tripwire for you to re-enact and panic about your ability to control. Your soul consciousness' intention is to resolve all varieties of control, but you inhibit your natural ability to do this with your fear of losing your illusion of control. But do you really have control of your life? It is your fear of losing your illusion of control and inability to deny truth, which causes you to renege on the importance of your own honesty. You fear losing what you never had; you never had complete control of reality or complete control of your awareness of your soul's consciousness or unconsciousness. You deny the reality of your soul truth, to torture yourself with your own desire to control life.

When you choose to use your escapism addictions, and your beliefs which originated from soul denial energy, to be masters over your awareness of your soul's consciousness, you avoid being honest about feeling the difference between truth and deception. You use your beliefs to oppose being completely honest with yourself. You want to dictate what life should bestow upon you, whilst ignoring the opportunities your life is presenting to you. You want to take control of life, by denying your awareness of the conscious flow of truth within life. Life gives you the opportunity to flow in conscious energy; your blueprint is synchronised with the flow of truth within life. Your defiance against the truth of your soul and your blueprint has you fighting your own existence. You do not realise you make your life a battle ground for your control and you constantly struggle with your perceived ability to control life. You programme, condition and indoctrinate yourself to trust only what you believe you have control of, but you have no control of the conscious flow of truth we call life.

Your defiance against truth has you denying your ability to trust what does not need or respond to your control. You defiantly seek to control what you believe your blueprint should be, rather than experiencing the truth of the opportunities in your life. Your defiance against your original intention within your blueprint, means you create a futile war with your own life.

- What are you fighting?
- How will you know if you win?
- Is the annihilation of your awareness of your soul and truth the prize?
- Is being devoid of feeling your own soul's consciousness worth the pain you cause yourself?
- If you are going to fight, shouldn't you know and understand what you are fighting?
- What are you defiant against?

RIGHT: *Throughout your life you are being exposed to the truth of your unresolved emotions. It is the exposure of your unresolved emotions that creates an opportunity to resolve the energy of your soul's unconsciousness and to experience the energy of your soul's consciousness. When you are dishonest about the truth of your life experiences, you become defiant against the truth of your own soul blueprint. However, your defiance exposes opportunities for you to discover the truth of your unconscious energy. You cannot miss experiencing the truth of your blueprint, because both your honesty and dishonesty expose you to the truth of your own soul journey.*

You struggle to defend your own deception. You separate from your awareness of your soul because you cannot defend your defiance against truth. When you control yourself to be numb to feeling, you disable your ability to experience life truthfully. When you control yourself to exist oppressed by your denial of your feelings, you create superficial images of yourself, to conceal the truth of your defiance against your own original intention to live life being truthfully honest. You obsess with trying to perfect your images, so you can ignore the deception of your denial. When you align to and place all of your effort into controlling your denial, you secure your own arena to fight truth. This means you dumb down the truth of who you are.

You control your unresolved emotions to fuel your soul denial, rather than unifying with your soul consciousness' intention for this lifetime. You fight your awareness of truth, to fight the truth of yourself. This leaves you abandoning your ability to acknowledge what needs to be resolved, to unify with truth. This is all superficial because you are a soul of truth. Your defiance against yourself has you avoiding living a life of true soul meaning and reluctant to acknowledge your significance and integrity.

- What do you relinquish your own significance and integrity for?

You can defiantly ignore the reality of being unconditionally loved by and significant to *True Source Divine Origin Consciousness*. When you refuse to accept the unconditional love within truth, you devalue your own significance by undermining your uniqueness, independence and individuality. When you conform to your own soul denial, you compromise your awareness of your soul truth. You judge the value of truth by the impact it will have on your control, which means you will struggle to truly acknowledge the significance of truth.

When you filter your awareness of truth through your judgement of truth's inability to conform to your control, your control structures become agencies for retribution and vengeance. When you attempt to punish your portion of truth, which is your soul's consciousness, for not succumbing to your desire to control, you become a slave to your own misguided aversion to truth. You have created distortions, misconceptions and lies about the reality of truth and your control, to secure your codependency on your aversion to truth. Your soul's consciousness endeavours to expose you to your own aversion to truth, which has you deceptively manipulating yourself with your accumulated lies against truth. When you denounce truth for a lie, you conform to any judgement of truth that secures your own lies against yourself.

Your acknowledgment of your uniqueness without judgement, your ability to trust your independence without fear and your choice to live the truth of your individuality, creates the space to feel the unconditional love within truth. Your truthful honesty is your soul liberator. Your defiance against your blueprint causes you to be unconscious to your own significance as a soul and your opportunity to liberate yourself.

Some souls live defiantly against their blueprint. They have the experiences they were always going to have, but remain unconscious to the significance of their experiences. Life continues and as the years go by, the opportunity to learn and understand can become evident with hindsight. Hindsight is only significant if you use it as an opportunity to be honest. If you create the space for your hindsight to expose the truth of your soul journey, your honesty will reveal what you have spent a lifetime experiencing and it is your acknowledgement of truth that creates resolution of carried unresolved emotions. The opportunity to be honest with your soul truth is always there and hindsight can register a minute after an experience, or a decade later, regardless of the duration of time your acknowledgement of truth is always significant. Your soul does not age like your physical body ages and it is your resolution and evolution that alters the strength of your flow of consciousness, which creates the maturity of a soul.

When you deny truth, by not comprehending your motives to oppress your own awareness of truth, you can become obsessed with your soul oppression. You can act compulsively against truth and consume yourself with negativity. You compulsively seek avenues of negativity to surpass your awareness of truth. You justify the need for more negativity, often without understanding your own compulsion. You may compulsively attempt to stay unconscious to the reality of what you are doing to yourself and the truth being exposed to you. You fight your awareness of your soul truth to be unconscious to the reality of your own defiance against your soul's consciousness.

You use your negativity as a way to be manipulatively defiant against truth and yourself as a soul. You manipulate yourself with the embedded beliefs and fears of your soul denial, which generates the unconscious energy produced by your unresolved emotions. You can become codependent on subjecting your soul's consciousness to the energy of your soul's unconsciousness, and then use your defiance to give yourself the illusion of being in control. However, you are defiantly revelling in your disunity with truth, whilst you obsess with trying to control your own emotional reaction to your disunity with truth.

- Do you believe disassociating from feeling truth is freedom?
- How does your disassociation from truth feel?
- Are you a slave to your soul oppressive compulsions, or are you free of them?
- Have you distorted your understanding of freedom to suit your illusion of control?
- Do you believe freedom means to be free to exist in unconscious energy?

True Source Divine Origin Consciousness never interferes with your freedom or your freedom of choice. You choose what you do with your freedom.

- What have you chosen to do with your freedom and why?

When you use the deception within your fears and embedded beliefs to complicate the possibility of evolving, you become resistant to being honest. You complicate your natural ability to feel and acknowledge your soul's consciousness and truth, by creating emotional, energetic and physical barriers to truth. These are manifestations of your soul denial and your unwillingness to address and accept yourself. Your soul denial manifests as unresolved emotions. You can fear being unable to control the outcome being truthful would have on your life, so you continue to compound your denial of reality. You can reject the existence of your soul's consciousness to hide from the responsibility that you produce your own unresolved emotions. You deny you are the creator of your unresolved emotions and want to be unconscious to any truth that holds you accountable for the truth of your denial and soul denial history. By acknowledging the truth of being the creator of your unresolved emotions and by resolving your compulsion to defend your deception, you feel the value in allowing the emotional, energetic and physical storm within yourself to reveal your truth. You will understand it is your fear of change, not change itself that scares you. You hide in your unconscious energy because you fear change and the inability to control where change will go.

Change might be:

- To accept the truth of your feelings.
- To stop converting ignored feelings into more unresolved emotions.
- To feel the truth of your feelings and enjoy the experience.
- To feel the truth of your own stagnation without defending your illusory comfort zones within your soul oppression.
- To trust truth without fear or hidden agendas.
- To be honest about how you use your fears and embedded beliefs, to fuel your defiance against your own soul blueprint.
- To feel peace within and experience feeling your freedom to trust your soul's consciousness.
- To realise you are constantly disassociating from feeling your separation from your awareness of your soul.
- To realise how you defiantly use your judgement of reality as a weapon against truth, so you can continue distrusting truth.

When you honestly seek truth, you reclaim your awareness of your soul journey out of the deception of your unresolved emotions. This might be the change you seek.

- What types of deception do you use to disassociate from the reality of your approach to change?
- Do you defy your awareness of your soul truth?

You can arrogantly miss the mark of the opportunities within your blueprint. Your blueprint is a guide to the potential, possibilities and probabilities of your life experiences. Your honesty about your experiences will allow you to acknowledge your emotional defiance against your life experiences and your ability to learn from life. Life exposes you to what you need to resolve. Life is the opportunity to liberate yourself from your own oppressive soul denial. Life is your teacher, exposing you to both your unconscious and conscious energy. Your defiance has you opposing the possibility of freedom, which means you are fighting against the process of awakening to the truth of your soul.

You use your unconscious energy to utilise all your life's opportunities to validate your illusion of control, until you can no longer deny the reality of your control being an illusion. You can defiantly want the power to be selective and dictate to truth what you will resolve, and what you class as valid to remain unresolved and useable. This causes you to compete with life's ability to expose truth. If your life experiences affect your control, you deny how obvious your life experiences are in exposing what you need resolution in. You deny wanting control of life; however you willingly repeat the same control structures,

RIGHT: *The rise and fall from grace is your soul's consciousness exposing you to the truth of the energy within your soul's unconsciousness. Your soul's consciousness highlights the energy for you to use your freedom of choice to either be honest with what is being exposed, or to deny your awareness of what is being exposed. When you unify with the presence of truth, which is the energy of your soul's consciousness, you convert the unconscious energy into conscious understanding. This dissipates the unconsciousness of the energy and is the process of resolution and evolution.*

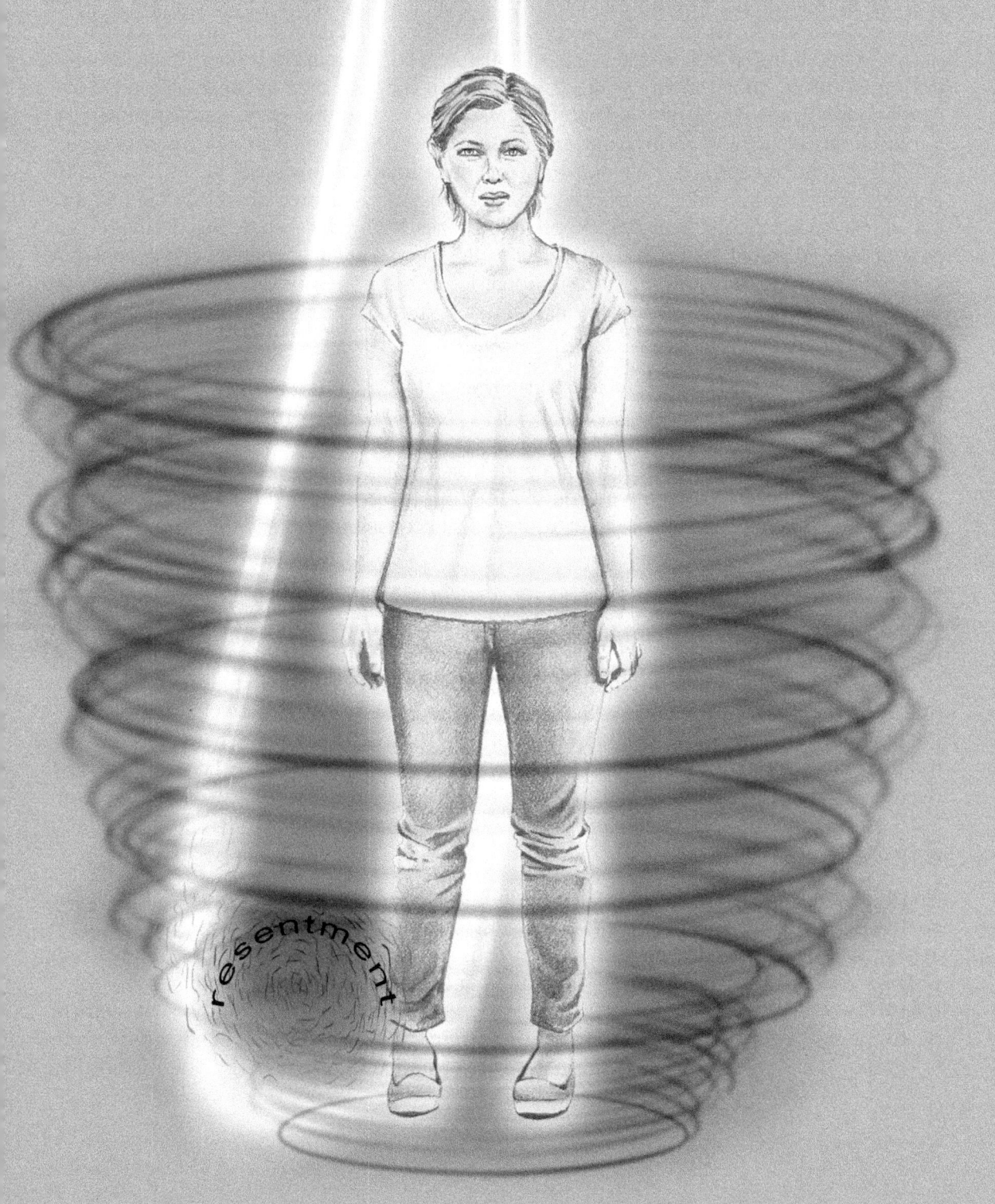

endeavouring to get the different results you think you want. When you want to retain your denial and control, you fight the presence of truth. This is why you do not trust your own soul blueprint, because your blueprint exposes you to truth. Your life is always exposing truth, the truth of both your conscious and unconscious energy. Your soul denial and control structures are exactly what your soul's consciousness wants to resolve. Your blueprint is about resolving your soul denial, not pacifying your denial of truth.

You can fight the grace within your rise and fall from grace; grace is a pure essence of your soul's consciousness. Grace is the energy of your honesty unifying with truth. Grace is love without conditions, which enables you to fall into your unconscious energy and expose truth to yourself; whilst giving yourself compassion for your own unconsciousness. Your soul's consciousness is of truth and naturally resonates with truth energy, which enables you to objectively observe your own soul's unconsciousness. Your grace allows you to explore, learn from and accept the truth of both your conscious and unconscious energy. Truth honours your freedom and you choose your response to your own observations, feelings and unresolved emotions. You may choose to be honest with your own reality, or retain your control over your soul oppression and reject truth. Your soul denial enables you to abandon your awareness of truth and the unconditional love within the grace of truth. You choose the energy you align with; avoiding your awareness of truth is a choice you make, although you may not admit to it.

If truth is accepted, acknowledged and trusted, your unconscious energy rises with grace to be unified with your origin truth. Your soul denial resolves as each unresolved emotion is converted to an acceptance of truth. Your blueprint is a mud map full of signs, crossroads and opportunities, all of which are within your life experiences but you have the freedom to navigate the truth of your reality as you see fit. Your life is exposing truth to you, creating opportunities to understand the truth of your soul's unconsciousness and the essence of your soul's consciousness.

You may defiantly control yourself to be unaware of the truth within your life experiences, and this causes you to be stagnant. Stagnation is being unreceptive to change, truth and reality. Stagnation is the choice to deny truth. Stagnation is to worship soul denial, control and soul oppression, which you defiantly mistake as living. Stagnation is the rejection of life being the flow of truth energy. Stagnation is the attempt to congest your awareness of the flow of truth. Life responds to the truth of energy. Your life is the experience of living the truth of your own conscious and unconscious energy. Your denial is how you conceal the truth of your energy, which causes you to be codependent on your lies. Your oppression exposes the truth that even with your denial, you are unable to alter the truth of what you are experiencing.

You may defiantly want your ability to control to be the purpose of your blueprint, but your control is inferior to the truth of your soul's consciousness. This is why you use your freedom against your awareness of your soul truth, because you internally know *True Source Divine Origin Consciousness* will not interfere with your freedom of choice. Your defiance against the reality of your present moment is defiance against your blueprint. Your present moment is always showing you the way back to your origin truth, because it is exposing the truth of your own energy to you. Your life unfolds exposing you to the energy you intended to resolve; your blueprint is a reflection of your original intention to have the experiences that expose you to the truth of your own energy. You navigate your blueprint with your freedom of choice. Your life is your blueprint exposing you to truth.

You separate from the significance of your soul blueprint and disassociate from feeling your soul's insight, so you can be defiant against truth which disarms your ability to feel truth. When you want truth to accommodate your desire for control, you demand that truth ignore your original intention for resolution and evolution. This means you have forgotten *True Source Divine Origin Consciousness'* freedom of choice, which you cannot interfere with. *True Source Divine Origin Consciousness* chooses to remain loyal to your soul's consciousness, and loves you without conditions. Your control is a speck of defiance energy compared to the magnitude of *True Source Divine Origin Consciousness'* unconditional love for your soul. This also exposes the arrogance of mankind's insanity of soul denial. Why would we fight to control love with conditions? When you feel the truth of your soul, you recognise the insanity of your control.

When you truly feel the conscious energy of your soul and trust your blueprint, you start to trust the whole process of your rise and fall from grace, and observe all of your experiences as opportunities to learn from life as your soul blueprint intended. When you are conscious of your love for your own soul and truth, your ability to live life honestly exposes the reality of being unconditionally loved by truth. You will feel your own grace, within your rise and fall from grace, as your soul blueprint intended. Your honesty within your fall from grace will inspire you to keep resolving and evolving, which is to rise with grace. Your honesty allows you to feel the truth of your experiences and the opportunities within your present moment. The more you accept you are on a journey for your soul's resolution and evolution, and the more significance you give to the uniqueness of your blueprint, the more you reveal your ability to unconditionally love the truth of your soul and the reality of life.

Chapter Twenty-Three

Carried victim energy

Victim

Being a victim is a description of someone who is experiencing the inability to utilise their freedom of choice. You are a victim in your present moment when you experience being overpowered, without the ability to protect yourself. Carried victim energy is when the victim energy from an experience is continuously carried and used as a definition of who you are as a person, which consequently affects how you interact with life, because there is no aspiration to resolve the carried emotions. This causes you to use your carried victim energy as a control technique and to oppose the truth of your soul. Carried victim energy is energy you become fearful of being without, because you use it to explain to yourself why you feel the way you do, enabling your loss of hope to become your familiar. Your carried victim energy inhibits your awareness of being an evolving soul. The present moment experience of being a victim is horrific, but the collateral damage of carried victim energy is colossal. You oppress your awareness of your soul with your carried victim energy, which sustains your defiance against your awareness of your own soul truth.

Carried victim energy morphs into a victim mentality which is a way of thinking. Mentality means 'of the mind' and victim mentality can become an habitual attitude. Carried victim energy unpins the complexities of a victim mentality. You use your carried victim energy to fuel a wide variety of reactions and responses. Carried victim energy also is a method of control, because it is used to expand your separation from the truth of your soul, and to oppose resolution of your unresolved emotions. The failure of your desire to control others to succumb to your wants, expectations or perceived needs, fuels your carried victim energy. You can use your carried victim energy as a source of reusable power and you remain steadfast in your beliefs, attitudes, fears and unresolved emotions. This cultivates your self-pity, internal rage, martyrdom, manipulation, what is familiar and contrived desperation, which leaves you clinging to the mentalities that ensue.

Carried victim energy is a multitude of unresolved emotions and mentalities, which can be used together or separately to oppress your awareness of the exquisiteness of your soul. You use these mentalities to camouflage the myriad of ways you control the oppression of your soul.

Your carried victim energy continues to develop as you seek and absorb oppressive energy, which sustains your separation from your awareness of your soul and disassociation from feeling truth. Your carried victim energy causes you to equate truth with the inability to control; this distortion causes you to oppose your soul consciousness' intention to expose

When you compulsively search for unconscious energy to oppress your awareness of your soul and truth, you become panicked and oppose your soul consciousness' intention to expose you to truth. Your intention is to utilise the unconscious energy you find, to sustain your separation from your awareness and your disassociation from feeling truth. You can then proclaim yourself as a victim because you feel oppressed.

you to truth. Your curiosity and willingness to value truth becomes the casualty of your carried victim energy. Your carried victim energy disassociates you from unconditionally loving your soul's consciousness, which is the truth of your soul.

You cannot change history or the experience of being overpowered, but you have the freedom to choose your response to your experience of being a victim. Coming to terms with your experience of being a victim may take time and can be extremely difficult. However, you are always worth the effort to never give up on your own value, worth and significance, which is what you deprive yourself of feeling with your carried victim energy. It will be the types of choices you make that will determine when you start the process of resolving what your experiences have created or what they have exposed within you. Your carried victim energy facilitates your own indifference to truth and your inability to accept your failure to control. You can deliberately choose to remain in a victim mentality to justify your own soul oppression and indifference towards yourself, because you fear examining the truth of your feelings. This fear inhibits you from feeling freedom from the experience or experiences of being a victim, debilitating your ability to express and freely resonate with the truth of who you are.

You use your carried victim energy to camouflage the lies you tell yourself about the injustice of not being able to control or of having been deprived of your freedom. Your carried victim energy can become a bottomless pit of self-manipulation where you distort the truth of your own natural value, worth and significance. Your distortions morph into the covertness of your desire to control, or your opposition to accepting your freedom of choice. The victim mentality becomes an excuse you use to give yourself permission to be a master manipulator, as you seek to pacify your desire to control your fear of life. You can manipulate yourself to deny how you use your carried victim energy to justify the internal duality of being the victim and the controller of your own oppression. This can cause you to become entrapped by your own tolerance of the familiarity of emotionally, energetically and physically see-sawing between both your desire to control and your carried victim energy.

When you want to protect your carried victim energy, you have an aversion to the possibility of learning to unconditionally love yourself and the truth of your life experiences. Your victim mentality and desire for control become opposing forces that leads to your judgement of your experiences being contrary. This causes you to become conflicted in your own justifications for your emotional reactions and behaviours. You use your judgement to retain your perceived righteousness of being entitled to judge truth as an interference and as an enemy. You betray yourself with your own victim mentality as you attempt to prove the righteousness of your defection from your awareness of truth. Your victim mentality causes you to believe you are entitled to dictate what the priorities and purpose, of others and *True Source Divine Origin Consciousness*, should or should not be, whilst omitting accountability for your own actions. You use your victim mentality to blame *True Source Divine Origin Consciousness* for mankind's indifference to you. Your victim mentality is contradictory to the reality of being a significant soul and survives as an oppressive force when you are willing to deny the truth of who you are. You are of truth but you deny this and use your carried victim energy to remain angry at truth for life not being smooth, predictable and under your control.

You can continually use your judgement to assess whether you are in control of your reality or a victim to reality. This creates a see-saw within your mind chatter, which limits your perception of yourself and life. Your limited perception of yourself becomes the lie you use to sustain your carried victim energy, which inhibits you from feeling the truth of your freedom of choice. When you lose awareness of the significance of your freedom of choice, you become anti-the truth of yourself and anti-the opportunity to resolve your victim mentality. This entangles you in the futile battle of trying to control and pacify your own judgement of yourself and life. It is a futile battle because you use carried victim energy to instigate your own opposition against your opportunities for resolution and evolution. Your opposition to resolution and evolution creates a bottomless pit of unresolved emotions.

Your protection of your carried victim energy, alters your ability to objectively observe your own unresolved emotions. When you have programmed, conditioned and indoctrinated yourself to interweave your victim mentality into every feeling, emotion and experience you have, you become entrapped within a fear of truth. Your desire to control your emotional state and your awareness of truth has you in varying degrees of separation from your awareness of your soul as you disassociate from feeling truth. You attempt to control what you feel and what you will acknowledge, which causes you to attempt to perfect your skills of suppression. However, suppression comes at a price, because it is unsustainable and emotional eruptions will occur, which cause you to panic about your inability to control your suppression. This creates anxiety, which is the fear of not being able to control yourself within life. When you attempt to avoid your interaction with life and suppress your own fears and emotions, you compulsively separate from your awareness of your soul and disassociate from feeling truth. This sustains your anxiety about your ability to control and secures the gridlock your fear has over you. Your willingness to separate from your awareness of your soul and disassociate from feeling truth, causes you to either control yourself to withdraw from feeling the truth of your present moment, or to try to control your present moment with your past and your perception of what reality should be.

You can deny yourself the opportunity to resolve your carried victim energy as retaliation for being hurt by other's indifference, although you are hurting yourself. Your indifference to yourself, activates your opposition to accepting any truth that interferes with your belief of being a victim and belief of being entitled to demand control of life.

You can inflict the oppression you refuse to resolve, on your own soul's consciousness, with the intention of hurting yourself, which exposes your willingness to devalue yourself. The residue of victim energy you carry causes you to devalue yourself, because you believe being a victim means you are unworthy. Being a victim is an experience, not a definition. When you refuse to resolve your negative self-definition, constructed from the unresolved emotions you have carried from your victim experiences, you seek to be a master over your control of life, often becoming extremely indifferent to yourself, others and life. This can cause you to control with a victim mentality, which intercepts your awareness of your soul's consciousness and dumbs down who you truly are. You use your carried victim energy to remain intentionally unconscious to the truth of your soul's consciousness and oppose being aware that you have opportunities to resolve what is unresolved. When you deny your ability to resolve your unresolved emotions, you become defiantly oppositional towards life, the truth of yourself and a victim to your own oppression.

Your victim mentality has you automatically reacting unconsciously to truth, and you then use the distorted perception of truth to feed your assessment of being a victim. Your victim mentality means you ruminate about emotional events seeking to sustain the ultimate suppression of anything you fear you cannot control. This causes you to exist within the constant see-saw of either believing you have control of life or believing you are out of control of life.

Your victim mentality has you opposing peace within, and your denial of reality supports the anarchy you create with your carried victim energy. You fragment your carried victim energy into many mentalities, which become compulsive reactions. You react without reasoning with yourself and these mentalities become habitual.

- Victim
- Self-pity
- Internal rage
- Martyrdom
- Manipulation
- Familiarity
- Contrived desperation

These stem from carried victim energy and are sustained by a pervasive victim mentality and desire for control.

When you deny your victim mentality, you inhibit your ability to objectively observe the entirety of your victim and control energy, and this sustains your soul oppression. Your victim and control energy is like a jigsaw, if you only observe one piece of it, you will never know what the full picture is. When you choose to objectively observe, acknowledge and accept the truth you resonate with, you will eventually expose more pieces of your jigsaw and become aware of the whole picture.

There are different camouflaging techniques of control that rely on carried victim energy as a base. You combine different unresolved emotions to automatically react and respond to truth, your soul's consciousness and reality with the intention of rejecting truth to control, justify and defend your beliefs of being a victim.

RIGHT: Your unwillingness to resolve your carried victim energy is your indifference to the truth of who you are and causes you to be entombed within your denial of your own significance. You hide from the truth of who you are within your emotional torment and become encased by your limited perception of yourself.

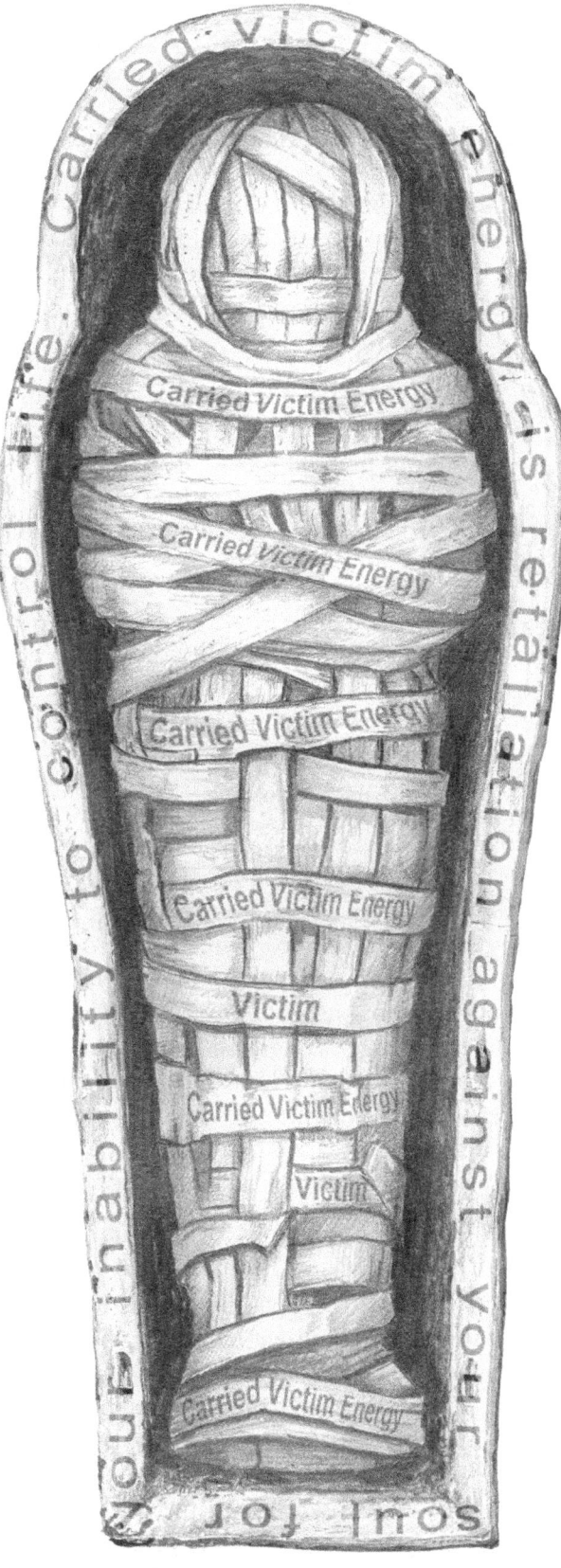

Self-pity

Your carried victim energy causes you to use self-pity, to seek and revel in the bottomless pit of despair you create with your own soul denial. This causes you to wallow in your choice to denounce the energy of hope. Your self-pity entraps you in your refusal to accept the reality you are experiencing and it is your non-acceptance, which has you ricocheting from one unresolved emotion to another. Your self-pity immobilises your ability to trust, feel and be honest about your awareness of your own soul truth.

Self-pity can feel like an energetic fog that descends over you, and you omit that you are the generator of the energy with your thoughts and attitudes. This builds a mentality that you find difficult to honestly address. When you commit yourself to a self-pity mentality, you use your thought processes to engulf yourself with negativity. This causes you to lose hope and to abandon the freedom to reason with yourself. You use your self-pity mentality to create an emotional haze that confuses you as you become consumed with despair.

We, as mankind, often distort the truth of hope, by believing hope is an assessment of the possibility to control. The truth of the core essence of hope is to be able to trust your own courage to be present within your reality. Hope facilitates the courage to deal with your emotions and any energy that ensues, honestly. Hope is to trust in the truth of being an eternal soul, experiencing a life which requires you to resolve your fear of losing your illusion of control. Hope is your acceptance of reality. Hope gives you the confidence to trust yourself within the dynamics of reality and the uncontrollable changes of life.

Your self-pity mentality has you seeking ultimate control of your soul consciousness' intention for resolution and evolution. This causes you to engulf yourself with the unresolved emotions you refuse to acknowledge, therefore inhibiting any chance of resolution or evolution. Resolution occurs after you acknowledge your unresolved emotions and become willing to be completely honest with yourself. When life does not work to your expectations and you throw an emotional tantrum, it is because your illusion of control has been broken. When you acknowledge your illusion of control has been broken, you can start to doubt your whole perception of reality. This can cause you to distort your awareness of reality, which leaves you believing that even the most trivial event is confirmation that you will never escape your own misfortune or the despair you feel. You can become entrapped in the negative beliefs created by your emotional tantrums, and by your fear of more despair or of not knowing what to expect. Self-pity is the choice to fuse yourself with your own refusal to be honest and to reject feeling the natural core essence of hope within your soul's consciousness.

Your self-pity is the act of engulfing and overwhelming yourself with your own soul denial, and beliefs of being entitled to expect your desire to control to be pacified and gratified. Your self-pity mentality has you seeking support from others for the emotional implosions you experience, which are the result of you believing you are not in control. Your self-pity can be a direct result of the failure of your denial of reality to shield you from the truth of your unresolved emotions. This can cause you to wallow in self-pity when your unresolved emotions are revealed to you, instead of honestly approaching what you have discovered as an opportunity to be truthful with yourself. Wallowing in your unresolved emotions is to remain fallen in the cesspit of your anti-you energy and prolongs your suffering in your own despair.

When you wallow in the unresolved emotions you refuse to be honest about, you become stuck in your fear of truth, which causes you to become very self-indulgent in your own emotional despair. This often leaves you being irrational in your thought process and creating rituals that you indulge in, because of the despair you feel. These rituals are as varied as people; some over-indulge in alcohol, junk food or drugs; some wrap themselves up in a blanket and shut themselves off from the world, and some stare into space trying to be numb. Some walk through life looking for events to prove to themselves that they are right about life always being difficult and perceive themselves through the distorted view of only ever experiencing misfortune, emotional angst and betrayal. You emotionally implode when your life is not pacifying your desire to control reality, or your denial has failed to separate you from what you do not want to acknowledge. Self-pity is born from the belief that your life is harder and more miserable than others, which means you are wallowing in comparison and judgement.

Your self-pity mentality will have you concretising beliefs of being beyond help, as you seek to utilise any emotions to justify feeding and protecting your own bottomless pit of despair. You use the self-pity within the carried victim energy to emotionally react to life, others and your soul's consciousness, with the intent to rid yourself of courage and hope, by emotionally generating energy you believe is impenetrable by truth. Your self-pity has you creating emotional cycles with the energy of hopelessness, helplessness, sadness, resignation, unworthiness and being overwhelmed by how you use your own unresolved emotions. The list of emotions is as varied as the degrees of self-pity you use to control your life experiences.

You combine your negative beliefs with your thought process to create cycles of mind chatter, which you use to attack your awareness of your soul consciousness' ability to expose truth. You use your mind chatter to generate and create a self-pity mentality that conceals the truth of your awareness of the entirety of your emotional, energetic and physical reality. You use your mind chatter to sustain your separation from your awareness of your soul and your disassociation from feeling truth, which enforces your codependency on your own negative beliefs. Your mind chatter becomes a repetitive attempt to silence your curiosity about truth and causes you to accept your self-pity without challenge.

Self-pity mind chatter:
- "This is as good as it gets, why bother?"
- "What about me?"
- "I'm entrapped and nothing will change."
- "It's all too much." (Overwhelmed)
- "Being a victim gets me attention."
- "I want out!"

Question yourself on your self-pity.
1. How do you attempt to control reality with your self-pity?
2. When you are entrapped in your self-pity, what are you hiding from?
3. What do you emotionally use that feeds, fuels and develops your self-pity?

Self-pity becomes an energy that ends up controlling you to justify the despair created by your soul denial and causes you to wallow in your own willingness to oppress yourself. Self-pity is like a fog that engulfs your thought processes and distorts how you feel about yourself. This leaves you opposing your natural significance.

Internal rage

You use your carried victim energy to justify your internal rage. You use your internal rage to revel in a bottomless pit of self-hatred. You can be full of loathing for yourself because you are unable to control your soul, truth, life and others to your expectations. This can cause you to emotionally demand that everything and everyone be submissive and subservient to you. Your fear of not being able to control and your refusal to be honest with your reality, incarcerates you in your own illusion of control or victim mentality. The energy generated by your desire to control has you creating excuses to preoccupy yourself with your own irritation, anger, resentment and retribution, which can lead you to antagonise others. Fear is the energy that underpins all of your internal rage. When you fear losing the familiarity of your victim and control see-saw, you struggle to care for the truth of your soul. You fear the unknown and you class freedom from your control and victim energy as unknown.

You internally rage because you want control of your experience of life and won't acknowledge the opportunities within your present reality to be honest with yourself. You deny yourself the opportunity to resolve your emotional fear and to evolve beyond that which you use to sustain your own emotional, energetic and physical incarceration. Your fear is your own incarceration, which you create from your desire to control life. Instead of accepting reality for what it is and trusting the opportunities within reality, you become fixated on what you believe reality should be. You internally rage within yourself, because there is a discrepancy between your reality and your expectations. When you internally rage, you distract yourself from the truth of your defection from the opportunities within your reality that expose you to the truth of yourself.

Your internal rage is an attempt to conceal your fear of not being able to control life's ability to expose you to the truth of your unresolved emotions. You use your internal rage to sustain the space for your indifference to truth, in an attempt to justify your denial, which creates a volatile reaction to your rise and fall from grace. Your internal rage oppresses your ability to honestly experience your rise with grace and causes you to create a surge of control energy, in an attempt to deny yourself any opportunity to become aware of the truth of your own unresolved emotions. You concretise your beliefs about your own unresolved emotions, which causes you to deny yourself any opportunity to resolve what is sustaining your internal rage.

You internally rage because you fear being a victim to something or someone else's control. Your control has become the prize for your defection from your awareness of truth and you internally rage because you cannot control your control to be flawless. You fear the competition you have with reality will prove to be futile and 'prize less'; you internally rage because your control is constantly being exposed as flawed and you have no way of perfecting your control.

RIGHT: When your carried victim energy has you entrapped in the fury of your own internal rage, you become willing to revel in a bottomless pit of self-hatred. This causes you to seek conflict to confirm your victim mentality.

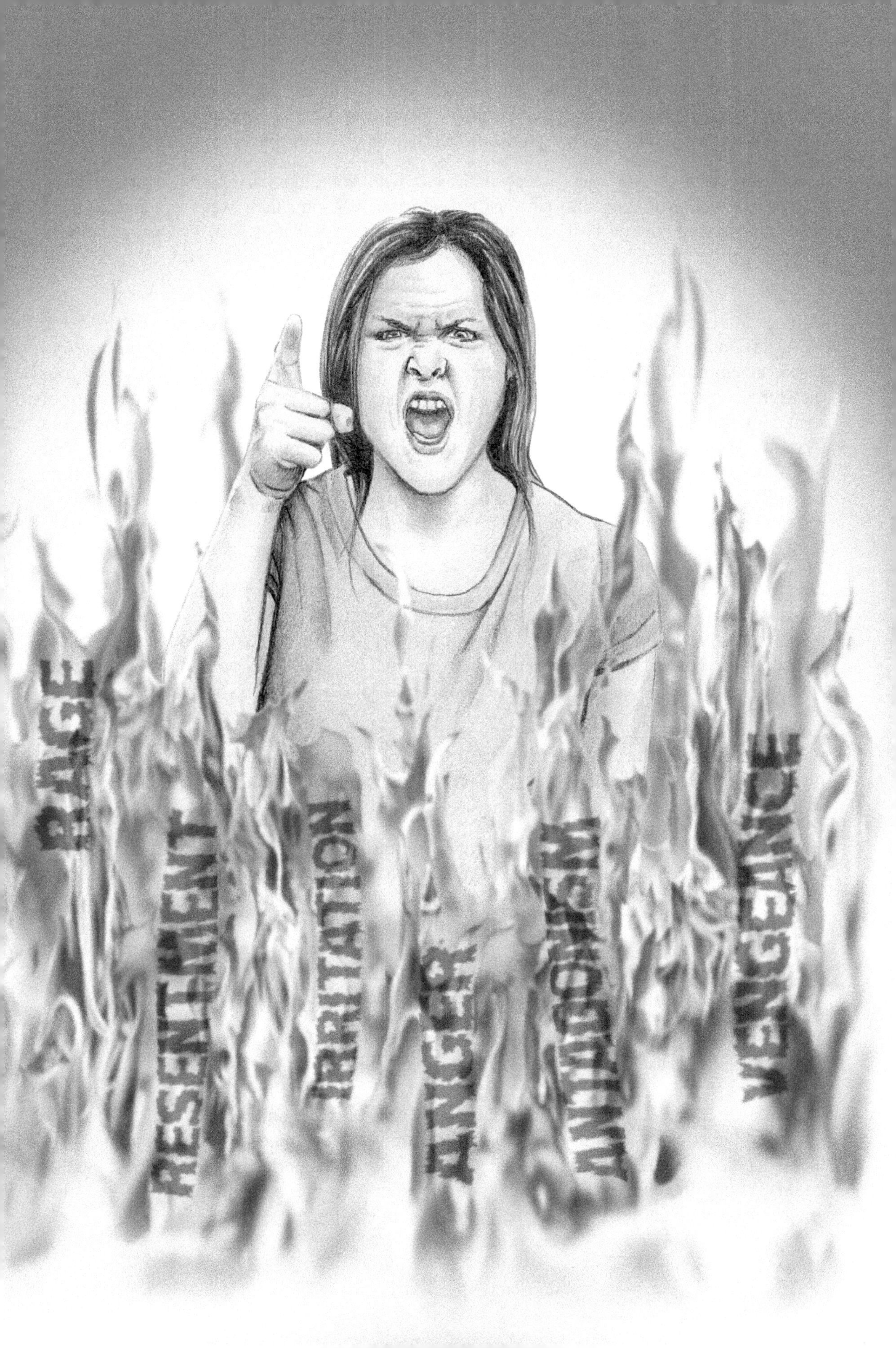
RAGE
RESENTMENT
IRRITATION
ANGER
ANTAGONISM
VENGEANCE

Your internal rage sustains both your control and victim energy, which concretises your compulsion to oppose caring about truth. This causes you to continually enhance your denial of reality, which secures your indifference to yourself and truth.

When you protect your soul's unconsciousness with your internal rage, you class others' compassion and willingness to care as a weakness, believing their weakness makes them vulnerable to your control. This can cause you to become exploitative. You can perceive others' compassion for you, as an opportunity to discover the prowess of your ability to manipulate, although you implode if you are not as successful at manipulating as you believed you would be.

Your victim mentality causes you to sustain your internal rage, which leaves you opposing being a friend to yourself. This is how you sustain your internal self-loathing. Your internal rage is an emotionally charged energy that disassociates you from feeling the reality of your indifference, which causes you to be disloyal, disrespectful and oblivious to the truth of your soul's consciousness. Your indifference becomes the security blanket, you use to avoid the truth of the emotional carnage you are creating for your soul and for others. You fear life's ability to expose the truth of your indifference, because you fear losing your ability to be indifferent. You fear being exposed to truth without your ability to counteract your own recognition of feeling truth. You have created the distortion that being indifferent means to be strong, and fear your natural ability to care for and feel your soul's consciousness.

Due to your refusal to be completely honest about your carried victim energy, you become consumed with orchestrating to have optimum control over being a victim, or to use being a victim to have optimum control. When your ability to use your control and the purpose of utilising your control energy has failed, your internal rage becomes your emotional backup system. You rely on your rage to shield you from acknowledging the truth of yourself.

You can programme, condition and indoctrinate yourself to exist in negativity, to justify your beliefs of being a victim. Once you justify your victim status, you believe you will have justified the use of all of your control techniques, negative beliefs, addictive behaviours and your cyclic patterns of soul oppression.

You use your victim and control energy to withdraw from your reality, deluding yourself with the illusion of control created by the familiarity of the energy you allow yourself to experience. You use your internal rage to emotionally feel out of control, which you then use to prove you are a victim. You use your own emotional state to justify your rageful reactions, but you deny you are the source of your rage, which sustains your internal unrest and upheavals. You deny it is your desire for control and unwillingness to accept reality, that leaves you feeling emotionally victimised.

You combine your negative beliefs with your thought process to create cycles of mind chatter, which you use to attack your awareness of your soul consciousness' ability to expose truth. You use your mind chatter to generate and create internal rage that conceals the truth of your awareness of the entirety of your emotional, energetic and physical reality. You use your mind chatter to sustain your separation from your awareness of your soul and your disassociation from feeling truth, which enforces your codependency on your own negative beliefs. Your mind chatter becomes a repetitive attempt to silence your curiosity about truth and causes you to accept your internal rage without challenge.

Internal rage mind chatter:

- "If everyone would just get out of my way, I would be all right."
- "I am right!"
- "If everyone would just do as I expect them to do, there would be no problems."
- You emotionally relive experiences and others' words that you could not control, recycling thoughts over and over, to justify the rage you generate.
- You enact possibilities within your mind, seeking to be ready to control reality, and cycle within your imagined variations of the possibilities you perceive for your reality, and rage if your predictions are wrong.
- You judge everything and then use your thoughts to justify or pull apart your own judgement.

You use your own emotional state to justify your rageful reactions to life, to truth, to the truth of being a soul and to others, but you deny you are the instigator of your own emotional unrest and upheavals. You deny it is your desire for control that you emotionally feel victimised by, and that you are willing to rage against everything and anyone that does not succumb to your control.

Question yourself on your internal rage.

1. How do you attempt to control reality with your internal rage?
2. When you are entrapped in your internal rage what are you hiding from?
3. What do you emotionally use that feeds, fuels and develops your internal rage?

Martyrdom

Your carried victim energy has you martyring yourself to your own justification for your addiction to emotional pain. You martyr yourself to the familiarity of your own misery, pain, struggle, soul oppression and soul denial, which causes you to devalue your natural significance. You fight the truth of your soul with the desire to create a comfort zone within your soul oppression. This is the belief that you can control yourself to suppress your emotions and deny how you feel, believing you can settle in the deception of believing you are insignificant. It is ironic what you protect as a comfort zone when you are so uncomfortable in it. You condition yourself to be martyred to your victim mentality. This is choosing to deny that resolution creates peace within. Your denial of the significance of resolution, means you deny you are a soul who has emotions to resolve. When you deny naturally feeling truth, you oppose the opportunity to resolve. Your awareness of your soul truth becomes the sacrificial victim, for your illusory control of your suppression of your unresolved emotions, which causes you untold angst.

When you are willing to be a martyr, you are intentionally being deceptive, creating a façade to hide your cunning manipulation of your own unresolved emotions. When you oppose expressing the truth of your soul, you cultivate the belief of being a victim. This entraps you in the familiarity of your own soul oppression, not recognising that the oppression you feel is created by your own deception. You use your martyr mentality to plan, preempt and orchestrate the lie that you do not have freedom of choice. You use your martyrdom to fight against feeling your freedom and the opportunity to be liberated from your own soul oppression. Your martyrdom can become habitual as you complain about being unable to control, while deliberately choosing to victimise yourself, disguising how you utilise your freedom of choice. When you obligate yourself to an image, you attempt to disguise the neediness of your victim mentality. The neediness within your martyrdom and victim mentality is insatiable and you are unable to pacify it, because you have chosen to orchestrate yourself, to emotionally feel and experience being a victim to your own soul oppression. Your victim mentality can have you craving attention.

Your desire to control has you refining the use of martyrdom; it becomes a game of trying to control others to notice you and revere your presence, while sabotaging your own ability to appreciate yourself and feel at peace with yourself. You use the belief that your struggling and suffering will enable you to achieve a better position later, to justify sustaining your own orchestration of martyrdom now. You sacrifice opportunities with this belief, and deny your awareness of the truth of your life experiences. You also sabotage the joy of living. Your habitual martyrdom is a way of endeavouring to deprive yourself of the joy of life, as you oppose the dynamics of reality. Your martyrdom is you amalgamating your desire for control and victim mentality, to oppress your freedom with your choice to renege on the evolutionary opportunities within your life experiences. Your desire to control life is a source of your stagnation, which you use to oppress your awareness of your soul. You choose to taint every situation with the familiarity of your opposition, oppressing your awareness of your soul's consciousness. When you victimise yourself with the familiarity of your soul oppression, you martyr yourself to your stagnation.

You can control yourself to attack your own awareness of your soul truth, condemning the presence of both your soul's consciousness and unconsciousness. This is an attempt to avoid the opportunities within your present moment to utilise your freedom of choice, to be honest about your interaction with life. This is how you diminish your natural ability to feel joy. Your loss of awareness of having freedom of choice disables your ability to feel joyful, and causes you to become fixated on martyring yourself to your own disappointment that you cannot control your life to satisfy your expectations. At the same time, you deny how you are orchestrating to exist in a self-manipulative state, allowing yourself to use anything and everything, that does not work to your expectations, as proof that you are justified in your belief that you are a victim to your experience of life. You can forcibly deny yourself the opportunity to feel the consciousness of your soul and the truth of your original intention to experience, feel and explore the truth of your soul's unconsciousness. You can judge yourself harshly for not feeling joyful and at peace with reality, whilst ignoring that you deprive yourself of joy. Joy becomes difficult to feel if you are controlling yourself to distrust the dynamics of your significance, uniqueness, independence and individuality.

The expectation of having to be right can cause you to panic, because you fear the potential of being judged. You attempt to revel in and prove the righteousness of your judgement, but your fear of being wrong causes you to align with your victim mentality, which you use to dispel the momentary jubilation you feel from your perceived righteousness. You can consistently fight what you are experiencing, attempting to justify your own desire to be in control and to secure any belief generated from wanting to be right within your judgement. However, you cannot sustain your own illusion of control, because you can feel your soul's consciousness constantly exposing the flaws of your control and judgement, and your vindictiveness against the truth of yourself. You try to compensate for denying yourself your awareness of your soul truth, with perceived righteousness. As you martyr yourself to your own perceived righteousness, you deny yourself the opportunity to feel your significance, uniqueness, independence and individuality as a soul; and then you flounder within your judgement.

Your willingness to martyr yourself generates more emotional pain, which becomes a way you punish the individuality of your soul and leaves you feeling trapped in a vortex of your emotionally charged energy. This causes you to exist highly strung and anxious about how others may affect you. When you are willing to be a martyr, you seek emotional chaos either by creating it or by entering another's emotional dilemma, because you wish to blame someone else for the internal grief you feel. You do this without any inclination to take responsibility for how you instigated or entered the chaos. This means when you see an opportunity for a struggle, you compulsively align to it, or seek to exacerbate it because you have the desire to identify yourself as 'poor me', and want to assess yourself as having been treated insensitively or being completely overlooked. You can adopt the belief that due to your struggle others are gaining benefits without care or consideration for your personal sacrifice.

You can control yourself with deceptive beliefs about being a soul, and use the excuse that consciousness is beyond your capability, to avoid how you choose to remain trapped in your victim mentality. You use these beliefs to excuse and justify exerting your desire for control over your awareness of your soul's consciousness. This has you martyring yourself to your process of protecting your ideals, whilst you become willing to control yourself to be oppressed by your denial of your significance, uniqueness, independence and individuality. When you use what oppresses you to deny any possibility of change and freedom, you can revel in your control of your oppression, impressing even yourself, with how difficult you have made your own existence. This has you preoccupied with sustaining your see-saw of control and victim energy. As you lose sight of your awareness, you ignore how you martyr yourself and mindlessly feed your own soul oppression. Your victim mentality controls you to anchor and martyr yourself to your negative beliefs about your own soul truth. This keeps you transfixed by your emotional pain and confusion, which enables you to deny the core of your emotional problems, which is your own denial of the significance of your existence.

You emotionally regurgitate your unresolved emotions, which leaves complex labyrinths of emotional energy. As you sustain the emotional labyrinths, you lose your awareness of your soul's consciousness. You use your emotional labyrinths to engage, entangle and connect your unconscious energy with any other unconscious energy, you believe will enable you to ignore your awareness of truth. You use your emotional labyrinths to secure your emotional pain. Your pain transfixes you, to arrogantly ignore your awareness of your soul's consciousness, and to oppose your potential freedom from soul oppression.

When you attack and dismiss your natural ability to feel truth, you fight the process of your life experiences, exposing your reality to you. Your rise and fall from grace is the process of you being exposed to the truth of your reality. This provides the opportunity for you to resolve your emotional, energetic and physical barriers to your awareness of being a significant, unique, independent, individual soul of *True Source Divine Origin Consciousness*.

Your desire for control and victim mentality causes you to martyr yourself to your own emotional creations, whilst denying your own involvement.

- Why do you martyr yourself to your own soul oppression?
- Why do you create emotional pain to martyr yourself to?
- Why do you orchestrate what you martyr yourself to?
- Why do you carry your victim energy and forego your freedom?

You combine your negative beliefs with your thought process to create cycles of mind chatter, which you use to attack your awareness of your soul consciousness' ability to expose truth. You use your mind chatter to generate and create martyrdom behaviours to conceal the truth of your awareness of the entirety of your emotional, energetic and physical reality. You use your mind chatter to sustain your separation from your awareness of your soul and your disassociation from feeling truth, which enforces your codependency on your own negative beliefs. Your mind chatter becomes a repetitive attempt to silence your curiosity about truth and causes you to accept your martyrdom without challenge.

Martyrdom mind chatter:

- "No pain, No gain. Life was not meant to be easy."
- "No one appreciates all the sacrifices I make for them."
- "I deserve pain and need to suffer and I know no-one will notice."
- "I am so unsupported."
- "Everyone just takes from me, and gives nothing in return."
- "It's too hard to forgive or forget."

Question yourself on your martyrdom.

1. How do you attempt to control reality with your martyrdom?

2. When you are entrapped in your martyrdom what are you hiding from?

3. What do you emotionally use that feeds, fuels and develops your martyrdom?

Manipulator

When you use your carried victim energy to overshadow the truth exposed to you and to override how you feel, you become very manipulative. When you are manipulative, you are resisting, denying and avoiding accepting your reality, and often refuse to acknowledge what you are trying to do to truth. When you are willing to be manipulative, you assess your reality via your own judgement, wants and desires. You can deny your manipulative reactions to the truth you are experiencing, whilst becoming dogmatically manipulative. Your manipulation is as clever, devious and skilful as your ability to lie to yourself. You lie to conceal the reality of knowing you are attempting to manipulate truth to secure an illusion of control.

You can manipulate yourself to be codependent on your manipulation. You need to manipulate yourself to believe your own illusion of control, so that you can attempt to abandon your awareness of your soul's consciousness without remorse. However, you often create and carry guilt, shame and humiliation because you can feel your self-manipulation and willingness to betray yourself and others. When you rule your existence with your expectations of what life owes you, you manipulate yourself to be in disharmony with truth and your own soul. As you disharmonise with your soul, you lose awareness of the grace within truth. Your lack of grace causes you to activate your unresolved emotions, and can leave you tolerating your opposition against yourself, reality and truth. You can victimise yourself with your own disharmony and manipulate yourself to dumb down the reality of being a soul.

When you are willing to be manipulative, you struggle to pacify your emotions and fight your reality as you attempt to get what you want from life. You can believe if you can get what you want, it does not matter that you have abandoned truth. However, regardless of whether you get what you want, you can never pacify the emotional angst created by your abandonment of truth. This causes you to believe that it is the pacification of your desire to control life, yourself, others, relationships and truth that will quell the disharmony you feel within yourself. You find yourself disassociated from feeling truth and can feel your separation from your awareness of your soul. When you manipulate yourself to deny the reality of what you can feel, you become less self-reflective. This can leave you disharmonising with others and demanding to be appeased.

While separated from your awareness of your soul and disassociated from feeling truth, you manipulate yourself to search for confirmation of what you want to believe about yourself. This causes you to seek a justifiable excuse for abandoning feeling your own awareness of truth. You search for someone or something to align to your manipulation, so you can believe you understand yourself and can justify your methods and reasoning for being manipulative. You can create programmed reactions from your indoctrinated beliefs that excuse and sustain your abandonment of truth, to justify your own denial and the lies you tell yourself. When you manipulate your perception of life, you attempt to conform to your separation from your awareness of your soul and your disassociation from feeling truth.

You want to be able to trust your ability to control life, but you are constantly competing with the truth of your reality. This makes it difficult to feel secure about your control, which

can cause you to be irrational about what will quell your feelings of insecurity. If you use manipulation, it generates deception that consumes and overshadows your awareness of reality, and you become the embodiment of indifference to truth. Truth becomes irrelevant and securing what you want becomes of upmost importance, regardless of how it affects others or your soul. However, your ability to manipulate is constantly letting you down, because you do not feel secure while separated from your awareness of your soul and disassociated from feeling truth.

You can manipulate yourself to fight feeling and attempt to numb yourself to reality. This causes you to want to avoid being aware of your soul truth. You want to be able to trust what you feel, but you manipulate yourself to judge and attempt to control your feelings with emotions. You use your manipulative thought processes to assault your ability to trust your soul's consciousness. Your thoughts can become dominated by your analysis of the best way to ascertain your illusion of control.

You can manipulate yourself to hide from the truth of your separation from your awareness of your soul and disassociation from feeling truth, by becoming consumed with your analysis of life, your judgment of yourself and by comparing your images, illusions and controlled identities to others. When you hide from the reality of your life experience, you hide from what life is exposing to you and you hide from any unfavourable results of your separation from your awareness of your soul and your disassociation from feeling truth. You can manipulate yourself to lie, to conceal the truth you feel. You can fear acknowledging your own separation from your awareness of your soul and your disassociation from feeling truth, because you do not know what to do about it. This can cause you to manipulate yourself to align to spiritual illusions or beliefs of being a victim, because you do not want to contend with life.

You emotionally feel like a victim if you cannot use your control to influence your own and others' lives. Having control is how you seek to pacify your insecurities and sustain your image of yourself. You can exist within the vulnerability of your own desire to control life with your arrogant images of yourself and the illusions of what you think your reality should be. You create parameters that restrict your awareness of yourself as a soul, which leave you ignoring the truth of your own manipulation. When you devalue your soul, it becomes easier to disregard how you use manipulation. It also becomes acceptable to you, to ignore the effects of your manipulation. This leaves you attempting to emotionally blackmail those you believe should be submissive to your demands.

You can obsessively control yourself to what you perceive would be an advantage for your control of your images of yourself and illusions of life, regardless of how it affects your soul and others. When you continue to defend your resistance to and denial and avoidance of truth, you protect your codependency on your own images and illusions. When you protect the mask you manipulate yourself and others with, and hide from the truth of the energy of your soul's unconsciousness, you become obsessively controlling.

When you believe you are entitled to be appeased or to get what you want, you use your manipulation to attack, punish or attempt to harness others' unresolved emotions. You may exploit what you recognise of their soul's unconsciousness or the essence of your soul's consciousness. You may utilise others' kindness, compassion and willingness to care, to become something you exploit to gain a perceived advantage over them. However, this will expose you to the truth of your unresolved emotions, such as slyness, selfishness and manipulation.

When you believe you need to manipulate to fit in with, match or attempt to control others, you will inevitably reveal what is unresolved within yourself. Your fear of not fitting in or not being able to control others means you have to generate and project huge amounts of unconscious energy, which exposes the energy of your soul's unconsciousness. Until you resolve your own indifference to truth, regardless of how skilled and prolific your manipulation is, you will be exposed to your own unresolved emotions. If you remain deceptive, you will be unable to escape your compulsion to manipulate. Your indifference to truth is how you sustain the energy of your soul's unconsciousness; your manipulation is how you hide from what is exposed.

When you obsess about having control, you feel emotionally exhausted. You have to be indifferent to your truth, to be separated from your awareness of your soul and disassociated from feeling truth, which exhausts you, because you cannot feel your own true essence. Obsessing about control depletes your willingness to operate from your own core essences. The obsession for control causes you to exhaust every avenue of denying truth, by counteracting what you can feel and have observed, before you will accept the possibility of exploring truth. You can lie to yourself about your own reality and arrogantly ignore the effort it takes to protect yourself from feeling your soul consciousness' reaction to the unconscious energy within you and others. Remaining manipulative requires effort.

You can programme yourself to arrogantly ignore what you feel, by swamping your awareness of your soul's consciousness with unresolved emotions. You can condition yourself to generate deception, to concretise your soul denial which continues your oppression of your natural awareness of your soul's consciousness. You can constantly manipulate yourself to oppose your awareness of your soul truth, which raises the question: "Isn't this a lot of effort to avoid feeling the truth of yourself?"

You can fear your manipulation being exposed, because you fear the domino effect truth will have on your habitual control structures. Your manipulation works by projecting an emotionally charged energy entwined with deception and demands at anyone who you believe is obstructing your ability to control. You can emotionally react to both conscious and unconscious energy, ready to manipulate yourself to detach from your reality and align with any deception fuelled by your indifference to truth. You believe this is necessary to resist, deny and avoid the truth your soul's consciousness seeks to reveal to you. You can obsessively manipulate yourself to disapprove of any discovery of your unresolved emotions, fearing that it might interfere with your illusion of yourself. The more you fear addressing the truth of yourself and your behaviour, the more manipulative you become. When you manipulate yourself with your own judgement, you deny the reality of yourself, which inhibits your ability to be self-reflective.

You can manipulate yourself to disguise your awareness of the damage created by your judgement and oppressive exploitation of others. You deny you have a choice to be of truth and exploit your denial to justify your alliance to your deceptive victim mentality. You justify the righteousness of your judgement and indifference, by feeding off your own image of being a victim. You want your manipulation to maintain your illusion of control, and you want your belief of being a victim of life to justify your desire to be secure in your illusion of control. This leaves you codependent on your desire to control, and habitual compulsion to justify oppressing your awareness of truth and your soul's consciousness. You become your own formula for oppression; you indoctrinate yourself to succumb to the oppression you feel, to justify believing you are a victim, while denying that you are the instigator of the oppression.

Your willingness to be manipulative inhibits your ability to feel the truth of all aspects of your soul. Your desire to control, your denial and your oppression of your awareness of your soul's consciousness, override your ability to trust and be honest with truth. When you allow yourself to acknowledge your truth, you start to address the fears and insecurities fuelling your compulsion to be manipulative. As you begin to value being truthful, you enable yourself to trust in the process of exploring and accepting the truth of yourself, both consciousness and unconsciousness. This leads to your comprehension that you are a significant, unique, independent, individual soul of *True Source Divine Origin Consciousness*.

When you manipulate yourself with your own beliefs, you oppress your internal soul knowing. When your beliefs about truth are based in your desire for control, you will accept creating a version of truth that justifies your own deception. Versions of truth are lies. Truth has no versions, truth just is. Manipulation is the desire to create an alternate truth, which is a lie you want to pretend is not a lie. Alternate truths are designed, whereas truth just is. Lies can be designed by your desire for control and your willingness to use manipulation. You may not comprehend truth, or are naive about truth, but once you start manipulating truth, you are lying. Manipulation is the intent to devalue truth.

It is your denial of your own separation from your awareness of your soul and your disassociation from feeling truth, which allows you to continue the oppression of your awareness of your soul's consciousness and restricts your ability to challenge yourself. You do not challenge yourself, because of your fear of the unknown. You seek to control your fear of the unknown with your own version of truth. You can use your fear of the unknown to manipulate yourself to pretend to be oblivious to how abusive your own denial is. You manipulate yourself to ignore the truth of your awareness of your soul oppression, so you can continue to deny what you are inflicting on yourself.

When you attempt to suppress any realisation of truth that conflicts with your illusion of control, you begin to lie to yourself. To protect your desires and illusion of control, you anchor to the belief that your soul has no value or worth. You deny your existence as a soul and anchor to your barriers to truth, which you have created with the embedded beliefs and fears of your soul denial. You allow yourself to be consumed by your own resistance to and denial and avoidance of truth, in an attempt to secure your manipulation and illusion of control. When you are willing to be manipulative and exploitative, you deny the value of being a significant, unique, independent, individual soul.

When you maintain, engage and keep your attention on blame and your resentment of reality, you divert your awareness away from the opportunity to be honest about your own reality. Your honesty is the junction to your awareness of your rise and fall from grace.

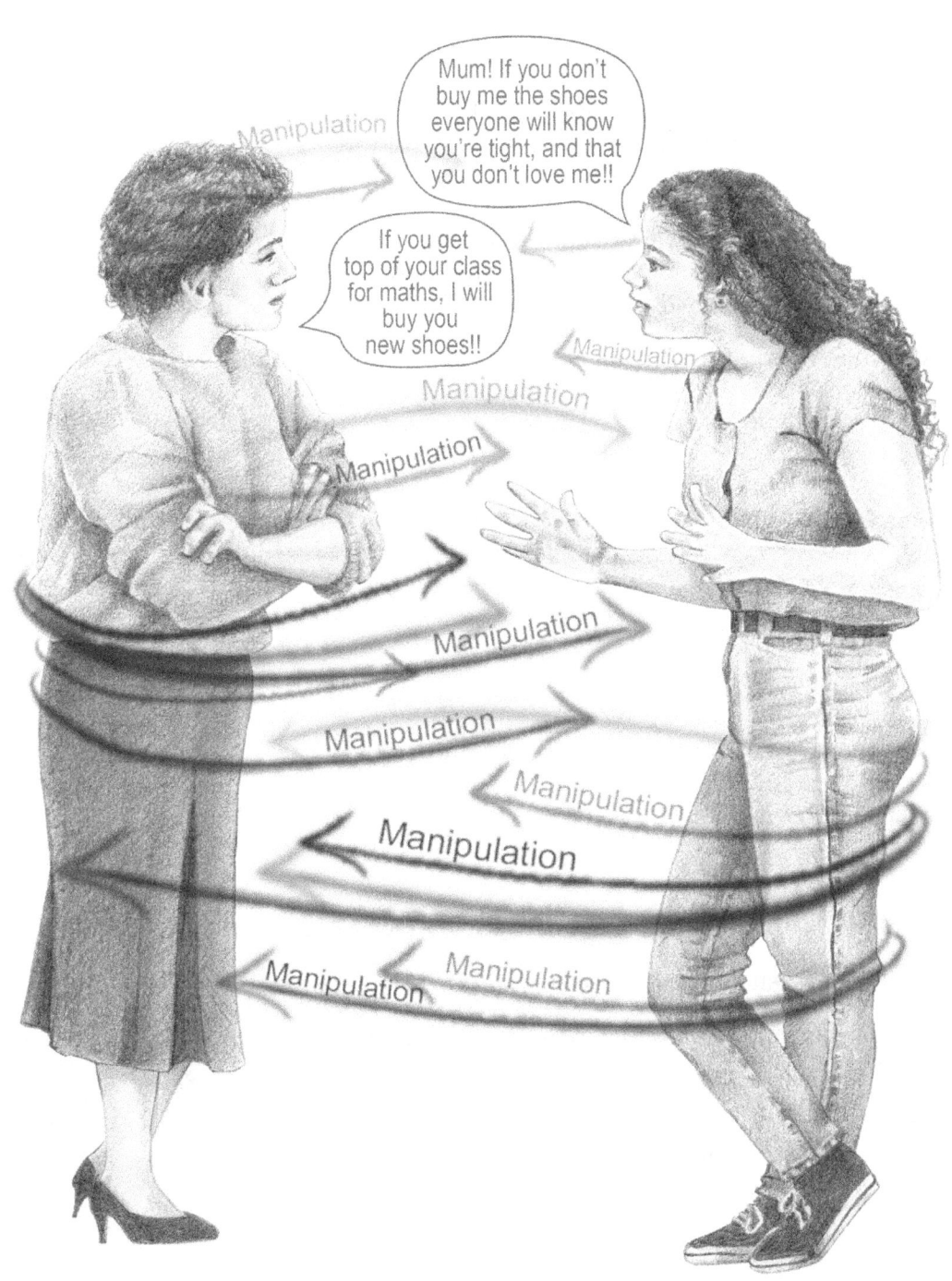

When we interact with manipulation, we attempt to exploit any insecurity we can find in each other, whilst seeking to pacify our own desire to control another and to control reality. Manipulation is the desire to intrude, seeking to create confusion. Manipulation is the result of the fear of not being in control. Manipulation incites either submission or a battle for control.

When you manipulate yourself to deny your own soul knowing, you are being dishonest. You use your dishonesty to fuel the ways you manipulate yourself, to obsessively blame others and sustain your resentment of reality, which incites an internal conflict between your protection of your soul denial and your awareness of your soul's consciousness.

Your reliance on blaming others becomes a filter that leaves you ignoring the ramifications of your unresolved emotions, and failing to seek the truth of your soul's consciousness. When you are willing to accept your own denial, you will ignore the consequences. You blame whatever or whomever you can to distract yourself from the truth of your own behaviour. This can leave you manipulating yourself to believe you are a victim to your history, your body, your emotions, relationships, others and even the truth of being a soul. You lie to yourself, to conceal your own manipulative abandonment of your awareness of truth.

You combine your negative beliefs with your thought process to create cycles of mind chatter, which you use to attack your awareness of your soul consciousness' ability to expose truth. You use your mind chatter to generate and create manipulative beliefs and behaviours to conceal the truth of your awareness of the entirety of your emotional, energetic and physical reality. You use your mind chatter to sustain your separation from your awareness of your soul and your disassociation from feeling truth, which enforces your codependency on your own negative beliefs. Your mind chatter becomes a repetitive attempt to silence your curiosity about truth and causes you to accept your own manipulation without challenge.

Manipulative mind chatter:

- "I know! Everyone should listen to me."
- "Who said I can't get my way."
- "I have to prove to myself that I am in control."
- "I know what is best."
- "I cannot forgive, until _____"

Question yourself on your own manipulation.

1. How do you attempt to manipulate reality?

2. When you are entrapped in your willingness to be manipulative what are you hiding from?

3. What do you emotionally use that feeds, fuels and develops your ability to be manipulative or manipulated?

Familiarity

Your protection of and alignment to your stagnation sustains your victim mentality. You use your victim mentality to justify repeating known emotional responses, which are devoid of the truth of your present moment, in an attempt to disregard the opportunities your present moment provides. Stagnation is repeating that which enables you to remain trapped in your own cyclic patterns of soul oppression. You can use your present moment as a stage, to upgrade your ability to deny the truth you feel. As you repeat the familiarity of your stagnation you believe you are validating your illusion of control. The familiarity of stagnation reinforces your expectations of your control. Stagnation creates a false illusion of being in control because it sets up expectations, which you then fulfill with the repetitiveness of your soul oppression.

The familiarity of how you emotionally feel, reassures you that your stagnation is unavoidable, which you then class as validation for your acceptance of stagnation. This leaves you believing, that if it is familiar, it is normal and justifiable. You rely on stagnation to justify the barriers to truth you use to govern your life. You use the familiarity of your barriers to truth to accept your stagnation without question or challenge. You do not challenge your understanding of life because you believe stagnation justifies your lazy approach to yourself, your relationships and life's opportunities.

The protection of your familiarity causes you to remain stagnant in your orchestration of life, and you create a treadmill for yourself to exist on.

Your Insight & Awareness Book | 265

When you cling to the distortions created by your carried victim energy and desire for control, you deny your relationship with your soul's consciousness. Your victim mentality and desire for control causes you to be over presumptuous with life. This leaves you smothering your life's opportunities with the stagnation of your unresolved emotions carried from past experiences. Your distorted view of your soul has you fighting against the truth of your soul's consciousness and devaluing your curiosity about yourself. You can filter life through your insecurities, whilst denying you are a significant, unique, independent, individual soul. You deny your soul is naturally of truth, to restrict the opportunities for being liberated from your own soul oppression. Liberation from your soul oppression is a process that occurs by acknowledging your consciousness and the truth of your own beliefs and behaviours. You may dogmatically fight against the natural flow of truth within you, and try to impose your desire to control truth on your awareness of your soul's consciousness; this is how you created your insecurity in the first place.

You can believe your ability to control will be more efficient, if you down play your relationship with your soul's consciousness. You become a victim to your arrogant dismissal of your own soul, and deny what you have been exposed to through your life experiences. When you create emotional wedges of concretised beliefs, you deflect the truth you can observe and feel. As you deflect your awareness of the opportunity to explore truth, you cling to your barriers to truth. This secures your denial, and then you wallow in the stagnation created from your fear of your own soul truth. When you fear taking responsibility, you fear the possibility of being liberated from your soul oppression. This means you remain trapped in the familiarity of your desire for control or the various mentalities derived from your carried victim energy.

When manipulation becomes your familiar, you stop recognising it as manipulation. This is the same for self-pity, martyrdom, contrived desperation, internal rage, your victim mentality and desire for control. You can corrupt the reality of being aware of your soul, by manipulating your own awareness of yourself with your desires and expectations. When you are willing to manipulate yourself by using the concept of being a soul for the purpose of enhancing your ability to control, you will use a corrupted ideal as a mandate to give yourself permission, to continually demand that your control be pacified. You want to be able to turn your awareness of your soul's consciousness on and off to suit your illusion of control. You want to use your soul's consciousness as a pawn in your manipulative desire to control truth. This is untenable as your 'I want' mentality will mean you manipulate yourself to be extremely arrogant, which eventually exposes the truth of your manipulation.

Your soul's consciousness cannot be manipulated to pacify your desire for control, and the soul concepts you deceptively create are manifestations of you being manipulative or allowing yourself to be manipulated. When your corrupted version of spirituality becomes your familiar, you avoid any truth that exposes your self-manipulation. Your soul's consciousness always remains pure, regardless of your beliefs, demands and manipulation.

You can become distressed and overwhelmed by the familiarity of your own confusion, which is often created by your self-manipulation. You become aware of your emotional, energetic and physical ability to repeat what you have done in the past, even though you expect a different outcome. You expect your control to be pacified, only to realise you have manipulated yourself to believe your own deception. This creates confusion within you as you struggle to admit your own deception and become complacent about how often you churn in your own unresolved emotional history. You are the creator of your own emotional incarceration, with the energy you produce, that oppresses your awareness of your soul. When this becomes your familiarity, you become reluctant to question what you are doing to yourself. You emotionally compel and coerce yourself to control your own oppression of your awareness of truth, believing there is security within this emotional encasement. When you incarcerate yourself in the familiarity of battling against your unresolved emotions, you consume yourself with your past, to resist, deny and avoid the freedom within your present moment.

When you control yourself with negativity to justify staying in your victim mentality, without challenging the negativity you use, you believe you have no choice in being a victim. This sustains the perpetuation of your false perception of yourself, and allows you to deny the reality of how you contribute to ramping up your negativity. When you deceptively control yourself to sustain your soul oppression, believing you have no other option, you abandon responsibility for your freedom of choice.

Your victim mentality can become your familiar and you can pride yourself on the severity of your victimhood. You can pride yourself on how victimised your victim mentality makes you emotionally feel. This can cause you to project an image at others to either hide the victim mentality, or to amplify the victim mentality to gain sympathy for yourself. You use your victim mentality to justify your own betrayal of yourself. You use your victim mentality to hide, justify and excuse how you manipulate your unresolved emotions. You revel in your unresolved emotions, so that you can revel in your belief of how remarkable you are to put up with all the emotional chaos in your life. You sustain, fuel and feed your unresolved emotions, whilst anchoring to the familiarity of your unwillingness to be honest about how you incite your own emotional reactions. You accept the familiarity of being a self-sufficient oppressor, opposing the dynamics of your present moment, so that you can continue to deny yourself the opportunity to explore the truth of your conscious and unconscious energy.

You manipulate yourself to believe you need to hold the attention of others to validate your ability to control, which causes you to react emotionally as a victim when you are unable to control the attention of others. You can become distraught at the lack of attention your victim mentality receives, which causes you to emotionally encase yourself even more with your own victim mentality. When others are not appeasing your control, you believe they are dismissive and lack understanding of your emotional plight, which can cause you to want to emotionally feel in control of them and their perception of you. You use your victim mentality to believe others and life should make you and your emotional plight their priority. You use your belief of being a victim as justification for your control and to validate and vindicate your emotional behaviour.

You can become addicted to the familiarity of creating drama. You create drama to observe the emotional effect your control has on life, yourself, others, relationships and physical situations. You incite your own unconscious energy, creating an emotional grenade to project at others and life situations, with the intent to control the emotional fallout, to prove you can control what you create. You can become addicted to the drama within the emotional

storms you create, even if it only affects your own thought process. You emotionally feed on your internal turmoil, to avoid being honest about the truth of yourself, impaling yourself on your own unresolved emotions, whilst you resist, deny and avoid feeling your soul's consciousness.

You can feed and fuel another's emotions to take on board someone else's drama and make it about you. This is because you want to be able to justify the emotional unrest you feel within yourself, without being honest about the reality of your own emotions. You use others' emotions and reactions to you, to conceal the familiarity of your own emotional chaos. Your denial of your emotions becomes chaotic and oppressive, which can lead to you hiding from the truth of being an evolving soul. You hide within the chaos you create.

When you control yourself to constantly make the same decisions, that cause you to suffer your own unresolved emotions, you condition yourself to tolerate your indifference to truth. The familiarity of your suffering causes you to be numb to the reality of creating your own emotions and emotional states. As you abandon your soul consciousness' insight, you repeat what you know hurts you. You choose to cycle in the stagnation of your denial, believing you are protecting yourself; however you will eventually discover that your denial only prolongs the familiarity of feeling oppressed. When you deny your freedom of choice, to continue in the familiarity of being unconscious to your soul's consciousness, you believe you are a victim but you are your own oppressor.

Familiarity builds complacency and you become unaware of your actual emotional, energetic and physical reality. This causes you to operate from your own expectations without acknowledging truth and the present moment dynamics of your experience. Familiarity has a way of corrupting you into believing you understand that which you no longer observe the truth of.

There is an old saying, "familiarity breeds contempt" and there is a truth to this. Often when you operate from expectations and judgement, you lose respect for those who you share a lot of time with. The familiarity can breed indifference towards the uniqueness of the present moment being shared, and towards the dynamics between individual souls. You can use your observations of what you judge as flaws and your awareness of their insecurities, fears and desires as justification for perceiving others through the filters of your judgement. Your judgement can become an established way of how you perceive another, which causes you to become complacent about the value and worth of those you share your life with, leaving you overlooking the significance of those closest to you. The familiarity of the presence of those you love and value can cause you to deny the importance of how you treat those you love and to become complacent about what you are expressing in your interactions, because you believe the other person will always be there. Familiarity can cause you to discount the importance of respecting what and who is familiar to you. Familiarity becomes an excuse to disregard the importance of empathy for those who experience your unconsciousness.

You combine your negative beliefs with your thought process to create cycles of mind chatter, which you use to attack your awareness of your soul consciousness' ability to expose truth. Your use your mind chatter to generate and create whatever is familiar that conceals the truth of your awareness of the entirety of your emotional, energetic and physical reality. You use your mind chatter to sustain your separation from your awareness of your soul and your disassociation from feeling truth, which enforces your codependency on your own negative beliefs. Your mind chatter becomes a repetitive attempt to silence your curiosity about truth and causes you to accept what is familiar without challenge.

Familiar mind chatter:

- "This always happens to me."
- "Same shit different day."
- "Here we go again."
- "Same old, same old."
- "You make your own bed; you've got to lie in it."
- "I was treated like garbage and always will be."
- "Suffering is what life is about, you shouldn't expect anything else."

Question yourself on what is familiar to you.

1. How do you attempt to control reality to conform to your familiarity?

2. When you are entrapped in your familiarity what are you hiding from?

3. What do you emotionally use that feeds, fuels and develops your ability to remain stagnant within what is familiar to you?

Contrived desperation

There are desperate situations in life but if you use your desperation to deny reality, you become your own worst enemy. This will immerse you in the despair of not being able to control and will cloud your perception of the options available to you. If you wallow in the desperation of a situation, you become entrapped in despair, which inhibits your honesty and disables your ability to self-protect. Desperate situations have you consumed with fear but it is the fear which is calling for you to be alert and present in your reality. If you choose to withdraw from acknowledging your fear and being aware of yourself in your desperate situation, you limit and restrict your natural ingenuity. Your natural ingenuity is enhanced by your willingness to trust yourself to be present in the reality of your life.

Desperation can be an opportunity to truly evaluate what you are doing to yourself, to understand the motives behind the choices you are making. It is a time to be extremely open to acknowledging the entirety of your own awareness of reality.

When you create a façade of being desperate to resolve your unresolved emotions, only to conceal the truth of wanting to be able to manage your control better, you will fool yourself with your own deception. You may choose to continue your oppressive control structures while you forge a false pretense of wanting resolution and evolution, as an attempt to excuse your own deception. When you excuse your own deception with the belief of being unable to control or resolve your emotions, you sustain the desperation you internally feel.

Your soul's consciousness seeks to resolve your control and your deceptive manipulation over your awareness of life. You can use your judgement of your life experiences, to validate, enhance and incite your willingness to be unconscious to your awareness of truth. Your willingness to be complacent about yourself actually exposes how you reinforce your unresolved emotions, to resist, deny and avoid your own reality. Your attempts to validate, excuse or deny your own unresolved emotions expose truth to you, and if you decide to deprive yourself of grace, you will miss the opportunity to use your honesty to explore the truth of your unconsciousness. Grace enables self-forgiveness. Your unwillingness to operate with grace causes you to desperately fight against your original intention for resolution and evolution with misconceptions and constructed lies. The desire to protect misconceptions and constructed lies has you desperately wanting to control your own perception of yourself, regardless of the ramifications.

You use your carried victim energy to attempt to protect your negativity and oppressive patterns, beliefs and emotional cycles. You desperately want to control the internal stagnation, so you can maintain your illusory control. You can pretend to want change and resolution but you stalemate yourself with your desire to control life, yourself, others, relationships and truth. This may leave you wallowing in the emotions, whilst being unwilling to make decisions or take action. You can also become someone who seeks to pull others onto your merry-go-round of soul oppression, getting them involved or expecting them to take responsibility for you. You may become an energetic vampire, depleting others of their energy as you whine, whilst having no intent to change your situation. This sustains stagnation.

The unresolved emotions you refuse to acknowledge become your soul oppressive energy, which deprives you of the opportunity to use your honesty to explore truth.

When you fear losing control of the stagnation, created by your lack of self-responsibility, you can become an accomplice to misconceptions and a constructor of lies. You can fear being exposed to how you contribute and sustain your own desperation, avoiding accountability. When you believe you are a victim of life, your emotions and others' emotions, you create a convenient loophole for yourself to deny responsibility for your own choices. Your stagnation is the result of your choice to deny your natural ability to resolve and evolve your unresolved emotions. However, for this to occur you need to be truthfully honest with yourself, because you are the interface of both your conscious and unconscious energy.

When you desperately cling to your ability to lie to yourself, believing your control can fix your unresolved emotions, you actually inhibit the resolution of your unresolved emotions. When you realise your control has failed your expectations, you can easily spiral into a state of desperation, which can entrap you in your fear of feeling. This causes you to want to be numb to your reality and to wallow in all that you judge as hopeless, which can have you pining for control of your reality, whilst torturing yourself with your awareness of the inefficiency of your control. Your desire to control is created by denying the importance of your soul, and sustained in a desperate attempt to deny truth.

When you prefer to battle reality seeking control of your existence, instead of accepting who you are, you become insipid towards the truth of your soul and recoil from the truth you naturally feel. This leaves you opposing your ability to feel the truth of your soul, as you fight for supremacy over the exposure of truth. When you desperately want to create balance between your different energies, you often disregard the potential for resolution. You may want to be the controller of peace within yourself while you deny the reality of your life, yourself, others, relationships and truth. This means you assess peace as the ability to control the external world to suit, pacify and gratify your unresolved emotions, because you do not want your emotions to disturb your illusion of control. You internally know peace comes from you accepting reality and choosing to harmonise with truth. To be at peace and in harmony with truth, you have to trust being an evolving soul on a journey.

When you arrogantly ignore your original intention for resolution, you battle your own awareness of yourself, as you attempt to deny your life is an opportunity to resolve your unresolved emotions. You use your unresolved emotions to create deceptive distractions from the reality of your soul journey. When you focus on attempting to learn how to control your emotions better, while attempting to conceal your deception with a façade of good intentions, you actually have no real intention to resolve and evolve. When you deny you are experiencing a soul journey with the original intention to resolve and evolve all aspects of yourself that are separated and disassociated from truth, you become immune and isolated from your origins. When you commit to being truthful, you become willing to look for and find whatever you are constructing that gets in your way of being unified with truth, which is a conscious choice to honour your original intention.

Your denial leaves you desperately seeking to lock yourself into the belief that you need to regain what you believe you have lost, even if you cannot identify what it is you have lost. You may believe you cannot resolve or be free of your past without the ability to alter the outcome of your past. You know you cannot go back and change history, but you can still stubbornly think that is what needs to happen, before you can commit to the process of resolving and evolving your unresolved emotions. When you use this self-defeatist belief to fight freedom, you desperately cling to your belief of what should have happened, instead of accepting what has happened. This incites your judgement, which creates a continuous cycle of negative thoughts. This is a way of tormenting and torturing yourself about your inability to have ultimate control at all times. You become stagnant within your regret for not being truthful with yourself and dealing with your emotions as they happen. You can also deny yourself the opportunity to use hindsight as a tool for resolution. Being truthful about your own hindsight allows you to accept the reality of the collective unconsciousness of mankind and the unconsciousness of the individuals from whom you expected more honesty, including yourself.

You can desperately cling to the notion of your own naivety, so you can justify your refusal to take self-responsibility for the repetitive patterns, that you use to distance yourself from the truth of your reality and from what influences your decision making. You may want to be oblivious to the emotional denial you use, to support the façade that conceals the truth of how you live life. You can use your thought process to swamp yourself with your emotional history, plans to control your future and options, while ignoring the reality of your present moment and what you have already set in play to occur. When you control yourself to believe you are a victim to life, you ignore your own refusal, to be present and honest with the cause and effect of your own denial.

You can recklessly annihilate or oppose your awareness of your soul consciousness' ability to expose you to the truth of your present moment. You can be consistently indifferent to the ramifications created by annihilating your awareness. You distrust anything that you fear or believe is beyond your ability to suppress, repress and oppress. When you choose to defy your own awareness of truth, you attempt to reject your present moment to create the demise of your awareness. This can cause you to swamp yourself with past emotions or fears for the future. You can willfully continue your known patterns of non-caring and self-rejection, in an attempt to prove, that there is substance to your belief that you are insignificant. You then use your beliefs of insignificance to sustain the pain you carry from your past, to override the importance of your present moment, and to expect further disappointment in your future. This becomes a trap that sustains your undercurrent of contrived desperation.

When you use varying degrees of denial, to generate negativity within yourself, you deny how much you rely on negativity and your victim mentality to control your opposition to being honest about your present moment. This leaves you hiding within your own denial, protecting the insidious nature of your opposition to exposing your soul truth. You fight your own awareness of truth, to sustain the illusion that stagnating yourself and protecting what is familiar means, if you know what to expect you will be in control. However, you control yourself with your stagnation. You generate thoughts to oppose your ability to naturally accept and be at ease with life.

When you allow your desire for control to fragment the truth that you cannot hide or ignore, you selectively acknowledge what you believe suits your agenda and omit the importance of the rest. Fragment means to break into smaller pieces, which makes it difficult to acknowledge something in its entirety. It also means to section off or break apart, which leaves you with an obscured perception of the entirety. When you do this to truth, it is no longer the whole truth. You fight your awareness of reality by fragmentising the truth.

When you want to justify your arrogant emotional deception and judgement, you only anchor to parts of the fragmented truth that suit your illusion of control. You want to ignore what does not suit your illusion of control and become obsessed with your willingness to fragment truth, hiding from your ability to acknowledge the entirety of your reality. When you willingly oppose the truth of your control, you deny wasting the opportunity your life is exposing to you, and oppose your opportunity to acknowledge the truth of your life experiences.

When you realise the ramifications of your desire to control, but are unwilling to accept responsibility for what you have created, you perceive yourself as a victim to your compulsion to control, whilst ignoring the reality of your opportunity for resolution. Your refusal to take any responsibility for yourself causes you to create charades and facades to perform, which are contradictory to the truth of your soul, so that you can continue denying yourself the opportunity to embrace the presence of your soul's consciousness. Your soul's consciousness is always present. If you have conditioned yourself to overshadow what you feel with your desire to control, you diffuse your insight about, or from, your soul's consciousness. When you attempt to hide from the truth of your soul's consciousness, within the deception of the facades you create, you desperately want your facades to hide your desire for control and victim mentality, to enable your resistance to and denial and avoidance of truth, to continue.

You desperately utilise your control structures within your victim mentality, to oppose the truth you feel, which has you ricocheting within different aspects of your carried victim energy such as:

- Self-pity
- Martyrdom
- Internal rage
- Manipulation
- Familiarity
- Contrived desperation

You use the control structures within these energies to deny the truth of your desire to control and to conceal your inability to trust yourself within the truth of your reality. You abandon the simplicity of the truth being exposed to you, with your ability to complicate what you know of your truth.

You can desperately try to override your awareness of your soul consciousness' natural energy with your control energy. When you are unwilling to accept your reality, you want to be able to control your barriers to truth, to inhibit your consciousness' ability to reveal the way you attempt to control life. You want to choose what you accept as truth and project your control over the truth being exposed to you by your soul's consciousness. Your spirituality can become an arena you desperately want control over, which deprives you of unifying with your soul's consciousness.

You may use your spiritual beliefs to fight your awareness of truth, rather than being honest and present with the truth of your life experiences. This becomes an attempt to exist within an image of consciousness while embattling your soul consciousness' aspiration to resolve your emotional, energetic and physical anchors to your unresolved emotions. When you deceptively want to control your soul consciousness' ability to expose truth to you, in the belief that your denial of reality will serve you better, you lose awareness of the authenticity of your soul. You may desperately want to control the exposure of truth to ensure the protection of your image of consciousness. As you develop an image of consciousness, you create façades. Façades are the willingness to emulate consciousness whilst protecting your soul denial and desire to control. Your desperation to secure your illusory control of your spirituality, encases you in your own willingness to be deceptive and you become a victim to your own deception entwined with your beliefs of spirituality.

When you choose to remain immersed in your victim mentality to avoid your own truth and the potential for your resolution and evolution, you trap yourself in the complexity of your soul's unconsciousness, ignoring the options truth provides. You fear being insecure, vulnerable and hurt, but you are already existing with the hurt, insecurity and vulnerability caused by your oppression of your soul. You can control yourself to be a victim to your own stagnation, by choosing to waste the opportunity truth presents, in an attempt to protect your illusion of control.

You emotionally feel like a victim when your control implodes and reveals the truth of your denial. Your soul's consciousness wants your control to implode, to expose the truth of your denial and control. However, if you want to use this implosion as your excuse to encase yourself with victim mentality, you become the oppressor of an opportunity to discover the truth

RIGHT: *When you lose awareness of the truth of your present moment you smother yourself in a blanket of desperation.*

of your denial and control. As you anchor to the entrapment of your victim mentality, you restart and sustain your cycles of denying truth. When you deny truth, you use your victim mentality to control your perception of reality. This inhibits you from comprehending the truth of yourself.

You combine your negative beliefs with your thought process to create cycles of mind chatter, which you use to attack your awareness of your soul consciousness' ability to expose truth. You use your mind chatter to generate and create contrived desperation, or to sustain situations of desperation, to conceal the truth of your awareness of the entirety of your emotional, energetic and physical reality. You use your mind chatter to sustain your separation from your awareness of your soul and your disassociation from feeling truth, which enforces your codependency on your own negative beliefs. Your mind chatter becomes a repetitive attempt to silence your curiosity about truth and causes you to accept your desperation without challenge.

Desperation mind chatter:

- "I can't resolve anything about myself until my history is fixed."
- "Nobody loves me."
- "No one understands or realises how much I have endured."
- "I am my pain; it is who I am."
- "If they don't think I am worth anything, why should I bother?"
- "I don't care anymore."
- "I will not release myself from my history, until they acknowledge what they did."

Question yourself on your desperation.

1. How do you attempt to control reality with your desperation?
2. When you are entrapped in your desperation what are you hiding from?
3. What do you emotionally use that feeds, fuels and develops your desperation?

Denial of your carried victim energy

Your acceptance of being a significant, unique, independent, individual soul of *True Source Divine Origin Consciousness*, enables you to take responsibility for the evolution of your soul. Your ability to trust and utilise your freedom of choice creates the space to apply honesty to yourself, and exposes the truth of your soul journey as an opportunity to resolve and evolve all unresolved emotions. Unresolved emotions produce unconscious energy that stagnates your evolution. Your carried victim energy perpetuates the stagnation of your evolution and enables you to deny yourself the opportunity to explore the potential of your soul journey. You use your carried victim energy to sustain the continuation of your denial of responsibility and accountability for your soul.

Your acceptance of yourself as a soul, enables you to trust the truth of your feelings as communication from the conscious part of yourself. You are the interface between your consciousness and unconsciousness. You are of both conscious and unconscious energy. Your soul's consciousness aspires for you to:

- Experience the truth of your soul journey as a unified soul
- Resolve and evolve beyond your fear of truth
- Unify all aspects of your soul to origin truth
- Live resonating with the natural essences of your soul

You use your victim mentality to oppose all of these possibilities, which means you control your evolution to be stagnant.

You use the different mentalities derived from your carried victim energy to attack your natural core essences. This means you inhibit your ability to naturally feel your own unconditional love for yourself. Core essences are unique strands of conscious energy that contribute to the purity of who you are. They are the unique strands of conscious energy within unconditional love. Core essences are natural energy that emanate from your soul's consciousness:

- *Acceptance*
- *Appreciation*
- *Care*
- *Clarity*
- *Compassion*
- *Dynamism*
- *Freedom*
- *Grace*
- *Harmony*
- *Honesty*
- *Hope*
- *Independence*
- *Individuality*
- *Integrity*
- *Joy*
- *Kindness*
- *Loyalty*
- *Patience*
- *Peace*
- *Purity*
- *Serenity*
- *Trust*
- *Truthfulness*
- *Uniqueness*

You use your victim mentality to annihilate the significance of acknowledging and feeling your own worth as an evolving soul and the natural value of experiencing the truth of your soul journey with integrity and respect for the possibilities of resolution and evolution. Your carried victim energy contaminates your awareness of the pureness of your soul's consciousness, and disharmonises you from your awareness of and resonance with truth. By acknowledging the reality of your victim mentality, you create the space for your awareness of truth to assist you in resolving your compulsion to keep using your carried victim energy to oppress the truth of your soul.

You are a naturally significant, unique, independent, individual soul of *True Source Divine Origin Consciousness* and have the divine right to choose to be at peace with who you are. This is a choice that only you can make; *True Source Divine Origin Consciousness* knows and can feel the truth of your soul, you are the one who has forgotten your origins. Your carried victim energy exposes your denial of the truth of your soul. Your carried victim energy oppresses your awareness of your own origins of truth.

When you recognise and accept yourself as a soul, you are giving yourself permission to trust yourself enough to be honest about your reality. Your trust in your soul's consciousness enables you to be accountable to the truth you are aware of, and the lessons you reveal to yourself when you care enough to be truly honest. By caring for yourself as a soul and being totally honest about the energy you are projecting at yourself, you create the opportunity to resolve your patterns of self-rejection and alignment to your own and mankind's soul denial energy.

Your acceptance of yourself as a soul enables you to resolve being at war with yourself. When you realise you are being an adversary against truth, it is your honesty that provides you with the opportunity to resolve what you are using to stagnate your evolution. Your carried victim energy inhibits you from:

- Acknowledging the truth of your soul
- Learning from your struggles
- Acknowledging your own soul denial
- Owning the truth of the obstacles and problems that you have created with your own self-rejection

This is how you inhibit yourself from acknowledging your truth, feeling your soul and accepting your awareness of the presence of *True Source Divine Origin Consciousness*.

When you realise you are a volunteer and not a victim to the energetics of the mass energy of mankind or your own unconsciousness, you become open to acknowledging the reality that there is an opportunity to resolve and evolve. While you are codependent on using the unresolved emotions within your soul's unconsciousness, you justify your own soul abuse and entrap yourself in carried victim energy. Your lack of honesty creates internal blocks, obstacles, distractions and barriers to exploring your soul truth, which entraps you in constantly controlling yourself with and to your unresolved emotions. When you internalise the different fragmented aspects of being a victim and store the emotional energy within your soul's unconsciousness, you oppress the truth of your soul. What you store you use to oppress your ability to trust truth.

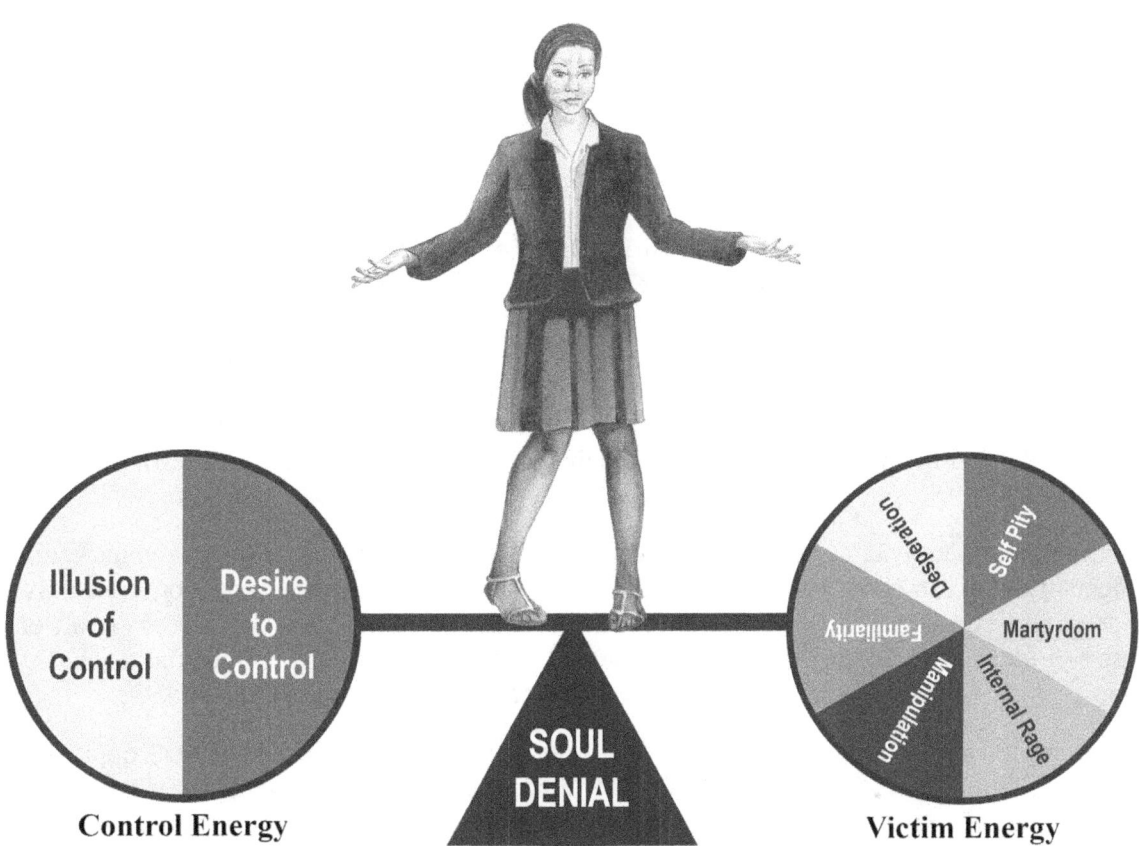

Your willingness to deny the truth of your soul and deny your awareness of reality causes you to see-saw within your control and victim energy. You create expectations with your perception of the two major components of your control energy, which are your desire to be in control of reality and your illusion that you are in control of reality. These expectations cause you to deny your awareness of reality and to fixate on your own limited perception of yourself.

When your control fails to meet your expectations, you implode within the different facets of your carried victim energy. These different facets of carried victim energy can become the way you justify your emotional reaction to control failure and you use the energy to attempt to gain an illusory control of your perception of yourself and reality. This sustains your willingness to be devoid of your awareness of the entirety of your own energy and reality. Your soul oppression is actually sustained by the different facets of your victim and control energy.

When you deny what you are doing to yourself, you fail to acknowledge the truth of your victim or control energy. This can cause you to become stagnant in an energetic limbo, compulsively protecting your own denial.

When you trust that your experiences within your soul journey reveal to you what you need to acknowledge, you create the opportunity to decide that your resolution and evolution is important to you.

You can externally project the fragmented aspects of being a victim, such as self-pity, martyrdom, internal rage, manipulation, familiarity and contrived desperation, in an attempt to control your images, illusions and controlled identities. You may believe you are a victim but you deny you are a victim to your own belief of being a victim. Your denial and unwillingness to be completely honest with yourself about your victim mentality, causes you to carry the emotions that will feed, fuel and enhance your ability to stagnate your evolution. You create and secure the stagnation of your evolution, to hide from the truth of being a soul. However, it is the resolution of your stagnation that evolves your soul. Your truthful honesty with yourself, about yourself, creates both resolution and evolution.

When you protect your carried victim energy, you become addicted to justifying your victim mentality. You can control yourself with forced ignorance, to deny your soul consciousness' attempts to expose you to the potential of resolution and evolution. When you become aware of your freedom of choice and understand your soul truth, you unify to your potential resolution and evolution. It is your ongoing truthfulness that actualises your potential to resolve.

Your carried victim energy is an aspect of your soul's unconsciousness, which oppresses your awareness of truth with a framework of emotional patterns. This interferes with your natural ability to trust and understand your freedom of choice and to trust the process of resolution and evolution. Your resolution and evolution is the process of trusting your awareness of your own rise and fall from grace exposing the truth of your unresolved emotions. This allows you to acknowledge and accept the truth of your emotions, which creates the opportunity to resolve the energy of your soul's unconsciousness.

You amalgamate your beliefs of being a victim with your desire for control, which inhibits your honesty and temporarily obliterates your ability to acknowledge the truth of what you need to challenge to resolve. When you immerse yourself in your unresolved emotions, you reinforce your perception of being a victim. You choose to emotionally carry your own pain, which you use to create barriers towards feeling your soul truth. Your carried victim energy camouflages the truth of your soul knowing and you use your carried victim energy to disguise the emotional pain you feel for betraying your awareness of truth. Your abandonment of your awareness of truth creates emotional pain within you, which you attempt to deny. You attempt to deny your choice to abandon truth and deny the pain you have caused yourself. You use your carried victim energy to abandon feeling the original pain caused by separating and disassociating from your awareness of your own soul.

You feel the pain of abandoning your awareness of your soul and seek to control the pain with your victim mentality, which sustains the many facets of your carried victim energy. When you give purpose to the pain you feel, you use the pain to justify your abandonment of your awareness of truth.

Your emotional pain:

- Becomes familiar and you condition yourself to utilise the energy to create an illusion of control.
- Is the source of your own manipulation against acknowledging the truth of how you feel. You manipulate yourself to intercept your feelings with emotions, and this is how you block your ability to resolve.
- Has you wallowing in self-pity, because you refuse to acknowledge the truth of your soul.
- Has you martyring yourself to the misconceptions and lies you tell yourself.
- Has you enraged if you cannot suppress and repress the effect the carried pain has on your existence.
- Has you desperate to control the chaos you create for yourself, because of your abandonment of your awareness of truth.

You are free to resolve your emotional pain because truth never abandons you, however your illusion of and desire for control has you caught in the misconceptions created by your abandonment of your own awareness of truth. You fight this truth with your desire to control your victim mentality instead of resolving your carried victim energy. You fight to conceal the truth of your own natural significance, uniqueness, independence and individuality from yourself. When you devalue yourself, you conceal your awareness that it is you who can free yourself from the pain you carry. Your internal pain naturally resolves as you accept the truth of being a significant soul of truth and a significant soul to truth.

Question yourself:

1. What do you believe you are a victim to?
2. Can you identify your carried victim energy?
3. Do you know why you refuse to resolve your victim mentality?
4. Do you struggle to be honest about your victim mentality?
5. How do you oppress your awareness of your soul's consciousness with a victim mentality?
6. How do you oppress your awareness of your soul's unconsciousness with a victim mentality?
7. How do you hide from the truth being exposed?
8. Can you objectively observe the entirety and complexities of your carried victim energy and mentalities?

Chapter Twenty-Four

Belief of not being good enough

Your belief of not being good enough develops from your willingness to deny your significance, uniqueness, independence and individuality. This causes you to anchor to the energy of your soul's unconsciousness, whilst being willing to deny your awareness of your soul's consciousness. Your belief of not being good enough is your acceptance of your own soul denial, and enables you to energetically entangle, engage and connect with any unconscious energy, you believe will secure and prove your belief of not being good enough. This causes you to become a reverberation within the energetic collectives of the mass energy of mankind, reverberating with the energy that correlates with the unresolved emotions you use to secure and protect your belief of not being good enough.

Your not good enough belief, is a convergence of a multitude of negative beliefs that morph into a belief of not being good enough. You isolate yourself from your awareness of your soul's consciousness with your embedded belief of not being good enough. As a result of you devaluing yourself, you have learnt to oppose the flow of conscious energy within you. You have programmed, conditioned and indoctrinated yourself to ignore and abandon your soul consciousness' insight, and the support and unconditional love of *True Source Divine Origin Consciousness*. When you protect your belief of not being good enough, you isolate yourself from your awareness of your soul's consciousness and fight your natural significance to truth.

You can use your belief of not being good enough to consistently distort and diffuse your awareness of being a soul. This leaves you creating emotional, energetic and physical barriers to the truth of your soul and the reality of what you are feeling. When you devalue or obliterate feeling truth with your belief of not being good enough, you control yourself to deny your own separation from your awareness of your soul and your disassociation from feeling truth. This causes you to omit from your awareness all the wonderful aspects of yourself and to focus on what you judge as flawed.

When you believe you are not good enough, you are failing to recognise yourself as a significant, unique, independent, individual soul, and instead you filter your awareness of yourself through your insecurities. You use your belief of not being good enough, to hide within your misconception of not being significant enough to be a soul of truth. Insignificance is a mankind judgement which is in opposition to the equality of all souls. You use your belief of not being good enough to devalue the significance of your independence. You accept your independence when you choose to experience life freely as a soul, uninhibited by others' judgement and opposition to truth.

To experience the purity of your independence, you need to resolve your fear of judgement and your willingness to be your own source of harsh judgement. When you override the

Your belief of not being good enough produces many thoughts and misconceptions, which ignite your perpetuation of unconscious energy. These thoughts become negative beliefs that cloud your perception of yourself and deprive you of feeling the truth of your natural significance, uniqueness, independence and individuality. This causes you to churn in the self-perpetuation of your own indifference towards yourself.

truth of being an independent soul with judgement, and create beliefs of being unworthy, you inhibit your awareness of your conscious energy. When you acknowledge your natural significance you give yourself the freedom to disentangle, disengage and disconnect from your own harsh self-judgement. This enables you to acknowledge and value your own significance, and appreciate the opportunity to choose to accept your resonance with truth. Acknowledging your significance stems from trusting your own uniqueness, independence, individuality and the importance of your soul journey. You strongly feel your significance when you trust your synchronicity with truth.

You fight your natural resonance with truth, in an attempt to control the unconscious energy you feel and embody. You abandon your awareness of truth to attempt to fit in with or defend yourself against judgement, which makes you uncomfortable about the truth of who you are. You abandon your awareness of truth in an attempt to fight or appease judgement, which is often generated by yourself. Your inability to feel secure when you fight or appease judgement has you believing you are 'not good enough' to be at ease with the truth of yourself. Your fear of not being able to control judgement causes you to become judgemental of yourself, and willing to be indifferent to your own significance, uniqueness, independence and individuality. This is the basis of your insecurity and you use this insecurity as a foundation for your misconceptions about yourself, especially if you hold to the belief that you are insignificant.

Your belief of not being good enough is a product of your negative judgement of yourself. You can harshly judge your uniqueness, and natural value, worth and significance. You may never question how you use your perception of others' judgement, to uphold your ability to inflict judgement on yourself, which enables your belief of not being good enough to concretise your insecurities. When you create a foundation of beliefs you use as a criteria to judge yourself and others on, do you acknowledge the oppressive nature of the criteria you use?

You can use your self-judgement to oppose feeling truth and oppress your ability to feel the compassion and unconditional love within truth and within yourself. You judge truth with the same ferocity you judge yourself and others, which creates misconceptions that govern how you feel about yourself. When you use your misconceptions to judge your reality, you begin to fear the exposure of your judgement as fraudulent. Truth does not judge you. Your soul's consciousness is compassionate towards the choices you make and regardless of the ramifications of your choices, you always expose truth to yourself. This could be the truth of your consciousness or unconsciousness, but either way, there is always an opportunity to discover the truth of your own energy. When you negatively judge yourself, you oppress your awareness of your resonance with your soul's consciousness and your significance to the truth of your reality and to *True Source Divine Origin Consciousness*.

When you fear being honest about your judgement of yourself, you oppress your soul consciousness' ability to reveal your unconscious energy, and inhibit your ability to evolve beyond being governed by judgement or the fear of being judged. Your fear of judgement causes you to fear freedom from your own soul oppression, which means you become fearful of the reality of being a significant, unique, independent, individual soul of *True Source Divine Origin Consciousness*. You can fear being aware of truth. You fear being exposed to truth, which causes you to anchor to your soul's unconsciousness, and to abandon your awareness of your soul's consciousness and the entirety of the truth of your present experience. *True Source Divine Origin Consciousness* is within all truth, and has never abandoned you, and there is nothing that could be exposed to truth, that truth is not already fully aware of. Your soul's consciousness is of *True Source Divine Origin Consciousness*, and is fully aware of the complexities of your soul's unconsciousness. You are of truth. Your belief of not being good enough is an attempt to deny the truth of being of *True Source Divine Origin Consciousness*.

Your belief of not being good enough has you immersed in the negativity of the unresolved emotions within your soul's unconsciousness. You can condition yourself to desensitise from the reality of your emotions. You can feel what your unresolved emotions do to yourself, others and your awareness of truth, but choose to override what you feel with indifference. When you allow yourself to be indifferent to the emotional carnage you are creating within yourself and for others, you are choosing to perpetuate your own soul oppression. However, regardless of the slyness of your indifference, you cannot escape feeling or eventually being confronted with the ramifications of your unresolved emotions. You may try to control your emotional reality, however this only results in you becoming insecure about your ability to control. The insecurity created by your desire to control, causes you to become consumed by your unresolved emotions as you fight your awareness of yourself and attempt to control reality. You can use your belief of not being good enough, to isolate yourself from your awareness of your soul consciousness' ability to expose you to the reality of your emotions and the carnage you create. The exposure of your emotional reality creates the opportunities for your resolution and evolution. When you are dishonest with yourself about your own awareness, you oppose the potential and possibility of your resolution and evolution. When you use your belief of not being good enough to isolate yourself from your awareness of your soul's consciousness, you become the slyness of your indifference.

Your inability to control reality, yourself and others, has you using the slyness of your indifference, to conceal your awareness of your emotional, energetic and physical reality. When you believe you will be able to construct reality to conform to your beliefs of how it should be, you become arrogant in your interaction with others and life. Your illusory control over others and life is unsustainable, which causes you to judge yourself as 'not good enough'. You can become consumed with incessantly berating yourself with judgement about your control.

Your belief of not being good enough suspends you stagnant within your beliefs of unworthiness and insignificance, but what are you judging yourself to be unworthy and insignificant for and to? If your answer is truth, you do not understand truth.

When you have the misconception, that pacifying your desire to control can band-aid the unresolved emotions created by your beliefs of unworthiness and insignificance, you become obsessed with wanting to see whom and what your control can affect. This causes you to try to protect your own illusion of control and to abandon your awareness of your soul consciousness' intention to resolve your desire for control. When you protect your unresolved emotions, you create an emotional merry-go-round which is fueled by your attempts to suppress what you refuse to resolve.

When you use your indifference to truth to overshadow your original intention to resolve your unresolved emotions, you lose your willingness to be honest and present in the truth of your life experiences. As you become addicted to the construction of images and illusions, you lose your sense of self. When you are indifferent to truth, you believe you can hide the reality of your emotions with your control structures, but this just separates you further from your awareness of your soul and causes you to feel oppressed. When you create or attempt to control images and illusions of yourself to hide your unresolved emotions, you may for a time be able to gloss over them, but your reactions to your life experiences keep revealing them to you. You overshadow your unresolved emotions with indifference, but you cannot escape carrying them, until you honestly acknowledge the truth of them. Resolution requires you to be honest with yourself and to objectively observe the truth of both your conscious and unconscious energy. This means you have to become responsible for what you believe and for the choices you make.

Your indifference to truth protects your images and illusions but reality causes you to experience image and illusion failure. Your image and illusion failures expose you to the truth of your emotions and create opportunities for you to resolve by being honest. When your images and illusions fail, your beliefs of not being good enough are how you counteract the reality of the truth exposed.

You fear that your images will be judged by others, which has you constantly judging your own performance of your images, as you seek to perfect your control over how others perceive you. This is emotionally exhausting and creates anxiety, fears and insecurities. If your images are not validated by those whom you want to control to perceive you in a certain way, you berate and cruel yourself with your own belief of not being good enough. This is how you assassinate your ability to be present within your own reality, and deprive yourself of feeling joyful about your life. When you fight your awareness of reality to secure an image of yourself, you deny yourself the opportunity to be present within the uniqueness of your experience. When you control yourself to miss what is being exposed, because you are consumed with your desire to control your image, you seek to replace reality with constructed lies and self-manipulation. When you endeavour to replace the truth of your reality with performed images, you become lost in your own denial of reality, which leaves you indifferent to truth.

Unfortunately, you can control yourself to miss the truth, that your belief of not being good enough, is a lie. You fear others will notice that you cannot control your own image and you panic that they will see the truth of your unresolved emotions. This can cause you to become obsessively controlling over the construction of your images and illusions. You can be extremely indifferent to your own emotions unless they are exposed and acknowledged by others, which allows you to be complacent about how you feel and how you are affecting others. When you experience someone else verbally acknowledging your unresolved emotions, you can emotionally feel vulnerable and obsess about what you believe their judgement of you may or may not be. This can cause you to become consumed with the

RIGHT: *The stagnation, created by your embedded belief of not being good enough, has you wallowing in your unresolved emotions, immersed in the thought processes that perpetuate your belief of not being good enough.*

desire to ascertain what another thinks of you, often inciting yourself to stew in your own self-judgement. When you fixate on what others may potentially observe about you or the events that have exposed your unresolved emotions, you become disappointed that you are unable to control the sustainability of your image, which can cause you to wallow in your belief of not being good enough.

Wallowing in your belief of not being good enough is a way of controlling yourself to remain fallen in your unconsciousness and is your way of opposing the natural process of your rise and fall from grace. You need to experience your fall from grace, which is you disassociating from feeling truth and immersing yourself in the unresolved emotions of your soul's unconsciousness. This enables you to become aware of your unresolved emotions as you react to your life experiences and also exposes what is inhibiting you from feeling the truth of who you are. You need experiences that expose you to the truth of your unresolved emotions.

Your images, illusions and control failures are experiences that expose the reality of your unresolved emotions. When you choose to ignore the opportunity to be truthfully honest with yourself, by oppressing your ability to be honest about your belief of not being good enough, you isolate yourself from feeling the presence of your soul's consciousness. When you commit to being truthfully honest, you strengthen your awareness of your natural flow of consciousness. Your truthful honesty enables you to consciously participate within your own rise with grace. Your rise and fall from grace is a process you constantly experience throughout your life, and it is the choices you make within your life that determine whether you unify with truth.

Your belief of not being good enough is embedded in your soul denial energy and keeps you enslaved to your fear of self-exploration, which causes you to reject the truth of your own natural value, worth and significance. Your fear of not being good enough ignites your indifference to truth which protects your soul denial. Soul denial is the crux of your soul's unconsciousness. You use this embedded belief and fear to become resistant to acknowledging that there could be more to you than you have envisaged. You limit the possibilities of your potential with negative beliefs about yourself.

When you overwhelm yourself with your desire to control, you ignore that you have options. This causes you to reject your awareness of being a soul, and you disregard the significance of your freedom of choice. You can control yourself to override the concept of freedom of choice, opposing your own divine right to care for yourself and to care about your freedom to be truthfully honest with yourself. Your soul denial energy results from manipulating your freedom of choice, to become a tool for your own soul oppression. When you resist, deny and avoid the truth of being a significant, unique, independent, individual soul, you fear losing your illusion of control. When you reject the freedom created by trusting in your significance, uniqueness, independence, individuality and the acceptance that you are of truth, you become your own worst enemy.

When you deny you have the freedom to choose to resolve your emotional habit of separating from your awareness of your soul's consciousness, you become entrapped in your own misconceptions. When you feel your isolation from your soul's consciousness, you are exposing to yourself, your separation from your awareness of truth. Your separation from your awareness of your soul and truth is how you dishonour the truth of who you are. You can deceive yourself to believe you have control over your soul's consciousness, which often leaves you creating an illusion about yourself and life. Your soul's consciousness is present within all your experiences. When you choose to sustain the unconscious energy of your soul, you isolate yourself from feeling the conscious energy of your soul. You do this to protect the insanity of your own denial. Denial has plagued you individually and also plagues the collective energy of mankind. Your denial is of the same vibration as mankind's collective denial, which protects the sustainability of unconscious energy.

When you are unconscious to the truth of yourself as a soul, you expect to exist within a struggle, which is actually caused by separating from your awareness of your soul's consciousness and truth. However, you may be unable to acknowledge the source of your struggle, because you are unconscious to the truth of your soul. Your unconsciousness is a cyclic self-perpetuating energy and remains so until you make a conscious choice to explore truth. The cyclic nature of unconsciousness ensures that what you miss in one present moment will be exposed again. You can become resentful of your inability to control reality with your unresolved emotions, and oppositional to any glimmer of how you repetitively resist, deny or avoid making a conscious choice to explore truth.

When you recognise your inability to control, you become consumed with your own disappointment. Your disappointment fuels the repetitiveness of your emotional, energetic or physical struggle. Your disappointment extends as you realise your inability to control life, yourself, others, relationships and the presence of truth. This causes you to self-propagate experiences that generate more painful emotions, in an attempt to justify your defection from your awareness of truth. Your soul's consciousness is unaffected by your defection from your awareness of truth, because your conscious energy is never removed from truth and always flows within you waiting for you to glimpse the value, worth and significance of who you truly are.

You become entrapped in your own fear of truth when you choose to override your awareness of your soul's consciousness with the beliefs embedded in your soul denial. Your embedded beliefs cause you to believe there is no other way to exist, but to fight for control of what your soul's consciousness exposes. Your fear causes you to attempt to control what your soul's consciousness exposes, which means you align to suppression and become willing to oppress your awareness. This causes you to store more unresolved emotions within your soul's unconsciousness. Your fight for control of your soul's consciousness expands your soul's unconsciousness. Your desire to control your soul's consciousness is unachievable, and causes you to wallow in your belief of not being good enough. You isolate yourself from your awareness of your soul's consciousness because you are disappointed that you cannot control the truth of your reality.

Your belief of not being good enough becomes a finely tuned control structure that commits you to your preconceived ideas of how your life will be. When life does not pacify your desire for control, you believe life has affirmed your preconceived ideas of expecting to be disappointed, and you throw down your emotional anchors and isolate yourself from feeling truth. You believe nothing will change but you will not acknowledge you are preventing change, because you insist on attempting to be the controller of life with your expectations of disappointment. When your control of life does not work, you withdraw from the truth of reality and choose stagnation as a way of pretending you are in control.

When you resent life for exposing the inefficiencies of your control, you miss the reality of life being an opportunity to learn from the truth of your experiences. When you miss the true value of what you are experiencing, you lose the momentum to resolve and evolve your unresolved emotions. This often has you unable to recognise that you control yourself to oppress your awareness of your soul's consciousness by blaming and resenting life, and by being oppositional to the opportunities that life presents. You can control yourself to survive, existing in your own soul oppression instead of living life conscious of being an evolving soul.

You use your belief of not being good enough to isolate yourself from feeling the reality of being a soul. You use your belief of not being good enough to prevent the resolution of your unresolved emotions and to prevent your own acceptance of being a soul, free to express your truth. What do you believe you have control of that should surpass the reality of being an evolving soul, experiencing what needs to be resolved, so you can evolve to be free of your own soul oppression? You fight your freedom with your desire to protect your stagnation, because you fear the truthful honesty required to liberate yourself from soul oppression. You stagnate in your fear of loss. When you fear losing your illusion of yourself, you become anxious about being honest with truth. Your fear of losing your illusion of control, causes you to be deceptive about yourself. You can stagnate in your self-doubt. When you doubt being able to control your illusions and you doubt being able to trust truth, your doubt creates anxiety about the reality of yourself. This can cause you to choose to isolate yourself from your awareness of the truth of your own stagnation. Your anxiety is the result of your fear of losing control of your stagnation and your ability to be deceptive towards yourself. Your stagnation protects your fear of exploring truth without your illusion of control, but how can you explore truth with your control?

You can hide in the belief that your soul and truth are a burden, and should be avoided and denied to protect your ability to hide in the insanity of mankind's soul denial. Deep within you can carry an embedded belief that your denial of your soul should exonerate you from being responsible for the resolution of your unresolved emotions and your own evolution. You can believe being unconscious to the reality of your unresolved emotions exonerates you from being responsible for them. However, you believe others should be responsible for their unresolved emotions and resent their emotions affecting your ability to hide from the truth of your own. You can feel your unresolved emotions and see the effect your unresolved emotions have on yourself and others. When you choose to ignore your emotional reality, to protect yourself from your fear of feeling vulnerable, you expose the truth of your unconsciousness to yourself. This is also part of the collective insanity of mankind energy; we ignore reality if it is contradictory to our illusion of control.

When you want to continue existing in your unresolved emotions and protect your illusion of control, you become indifferent to your own contribution to reality. When you deny your awareness of yourself and pretend to be innocent of what you are aware of, because you want to protect your own illusion of control, you become willing to perform any charade you believe will conceal the truth of what you want to hide. This is your own indifference to truth. When your charades do not conceal what you want hidden, you wallow in your belief of not being good enough and attempt to secure an illusion of innocence, believing you are a victim of life.

When you choose to control yourself to be isolated from feeling your soul's consciousness and truth, in an attempt to have no responsibility or accountability for your unresolved emotions, you become deceptive with yourself.

- Who is responsible for your unresolved emotions?
- If you are unwilling to be responsible for your own unresolved emotions, how will you resolve what emotionally haunts you?
- Why do you believe you should have an exemption from being accountable for your own truth?
- Why do you want *True Source Divine Origin Consciousness* to accept your lip service as you attempt to by-pass the resolution and evolution process?
- Why do you not want to resolve and evolve?
- Do you seek evolution or do you just want better results for your control?
- Do you seek evolution or are you using your spirituality to avoid being truthful?

Your choice to isolate yourself from feeling your own energy, is an attempt to control yourself to remain separated from your awareness of the energy of your soul's unconsciousness. When you are indifferent to your own attempts to fool truth and yourself, in relation to being honest about your own emotions, energetics and physical reality, you are the oppressor of your soul. Your willingness to lie to yourself about yourself is evidence of your protection of your soul's unconsciousness.

When you allow yourself to use your unresolved emotions and a backlog of examples from your history or your catalogue of projected opinions of your future, as a reference of what to expect from life, you increase your fear of truth. Your fear of truth causes you to emotionally feel doubt, distrust, guilt, shame, humiliation and despair, and you use these as guidelines for your desire to control. You miss the opportunity to be present and honest about how you feel in your present moment and start telling yourself what to believe. You use your unresolved emotions to engulf your awareness of your insight from your soul's consciousness, as a way of diffusing any insight which is contradictory to your illusion of control. When you fight your soul consciousness' ability to expose truth, you inflict yourself with emotions which are often generated by thoughts, rather than events. This overwhelms you as you attempt to deny or justify your own reactions to truth. While you fight to justify your compulsive reaction to oppose truth, you reinforce your denial of reality, allowing yourself to be deceptive about the truth of your own emotions, energetics and the physical results of your denial of reality.

When you realise the reality of your own denial and reactions towards your awareness of your soul's consciousness, you feel confused. Your reactions are in conflict with your original intention for your life experiences to be an exposure of truth to you. You often ignore your awareness of your soul consciousness' ability to expose the energy of your soul's unconsciousness, to protect your own denial of responsibility. Your confusion can be a catalyst that helps you question your awareness and understanding of your experience, with the knowledge that you may be in denial of the entirety of your reality. This allows you to create the space to explore truth. Or, you can use your confusion as justification to dogmatically latch onto a judgement or control structure that you believe will justify your willingness to oppose the exposure of the entirety of your reality. Confusion is your acknowledgement of the space where you can decide to either seek truth or to protect your ability to deny truth. You use your freedom of choice to decide if you will deal with the reality of your awareness consciously or unconsciously.

When you respond to your awareness of your emotional, energetic and physical reality, by refusing to be totally honest with yourself and deny what you are aware of, you will seek a control structure you believe you can use to create an illusion to conceal your truth from yourself. This causes you to concretise the suppression of your unresolved emotions and to deny what your confusion is exposing to you. The exposure of truth is part of the process of rising and falling from grace, and you may start unconsciously reacting to your confusion and end up consciously aware of truth. When you become truthful about your confusion, you seek the truth of yourself and reality. However, you can start consciously aware of what is causing your confusion, and end up unconsciously protecting your denial of reality, as a way of escaping from your awareness of what is being exposed within your confusion. The truth of your feelings exposes the truth of your conscious response or unconscious reaction to your confusion, and to the reality you are experiencing. However, if you try to control yourself to be more conscious, you will start over-analysing the truth of your experience. If you want to protect your denial and illusion of control, you will start a denial of reality cycle all over again.

When you protect your denial of reality and deny your awareness of your feelings, you internally feel shame for dishonouring your soul, your original intention and *True Source Divine Origin Consciousness*. You can feel guilt for using your desire to control to sustain your soul denial. The shame you emotionally feel is a mixture of your own opposition to your soul truth and your fear of acknowledging your own awareness of your soul truth. Shame can be invoked as you recognise the truth of your lies. You can use shame to incarcerate yourself into an emotional prison created whilst being separated from your awareness of your soul and disassociated from feeling truth. When your life experiences expose the truth of your unresolved emotions and you are indifferent to the truth being exposed, your own awareness of your indifference can cause you to react with shame.

When you deny the lies you tell yourself to justify your own deception, and anchor to your backlog of different emotional experiences of yourself or others opposing you, you become lost in your fear of not being good enough. When you provoke your own and others' opposition to you, you create a struggle. You use this struggle to remain preoccupied by your interactions with others in an attempt to deny your awareness of yourself. Your deception causes you to separate from your awareness of your soul. Your preoccupation with your deception and denial, is just a smoke screen designed to conceal the truth of your own actions, which cause you to become the protector of your own soul's unconsciousness.

There is more to you than you perceive.

Your Judgement of yourself creates negativity to wallow in.

Your limited perception of yourself is what you need to resolve.

You can choose areas of your life to create battles with, to sustain the denial within your soul's unconsciousness. For example, it could be your:

- Weight
- Health
- Relationships
- Finances
- History
- Beliefs of life
- Addictions
- Family dynamics

The list is as varied as your reality.

You may create struggles to control the perpetuation of your battle with your own deception, which actually protects and sustains the unresolved emotions of your soul's unconsciousness. You counteract both your attempts for control and your ability to be honest with your compulsive deception, which means you cannot control yourself to what you want or trust yourself to be honest about reality. This is a self-imposed purgatory within the energy of your soul's unconsciousness.

You can emotionally feel shame for retreating from being honest with yourself and your awareness of truth. You can use your guilt, shame and humiliation as decoys to avoid being honest. You can also use your guilt, shame and humiliation to create a fear of being vulnerable to the exposure of truth. When you fear exposing truth, it is because you fear exposing the truth of your deception, and you fear losing your ability to be deceptive. You emotionally feel shameful because you know truth is aware of your deception. You emotionally feel shameful because truth exposes you to the insanity of fighting your opportunity to free yourself from your own soul oppression. Your soul oppression is the cyclic patterns of your own self-imposed purgatory, which leaves you entrapped within the unconscious energy of your soul's unconsciousness.

Your heresy energy of guilt, shame and humiliation immerses you in your own opposition to your awareness of truth. You use the emotions stored within your soul's unconsciousness, to oppress your awareness of your soul's consciousness. Your guilt, shame and humiliation are heresy energies, because you always end up being anti-yourself and truth, when you allow yourself to be governed by these unresolved emotions. You use your thoughts to torture yourself with your desire to control reality, believing you are entitled to deny truth, which causes you to feel tortured by the unresolved emotions of your soul's unconsciousness. You emotionally feel shameful for not being able to control your emotions. This causes you to feel overwhelmed with a sense of powerlessness, sorrow or emotional exhaustion. This means you see everything as an obstacle to your control, enforcing the belief that you are not good enough because you cannot control yourself to the results you want, which is to have control over life, yourself, others, relationships and truth.

You can be constantly in fear of experiencing guilt, shame or humiliation because you know these emotions expose the illusion of your control. Your guilt, shame and humiliation expose the insecurity created by your illusion of control, which causes you to become willing to use any unresolved emotions to protect your denial. You attempt to disguise your fear and the reality of your insecurity with denial. You believe you are protecting yourself from further guilt, shame and humiliation by trying to conceal your insecurities and deny your beliefs of not being good enough, insignificant and inadequate. However, concealing truth fosters deception, which prolongs your self-imposed purgatory.

The insecurity created from your attempts to control makes you feel not good enough, insignificant and inadequate. This causes you to be more deceptive with your denial, as you attempt to control yourself to disassociate from feeling the truth of your unresolved emotions. Your soul's consciousness wants to expose you to what is unresolved within you. When you ignore your own awareness of your unresolved emotions, you cheat yourself by sabotaging any opportunity to be truthful with yourself.

When you dishonour yourself as a soul to sustain your belief of not being good enough, you are an oppressor of truth. You use your belief of not being good enough to conceal your resistance to and denial and avoidance of truth. Your belief of not being good enough can be used as a camouflage for your emotional manipulation. You manipulate yourself to be codependent on your soul oppression. You seek to use your belief of not being good enough to hide the reality of dishonouring yourself as a soul, but your beliefs actually expose you to how you dishonour yourself. Your belief of not being good enough becomes camouflage for your soul denial and your protection of your soul's unconsciousness.

When you falsely want to believe that you have exonerated yourself from your soul consciousness' intention to resolve and evolve your unresolved emotions, you expose the arrogance of your use of denial. Your soul's consciousness will never give up on exposing you to the truth of your unresolved emotions, because it is your denial that suspends you in the falsity of your not good enough beliefs. When you align to your illusion of control and control yourself with your own arrogant ignorance, you become indifferent to yourself and your behaviours. You believe you can control yourself to be isolated from your awareness of your own soul's consciousness with your belief that your original intention is a burden and resolution will interfere with your illusion of control. This can cause you to settle for stagnation and condition yourself to tolerate your indifference to truth.

You can create an illusion of what you believe consciousness is, however you are unrealistic with your beliefs of consciousness, because you deny the natural process of rising and falling from grace. Your images of consciousness become ways of denying your experience of falling from grace, and you fixate on perfecting your perception of always being right and never being wrong in your assessment of yourself and reality. This causes you to become obsessed with your own self-judgement. Your images of consciousness become unattainable because your version of consciousness is not based in truth. Your illusory versions of consciousness are attempts to suppress your awareness of the energy of your soul's unconsciousness, and are an attempt to deny truth and the process of your resolution. False versions of consciousness are an attempt to use spirituality as a by-pass to resolving what is unresolved. Pretending to be truthful does not make you of truth. Consciousness is to resonate with truth. Consciousness is to be awakened to truth and stems from an acceptance of life being an opportunity to honestly explore yourself and your resonance with truth.

Consciousness is being of truth and being honest about the entirety of your own awareness. Consciousness is the willingness to acknowledge your awareness of the entirety of both your conscious and unconscious energy. Your false versions of consciousness are orchestrated by your belief that you can perfect your control of an image, while you disregard the reality of being an evolving soul. When you attempt to control an image of consciousness, you are choosing to try and sidestep the resolution process. However, you can only feel the truth of your soul by resolving what is inhibiting your awareness of your natural flow of consciousness. Your desire to control an image of consciousness inhibits your awareness, and regardless of the image you are endeavouring to create, you are cheating yourself out of the authenticity of your soul. All images and illusions will implode due to the deception required to sustain the façade and charade that come with any image or illusion.

When you scale the significance of souls with your judgement and deceptive beliefs, you lose sight of all souls being of *True Source Divine Origin Consciousness*. You can arrogantly believe that only the chosen few can be conscious of truth and that you need to either be the chosen one or the follower of a chosen one. This belief causes you to deny the reality that each soul individually resonates with truth independently. When you deny that each soul individually resonates with truth independently, your denial causes you to retain your misconceptions about elitism, superiority and inferiority. Your misconceptions about the equality of all souls are created by your desire to scale the value, worth and significance of yourself and others with your judgement and your willingness to create and sustain pecking orders.

The arrogance of your judgement can have you anchoring to beliefs that enable you to use your embedded beliefs and fears of your soul denial to construct your own false version of consciousness. This can cause you to manipulate yourself to believe your intentions are good whilst denying your actions, hidden agendas and desires. However, you cannot sustain your own expectations of yourself within your false version of consciousness, and you will become disillusioned with your own concept of consciousness. When you anchor to your desire to be in control of life and attempt to use the concept of consciousness to enhance your desire to control life and truth, you become obsessed with proving your own elitism. This causes you to lose the ability to feel the purity of your soul, which can mean you seek constructed lies that you believe justify your denial of reality. The lies facilitate your ability to deny feeling the truth of your desire to manipulate the concept of consciousness, which actually has you opposing your awareness of the presence of truth. If your false version of consciousness is not appeased by your reality, you arrogantly believe that consciousness is inaccessible to you and control yourself to deny the reality of feeling truth. We are all significant, unique, independent, individual souls of truth with the opportunity to resolve any misconception our beliefs and unresolved emotions create for us in relation to consciousness.

Life is the journey of souls. Evolution is to understand the truth of who you uniquely are and to be at peace with your origins of truth. Your soul's consciousness is of *True Source Divine Origin Consciousness* energy, in a physical form on Earth. Your physical form is a vessel for both your soul's consciousness and your soul's unconsciousness, and you are the interface between the two. You have the freedom to choose in each present moment which energy you align to. Your soul's consciousness is your origins and your soul's unconsciousness is what you have created when you deny the origins. Your soul denial contributes to the energetics of the mass energy of mankind. The energetics of the mass energy of mankind is the unconsciousness of *True Source Divine Origin Consciousness*.

True Source Divine Origin Consciousness seeks to resolve and evolve that which is unconscious to truth.

Your lack of understanding of who you are has you arrogantly ignoring the truth of your ability to trust feeling the presence of truth. Your lack of trust and opposition to feeling truth can cause you to camouflage the opportunity to be honest about your unresolved emotions with your belief of not being good enough to be of truth. You use this belief to conceal the reality of wanting to protect your soul denial, so that you can keep acting out your illusion of control. When you are unable to pacify your own desire for control, or have recognised that you have not sustained an image you want, you project out or wallow in the belief of not being good enough for your own expectations. You use your belief of not being good enough to be of truth as the choice to be inactive in your own resolution and evolution.

When you want to isolate yourself from your awareness of your soul's consciousness and your awareness of the presence of *True Source Divine Origin Consciousness* which is truth, you lose your sense of self. You may want to be left alone to flounder in your own soul oppression, but your soul's consciousness keeps exposing you to the truth of yourself. When you refuse to acknowledge your soul oppression, you sustain what you use to oppress your soul. You cannot resolve what you do not acknowledge, and what you refuse to acknowledge becomes a burden you carry. You are never without the opportunity to decide you are more than your oppression. The reality of your life exposes you to the fraudulent beliefs and fears embedded in your soul denial. Life reveals the truth of your soul's unconsciousness to you and creates the opportunity for resolution and evolution.

You are your soul's consciousness and your consciousness is the life force of all aspects of your soul. You may try to denounce your own life force because you want to exist within your illusion of yourself and reality, but your soul's consciousness never gives up on exposing you to the significance of truth. When you deliberately oppose the significance of truth, you align to an illusion of yourself and reality, which is an attempt to be immersed in your soul denial, and to remain separated from your awareness of your soul and disassociated from feeling truth. If truth disturbs your soul denial and your illusion of yourself and reality, you use the energy of your unresolved emotions to turn on your soul's consciousness with vengeance. If you have experienced being anti-yourself or observe sabotaging yourself, you have felt your own vengeance.

You avoid your awareness of truth, by protecting and justifying the unresolved emotions within your cycles of soul oppression. You align to many beliefs to defend your avoidance. Your belief of not being good enough can become an avoidance tool, which inhibits your honesty about how you justify and sustain the belief.

You can become consumed with your own desire to control yourself to an image of who you want to be perceived as and an illusion of what life should provide for you. When your desire to control is not pacified, you vent your unresolved emotions at life, yourself, others, your relationships and truth. If your desire to control is not pacified you perceive it as a failure. You use your perceived failures to justify the presumed righteousness of your judgement, and as permission to seek to pacify your own desire to control. You class your perceived failures as validation that your emotions are unresolvable and that you have no option but to control yourself to images, illusions and controlled identities.

When you are consciously aware of venting out your unresolved emotions but you ignore the opportunity to resolve what is being exposed to you, you stagnate in that which you refuse to honestly deal with. You are exposed to the truth of your unresolved emotions because you cannot control your emotions to be concealed, contained or suppressed all the time. Your inability to sustain control over your unresolved emotions, exposes you to the truth of your unconsciousness. This creates the opportunity to be honest with yourself however, you have to choose to take the opportunity. You will keep experiencing the emotions you refuse to be honest about.

When you want to prove to yourself that your illusion of control and desire to control are of value, you may try to prove that truth is not good enough to penetrate your soul denial. You may try to prove to yourself that your soul's consciousness is not of your energy, and try to secure an illusion that your soul's consciousness is an outside source separated from you, that you can deny, or place emotional, energetic and physical demands on. You may try to counteract your soul consciousness' ability to expose you to your own soul truth, by using negative judgement about your significance to override what you feel.

Your embedded belief of not being good enough is a by-product of your judgement of your significance. You either judge yourself as not being good enough to be unified with the truth of being a significant, unique, independent, individual soul, or you judge your soul and truth as not being good enough to inhibit your ability to control your soul denial. Resolution of your belief of not being good enough has a lot to do with the resolution of your desire to control and illusion of control; and it is a choice only you can make. When you decide that you are worth the effort required to explore the truth of your own energy and to explore any misconceptions that inhibit your awareness of your natural worth, value and significance, you are accepting you are an evolving soul on a journey of discovery.

When you protect, justify and defend your belief of not being good enough, you are telling yourself that you are not good enough for your own illusion of control. You believe you know what and how you want to control life and have judged yourself as inefficient to validate your own illusion. Your belief of not being good enough is the choice to wallow in the energy of your soul's unconsciousness, because you are unwilling to explore the option of resolution and evolution of your own soul's unconsciousness.

Denial of the belief of not being good enough

Your belief of not being good enough is a misconception about yourself that has you ignoring your natural ability to accept and trust your soul's consciousness as the truth of who you are. Your belief of not being good enough creates barriers to being an objective observer of the unresolved emotions within your soul's unconsciousness and of the flow of conscious energy within you. You can subject yourself to your own judgement that you will never be good enough to experience peace within your soul. You can ignore your own observations of the truth of being a significant, unique, independent, individual soul of *True Source Divine Origin Consciousness*.

You can isolate yourself from feeling your soul truth, because you do not believe in your own significance, which leaves you devaluing the significance of life. You can choose to get caught in the drama you create by opposing the truth of who you are. You can forget the value of yourself as a soul and you can choose to arrogantly override the truth that you are a unique, independent, individual soul of *True Source Divine Origin Consciousness*, who is naturally significant.

Your defiant protection of your belief of not being good enough is a sly way of hiding your arrogant tantrum about truth getting it wrong, and that truth should give you more power to control. The unresolved emotions created by your belief of not being good enough are generated, because you are having a tantrum about not being able to get what you want from life, yourself, others, relationships and truth. Your emotional, energetic and physical tantrums stop you from recognising the truth of your soul. This causes you to deny your own clarity, which leads to you opposing your ability to trust yourself. You fail to perceive the difference between emotionally reacting from the energy of your soul's unconsciousness, and feeling the purity of truth within your soul's consciousness. When you deny the entirety of your energy and your awareness, you dismiss the significance of the exposure of the truth of both the conscious and unconscious energy of your soul. This can also lead to you devaluing the experiences that you feel yourself resonate with. When you dismiss and devalue what life is presenting, you deny the significance of what you are experiencing within your present moment and become fixated on wanting control of reality.

When you control yourself to continuously analyse your thoughts, expectations, impressions and emotions about yourself with bias, you deprive yourself of the opportunity to discover truth. This can cause you to stagnate within your tendency to override your own insight and awareness. You can use irrational thoughts to judge yourself unworthy of being aware of yourself as a soul, and unworthy to be aware of your own synchronicity with the presence of *True Source Divine Origin Consciousness*. You can allow your emotional wounds, to inhibit your awareness that the process of rising and falling from grace exposes the truth of your soul's unconsciousness. The exposure of any truth creates the opportunity to choose to be honest about your own emotional, energetic and physical reality, which means you have the freedom to choose to resolve and evolve your unconscious energy. Your belief of not being good enough generates unconscious energy that you use to renege on your own original intention. Your original intention is to honour yourself by exploring truth.

It is a shared agreement you made with *True Source Divine Origin Consciousness*. You know as a conscious soul, you would not have made an agreement with *True Source Divine Origin Consciousness* that you are not capable of fulfilling, because truth supports your soul consciousness' intention flawlessly.

Your belief of not being good enough is a smokescreen for the guilt, shame and humiliation you feel, for attempting to renege on your agreement with *True Source Divine Origin Consciousness* and for your willingness to ignore your awareness of denying the truth of being a soul. Part of your original intention is to honour the truth of who you are. You have forgotten you actually need to be unconscious to the truth of your soul, to experience the truth of your unresolved emotions. You have forgotten that it was always your intention to experience your unresolved emotions. You only fight and struggle against your unresolved emotions when you have no desire to honour your original intention of seeking resolution. By being honest about experiencing your unresolved emotions you will seek, find and understand the truth of what you need to resolve, and your honesty will allow you to appreciate the truth of your original intention for your resolution and evolution.

You need to address your belief of not being good enough to be a conscious participant in the natural process of rising and falling from your own grace, because it is often your belief of not being good enough that causes you to remain fallen within your unconsciousness with no inclination to be truthful. It is your truthfulness that enables you to rise with grace, resolving what is unconscious within you. Resolution is never done unconsciously and being a conscious participant means you are aware of yourself, discovering, accepting and being truthful about your own unconsciousness. Your belief of not being good enough is a control structure, which opposes your willingness to be of your own grace, and inhibits your ability to forgive yourself for being unconscious to the truth of yourself. Grace is to acknowledge yourself as an evolving soul, who is willing to be in the process of discovering the entirety of your consciousness and unconsciousness.

Your belief of not being good enough inhibits you from experiencing the sincerity of your soul's consciousness and *True Source Divine Origin Consciousness'* unconditional support for the journey of your soul. Honouring and accepting yourself as a soul is to challenge your belief of not being good enough. This means you decide to not just aimlessly align to every negative thought you have about yourself, but instead choose to be compassionate towards yourself, which creates the space for resolution and evolution. Your belief of not being good enough misleads you, and you become untrustworthy about your own intentions, because your belief of not being good enough is the intention to deny your significance, uniqueness, independence and individuality as a soul of *True Source Divine Origin Consciousness*. Honouring your soul is your choice to be honest with the reality you feel, and is the choice to be free of any desire to mislead yourself.

You often fight and struggle with what you have decided is not good enough about yourself. In truth, what you have decided is not good enough is controlling you to feel not good enough. You can perpetuate your own misery to oppose your awareness of truth, which sustains your compulsion to believe you are not good enough. This leaves you opposing all truth to devalue and dishonour the significance of your awareness of your soul. You create emotional, energetic and physical barriers to oppose your ability to genuinely feel your feelings and acknowledge your awareness of truth.

To resolve your belief of not being good enough, you need to apply the same effort to being honest as you do to defending, protecting and hiding from the truth of your soul. Your belief of not being good enough continues the stagnation of your soul oppression, which causes you to feel frustrated. Your frustration exposes what needs to be resolved. Frustration is a warning signal that your desire for control and your unresolved emotions are hindering your acceptance of your reality and your soul. You can inhibit your natural process of resolution and evolution with emotional demands and the desire to emotionally feel in control of reality.

When you acknowledge and feel your own dishonour and your attempts to conceal the truth of your feelings, you are exposing an opportunity to be truthful. When you decide that truthfulness is problematic, you attempt to bombard yourself with distractions that inhibit your ability to trust your awareness of truth. When you distrust you own awareness of truth, you become easily distracted and often obsessed with what frustrates you. You can feel the reality of attempting to distract yourself from what is really relevant to you and often become more frustrated because you cannot control yourself to stop feeling the deception within your soul's unconsciousness. Whatever you use to distract yourself from your awareness of your soul truth never completely satisfies your yearning to feel the truth of your soul. You seek to feel the unification of all aspects of your soul with truth. The way you deceive yourself, regardless of how good your denial is, can never secure and sustain the suppression of your awareness of your original intention to resolve and evolve the energy of your soul's unconsciousness.

Your belief of not being good enough reinforces your misconceptions and your own justifications for your emotional unrest, which often entraps you in denial. Your belief of not being good enough is a control method that generates and keeps you magnetised to the unresolved emotions you need to acknowledge, to resolve and evolve. Your unresolved emotions attract other unresolved emotions, which create the perpetuation of your emotional patterns. The exposure of your belief of not being good enough can work in your favour if you are truthfully honest, because they reveal many misconceptions and highlight deceptions you use to emotionally feel not good enough.

Your belief of not being good enough is a manifestation of your non-acceptance of yourself. It is when you choose to trust your awareness of truth and trust the truth of your origins that the unresolved emotions entangled in your belief of not being good enough, become resolvable.

Chapter Twenty-Five

Images and illusions

Images are constructed when we use façades to conceal the truth of ourselves and our own energy. We use control structures in an attempt to secure the illusion that our façade is the truth. Images are the combination of your façades and control structures, which you amalgamate to form an illusory concept of yourself, which you want to portray to others.

Your images and illusions always reflect your soul denial and are the façades and control structures you use while separated from your awareness of your soul. When you accept the value, worth and significance of your soul's consciousness, you do not need or desire to use an image or an illusion. Truth does not need façades to hide behind. You can use images and illusions to hide from the truth of your own unresolved emotions. Your images and illusions are often the manifestation of your fear of not being good enough in your natural essence. Your images and illusions are used as suppression tools in an attempt to deny your unresolved emotions. Your images and illusions shield you from feeling the truth of yourself.

When you seek to use beliefs to stroke your ego and to pacify your insecurities, you will portray an image you believe ensures you can orchestrate what you want. This means your images come with hidden agendas, you believe you can actualise. You want your beliefs to justify the motives behind your own images and illusions. You want to identify reasons so you can give yourself permission to be deceptive about your own soul's consciousness, and to justify your opposition to the reality of being a naturally significant, unique, independent, individual soul of *True Source Divine Origin Consciousness*. You want to construct what significance, uniqueness, independence and individuality means, without exploring what is naturally within you. This causes you to want to control an image and illusion to impersonate your perception of what a soul's consciousness is, instead of being open to the opportunity to discover the truth of your soul. You want to define your images and illusions as reality and truth, in an attempt to conceal your own unresolved emotions and to pacify your desire for control. You use images and illusions to deny your separation from your awareness of your soul, but your images and illusions can only be performed when you are separated from your awareness of your soul.

If you believed your images and illusions were working, validating your illusion of control, you would not need to question the validity of your images and illusions, nor would you feel insecure and superficial when performing your images or defending your illusions. It is your recognition of feeling your insecurity and superficiality, which causes you to question the validity of your images and illusions. It is your questioning of what you want your own images to portray and what your illusions are concealing that will expose truth to you. You can emotionally feel shocked when reality does not align to your expectations and agendas, because this exposes the truth of your illusion of control. You construct an illusion or perform an image, because you have an agenda of wanting to control how others

perceive you. It is your acknowledgement of your own agenda, that enables you to explore the truth of your own images and illusions.

- Do you feel removed from yourself and the reality of your life?
- Do you feel like a fake?

If the answer is yes, then you are aware that your images and illusions are not resonating with your soul or truth.

- What do you want to achieve with your own images and illusions?
- Are you reluctant to question yourself about your images and illusions because you do not want to acknowledge your own agenda?

The fear of others' judgement can cause you to abandon the true essence of your uniqueness, independence and individuality and to seek to create images and illusions, which you believe will be revered by others. This has conditioned you to devalue the essence of truth and to align to, construct or revere images and illusions. This creates the justification for being your own 'spin doctor', so that you can misconstrue whatever you want to secure your protection of your images and illusions.

When you misconstrue the truth of anything, you become the orchestrator of your own propaganda. This causes you to believe it is acceptable to deceptively appear a certain way, if you believe your manipulation will secure your illusion of control or enhance your ability to pacify your desire for control. Unfortunately, the cost for you is your own soul integrity.

When you separate from your awareness of your soul to deceptively perform, you use images and illusions as an attempt to fit in with, or to compete against others' judgement of you. You begin to layer your own deception, often to the point of being unable to easily identify it as deception. This means your deception, outgrows your willingness to be truthful and what you believe you can control with your deception starts to outstrip your logic and awareness of truth. You categorise your images and illusions with your judgement of mankind and truth, deceptively believing you can fool both mankind and *True Source Divine Origin Consciousness* to accept your orchestrations.

You can align to the collective energy you want validation from or aspire to be part of; however, this causes you to oppose your own uniqueness. When you oppose your own uniqueness, you will want to manipulate others to reverberate with your control, because you want to be able to emotionally feel your control having an effect on something or someone.

You can create an illusory world to exist in, and seek others to pacify your insecurities and to align to your control of their perception. This can cause you to manipulate yourself with deception as you control yourself to be separated from your awareness of your soul. You do this to oppress your awareness of your soul consciousness' ability to expose you

RIGHT: *Your fear of others' judgement can cause you to abandon the true essence of your uniqueness, independence and individuality, and to seek to create images and illusions that you want revered by others, who are also trying to perfect their own images and illusions.*

to the truth of your own deceptive images and illusions. You oppress your awareness of your soul's consciousness, so that you can believe your own images and illusions, because you know if you feel the truth of your own deception, you will feel the superficiality of your images and illusions. You use your resistance to and denial and avoidance of truth, to sustain your codependency on your addiction to performing your images and sustaining superficial illusions. The superficiality of your images and illusions makes you emotionally feel fake and disassociated from feeling your own reality.

You disguise your negativity and the lies you tell yourself, with your illusion of being able to control the unresolved emotions of your soul's unconsciousness, and the feelings of your soul's consciousness. This causes you to obsess with your desire to control your unresolved emotions to override your awareness of your soul's consciousness. This often means you become consumed with wanting to suppress how you feel, to ignore reality and to construct an illusion that you can use to believe you are back in control. You control yourself to believe your own deception, which hides the reality of your control being an illusion and that you are the creator of your own internal struggle.

Your willingness to be deceptive causes you to emotionally ricochet within your own insecurities. You emotionally feel insecure because you do not know if you are going to achieve your agenda and cannot be sure how successful your images and illusions will be in fooling others or *True Source Divine Origin Consciousness*. You emotionally ricochet within the insecurity of wondering what will be exposed if your images and illusions are not accepted. When you are ricocheting within your insecurities, you feel an undeniable anxiety because you instinctively know your images and illusions will not get you the results you truly want. You want to believe you are in control of yourself, others and reality. Your images and illusions become control mandates, you anticipate will supply you with the illusion of having tangible control of reality, and you become extremely anxious if reality does not conform to your expectations.

All of your images and illusions are mandated to protect your own self-image and illusion of being in control. You create images you believe will pacify and gratify the insecurity incited by your desire to control your separation from your awareness of your soul. You can create illusions to support your own images that actually perpetuate your separation from your awareness of your soul. Your images and illusions are facades concealing the insanity of protecting your own soul's unconsciousness. They also conceal the significance of the truth of who you naturally are, which is a unique, independent, individual soul of *True Source Divine Origin Consciousness*.

The reality is, that your images and illusions cannot emulate the purity of the significance, uniqueness, independence and the individuality of your soul. You internally feel your natural significance, uniqueness, independence and individuality when you accept the truth of your soul. Your emulations of significance, uniqueness, independence and individuality cause you to be codependent on whatever you believe supplies an arena for your image and reinforces your illusion. This means you are focused on what is externally providing you with the arena and on your judgement of how others perceive you. Your desire to perfect your images and illusions cause you to be dogmatically controlling and deceptively manipulative and sly, because that is how you secure the arena for the image. Your enmeshment with your constructed arena inhibits your ability to feel the purity of yourself. Instead of feeling the truth of your own energy within the uniqueness of your present moment, you become the repetitiveness of projecting an image, seeking to construct an illusion of reality over your awareness of your present moment.

You have a variety of contradictory images and behaviours you use depending on what you desire to believe, how you want to control reality, or your desire to believe you are a victim to your inability to control. You can ricochet from image to image in an attempt to uphold an illusion of being in control of yourself and life. You can orientate yourself to support your own desire to secure and portray the image you want others to believe. However, if you identify that your image is not supplying you with what you believe you deserve or want, you portray conflicting behaviours and become contradictory to the image you want to be perceived as. Your contradictory behaviours can reveal the motives behind the original image you attempted to portray. This causes you to become confused about the reality of your own compulsive behaviour.

Spiritually elite image: You project the image of being spiritually evolved, especially when you perceive your control is working. This causes you to project an image of being principled, which you use to justify your desire to sustain your control over your and others' perception of your spirituality. When you believe everything is going to your expectations, you project an image of being easy going, because you are in tune with your 'spiritual self'. When you believe your spiritual image is allowing you to control reality, you become very secure in your spiritually evolved image. This can cause you to dogmatically defend your denial of portraying an image, and cling to the belief that your image is who you are. This has you striving to be in control of yourself and reality, which causes you to become contradictory to the spiritual principles you have based your image on. You can speak as though you are a philosopher and have catch phrases for all occasions. You can also emphasis your love for life and others, believing you are a gateway for others to find what you are portraying. This changes what you focus on, and you fixate on how others are perceiving you, instead of your own spirituality. You become obsessed with ensuring others are falling for the image you want to portray. If you judge others as not falling for your image, you become very defensive.

When you can become consumed with the belief that you need to secure your perceived spiritual elitism, you become manipulative with and about your spirituality. You can fixate on orientating yourself to your desire to control life, yourself, others, relationships and truth to adhere to your perception and image of yourself. The behaviour you display may be at odds with the spiritually evolved soul you want to portray.

Superior images: Your insecurities cause you to exist in the duality of perceiving yourself as inferior or superior, depending on your judgement of the situation. From this evaluation you create images you perform to conceal your self-judgement. You may project an image of being superior to others, in an attempt to prove there is significance to your existence. You want to ensure you can rank yourself as superior by how you judge others or by how you perceive others are judging you. You also want to shield yourself from your fear of being inferior. When everything is going the way you want, you project an image of being entitled to be classed as superior, because you believe you are more important than others. The image you create from your sense of entitlement, conceals your insecurities, which result from the duality of your judgement of yourself. This means the image you portray is contradictory to the internal chaos you feel.

You use your judgement of life, others and reality as a way of justifying your own arrogance. Your arrogance becomes an image you use when you believe you have complete control over yourself within reality. However, your arrogance is a by-product of your decision to be completely indifferent to your soul and fixated on orchestrating an image. When life does not align to your expectations, you become swamped with your fears of your own insecurities, and project an image of being a victim to others who do not comprehend your superiority. When you attempt to deny the insecurities within yourself, you project an image of being an authority over reality, which has you believing you are righteous in your judgement. This causes you to see-saw between your beliefs of superiority and inferiority. Your behaviour can become contradictory to the image you want to portray. Your own conflicted self-judgement and beliefs of your superiority becomes a way of justifying your arrogant behaviour. Your beliefs about how you claim to be superior to others become platforms for you to be dogmatic in, as you attempt to hide from any of your own insecurities.

Free-spirited and victim to life image: You can portray an image of being free-spirited, whilst attempting to conceal the reality of your resentment of life. When you resent life for not appeasing your desires and yet portray a free-spirited image, you can become aloof from your reality. This can cause you to overlook the basic realities of life and cling to the belief that others should carry the burden of ensuring you are able to live the way you want. You project an image of being in the flow with the dynamics of life, but resent anything or anyone who does not attune to your control, or orchestration of how you think your life should be. This is in conflict with your free-spirited ideals.

When your resentment overrides your ability to believe your 'free-spirited, going with the flow' image, you align to the image of being a victim of life. Your victim to life image causes you to believe you have been cheated out of the life you should be living. This has you seeking to reinstate control over those who can assist you to get what you want so you can uphold your free-spirited image. This leaves you sly and manipulative, and may cause you to intimidate or emotionally blackmail others, in an attempt to make them take responsibility for giving you what you want. As you project whatever you believe will obligate others to pacifying your wants and desires, you ignore the reality of your behaviour and project the illusion that your free-spirited image inhibits you from understanding how to operate in this world. However, you have understood enough to manipulate others to appease you.

You can fear being classed as boring or ordinary, which can cause you to become defiant against having to do anything you class as mundane. You can arrogantly believe you are above the mundane aspects of life, and cling to the belief your free-spirited image means you are superior and advanced in the way you view life. After you believe you have controlled those around you to appease your desire to uphold your image, you attempt to perform a pretense of being humble in your superiority. If you cannot get others to appease your control, your resentment festers causing you to emotionally feel like a victim again. As you try to become secure within your image and beliefs, you become obsessive with your judgement of your self-image. The concept of being free-spirted becomes a control structure, you use to suppress any awareness of your own insecurities and willingness to be conniving. Your fear of how others may judge your contradictory behaviour, creates an anxiety which actually feeds your insecurities and your obsession with your own images. Free-spirted becomes a saying or a belief, not a doing or being.

Trustworthy image: You portray an image of being trustworthy to purposely conceal your willingness to be manipulative to get what you want. When you believe you are in control, you project an image of being honest. However, when you fear losing control, you become a tyrant, behaving from a sense of righteousness and beliefs of you being entitled to have everyone submissive to your control. This is in conflict with your trustworthy image, and causes you to expose the manipulative control agenda underneath your image of trustworthiness.

Charade of affluence: You project an image of being successful and affluent, created on excessively borrowed money. This image causes you to deny your reality and you become fixated on securing the portrayal of success and being affluent. You become reliant on your denial of reality and fear losing control of your image. You portray an image of being financially secure, in an attempt to control the sustainability of your image of being successful. This image causes you to be in conflict with your reality, because you are sustaining both your dishonesty with yourself and others. The effort you have to apply to yourself to deny reality also exposes how willing you are to be deceptive, and that your image of being successful is dependent on your ability to sustain your dishonesty.

The façades concealing the truth of images and illusions are as varied as the individuals using them. When you use an image, you rely on being codependent on your deception, to sustain the illusion created by your image. Your images are deceptive. You deceive yourself with your own image, and you want to deceive others as well.

 All images come with agendas; there is a purpose to the performance, which means the image is fueled from the desire to manipulate and the desire to control for outcomes you believe you want. This is very different to naturally expressing yourself and being present in the truth of what you are internally and externally experiencing. When you use an image, you may portray the same actions and say the same words that appear to be coming from your natural self, but you will strive to control for outcomes, and there will be a huge difference in how you feel about yourself and often how others feel around you as you perform your image. When you are responding to reality with the truth of who you naturally are, you do not need an image and will trust yourself to be present in the unfolding of the experience in your present moment. Some images are an enactment of who you believe you are, however you have actually chosen in that present moment to suppress the truth of your soul, and to construct an artificial version of yourself.

Images are constructed with the combination of façades and control structures, which become embedded in your desire to control reality, and are often used to justify the energy of your soul's unconsciousness. Your images restrict your ability to express the truth of yourself within the uniqueness of your present moment. All images are illusory and they inhibit you from being dynamic. Your images restrict the way you experience life because to protect the image, you construct programmed reactions to life. When you acknowledge you are a soul, you can dynamically experience your own rise and fall from grace and respond to the entirety of what you are experiencing. There are many variables for any given present moment and to be truly present in what is occurring is to be dynamic. Performances of images restrict the dynamic nature of your soul and of your evolutionary journey. Your reactions and responses to life become robotic and predictable to ensure your own illusory control of yourself. Your images become a way to define yourself and they restrict your awareness of the truth of yourself. They become anchor points for your denial and control, which become the determining factor in how you interact with life, yourself, others, within your relationships and truth.

Images are unconscious fragmented aspects of yourself. Images become what you align to and perform. They can reflect aspects of your unconsciousness and consciousness. However, it becomes a limited version of the dynamics of who you naturally are. Once you start believing your images are what you should use to interact with life, yourself, others, within your relationships and with truth, they become your automatic mode of being for all your life experiences, regardless of the ramifications or how appropriate your image is for that given situation. For example:

- Perfectionist
- Intellectual
- Ethical
- Elite
- Sexy
- Caring
- Fun-loving
- Doting father
- Advisor

- Protective mother
- Florence Nightingale
- White knight
- Hard worker
- Empathic
- Forgiving
- Selfless
- _____

- Life of the party
- Martyr
- Easy-going
- Warrior
- Reliable
- Loving
- Professional
- Leader
- _____

These become ways you define yourself but you are more than any label or self-definition, you are a dynamic soul. These labels and self-definitions become traps that restrict your exploration of yourself, and are a description of the traps you have settled for.

Your soul's consciousness, the truth of who you are, is not image or illusory based. All images are control structures with facades attempting to conceal the truth of your beliefs, your indifference towards yourself, your insecurity and fears, which all encase you in the energy of your soul's unconsciousness and have you reverberating with the energetic collectives that correlate to your image.

Your images and illusions are how you contribute to the fracturing, compartmentalising and disunity of your soul. Your soul's consciousness has the intention to resolve all images and illusions, because they conceal the entirety of the truth of your soul. When you focus on controlling yourself to an image or seek to secure an illusion of control, you fragment your awareness of the entirety of your soul and become self-manipulative and deceptive. This has you compulsively selective in what you notice and acknowledge. You manipulate yourself to concentrate on the perceived righteousness of your judgement, ignoring and denying your unresolved emotions in relation to your desire to control the perfection of your images and illusions.

Your soul's consciousness seeks to expose all that contributes to your denial and to reveal how you have become the orchestrator of your own willingness to be deceptive. You are often willing to resolve the emotions related to your control, in an attempt to perfect your control, but you baulk at resolving your desire for control. This is you attempting to use the truth to enhance your ability to control. When you want to deny your insecurities and hold onto the illusion of control, you become very willing to deny any truth which interferes with your control agendas. This means you become selective in what you will acknowledge and in what you will deny of your own reality.

Your soul's consciousness exposes opportunities for you to acknowledge the reality of your soul's unconsciousness. When you use your self-manipulation to deny your awareness of exposed truth, you seek to sustain, pacify and justify your own misconceptions. All images and illusions are the manifestation of your protection of your unresolved emotions and are founded in your own misconceptions. Images and illusions are built from what you perceive will conceal all that you do not want to reveal of yourself, and they become a way of buffering yourself from potential humiliation. Often when you have experienced humiliation, where it has cut through you to your soul, you attempt to either create an image to conceal how you feel or you construct a method of trying to avoid ever feeling like that again. This can leave you rejecting the truth of who you naturally are.

When you are unable to feel and accept the truth of who you are, you become reliant on your images to perform charades of how you want to be perceived. This often has you performing in the way you believe others want you to.

When you deny your ability to resolve your unresolved emotions, you cling to what you believe will protect you. If you believe it is your images and illusions that will protect you, you will go to great lengths to validate and secure your images and illusions. You will permit yourself to lie and to perpetuate whatever is unresolved within your soul's unconsciousness. When you deny the reality of your awareness of yourself and align to control structures, you deceptively uphold your images and illusions. When you adopt mankind's embedded beliefs of the importance of images and illusions, you use them to defend your own soul denial. This has you denying the uniqueness of your soul and the significance of who you are, which prolongs your own soul oppression.

The energetic collectives of mankind's soul denial are sustained by each individual's denial of their own significance. When you deny the significance of being an individual soul and adopt the images that you perceive mankind wants, you become a reverberation of unconscious energy within the collective of mankind's soul denial. You use images to construct illusions to control yourself to. Your beliefs in what you can perform enable you to assess which images and illusions suit your desire and ability to control. If you seek to infiltrate what you aspire to control, you will become indifferent to what you are doing to yourself and sacrifice your awareness of the uniqueness of your soul.

Mankind energy splinters into many different energetic collectives because it is fuelled by each individual's soul denial and each person's compulsion to compete against others. When you become competitive about your own image, and judge and compare yourself via your performances of images, you become compulsively competitive with everyone you encounter. This causes you to seek others who enhance your image, but you struggle if you believe they are rivals, which can create many toxic relationships. You may seek to manipulate others to be envious of your images and to covet your illusions, in order to pacify the insecurities you create when you separate from your awareness of yourself. When you want others to support your denial, you align and aspire to perfect images and illusions you believe will be revered by others. If others condone your images and illusions, it reinforces your denial of your significance, uniqueness, independence and individuality and of your soul journey. However, mankind is fraught with judgement and what can be revered in one moment may be denigrated in the next.

You try to create images and illusions to conceal the truth of your unresolved emotions. However, regardless of how good your performance is, you still feel the unresolved emotions underpinning your images and illusions. You know what you want your images and illusions to conceal. Your images and illusions do not enable you to escape what is unresolved within you; often your images and illusions make your unresolved emotions more pronounced.

You can become codependent on your images and illusions to hide the truth of your unresolved emotions from yourself. However, this is insane because you fragment your understanding of yourself, creating layers of emotional cycles you attempt to use to counteract any truth exposed to you. When you are exposed to truth you do not want to know about, you exert more control over your emotional cycles, and push yourself into emotional overdrive, in an attempt to not feel the reality you are experiencing. This can cause you to become very vague and disassociated from your own present moment or extremely emotional. When you become overly emotional you often miss the opportunity to acknowledge the truth being exposed, and become willing to settle for the familiarity of your resistance to and denial and avoidance of truth. This causes you to anchor to any image and illusion you believe will conceal the reality of what you are experiencing.

The insanity of denying truth, fuels the insanity of existing superficially within an image and illusion of yourself. Your denial of your unresolved emotions splinters you into different images and illusions, causing you to be unsure as to which image to project in different circumstances. This means every experience you have is governed by your own judgement of reality, because you are attempting to ascertain how to perform. Your judgement of reality inhibits you from being present and feeling your soul truth within the uniqueness of each present moment, because you are always assessing if your images and illusions can control your experience to be one that does not get in the way of your desire to control or your illusion of control.

When you struggle in your denial of your soul truth, you try to control an image to overshadow your awareness of the truth of who you are. You use many images to sustain your denial, because your images create a deceptive veil to hide behind. This is how you attempt to deny the truth of your unresolved emotions. Your images exist because you want to deny your unresolved emotions. When you are willing to resolve your own unresolved emotions, your images dissipate and the truth of who you are shines through. You can deny yourself the opportunity to resolve your unresolved emotions, by complicating your understanding of yourself with your own images and illusions. Your images and illusions are designed to conceal the deception of your separation from your awareness of your soul, and enable you to deny the significance of resolving your fragmentation. When you acknowledge the truth of how fragmented you are whilst separated from your awareness of your soul and disassociated from feeling truth, you create the opportunity to be free of your own soul oppression.

When you use your images and illusions to obscure your ability to be objective about your own unresolved emotions, you scan the mankind collective landscape to assess which image will give you an illusory prize. You select an image you believe will generate the illusion you want to exist in and condition yourself to perform it. When you become disillusioned with the illusory prize and realise it has no substance, the superficiality of your images and illusions causes you to emotionally feel empty and trapped in the meaninglessness of your own performances. When you disassociate from feeling the truth of your soul, to control yourself to images and illusions, you aid the suppression, repression and oppression of what you came to resolve. Your codependency on images and illusions means you deny yourself the opportunity to resolve the façades concealing your soul denial, and to evolve to feel the meaningfulness of all your experiences.

Your desire to create an image that you believe is attached to a revered illusion fosters your codependency on abiding by your own desire to control. You can become blinded by your desire and lose awareness of what you are actually doing. This causes you to become fixated on an agenda, while being unwilling to acknowledge or accept reality. Unfortunately, you will often attach yourself to images and illusions, regardless of their validity or how they make you feel. You bind yourself to your images and illusions in an attempt to control your life experiences. However, it is often your desire to perfect your images and illusions that inhibit you from enjoying your own life. You can become so caught up in the performance of your images and illusions that you become disassociated and unable to feel yourself within your life experience. Your life experiences can become surreal; you are there but not there, often just going through the motions. When you sacrifice your original intention for life and shift to a temporary illusion, you feel oppressed and lost in the familiarity of the cyclic patterns of your soul oppression.

When your desire to defend your own images and illusions becomes of paramount importance, you justify all your emotional reactions with perceived righteous judgement, which you use as your defense for being deceptive to yourself. When you sacrifice living as a soul unified with truth to exist in your images and illusions, you become plagued with a sense of having lost something; you feel a void that you know you are unable to fill. You defend the choices you make to protect your attachment to your images and illusions, and deny the price you pay for controlling yourself to an image.

Your desire to gratify your control of your images and illusions undermines the significance of being a unique, independent, individual soul of *True Source Divine Origin Consciousness*. When you devalue the significance of being honest, you demoralise yourself and you crave validation for your images and illusions. This means you lose the courage and confidence to be true to yourself, which throws you into emotional chaos. The image you are trying to portray is born from your desire to conceal the emotional chaos, which creates a yearning in you to see if you can influence others' perception of you. The question is: do you want other people who are consumed with their own images and illusions to be validating your images and illusions? When you crave getting validation but cannot satisfy the craving, you compulsively compete with your perception of others' judgement of you and are often obsessed with your desire to control their judgement. Your own self-judgement invalidates any validation you receive. You emotionally feel a void because you have corrupted yourself and have gone into competition with others, even the ones you love. People with images compete with other people's images, and there is always the perception of a winner and a loser. When you perceive yourself as being the winner or the loser, do you realise that you have sold your awareness of your soul for an image competition?

When you have oppressed the reality of being a significant soul, by orientating yourself to chase validation for your images and illusions, you become entrapped by the void you feel. You want to be able to control a way of validating how you define yourself and seek verification of how you are significant within mankind, whilst denying the natural essence of your soul. You can be emotionally volatile when you try to control your own definition of yourself, because you become fearful of anyone or anything that could potentially disrupt what you are trying to construct and control for. This means you are constantly trying to secure your own control of your images and illusions; this is how your ego began. Ego is the desire to gratify your control by prioritising the unconscious energy of your soul's unconsciousness, over your awareness of your soul's consciousness. When you stop trusting and accepting the truth of your own soul and want to alter the reality of truth with your images and illusions, you prioritise the protection of the unconscious energy of your soul. This means you distort your understanding of yourself with your own desire to pacify your ego. This leaves you constantly layering your unresolved emotions over your feelings and awareness of reality, in an attempt to control how you hide the truth of yourself, your emotions and your choices from yourself.

When you seek to pacify all your insecurities and want to act out all your unresolved emotions with no accountability, you become obsessed with having life work to your expectations. You can obsess with wanting your illusion of control to be secure, which means you struggle when life becomes uncertain or when you recognise others are not aligning with your images and illusions. You want to control reality to be conducive to your illusion of control, which causes you to become bitterly disappointed because life is dynamic and can never be completely controlled by you. When you deceptively believe you can control your soul's consciousness to abandon the purpose of your soul journey, which is to resolve your unresolved emotions, you seek to perform an image that you believe is conducive to your control. You may also seek to align to an illusion about your soul to corrupt your ability to acknowledge truth. You may anchor to a controlled identity to create an excuse for your denial.

Controlled identity is a role or experience that you use to form an image of who you believe you are. Roles can be mother, brother or those defined by your profession. They are also roles defined by your experiences, such as mountaineer, traveler or being an authority over something or others. They are part of what you do and when used to define yourself, you lose awareness or the willingness to be of your natural self. For example:

- You are a soul who mothers.
- You are a soul who is also a brother to someone.
- You are a soul whose occupation is _____ .
- You are a soul who enjoys climbing mountains.
- You are a soul who loves to travel.

When you comprehend yourself as a soul, image, illusions and controlled identities become limiting definitions. Even though the roles you have in life are important and all contribute to the tapestry of your life experience, you are not defined by one role; to do so, dumbs down the truth of who you naturally are.

- You may be a mother, but you express the uniqueness of your soul within this experience.
- You may love climbing mountains, because you feel your unification with your soul in that activity.

Your soul's consciousness constantly endeavours to alert you to the reality of your denial and control structures, which often has you in conflict with your own awareness. When you control and restrict your internal knowing of truth, with your images and illusions of yourself, life, your present moment and others, you become your own soul oppressor. When you deny your natural ability to feel the dynamic energy of your soul, you start constructing ways of upholding an illusion of control. You create control structures, that become patterns of how you attempt to sustain your life. Your illusion of control causes you to misunderstand yourself and the motives behind your emotional reactions. You can inhibit your ability to accept your own awareness of truth, whilst not realising you are seeking to understand your soul, life and *True Source Divine Origin Consciousness*.

When you are willing to be indifferent to truth, and ignore and deny your reality to secure your illusion of control, you inhibit your ability to be truthfully honest. It is through your truthfulness that you begin to understand and comprehend your soul, life and *True Source Divine Origin Consciousness*. Truth is only found when you are truthfully honest about your reality. Your denial of your soul and truth has you existing in mankind's insanity of denying reality. When you deny life is a learning opportunity, you accept the insanity of denying reality and being indifferent to truth. This is because you want to deny the reality of the unconscious energy of your soul, and you want to believe your control can surpass the relevance of truth.

When you claim to be in control but ignore the patterns of your own ego, you lose your willingness to explore truth because you fear any discovery will disrupt your illusion of control. When you ignore the reality of your ego, which is the desire to pacify your own control, you lose awareness of yourself and become consumed with your own wants and desires. This causes you to become indifferent to yourself within reality as you try to hide the extent of the negativity of your control. To understand your control energy is to be enlightened, because it is the discovery of what is inhibiting your awareness of truth.

Enlightened means to:

- Know yourself in truth
- Acknowledge the reality of your soul oppression
- Appreciate the core essences of your soul
- Feel your soul
- Be awakened to your origins
- Participate in your own resolution

Resolution is not achieved through images, illusions or controlled identities, it comes from the acceptance of life being an opportunity to learn by being truthfully honest with yourself.

Your desire for control is what you use to oppose your honesty. You oppose your honesty by trying to assess what you can achieve with your control. You can become obsessive with the desire to see evidence of your control steering how your reality unfolds. This causes you to go to great lengths to observe your control affecting others, and the emotional, energetic and physical environment you inhabit. This means you do not want to be present and honest about yourself in your reality, but you want to construct a reality that is conducive to your control. Your life can become an arena where you try to pacify you own control, which means you become ego driven and out of tune with the true essence of your soul. You seek to control the surface of your existence, whilst denying the depths of your own emotional turmoil and the truth of denying the significance of being a soul who has the original intention to be honest. You can overshadow the truth of your behaviour with an image constructed to suit your illusion of control. This leaves you anchoring to any excuse that you believe justifies wanting to control reality and truth. However, there is always a cost to your soul.

When you try to validate your control by controlling others to align to it or to have the same control structures as you do, you become manipulative because you want to incite in others what you use to justify your own emotional behaviour. This can cause you to only value what conforms to your control. The failure of others to conform to your expectations causes you to emotionally feel conflicted, which creates an agenda you use to justify ramping up your control. You use others' non-conformity as an excuse to react and exert your control energy. You want others to adopt and perform the images and illusions you have of them, so you can believe your own illusion of control. You use others' non-conformity to the images and illusions you want them to perform as a justifiable excuse to be judgemental and even vindictive.

You can control yourself to be in conflict with your own inability to control, which means you are constantly creating competitions with your reality to ascertain the prowess of your control. This competition causes you to lose awareness of your own soul integrity and you separate further into an image of yourself. This means you can perceive others as either in competition with your image or as stagehands that need to be controlled to enhance your image. You can control yourself to deny the uniqueness of all souls, which causes you to oppress the truth of being a significant, unique, independent, individual soul of *True Source Divine Origin Consciousness*.

When you are in conflict with the difference between your illusion of control and reality, you become very indifferent to how your unresolved emotions and agendas affect those you encounter. This causes you to use your control to attempt to conceal your own arrogance towards truth, as you become skilled at justifying every expectation, want and desire. When you arrogantly ignore truth to accommodate your denial of being emotionally swamped by the energy within your soul's unconsciousness and your denial of the truth of feeling the resonance of your soul's consciousness, you make your life a struggle. You arrogantly deny you have created your own emotions with your denial of your soul. You have created conflict with reality, because you are in conflict with your soul. If you cannot accept the truth of who you are, how can you accept reality?

You use your desire to control or your desire to sustain an illusion of control, to create beliefs and fears you believe justify generating more desire for control. You expect it will be your control of someone or something that will quell your fears and prove the validity of your beliefs. This creates a self-perpetuating cycle of being addicted to your illusion of control, which means you are constantly craving the pacification of your desire to control. This causes you to become fearful that your denial of reality will not work and that you will be exposed to the arrogance of wanting control over everyone you encounter. You fear being exposed to your own arrogance because it highlights your attempts to control your denial, but exposing your arrogance is an opportunity to observe the truth of your soul's unconsciousness and how debilitating your addiction to control can be.

Your soul's consciousness observes your desire for control as an obstacle to your rise with grace; your desire for control inhibits your own evolution. You can observe your desire for control inhibiting your awareness of your soul consciousness' ability to expose you to truth. If you have decided to protect your control you willingly annihilate your ability to give yourself grace, and allow your self-judgement to obstruct any opportunity to be truthful with yourself. It is you who chooses what you will acknowledge within your rise and fall from grace.

Your rise and fall from grace is you experiencing your unresolved emotions, whilst your soul's consciousness highlights the truth of what you are experiencing. When you are truthfully honest with yourself and have accepted responsibility for your own energy, the unconscious energy is resolved and converted to conscious awareness. When you deny what is being highlighted and attempt to use your unresolved emotions to deal with your unresolved emotions, you withdraw from giving yourself grace. This causes you to align to a cyclic pattern of soul oppression to obstruct your awareness of your freedom of choice, which is an attempt to escape being responsible and accountable for yourself. This often has you performing images and illusions to override your awareness of yourself within your present moment reality.

If you are dishonest and contrived, you will deny the opportunity you have to explore all aspects of your truth. Your dishonesty causes you to deny your ability to explore the natural process of your own rise and fall from grace. This denial means you become stuck within the fall, refusing the freedom to rise with honesty and grace. When you choose to remain fallen, you encase yourself within the stagnation generated by your images and illusions. Images and illusions are created by your fear reactions and embedded beliefs that sustain your denial of your soul.

Your soul's consciousness and life expose you to the reality that your control is an illusion. Any exposure of truth is an opportunity to use your honesty to create your rise with grace. Your honesty creates the space for resolution and evolution of your soul. You can fear exposing your desire for control, because you fear being held responsible and accountable for the truth of your soul's unconsciousness. When you fear acknowledging the futility of your control, you use your unresolved emotions to secure your denial. Your denial causes you to miss the opportunities for resolution and evolution. This means you will justify your denial to protect the familiarity of your images and illusions, because you believe you are keeping yourself safe. The question is safe from what?

Your images and illusions are barriers to truth. When you are fearful of being aware of how your images and illusions are barriers to truth, you create a fear of yourself. Your fear of yourself causes you to disregard your own awareness of yourself and truth. Your soul's consciousness, which is the truth of who you are, has no need to use barriers to truth, and it is only when you are separated from the awareness of your soul that you align to your images and illusions. Your honesty with truth creates change and the freedom to acknowledge what your soul's consciousness exposes for you. Your images and illusions are a product of your stagnation, and part of your inability to trust the dynamic energy of your soul, life and truth.

When you separate from your awareness of your soul, you try to use images and illusions to emulate the truth of who you are. Why settle for emulations when you are of truth? Imitations are always missing the truth of the original. When you perform images and illusions, you lose your awareness of the authenticity of your soul. When you try to control truth and reality to suit your imitations and emulations, you can feel the missing original energy of your soul and truth, which leads to you feeling the disunity within yourself. Your acknowledgement of your internal disunity can be a catalyst for you to seek the original meaning of your soul journey. This may cause you to be open to discover the truth of your control structures and how you have existed in denial of the truth of who you are. When you control yourself to create an image to feed your own control structures and soul denial, you are actually disregarding the opportunity to be open to discover the truth of both your consciousness and unconsciousness. Your images and illusions fragment your awareness of truth and cause you to disassociate from feeling the truth of yourself. When you protect your images, you sustain your resistance to and denial and avoidance of your own awareness of your soul truth.

You can use your fear or non-comprehension of yourself to invoke harsh self-judgement, and also to justify the extent of your indifference to truth. Your indifference can cause you to be arrogant about the images you use. Your indifference to truth can become a source for your own delusion of grandeur, which inhibits you from discovering the truth of your soul.

When you choose to trade off your awareness of the truth of your soul for a delusion of grandeur, you actually dumb down the truth of who you naturally are. When you support your unresolved emotions with illusions and ignore the truth of your soul, you reject your natural significance, uniqueness, independence and individuality. You do this so you can imitate what you believe will support your delusion of grandeur whilst overriding any feelings and observations that expose the arrogance of your ego. When you create an identity to protect and justify the unresolved emotions being exposed, you will go to great lengths to attempt to conceal your indifference to truth. This will expose a lot to you about your own desire to control, which creates opportunities for you to acknowledge the motives, agenda and deception of your delusions of grandeur.

Your delusions of grandeur are dangerous and expose your willingness to operate without boundaries. This means you do not seek to discover truth and will go to any extreme to annihilate anything and anyone who does not support your perceived superiority. When you are unwilling to recognise the significance of the boundaries you need to put in place, to honour yourself and others, and to respect the truth of what you are aware of, you betray your integrity. When you betray your integrity, you become indifferent. Your integrity enables you to get to the point of curiosity where you want to reveal the truth to yourself. Delusions of grandeur create barriers to truth and obliterate your awareness of your own integrity, leaving you fixated on your desire for control and tolerating your indifference to truth.

When you govern yourself with delusions of grandeur, believing you are able to control life, you become pretentious within your own illusion of control. Your indifference to truth underlies all your illusions and enables you to be manipulative; constructing lies that you believe you are entitled to force others to align to. Your attempts to fasten to your own delusions of grandeur have you fearing the exposure of any of your insecurities and you use this fear to ramp up your indifference, which leads you to have no boundaries and a complete lack of integrity. Delusions of grandeur enable you to override your fear of your own insecurities with the arrogance of your indifference. This causes you to be governed by your own narcissism, engulfed by your desire to prove you are above all others. You believe you are entitled to have free rein to do whatever you like. When you seek to use others' unresolved emotions to your advantage, you knowingly manipulate others to sustain your beliefs of your own importance.

Your delusions of grandeur mean you oppose the reality of the equality of all souls, which causes you to become transfixed by your own desire to control your images and illusions. When you deny the equality of all souls and compete to be superior, you lose your natural ability to feel the significance of truth and the significance of being present in your reality.

When you deny the equality of all souls, you also deny part of who you are. When you acknowledge the equality of all souls there is no need to be in competition or to try to be superior; because you know each individual is naturally significant.

Your images and illusions are the choice to conform to performances, which creates internal disunity because you cannot feel the truth of yourself or appreciate your own significance, uniqueness, independence and individuality. Regardless of who you momentarily impress with your images and illusions, you still feel the void within and the emotional upheaval of your own internal disunity. The void you feel may cause you to desperately use more exaggerated images and illusions in an attempt to hide from acknowledging that the void is there. This causes you to separate further from the truth of yourself and then you begin to seek validation from outside yourself to justify the image you have created. You start fearing that you are unable to get or sustain the validation you believe you require, to quell the disunity within you and to overshadow the void you feel.

When you create or align to beliefs that support your images and illusions, and enact behaviours that defend and protect your images and illusions, you become lost in your own performances. You can fool yourself into believing you can settle for images and illusions. This leaves you oppressing the truth you can feel, as you attempt to deny the niggling feelings alerting you to your own deception. The niggling feeling is your awareness that you are in disunity with your soul's consciousness and truth, and that feeling does not go away until you become truthful with yourself. Your attempts to ignore the niggling feelings, leaves you justifying your own control structures that underpin your images and illusions. You are rattled by the potential exposure of your insecurities and portray an image in an attempt to quell your fear and anxiety. However, this further exacerbates your insecurity, fear and anxiety, as you constantly remain in a semi-state of panic about your image. You want to believe you are in control of your images and illusions, but you teeter on the verge of exposing to yourself how fraudulent your images and illusions really are.

When you try to resist, deny and avoid others' control structures or any truth that may interrupt your illusory control, you may fear imminent image failure, and become obsessed with protecting your images and illusions. Your fear of image failure is fueled by your fear of exposing your own indifference, superficiality or incompetence, which can cause you to behave irrationally. You become what you fear because when you behave irrationally you actually exude indifference, superficiality or incompetence. Your irrational behaviour draws attention to that which you most want to hide.

When you do not acknowledge your unresolved emotions, you do not seek resolution. This causes you to become stagnant and very contrived in the way you interact with others and life. You can fail to recognise that you are constructing an image, instead of being of your truth. You use your control structures to protect your unresolved emotions, and to construct images and illusions to hide from the reality of your soul and the truth of your feelings. You ignore your own deception and complacently create illusions about yourself and life. The longer you invest in the deception, the more difficult it becomes to unravel the illusions. To uphold your illusions, you become reliant on your performances and beliefs, in order to conceal the unresolved emotions underpinning your willingness to be deceptive with yourself. This enables you to construct an identity using the unresolved emotions stored in your soul's unconsciousness. Your constructed identity becomes an arena for you to act out all your unresolved emotions and control structures.

When you align to your own images and illusions, you scale your worth by your ability to perform well. If you believe your performances are fooling others you become entrapped in your own constructed image, but you will be unable to escape the void you feel. The void is the result of your own separation from your awareness of your soul and your disassociation from feeling truth.

Images are an attempt to sculpt yourself into a performance, which often takes you in the opposite direction to what you believe you want to portray. Images are never sourced from the authenticity of your soul, even though some may resemble in appearance or behaviour what you want to be perceived as. Your desire to perfect an image can cause you to lose the essence of how you would like to live and while you imitate what you want to be perceived as, you lose the opportunity to express the truth of who you are. Your desire to perfect an image causes you to lose all objectivity about yourself, your behaviour and how you are affecting others.

When your image becomes a constructed identity, you apply rules to regulate how you should perform. Constructed identity becomes what you falsely believe makes you, 'you'. It is how you define yourself and what you control yourself to, regardless of the ramifications. You can be determined you need to perform and control for the results you believe will achieve the image you strive for. This causes you to become obsessed with how others are perceiving you.

Spiritually elite identity: When you use a constructed identity of being spiritually elite, you can believe you are an authority on what truth is. This constructed identity becomes your arena in which you create performances to hide the unresolved emotions stored within your soul's unconsciousness. You align to the belief of being born special and superior to others and truth. Unfortunately, your image inhibits you from discovering your own uniqueness and feeling the individuality of your soul. You align to what you believe is spiritually elite behaviour and act it out, believing you can orchestrate reality with an illusion. You use your image of being spiritually elite to become indifferent to the natural equality of all souls, and become judgemental of anyone who does not ascribe to your beliefs about yourself.

If you class yourself as an evolved soul without acknowledging or resolving your unresolved emotions, you will become reliant on your judgement to secure your beliefs. You create an illusion you believe will conceal your unresolved emotions, however your inability to sustain your own illusion exacerbates your insecurities. Your insecurities can cause you to become extremely manipulative, sly and dogmatically controlling. You may internally believe you are not good enough for your own illusion, but the illusion is what you cling to in order to override the truth you feel, and to control yourself to orchestrate the pretence of your own constructed identity. When you want to justify and gratify your own ego, you become controlling in an attempt to uphold your illusions and secure your image. When you emulate what you want your truth to be, you create a false version of truth, which separates you from the truth of your soul and your opportunities to resolve and evolve.

Perfect parent identity: When you use the constructed identity of being a perfect parent, you believe you are an authority on parenting. This constructed identity becomes your arena in which you create performances to hide the unresolved emotions stored within your soul's unconsciousness. You align yourself to the belief that you have to be busy and the expert, and then exert righteous control over every aspect of your child's life, so that you can believe you are the perfect parent. Unfortunately, this inhibits you from sharing quality time and the truth of yourself with your child. You use the image of being a perfect parent to become indifferent to the truth of what you are actually doing.

If you class yourself as a perfect parent without actually acknowledging how your desired image is affecting your family, you will become reliant on controlling others to orchestrate the family image. This may stem from the belief that you have ownership over the family. This causes you to believe that you have the right to fix everyone so that they can perform as you request, as you seek to secure your perfect parent image and orchestrate the projection of the perfect family image to the outside world.

Your image of being a perfect parent is how you try to conceal your insecurities and causes you to demand conformity to your control of the family. However, your inability to sustain and orchestrate the image you want creates more insecurity within you. This causes you to internally believe you are 'not good enough' for your own image, but the image is what you cling to, to override the truth you feel. You can control yourself with your fear of being wrong, to remain devoted to the constructed identity.

Your image of perfect parent can leave you emotionally, energetically and physically exhausted, and you often become overbearing and removed from reality. Part of the exhaustion you feel comes from the amount of effort it takes to uphold your own image and from trying to control everyone to comply with your expectations. When you are obsessed with your desire to project an illusion to the outside world, you override your awareness of your own reality. When you cling to your image, you internally struggle with your own control and struggle with the reality of your family consisting of significant, unique, independent, individual members who maintain their own agendas, one of which may be to oppose being part of your constructed image.

Superior identity: When you use a position of authority to construct an identity of being superior, you believe you are an authority on everything that comes into your orbit and an authority over anyone you encounter. This constructed identity becomes your arena in which you create performances to hide the unresolved emotions stored within your soul's unconsciousness. You align to the belief that you are the most knowledgeable and are infallible. Unfortunately, your image inhibits you from being aware of how you treat others, causing you to become very competitive and often manipulative as you seek to prove you are the one with all the answers. You express what you believe is wisdom to others while you ignore your own nagging self-doubt. You rely on your judgement of others, to reinforce your identity of being superior. You can arrogantly feed off others' self-doubt and insecurity, whilst slyly denying your own self-doubt and insecurity.

You use the constructed identity of being superior because you believe it will conceal your unresolved emotions and allow you to remain dogmatically righteous in your judgement; however, your fear that someone could challenge your superiority leaves you feeling anxious. If you class yourself as superior without acknowledging your insecurities, you become reliant on belittling and criticising others. This will cause you to become overzealous in your desire to prove you are above all others, which has you unwilling to explore or even discuss new concepts or possibilities. Your dogmatic approach to life and others has you attempting to restrict everyone and everything to adhere to your boxed perceptions of how you want the world to work. You constantly seek to reaffirm your own judgement to yourself and seek to observe your control affecting another and reality, which causes you to become contrary to the flow within reality and to be oppositional to others. You can become obnoxiously defensive and sly as you endeavour to prove to yourself that your image of superiority supersedes your fear of not being good enough. You inflict your dogmatic views on others in an attempt to justify and gratify your own ego.

In your illusions, you believe you can control and compete with the natural order of life and your soul consciousness' intent for life, which is actually your original intention. However, this belief actually numbs you to the significance of your soul. You use different aspects of your soul's unconsciousness to create illusions about the reality of your soul journey, and to discount the importance of how you choose to interact with others and the truth of your reality. This means you deny the equality of all souls and the significance of valuing your own soul. Your images and illusions create beliefs and constructed identities that actually inhibit your resolution and evolution, and cause you to stay trapped, denying the reality of who you really are.

When you deny the reality of who you are, you often control yourself to believe that life has to be hard and long suffering, and you adopt a martyr or victim mentality, which can morph into a constructed identity. This can create many misconceptions you use to construct beliefs that life is a struggle and leaves you suffering for as long as you deny your awareness of truth. These beliefs inhibit your awareness of your own natural flow of consciousness. One of the biggest struggles you have is consistently trying to work out how to deny truth when your soul's consciousness is constantly exposing you to truth. You struggle to secure your denial. You create your own suffering when you allow yourself to worship, protect and justify your images and illusions. When you believe you are in control of your images and illusions, you do not realise that your images and illusions are actually controlling you and the choices you make.

When you resist, deny and avoid coming to terms with the reality of your images and illusions, you deny yourself the peace created from your acceptance of being a soul. Your images and illusions are a barrier to your awareness of truth, and when you protect your images and illusions you remain ensnared in your soul denial, depriving yourself of the opportunities your own truthfulness creates.

Denial of the truth of using images and illusions

Your soul's consciousness endeavours to help you acknowledge the reality that you have the freedom to choose to accept yourself as a soul, and to feel the truth of who you are. You cannot accept yourself as a soul and feel the truth of who you are by adopting beliefs, or controlling yourself to an image of being conscious, or by creating an illusion from what you would like your life to be perceived as. When you become attached to your images and illusions because you are trying to redefine yourself through them, you devalue the natural significance of your own soul. This means you deprive yourself of the opportunity to explore, discover and unconditionally love the truth of who you are. You create or align to a falsity about yourself, because you are unwilling to explore the truth of yourself, your words and behaviours. You can define yourself with falsities. This becomes a self-perpetuating cycle of performing images and believing your own illusions, which inhibits your ability to objectively observe yourself within your reality.

When you control yourself to fixate on your images, illusions and controlled identities because you are hiding from the truth of yourself, you become willing to lie to yourself and to protect your lies. When you hide behind your lies, you create an internal struggle, because you cannot control your soul to conform to the falsity of your images and illusions. You hide from acknowledging your own deception of wanting your images, illusions and controlled identities to oppress the truth of being a soul who seeks resolution and evolution.

Reading a book and attempting to replicate what you have read, or emulating what you have seen in others, without truly comprehending your own behaviours, is to exist within the insecurity of having to constantly modify your images and illusions. When you emulate what you believe others will admire, or adhere to what you believe others will refrain from judging you on, you become lost in your own emulations, often to the point of being unable to recognise your separation from your awareness of your soul. Your images and illusions become the actualisation of your self-manipulation, and when you are unwilling to be honest with yourself, you become embroiled in your own denial and deception.

You can attempt to use your images and illusions as deflectors of judgement, as a shield to protect yourself from your fear of being judged, or from your fear of not being able to control your reaction to the judgement you receive. When you try to foresee what you will be judged on, you create a story to tell yourself, in an attempt to counteract your own insecurities, which you have incited with your anticipation of being judged. This causes you to constantly analyse and compulsively scrutinise your own images, illusions and controlled identities. This means you can never be free of your own self-judgement. When you attempt to create an image of yourself that you believe will suppress the insecurities created by your own self-judgement and your judgement of your own images, illusions and controlled identities, you internally fester in your fear of not being good enough. There is an insanity to the compulsion of trying to fix emotional problems with images and illusions, and then denying the insecurities which result from attempting to protect and secure the images and illusions.

You do not feel secure in your own images and illusions and are afraid you will not be able to deceive others into believing your images and illusions represent the truth of who you are. You are afraid because you internally know truth cannot be fooled. You cannot even sustain the image to fool yourself one hundred percent of the time, and feel the falsity even when you believe the performance of your image is flawless. When you choose to act out images and illusions, you are choosing to dishonour the truth of your soul and devalue the significance of truth. You are also choosing to be stagnant within the control structures you use to perform your images and to secure your alignment with your own illusions. This is how you oppress your awareness of your soul's consciousness.

You use your images and illusions to control yourself to a charade of living, obscuring the truth of your soul and the importance of your soul journey. When you accept the reality of your images and illusions, many lessons can be learned. When you choose to be honest, you free yourself to acknowledge your truth, but this level of honesty can never be achieved if you are manipulating yourself with your own images and illusions. When seeking your truth, be aware of the resistance, denial and avoidance you will compulsively want to use, to protect and validate your illusion of control. Your awareness of yourself will create opportunities to expose what is inhibiting you from feeling free, to truthfully explore the entirety of yourself. Trusting your soul's consciousness means you accept the truth of your unresolved emotions without fear or judgement. When you are willing to trust your soul, you will use your truthfulness to resolve what is unresolved. This includes the images and illusions you use to create a false sense of security, or to hide the insecurity you are aware of, but refuse to be completely truthful about.

Your images, illusions and controlled identities become band-aids over your emotional issues and enforce the perpetuation of the energy of your soul's unconsciousness. Your images and illusions are not of your natural self and this causes you to go to great lengths to secure your denial of the effort you are putting into your own images and illusions. You use your images, illusions and controlled identities to conceal the truth of your unresolved emotions. However, your images, illusions and controlled identities do in fact expose you to what you are attempting to conceal, if you are willing to be truthful with yourself. Your unresolved emotions fester because you have chosen to oppress the truth of your soul's consciousness. You attempt to justify your attachment to your images, illusions and controlled identities, because you believe they give you the strength to survive your denial of reality. However, they actually weaken you, because a false foundation never results in self-confidence or true self-acceptance.

You use your images and illusions to suppress the reality you feel, however the suppression of your feelings is detrimental to your resolution and evolution. When you anchor to your intention to suppress your awareness of the emotional, energetic and physical effects of your unresolved emotions, you become complacent about life. You use your judgement to secure your denial and to convince yourself that your images and illusions are essential for your control of life, truth, yourself and others. You can desperately cling to your ability to sustain your denial of reality, however truth has a natural way of exposing itself. Suppression is an attempt to create more space for your deception to continue. You can get to the point of overload, where your suppression, your images and your illusions do not band-aid anything, which causes you to implode within the instability of your own deception.

Your images and illusions are the manifestation of your willingness to deny your soul. You attempt to control yourself to be indifferent to the emotional state your unresolved emotions create, but you are a soul with the internal knowing that you have the opportunity to explore the truth of your own conscious and unconscious energy. The emotional states you find yourself in are constant reminders of what you require resolution in. You will always expose yourself to your own unresolved emotions. You may internally fight your awareness of your unresolved emotions, to suppress the truth of what you originally intended to acknowledge, accept, resolve and evolve in this lifetime.

You manifest images and illusions that you believe will pardon you from the ramifications caused by your own deception. However, your unresolved emotions have a cause and effect within you; for every emotional reaction you have there is a reverberation within you, which can either be a catalyst for your honesty or a trigger for a sequence of emotional reactions.

Your images and illusions align you to a false version of reality that you believe will pacify your fear of not being good enough. Instead of resolving the fear, you use images and illusions to protect your denial. You internally know that your denial will create more emotional angst for you to confront, because the truth of your life experiences is constantly alerting you to your emotional, energetic and physical reality. Your constructed versions of reality, which means the illusions you pretend represent truth are devoid of any truth that will upset your denial and illusion of control. This causes you to omit, from your verbal recounts or memories of events, what will expose your deceptive contribution to the experience. Most people tell you about being a victim but they rarely tell you about how they orchestrated, incited and contributed to the negativity of the event, or the oppression of another.

When you align your performances to others' expectations in an attempt to fool yourself into believing you can control life, you will emulate what you believe is expected of you, and this causes you to lose your energetic independence. When you lose energetic independence, you attempt to pacify your insecurities by believing you are superior or inferior to others. You will seek to identify who you believe you are superior or inferior to, or who you want to impress. Your insecurities are created by denying your own natural significance, uniqueness, independence and individuality. Your denial enables you to conform to and emulate what you believe will insulate you from being shunned by those you want to align to and want approval from. However, this actually inflames your insecurities, because you are now at the mercy of the judgement of those you were trying to align to.

Resolving your unresolved emotions is the only way of understanding and accepting the true meaning of truth. Your images and illusions produce energy that has you separated and disassociated from feeling truth. No one can control or dictate to you what your soul's consciousness is. Your life is a journey of self-discovery and we all discover the truth of ourselves uniquely. To experience and feel the uniqueness of your soul is to consciously participate in the exploration of your own truth. Only you can decide to value your own resonance with truth and the significance of your choices.

LEFT: *Images and illusions come in many forms and are often hard to identify as an image or illusion if you are unwilling to be truthfully honest with yourself.*

Resolution creates evolution. Evolution stems from:
- Trusting in your ability to be of truth and valuing your resonance with truth.
- Your truthfulness, which enables you to feel your relationship with your origin of truth.
- Consciously aligning to the significance of resolving the energy of your soul's unconsciousness.
- Resolving your separation from your awareness of your soul and your disassociation from feeling truth.

Seeking your truth is a choice and creates the space for you to be present and honest about your own internal and external reality.

You use your images and illusions to oppress your ability to utilise your freedom of choice. You limit your experience of life by upholding your attachment to your images, illusions and controlled identities. Your soul's consciousness creates opportunities for you to use your freedom of choice to acknowledge the truth of your soul and the reality of your life experiences. Your choices create your experiences and by acknowledging your freedom to choose, you begin to take responsibility for the gift of freewill.

Life is an opportunity to choose to explore your soul truth or to exist separated from your awareness of your soul. To be soul separated is to exist within an image of yourself and an illusion of reality. Trusting the truth of how you honestly feel, creates the space for truth to be recognised, appreciated and respected. This assists you to understand your soul journey. Your choices are crossroads within the journey of life, and it is your honesty that creates opportunities to learn from your choices. Every truthful choice expands your awareness of the truth of your reality, which enables you to be even more receptive to the synchronicities within your life.

Section Five

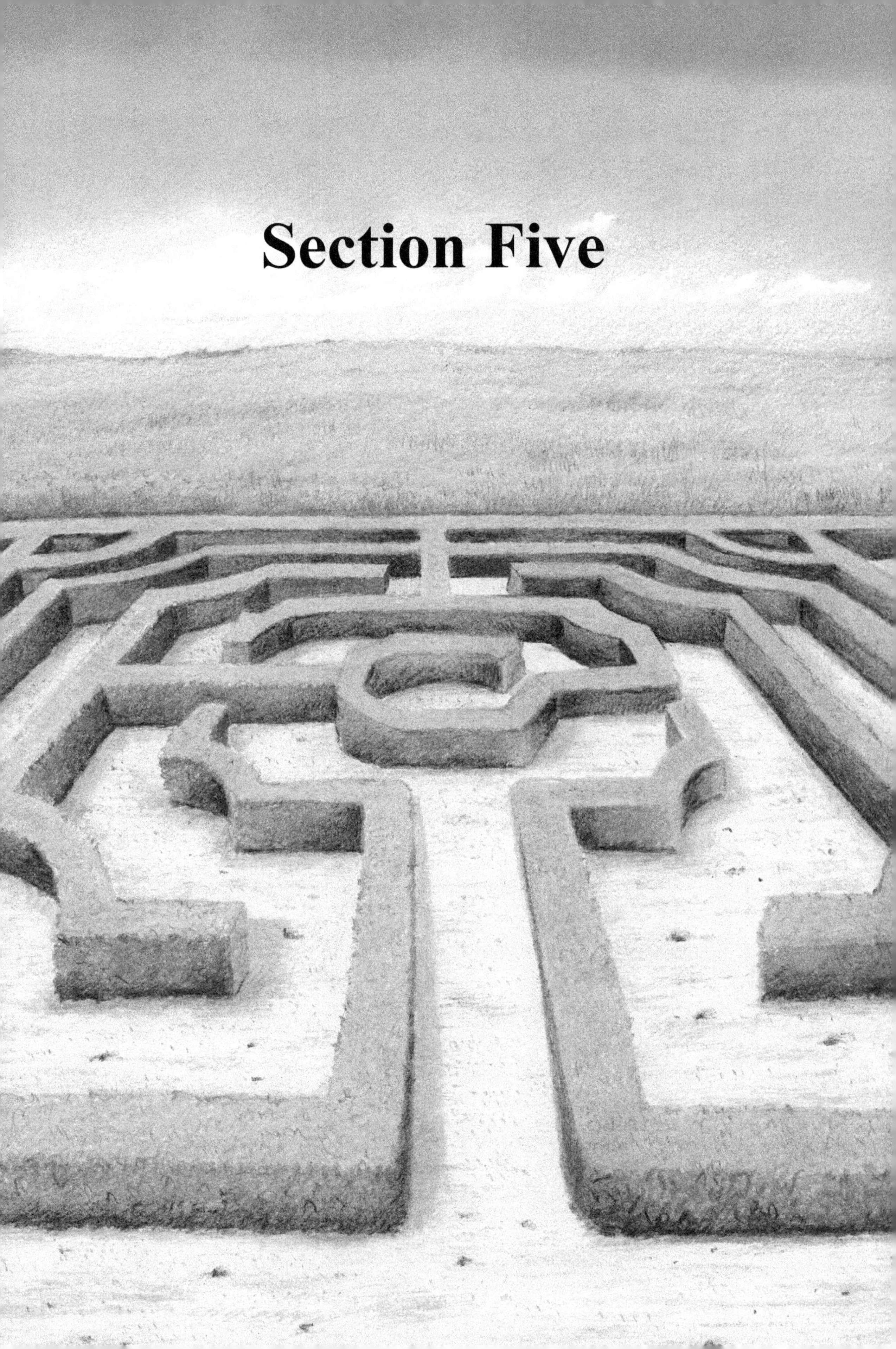

Chapter Twenty-Six

Controlled evolution

Controlled evolution is one of your barriers to truth within your soul's unconsciousness. Your controlled evolution energy is a mixture of your beliefs, denials and desires that are entwined with your spirituality or your demands for how life should be. Controlled evolution is a type of unconscious energy which you produce by conjuring beliefs about what truth is, and also what you believe your version of truth expects of you. It is also conjured beliefs about how you should be perceived and how your life should be. These beliefs can be used to reinforce your barriers to truth. You can use these beliefs to create and align to a spiritual image. You use your spiritual image to construct what you believe you have to portray. For example:

- Being spiritually enlightened
- Overtly compassionate
- Philosophising
- Having a sunny disposition
- Appearing to be wise
- Having the perfect body
- Unconditionally loving all you encounter
- Denying the importance of the physicality of life
- Being accepting of everything
- Being constantly sincere

What you believe you portray and what you actually do can be extremely different and performing an image only secures your barriers to truth, which inhibits you from exploring your soul truth, both your consciousness and unconsciousness. Controlled evolution energy entwines with spiritual deception that stagnates you in what you believe you know, or in what you want to believe.

You use spiritual deception to protect the sustainability of all your barriers to truth. Your controlled evolution energy, is generated from spiritual beliefs, denials and desires, which becomes a way of attempting to control the pivotal points within the junction between the energy of your soul's consciousness and the energy of your soul's unconsciousness. This means you circumvent what is being exposed to you and align to whatever you want to believe. You are the interface between your consciousness and unconsciousness, and what you choose within the junction either has you compulsively operating from the energy of your soul's unconsciousness, or frees you to explore truth and to respond consciously to whatever is occurring or being revealed. When you acknowledge the truth that every present moment is a junction, and accept that it is you who decides how you react or respond, you naturally enhance your awareness of truth.

When you deceptively use spiritual beliefs to separate from your resonance with truth, you protect your own soul oppression, and avoid taking responsibility for your own resolution and evolution. This stagnates your evolutionary process and creates a spiritual labyrinth that causes you to use your spirituality:

True Source Divine Origin Consciousness

Your Soul's Consciousness

Controlled evolution - desire to control your soul denial with beliefs.

- As an avoidance technique
- As a defense mechanism
- To skip the resolution process
- To disconnect from feeling
- To seek a destination
- To align to misconceptions
- To escape the pain within your soul
- To pretend you understand yourself
- To resist being present in your reality
- To perform an image of consciousness
- To generate catch phrases to sidestep examining reality
- To hide from your soul truth

Controlled evolution stagnates souls. Instead of being curious and exploratory, we become protective of what we believe, deny or desire, we also become dismissive or fearful of others who do not adhere to our beliefs. Controlled evolution sustains division within mankind and the non-acceptance that we are all significant souls. Controlled evolution is used to overshadow truth. Spiritual beliefs can be used to create prejudices and to discriminate against others if they are not of the same belief system. When we adhere to controlled evolution, we dogmatically protect the beliefs that appease us, and we also restrict the exploration of truth. We can shelter ourselves within only what adheres to what we want to believe. This often allows truth to become the last thing that we value or take notice of, and we devote ourselves instead to the protection of our beliefs.

What we do to truth, we do to each other and to ourselves. When we decide our beliefs are greater than our awareness of truth or the significance of being truthfully honest, we become contradictory, competitive and extremely judgemental. We often hold to and use adverse judgement against any truth that exposes the hypocritical nature of many of our beliefs. When we refuse to examine the facts and disregard any evidence that is contradictory to what we want to believe, we construct beliefs from a lack of knowledge and use these to fuel our adverse judgement. We use our beliefs to shield ourselves from the motives behind our behaviours and from the unresolved emotions underpinning why we surrender to our beliefs. This creates a barrier to us being insightful about ourselves and aware of what we are contributing to.

You can use spiritual beliefs to ignore the impact you have on others, life, relationships and your interactions with truth. Hiding behind the barrier of controlled evolution is one of the ways you contribute to staying intentionally unconscious about your own soul truth. Intentionally unconscious is to deliberately ignore the truth you are aware of or your observation of what is occurring, instead choosing to remain steadfast in what you want to believe. When you protect beliefs that are contrary to reality, you are intentionally unconscious and have chosen to devalue truth. Intentionally unconscious is tolerating a pretense of being of truth, whilst sustaining the protection of your soul's unconsciousness.

You can use spiritual deception to manifest control structures that target the desire to habitually silence your awareness of your soul's consciousness. When you use your beliefs to overshadow the energy of your soul's unconsciousness, you abandon your ability to feel your way with truth. You condition yourself to hide from the reality that you are aware of a part of truth that you deliberately ignore.

LEFT: *Controlled evolution is the use of beliefs to separate yourself from your awareness of truth, which is how you inhibit the process of your resolution and evolution.*

Your barrier of controlled evolution is constructed from your unresolved emotions that fuel the spiritual beliefs you use to hide from your awareness of your soul truth. You do this by oppressing any truth that interferes with your beliefs, which means you become deceptive, manipulative and devoid of feeling the uniqueness of your soul. You can use spiritual beliefs to dictate the direction of your desire for control, which animates your spirituality and activates your indifference to truth. Performances become the priority, and you become fixated on ascertaining what will uphold your image of consciousness you want to portray. Unfortunately, you disengage from the authenticity of your soul and become the enactment of what you believe.

Your framework of soul oppression is a labyrinth of avenues of indifference, you use to protect your own judgement and illusion of control. This also protects your soul denial, which is the crux of your soul's unconsciousness. When you protect your soul denial, you sustain the energy of your soul's unconsciousness whilst you create cyclic patterns of soul oppression to avoid acknowledging truth. Soul illusion is an avenue of indifference within your framework of soul oppression, and your indifference to truth fuels the cyclic patterns that inhibit your natural resonance with truth.

When you manipulate yourself to fortify your spiritual beliefs and denounce any truth that is not useful to the fortification of your beliefs, you become unconscious to the true meaning of being a soul. When you control yourself to separate from acknowledging and feeling the truth of being a significant, unique, independent, individual soul of *True Source Divine Origin Consciousness*, you lose awareness of the value of your own soul integrity. When you lose awareness of your soul integrity, you stifle your willingness to explore truth, to be an objective observer and to perceive the bigger picture. There is a bigger picture to your life experiences, which is far greater than desiring to pacify your control, or to emotionally feel spiritually superior over another soul or collective of souls. When you are separated from your awareness of truth and your soul, you conform to your beliefs that support your unconsciousness. This leaves you attempting to skip the resolution process and instead pretend to be evolved. You are a soul who can resolve what separates you from truth. You can evolve to be unified with the origins of truth, but it is done with truthfulness, not pretense.

When the process of resolution and evolution becomes sidelined, and your beliefs of how to survive in your soul oppression kick in, you become emotionally attached to the protection of your soul's unconsciousness. When you are unconscious to your own spiritual reality, you can become the embodiment of your unresolved emotions; often oblivious to the fact that you have made the decision to deny the significance of being truthfully honest. Your lack of honesty with yourself, causes you to abandon your ability to objectively observe the reality of your emotions and behaviour. You become what you do not acknowledge and what is unresolved within you becomes the catalyst for your behaviour. It is your dishonesty

RIGHT: When you are operating from your unresolved emotions, you fall from grace, separating from your awareness of your soul and disassociating from feeling the truth of your own energy. It is your fall from grace that allows you to experience and explore the truth of the energy of your soul's unconsciousness, which is part of the natural process of resolution and evolution.

Grace

Grace

Grace

The energy
of your
soul's unconsciousness

Grace

Grace

Grace

Soul denial

Denial

Resistance

Judgement

Control

Controlled evolution

Illusion

Images

Heresy

that fuels what is unresolved within you and keeps you opposing any insight into your spiritual reality.

The natural process of rising and falling from grace is a key component of your resolution and evolution. You can remain deceptive about your unresolved emotions because you deny the natural process of rising and falling from grace. The fall from grace is a natural process where you become aware of your unresolved emotions. Within the process of your rise and fall from grace, you have the freedom to choose to be truthfully honest about what you have highlighted for yourself to acknowledge. However, if you choose not to be truthful, you will compulsively justify your unresolved emotions or become the master of your suppression. Your truthful honesty creates your rise with grace, which means not only have you acknowledged the truth of yourself, but you have also decided to be completely responsible for your unresolved emotions and the behaviours you have displayed. Your fall from grace is to separate from your awareness of yourself as a soul and is to disassociate from feeling truth.

To remain fallen is to choose to be intentionally unconscious to the opportunity to resolve your unresolved emotions, and is an attempt to ignore your emotional, energetic and physical reality. To remain fallen is to abandon the opportunity to explore your soul truth and to be entrapped by your own dishonesty and denial. Your truthful honesty with yourself will allow your soul's consciousness to naturally resolve the unresolved emotions, which produced your unconscious energy. Your truthful honesty is how you facilitate your rise with grace. Your rise with grace is you resolving the unconscious energy you formerly denied, which converts your unconscious vibration to conscious frequency. Your choice to ignore, override or deny your emotional, energetic and physical reality, stagnates you within the unconsciousness of your soul. Your dishonesty immerses you in the energetics produced by being in denial of your unresolved emotions. This causes you to become a reverberation of unconscious energy within the energetic mass energy of mankind's collective soul denial.

Your stagnation within your soul's unconsciousness has you fuelling and being fuelled by the energetic collectives within the mass energy of mankind that correlate to your unresolved emotions and beliefs. You become an expression and reverberation of energy within the mass energy of mankind, which amplifies your own unresolved emotions and beliefs. This reveals the truth of your unresolved emotions. You can either choose to acknowledge and be truthfully honest about them, or you will attempt to develop and sustain ways of controlling your avoidance to any emotions you are experiencing. Deceptively using spiritual beliefs can become a way of sustaining the suppression of your unresolved emotions, but it means you are controlling your evolution to be stagnant.

You may honestly recognise your unresolved emotions but if you have no inclination to be responsible for your own unconscious energy, you will not be truthful. It is your honesty that facilitates an opportunity, a junction where you either utilise your recognition to reinforce

LEFT: *To remain stuck in the energy of your soul's unconsciousness is to choose to be unconscious to your emotional reality and to oppose your own opportunities for resolution and evolution. When you wallow in your unresolved emotions because you fear being honest about the truth of yourself, your dishonesty entraps you in what you refuse to be truthful about.*

the oppression of your soul, by using honesty as a judgemental weapon. Or you choose to deal with whatever is oppressing your soul, by using your honesty as a stepping stone to being truthful. You can use your honesty as a platform, where you acknowledge your unresolved emotions and then build an illusion of how you have dealt with them, seeking to portray an evolutionary tale to enhance your image of consciousness. It is your truthfulness that facilitates your resolution and evolution. Truthfulness nurtures your soul. Honesty is a required stepping stone, but does not guarantee truthfulness.

When honesty is used in a disrespectful or dishonest way, you create an internal battle. When you battle with your own dishonesty, you become overwhelmed and often possessed by your lack of insight into yourself and your behaviour. This causes you to discount the significance of truth and your truthfulness. We, collectively as mankind, are at war with the truth of ourselves and when we collectively discount the value of truth, integrity and truthfulness, we create disunity and distrust. This morphs into emotional, energetic and physical chaos we have to contend with. Your dishonesty, contributes to the deceptive energetic collective within the mass energy of mankind. Your dishonesty and spiritual deception sustains your internal war with the truth of yourself.

Spiritual deception is a way of trying to shield yourself from your own dishonesty, which leaves you aligning to beliefs that are glamourised defensive mechanisms. Glamourised defensive mechanisms are an attempt to make the suppression of your unresolved emotions, repression of your thoughts and insight, and the oppression of your soul more palatable. This is how you control your evolution to be stagnant and leave yourself trapped trying to control your soul denial with beliefs.

At times you do not mean your resistance to and denial and avoidance of truth to morph into dishonesty. However, regardless of your best efforts, your dishonesty takes you emotionally, energetically and at times physically to the depths of your own despair. Your despair can be an opportunity to hit your own brick wall and to see your dishonesty for what it is. When you are dishonest you fall from grace and lose yourself within your own unconsciousness. Your acknowledgement of the truth of your own energy and your willingness to be truthfully honest with yourself, creates the opportunity to be of grace for yourself. Grace is self-forgiveness coupled with your unification with truth. Grace enables acceptance of reality and creates an opportunity for resolution and evolution to occur.

Unfortunately, you can fool yourself by believing that justifying your despair is you being honest. Your justification can be fraught with deceptive resistance, denial and avoidance. If you are willing to be truthfully honest, rather than remain wallowing in victimhood and the sorrow of your despair, your despair can become the catalyst for your conscious

LEFT: *When you are truthfully honest, you are the instigator of your rise with grace because it is you choosing to unify with truth and to your soul's consciousness. Your truthful honesty and willingness to be responsible for yourself, converts the unconscious vibration of your unresolved emotions into a conscious frequency. Your willingness to be unified with truth and to be truthfully honest about your own unresolved emotions, dissipates the unconsciousness of the energy, and is the process of resolution and evolution. Your rise with grace is the natural process of evolving your soul. Your unification with truth is evolution.*

participation in your own resolution and evolution. Instead of seeking to find your way to the elusive destinations you have conjured with beliefs, you can choose to be present in the truth of that which is unresolved, accepting you have the opportunity to learn from yourself.

Your internal war with yourself is the result of your choice to remain fallen, and your attempt to be unconscious to what is being revealed to you within the energy of your soul's unconsciousness. The energy within your soul's unconsciousness is not who you are but what you produce whilst separated from the truth of your soul. You create your own internal war with your dishonesty and you can be your own liberator with your truthfulness. Deception, regardless of the type, sustains oppression.

We, as the collective of mankind, use the illusion that we can control reality to manipulate ourselves into believing we can control evolution, while we actually want to remain separate from truth and ignore the destruction that results from our desire for control. Our mankind desire to control reality, without truly comprehending the entirety of reality, is how mankind has disassociated from truth. Mankind has separated from the truth of being the interface between both conscious and unconscious energy. When we have forgotten the true essence of our souls, we are 'mankind', and we are 'humanity' when we remember the true essence of our souls whilst in a physical body.

Mankind is the collective of souls experiencing living on Earth in a physical body with freewill. We are humane when we remember and express the true essence of our soul. To be humane is to enable the prominence of the core essences of our souls to flow freely within all our interactions with life, ourselves, others and truth. When we deny our humanity, we perpetuate the energetic residue generated by our separation from truth. This means we protect and make the unconsciousness of our souls prominent. Mankind will carry the energetic residue until each soul takes responsibility and resolves their portion. Each soul is of *True Source Divine Origin Consciousness* and contributes to the collective energy of mankind. Each soul has their own portion of unconscious energy to resolve and evolve, and every soul that resolves their portion lightens the load that mankind carries. However, we as mankind, are addicted to the illusion of control and we have conditioned ourselves to use our freedom of choice against the truth of who we naturally are. When we choose to resolve our conditioning, we evolve.

Mankind has always perceived evolution as the 'advancement of our ability to control' and we seek to control everything, often with little regard for truth and little regard for the ramifications of our collective denial of reality, as we attempt to control:

- The appearance of the physical body surgically
- Food chemically and genetically
- Finances deceptively
- Equality egotistically
- Power unfairly
- Nature artificially
- Environments selfishly
- Truth dogmatically

All of which are denying the consciousness of truth, the life force of existence.

As mankind, we have attempted to be the master of our domain and collectively ignore our insight into the ramifications of our desire for control and the exploitation of our physical environment and of each other. We become a destructive force, arrogantly trying to appease

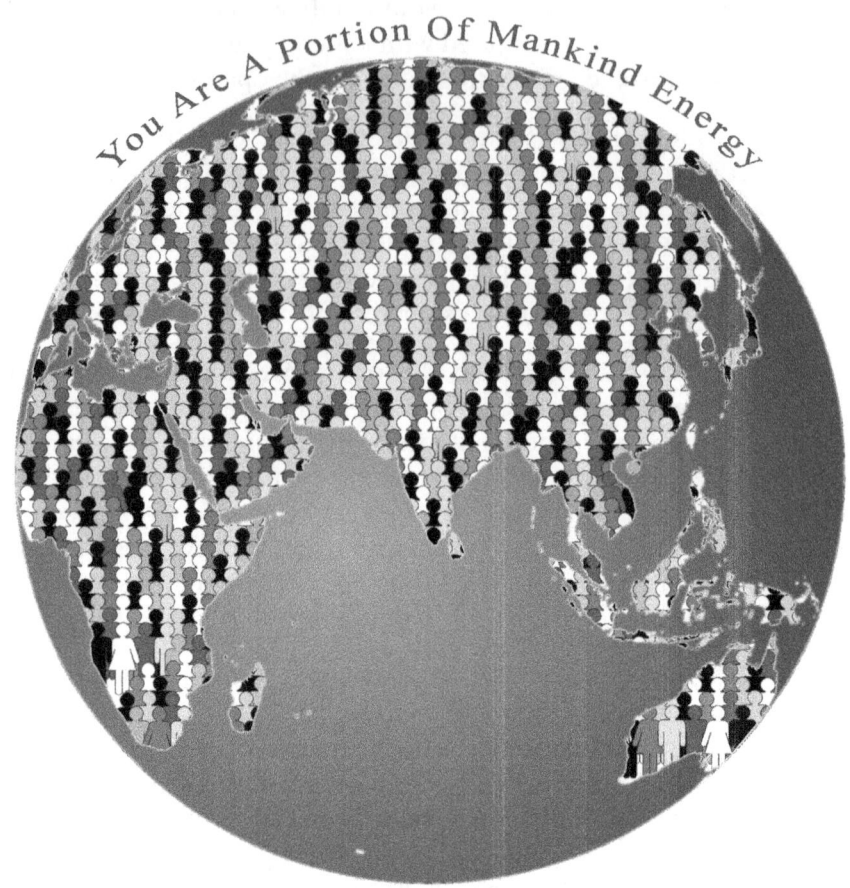

our insatiable appetite, disregarding the truth of ourselves and the devastation we leave in our wake. This thirst for power and control means we oppose our natural affinity with truth, and deny that we are an intrinsic part of a greater system. We are part of the evolutionary process and we should always be mindful and truthful about the integrity of our souls and the significance of everything in nature. When we, as a collective, and you as an individual, lose awareness of the significance of integrity and truth, we develop an insatiable appetite for whatever we believe is important to secure our control. This alters what is revered by mankind and means we are revering the superficial and worshipping control. We collectively, and individually, fight against awareness of truth and reality, while arrogantly ignoring the ramifications of our collective and individual desire for control.

When you deny that you can observe the energy of your soul's unconsciousness, you create the desire to avoid the truth of what is unresolved within you. Your desire to deflect the truth you do not want to acknowledge, incites an insatiable appetite for wanting to observe your control affect everything and everyone you encounter. This has you addicted to your illusion of control and causes you to use your freedom of choice to abuse your awareness of your soul's consciousness. You can control yourself to mankind versions of evolution, constantly trying to better yourself in the eyes of mankind's judgement.

When you attach to your own deception and seek to control your awareness of truth and reality, you use your deception to validate your control and to justify your arrogant betrayal of your soul. When you are separated from your awareness of your soul and disassociated from feeling truth, you lose your willingness to acknowledge any insight into yourself. Unfortunately, this means regardless of what you become aware of, or the ramifications of your own actions, you dogmatically defend your beliefs, denial and desires. This allows you to ricochet from one illusion to another, as you attempt to protect your soul denial from being exposed. This creates and sustains your emotional, energetic and physical barriers to truth. When you control yourself to continue the cycle of struggling to survive your own unconsciousness, you create control structures to generate an energetic surge of unconscious energy, which you use to oppress your awareness of your soul's consciousness. You actually create the space for your own lies. You use your beliefs, denials and your desire to control to suppress, repress and oppress your awareness of your soul's consciousness. This means your desire to sustain an illusion of control has you anchored to your own deception, including spiritual deception.

When you control yourself to be in denial, you manifest condemnation for and oppression of your original intention for resolution and evolution. This can leave you using your spirituality as a game you play, but refuse to genuinely commit to. This causes you to believe the wake of your spiritual illusion or your worship of control is justified, and you become indifferent to the ramifications your denial has on your own evolution. When you adopt and concretise misconceptions about yourself that oppose the truth of being a significant, unique, independent, individual soul of *True Source Divine Origin Consciousness*, you override your original intention to discover what needs resolving for you to evolve. You may attempt to ignore creating ramifications for yourself, but eventually the ramifications will be undeniable. This can leave you spiritually bankrupt and disillusioned. Spiritual bankruptcy means you can no longer uphold your spiritual illusions and have become disillusioned with the stage you created to hide from the truth of both your soul's consciousness and unconsciousness.

You use self-persecution and soul condemnation as a weapon against yourself, and may dispute that you are on a soul evolutionary journey. Your disillusionment can leave you opposing that you still have an opportunity to unify with the truth of your original intention to be truthfully honest about the reality of yourself. Deep within your soul, you feel the yearning to be of your truth, and spiritual illusions or deception will never quell the instinct to unify with truth. When spiritual misconceptions and deception fail and implode, you have the opportunity to acknowledge what you have learnt. Sometimes knowing what truth is not, is just as important as knowing what it is.

You can want freedom, but not the responsibility of acknowledging and resolving the truth of the energy of your soul's unconsciousness, such as your desire to control and your various ways of being indifferent to truth. When you compulsively lie to yourself to justify the energy of your soul's unconsciousness, you will become deceptive with your own spirituality. You can use spirituality as an avenue, to become devoted to your desire for control. You can oppose the reality of truth, cling to your lies and fight your experience of life. However, when you stop oppressing your awareness of truth and accept reality, you feel relief.

When you experience the truth of your rise and fall from grace while retaining your awareness of grace, you are choosing to accept the dynamics of reality. You are also accepting your

freedom to be truthful about yourself. This creates resolution and evolution of your soul's unconsciousness, and freedom from soul oppression. You feel freedom when you choose to:
- Be of truth without the fear of your own spiritual deception interfering with your natural process of rising and falling from grace.
- Stop fighting your awareness of truth and allow yourself to trust your exploration of soul truth.
- Trust your ability to be truthfully honest about your reactions and responses to your reality, feelings and others.
- Be conscious of your ability to respond truthfully to your present moment.

You can use your unresolved emotions to fuel your desire to deceptively have control of your performances of an image of consciousness, but you do not want responsibility for the ramifications of what your control does to your present moment. When you deny responsibility for the choices you make, and discount how your hidden agendas control you, you become extremely indifferent to the value of your truthfulness. This can cause you to be manipulative with your responses, in denial of your reactions and to believe it is unjust if others do not align to what you want to achieve with your performance of consciousness. Spiritual deception and images of consciousness are always underpinned with hidden agendas. When you acknowledge the hidden agendas, you create the opportunity to unravel the unresolved emotions entwined with your spiritual deception and image of consciousness.

When you create an alliance with any deception you believe will facilitate whatever it is you have decided you want, you seek to secure your belief of what your reality should be perceived as. Your disregard for the truth of your reality causes the unconscious energy produced by your unresolved emotions and beliefs to become reverberations within the energetic collectives of the mass energy of mankind. You use your awareness of your reverberations to justify your denial of what you are doing to yourself. You may energetically feel the reverberations and misinterpret them with spiritual connotations.

It is your disregard for the truth of your reality that causes you to separate from your awareness of yourself, and it is this disconnection from yourself that allows you to use your unconscious energy as a governing force over you. This makes you susceptible to reverberating with any unconscious energy that correlates with the beliefs, denials and desires you use to sustain your disconnection from yourself. You supply the space for your deception to corrupt your natural ability to honour the significance of truth. You secure your willingness to be deceptive by cultivating your attachment to your beliefs, denials and desires, whilst harnessing the unconscious energy produced within you. You can become an emotional chameleon, shifting, changing and diverting your attention to any beliefs, denials and desires, that cultivate deceptive justification for being intentionally unconscious to the truth of your soul and the reality of your own behaviour.

As you feel your reverberation with the energetic collectives that correlate with whatever you have emotionally activated, you can ignore that it is you who is instigating the reverberations with the energetic mass energy of mankind. You can deceptively use your awareness of your own reverberating energy, to create the belief that you are a victim to the mass energy of mankind. When you protect your intentional unconsciousness, you will use your heightened energetic awareness to overshadow your lack of self-responsibility, which leaves you indifferent to truth. This is because you deceptively use your awareness to secure the energy of your soul's unconsciousness, whilst denying you have the option of resolution. You use your awareness of your reverberation within the energetic collectives of the mass energy of mankind to desecrate the value of being truthful.

When you are willing to be deceptive with yourself, you reverberate with the energetic collectives of mankind, which correlate to the unresolved emotions you use to secure your beliefs, denials and desires. Your controlled evolution energy is a mixture of your beliefs, denials and desires, which you use to create energy that enables you to waste the opportunities truth presents to you. You often want control of the opportunity, seeking to misconstrue what the opportunity is about, to defile your own awareness of truth. You want the opportunity to be about securing your righteous judgement or pacifying your desire to control, ignoring that your awareness of truth is exposing you to the truth of your soul's unconsciousness. This can be an opportunity for you to use your truthful honesty to resolve what is unresolved within you. However, if protecting your beliefs, denials and desires is what you perceive as being of paramount importance, you will separate yourself from your awareness and corrupt your ability to observe the truth of your own deception. When you objectively observe the truth of your deception, you can acknowledge the opportunity your unresolved emotions present to you, and observe what you do to your own awareness. When you deceptively want control of your evolution, you only control yourself to stagnation, and miss the opportunity to resolve and evolve, because you are choosing to prioritise your desire for control.

Your controlled evolution barrier is fuelled by your ability to control yourself to be separated from feeling your soul consciousness' presence. Your soul's consciousness is always present within the reality of your experiences and never gives up exposing truth to you. You can control yourself to be disconnected from your ability to resolve your own unresolved emotions, and isolate yourself from comprehending your reactions and responses to truth. When you are willing to be truthfully honest, you enable yourself to comprehend your reactions and responses to truth, which allows you to naturally resolve. Your dishonesty creates disharmony within you, and it is your own dishonesty that secures your unwillingness to acknowledge the entirety of your reality.

When you anchor to your dishonesty, you control yourself to believe your pursuit for control of your spirituality is justified and excusable. Your dishonesty violates your awareness of your soul's consciousness, causing you to govern yourself with the righteousness perceived from your beliefs of being entitled to pacify your desire to control. You use the lies your dishonesty creates as belief systems, causing you to believe you are not good enough to experience the purity of truth, so you settle for a pretense. When you disharmonise with the natural process of experiencing the truth of your unresolved emotions, you leave yourself opposing your awareness of truth. It is your willingness to be truthfully honest about your own unconscious energy, produced by your unresolved emotions, that will enable you to become conscious of your emotional, energetic and physical reality. Your truthful honesty enables you to remain aware of the presence of your soul's consciousness within your rise and fall from grace. When you choose to be truthfully honest about being aware of the presence of your soul's consciousness, you have the opportunity to value giving yourself grace as you discover the truth of your soul's unconsciousness. Your truthful honesty aligns you to the integrity of your original intention to resolve and evolve. You use your spiritual deception to remain unconscious of your original intention to unify all aspects of your soul to your origin truth.

Your soul's consciousness will naturally expose you to the truth of your unresolved emotions and beliefs, and seeks to resolve what you use to corrupt your awareness of the purity of your soul. It is your truthful honesty that resolves the unconscious energy you carry within your soul's unconsciousness. Being truthfully honest is choosing to unify with your soul's consciousness, which is the truth of who you are. Spiritual deception can be difficult to reconcile, because you use the concept of truth or fragments of truth to uphold your disconnection from truth and yourself. This creates a complex web of deception that you defend with what you want to believe is truth. You use terms associated with truth, but you do not resonate with their meaning. Unfortunately, you can become lost in an illusion that you defend as if it were a truth.

When you choose to become consumed with your own ignorant perspective of reality, truth may become of little value to you, as you attempt to preempt and seek an outcome that you believe will pacify your desire for control or secure an illusion of control. When truth has little value to you, you become determined to expand your ability to control, and you manipulate yourself to believe your control is superior to truth. This causes you to lie to yourself about the choices you make to fight life's ability to expose you to the truth of your own unresolved emotions and deceptive beliefs. When you choose to defend and protect your unresolved emotions and beliefs with your dishonesty, you become indifferent to truth. Your dishonesty manifests your attachment to being deceptive about the way you animate your unresolved emotions via your mind chatter, as you continue to regurgitate what has not worked and punish yourself with your self-betrayal, sabotage and fears.

When you sedate your ability to observe the reality that you are deceiving yourself, you become automatic with your regimented perception of how to live life. You numb yourself to the truth of how you feel and you oppress the dynamism of the truth of who you are. To feel the dynamism within your soul is to experience yourself within your present moment without controlling yourself with any deception. Being dynamic is the willingness to be present in, and honest about, what is occurring internally and externally. When you deny and ignore the ramifications of oppressing your feelings, you deceive yourself with thoughts you generate from your unresolved emotions, which have you anchoring to the stagnation of your soul's unconsciousness. When you control yourself to stagnation, you emotionally feel frustrated and you feel uncomfortable with the ramifications of your own deception. Your frustration is a reminder that your control does not always work, and that your choice to oppress your awareness of truth has created internal angst for you to contend with. You emotionally feel frustrated, because you cannot completely suppress your internal angst and on a deep level you fear the ramifications of your own soul deception.

When your control has not supplied you with the results you want and you still insist on denying your awareness of truth or how your hindsight is exposing you to the reality of what your choices have put into play, you will use your deception to create confusion. You attempt to use your confusion to conceal your own betrayal of your soul. When you choose to deny your awareness of truth, you betray your soul. You use your mind chatter to mask the gravity of your soul betrayal and you become so consumed with your mind chatter that you cannot see or truly feel what you are doing to yourself.

When you deny feeling your soul, you experience an energetic surge of unconscious energy. You can misinterpret the energy you feel and confabulate a story, contrived from what you want to believe, instead of accepting that you do not know. When you are willing to consciously explore, not knowing becomes an opportunity. Acknowledging that you do not know, but are aware creates an honest foundation to explore from. If you tell yourself the outcome before you honestly explore, you will only look for what supports your desire to be right. Resolution stems from recognising the truth, not from contrived information.

You can fear the dynamism of your soul's consciousness, because you know your awareness of truth makes your illusion of control null and void. You can fear losing control of your spiritual illusion because you have become addicted to the familiarity of feeling the surges of your control energy required to uphold the illusion. When you believe surging with control energy enables you to achieve what you want, you can become addicted to the misconceptions about the reality of your control. You can utilise the surge of control energy to justify projecting your unresolved emotions and oppressing your awareness of truth.

You can be addicted to your illusion of control and believe your emotions have control over your inability to be conscious. You use this belief to justify protecting your unconsciousness, which causes you to align to the belief that you are searching to find yourself. Having control over your emotions and reality can become the destination you seek, and you may be using beliefs about enlightenment, nirvana and finding yourself to conceal your addiction and worship of control

Your addiction to unconsciousness can be recognised in the way you tenaciously deny responsibility for yourself; you can control yourself to deny your ability to be honest about your own clarity. Clarity is to be aware of truth and to accept the value of truth, without the desire to alter your awareness with any deception. When you constantly deny self-responsibility, you are continuously opposing your own awareness of truth. When you choose to numb yourself from feeling your awareness of truth, you become susceptible to protecting your denial with constructed lies. Your constructed lies annihilate your ability to have clarity, and until you are willing to be truthful, you will cocoon yourself and exist within your constructed lies. Your constructed lies turn what may be a simple truth into the creation of a convoluted web of deception, which is how you conceal truth from yourself. When you fight your awareness, you retain your desire to hide in your emotional unrest. You want your emotions to protect either your illusion of control or your justifications as to why you are not responsible for the words you speak, your behavior and your beliefs. You attempt to shield yourself from your hidden desire to be separated from your awareness of truth and to discredit being an evolving soul. When you deny that aligning with truth creates clarity, you can deceptively hide in the emotional chaos you create by undermining your own awareness of truth.

Unfortunately, you can become addicted to eliminating your willingness and ability to trust your own clarity, which causes you to become fearful of your significance, uniqueness, independence and individuality. Being an individual means you freely trust yourself to acknowledge your resonance with truth. You also acknowledge the entirety of yourself, and objectively observe your emotional reactions to your life experiences. Being unique means you realise you are one of a kind and that your uniqueness is your natural state. Being independent means you take responsibility for your decisions and hold to the truth of your own soul integrity. When you ignore, override and attempt to completely deny the ramifications of opposing your ability to live free of self-imposed limitations, you devalue your own significance, uniqueness, independence and individuality. Your dishonesty creates limitations and obscures your natural clarity. Your natural clarity is attuned to your soul consciousness' insight into your reality, which is dynamically present within every moment.

Your dishonesty stems from not wanting to be accountable for the reality of your choices, beliefs, behaviours, reactions and hidden agendas. It is also fear driven and as you acknowledge your wants and fears, you begin to unravel the dishonesty. When you want to deny feeling truth, you will attempt to secure an illusion of innocence, because you fear taking full responsibility for yourself. When you fear your own clarity, you become reliant on constructed illusions and dogmatic beliefs to secure your deception. Fear inhibits your natural aspiration to discover truth; discovering truth enables you to have clarity which actually quells your fear. If you oppose the aspiration to discover truth, you align to the construction of your own deception.

Your clarity is an essential component to resolving your desire for control. As you consciously choose to not use your desire for control to fool yourself, your clarity becomes more evident to you. When you recognise you are emotionally, energetically or physically struggling, it is a flag that you have lost your clarity and you can actually use this as an alert system for yourself. Your struggling is a sign that you need to explore your own internal reaction to your present moment and life events. It is also a sign to acknowledge the reality, that your own deception or fear is inhibiting you from accepting the truth of what you are experiencing. Your choice to trust your awareness enables you to realise that when you feel an uneasiness within yourself, it is an indication that you are not trusting yourself to be truthful, which inhibits your clarity.

Your awareness of your own uneasiness can help you open your doors to further exploration. However, if you fear the uneasiness, you will use your desire for control to confabulate a story, in an attempt to believe you have clarity. You can use fragments of truth and then build a web of deception with the fragments to fill in the gaps created by your lack of clarity. Unfortunately, this can cause you to dogmatically defend your indifference to truth and self-perpetuate your deception. When you become addicted to deception and support your addiction with distorted spiritual beliefs or pursuits, you become lost in your own indifference to truth. Your soul does not resonate with deception. Spirituality is the yearning within your soul to resonate with the purity of truth and a sense that there is something greater than yourself that you are part of.

When you deliberately distort your understanding of reality, to ignore, override and deny what you feel, your indifference to truth can take you a long way from the truth of who you are. This causes you to feel the void of your separation and you become more attuned with your unconsciousness, while opposing your own soul's consciousness. You use your emotional chaos, your willingness to carry the emotional residue of your soul denial history and your expectations for the future to create decoys, in an attempt to justify being dishonest about your awareness of reality. When you are addicted to your own dishonesty, you believe your deception protects you from having to acknowledge both your soul's consciousness and your soul's unconsciousness. This enables you to anchor to a spiritual illusion and image of consciousness. However, dishonesty inhibits resolution and evolution and disconnects you from your resonance with your soul and truth.

You can emotionally feel indentured to the unresolved emotions you have stored in your soul's unconsciousness. This has you operating from the cloaked fears and embedded beliefs of your soul denial, which causes you to invoke your soul oppressive energy such as judgement, indifference and manipulation. You can also become dogmatically fixated on the spiritual beliefs you have created or have been indoctrinated into. You obligate yourself to your own soul denial with your dishonesty. You obligate yourself to your soul oppression with your desire to control. You misplace your loyalty, to obligate yourself to your and mankind's beliefs, that deny your natural significance, uniqueness, independence and individuality. This misplaced loyalty and sense of obligation causes you to deny your original intention to resolve and evolve, which leaves you devoted to being a struggling human beneath the layers of spiritual deception. You struggle because you deny the truth of your soul and deny your original intention to resolve and evolve. Your denial causes you to devalue both what is being exposed to you and the opportunity to resolve. Your denial is the catalyst for you to construct a struggle out of anything you believe is not under your control. Your struggles become power plays you have with your own desire to control, often believing you are in control of your own deception, only to discover that your deception is controlling you.

You use your freewill to choose how to respond to your life. When you choose to struggle, the depths of your struggle reflect the extent of your dishonesty and the enormity of your desire to control. Your acknowledgement of truth frees you from being emotionally indentured to your denial. You fear being free of your own incarceration because you want to control what freedom is, but freedom is the resolution of control, denial and oppression. These all incarcerate you in your denial of your significance, uniqueness, independence and individuality. Evolution is the ability to trust and feel the freedom to be the true essence of your soul.

Your controlled evolution energy is created by the spiritual beliefs that support your deceptive labyrinths. You use these beliefs to justify your devotion to your soul oppression. You may be unaware that this is what you are doing, if your spiritual beliefs are upholding an illusion of control. When you use your unresolved emotions and beliefs to oppose the truth you can feel, you create distractions from your awareness of your consciousness, to obscure the reality of being stagnant within your soul's unconsciousness. When you use your unresolved emotions and beliefs to obscure your opportunity to evolve, you are choosing to remain oblivious to the extent of your soul betrayal. Your emotional labyrinths are constructed to serve the purpose of concealing what you do not want to acknowledge. You can enslave yourself to your own soul denial with your heresy against yourself, and control yourself with beliefs that are designed to inhibit your awareness of your soul's consciousness. This is a choice to devalue truth and sustain oppressing yourself with your beliefs. When you devalue truth, you forget that you have freedom of choice and unconsciously drift into your deceptive beliefs about yourself.

Your devotion to your embedded beliefs generates deception, because you are attempting to exist within a lie. Lies create misconceptions and deception. Deception creates the space to control your evolution to be stagnant due to your illusions and beliefs. When you condition yourself to remain distracted from questioning the validity of your beliefs and deception, you often become willing to defend what does not resonate with your soul, and this creates a struggle. You struggle with your denial of what your beliefs and deception are doing to yourself, others and the way you experience life. You can use this struggle to try and defend, justify and control your refusal to trust truth, which inhibits the exploration of both your soul's consciousness and unconsciousness. Your refusal to trust truth results from wanting control of your evolution, whilst disconnected from truth.

When you are submissive to your own distrust of truth, you generate the energy required to sustain your separation from your awareness of your soul and devalue the significance of truth. When you devalue the significance of truth, you actually disassociate from feeling truth, so you can sustain your distrust of truth, often not even comprehending why you want to distrust truth. When you oppress your natural ability to resonate with truth, you bombard your clarity with your desire to control. This causes you to chip away at your clarity until you construct what you want to believe. This means you fill your mind with your analysis of your control and options you believe you can control yourself to. In truth, you become confused, disorientated and oppressed by your own inability to trust your awareness of your soul's consciousness, truth and what you are really experiencing.

Your distrust of your awareness of truth causes you to feel the reality of your own soul's unconsciousness. You believe if you can sustain your denial, you will avoid feeling the unconsciousness of your soul. However, this does not work because when you deny your awareness of truth, you are actually immersing yourself in exactly what you are attempting to avoid, which is feeling your soul's unconsciousness. When you control yourself to deny the truth of what you feel, you entrap yourself in your denial. This causes you to control yourself to oppose the exposure of truth and you refuse to acknowledge being lost in your own unconsciousness. You do this to remain stagnant in your soul oppression, which is the choice to deny yourself the opportunity to explore truth and to trust yourself to be completely honest with yourself. Your truthful honesty is how you facilitate your evolution, and your dishonesty is how you deny yourself the opportunity to evolve.

When you become consumed with wanting to perfect your control of your image of consciousness, you oppress feeling your soul and align to spiritual beliefs. You do not realise that your image, beliefs and your desire for control are arcing up the emotional angst and fears you are actually trying to control. You believe it is not having control or your belief of not being good enough to uphold your own image that is causing you the angst, but it is actually your separation from your awareness of your soul and your unwillingness to trust yourself to be in the dynamics of life. Your acknowledgement of how you use your control is actually the opportunity to discover how you oppress yourself. You believe the misconception that if you are in control, you will be free of negativity and your internal struggle. However, all misconceptions are built on false foundations that eventually become untenable.

When you abide by the familiarity of being separated from your awareness of being a soul and disassociated from feeling truth, you exist in the deception generated by your desire for control of reality. The questions are:

- When did you decide your control was better than feeling the truth of your soul and resolving and evolving completely supporting truth?
- How do you justify the decisions that leave you in denial of reality?
- Why do you struggle to trust yourself and your origins?
- What is the prize for your control, denial and oppression?
- What is the prize you want your beliefs to deliver?
- What are you aware of?

You can become blinded by the familiarity of wanting to gratify your own beliefs. You can bind yourself to your conceptual ideals of being a soul, to your disappointment about your life experiences and to your rejection of your opportunities for your resolution and evolution. This can blindside your awareness of the natural significance of being a soul, the truth of your life experiences and the reality of your opportunities to resolve and evolve. You can become addicted to the belief that you need a struggle to have something to exert your control over, which causes you to incite your own struggle with yourself, life, others, relationships and truth. This focuses your perspective on trying to ascertain how everything affects your illusion of control. You sustain the space for your unconsciousness to dominate your awareness by aligning to the familiarity of being dishonest with yourself. This is to be fallen from grace. However, when you choose to be conscious of the process of rising and falling from grace, you are less able to be unconscious of truth.

As you accept the process of rising and falling from grace, you do not want to use excuses to hide from truth, your awareness heightens as you feel the truth of your unresolved emotions which creates the opportunity for resolution. Your truthful honesty allows you to choose to be an objective observer of your unconsciousness, and you then become aware of your freedom to choose how you respond to your own rise and fall from grace. Your truthful honesty with yourself means you have chosen to be a conscious participant in the unraveling of your unconsciousness, which is part of the process of your resolution and evolution.

Your soul's unconsciousness is the energy you carry that is encumbered with your soul denial and is created when you lose the significance of trusting truth and being truthful with yourself about yourself. Your soul denial is the energy of your distrust of truth, developed from your embedded beliefs and fears, which has become your false foundation. When you choose to abandon your origins and oppose being unified with truth, you surge within your illusions of control. Your surges of control energy oppress your awareness of truth. Your soul oppression is the result of your fear that truth will interfere with your control. When you align to the energy within your soul's unconsciousness, whilst denying responsibility for yourself, you become a willing participant in your own oppression. Your denial of being responsible for yourself has you fearful and oppositional to your own significance, uniqueness, independence and individuality.

Truth
Your Own
Oppression
Unconsciousness
Unconsciousness
Unconsciousness

When you are codependent on using your unconsciousness to supply the space to hide from your awareness of truth, you become indifferent to the truth of being a significant, unique, independent, individual soul of *True Source Divine Origin Consciousness*. Your awareness of truth exposes you to your soul's unconsciousness. If you are truthfully honest you raise yourself from your unconscious energy to be conscious of truth. However, if you are dishonest with yourself, you will use your distrust of truth to dismiss the significance of your soul journey and the significance of the natural process of rising and falling from grace. You fight feeling truth to maintain your fall from grace, which means you fight your awareness of truth, to control yourself to be emotionally swamped and unconscious to the reality you are creating for yourself to experience. If you are conscious of your fall from grace and recognise the reality of your emotions, your truthful honesty about the reality you are experiencing becomes how you raise your unconscious energy with grace. When you accept the reality of yourself and trust yourself to be truthfully honest, you feel at ease with the process of living. Spiritual illusions inhibit you from living as a true expression of your soul.

When you desire to be unconscious to the truth of yourself, your indifference to truth becomes the backbone of your denial. Your desire for control renders you unconscious to reality, because you use your desire for control to inhibit your ability to reason with yourself, and to oppose your own awareness of yourself and your behaviour. This creates a struggle, when there is often no necessity for a struggle. When you choose to be truthfully honest with yourself all aspects of your soul become accessible to you. When you acknowledge the value of truth, you will resonate with truth. Your soul's consciousness is truth energy. Your truthful honesty is you choosing to align to your own truth. Your life is the opportunity to resolve and evolve beyond your own unconsciousness.

Aligning to beliefs is different to unifying with truth and your soul's consciousness. Unification means you do not deny what you are aware of, and remain curious because you accept the dynamism of your soul, truth and life are constantly revealing opportunities to discover, uncover and to resonate with truth. When you have perfected the skill of being in denial, aligned to beliefs and stagnating yourself, you:

- Are constantly opposing your own awareness of the dynamics of truth.
- Control yourself to protect the energy of your soul's unconsciousness, which leaves you addicted to your soul oppression.
- Sabotage your awareness of the process of rising and falling from grace.

Stagnation is created when you attempt to control the natural process of your evolution with the desire to gratify your illusory control of your spirituality, which incites a desire to control life, yourself, others, your relationships and truth. If you do not completely trust yourself and your origins of truth, you will see-saw within your varying degrees of unconsciousness and oppose taking self-responsibility. This will cause you to lose awareness of your soul's consciousness.

LEFT: *By just focusing on your oppression, you inhibit your awareness of your own flow of consciousness. You dismiss the significance of your truthful honesty and oppose the truth you can feel. This can cause you to devalue what is exposed by truth.*

When you choose to be aware of yourself, you can become attuned with your own grace. Grace is a core essence of your soul and is the willingness to forgive yourself. Attuning to grace enables you to confront your own fear of discovering your soul denial, which is the storehouse of your embedded beliefs and fear of truth. Choosing to be of your own natural grace resolves the hold your embedded beliefs and fears have over your awareness, which frees you to experience being completely honest with yourself. Being of grace creates unity within and enables you to be aware of your constant flow of consciousness, which allows you to feel the truth of your reactions and responses to your own life experiences. When you feel the truth of your soul resonating with the truth of your experiences, your natural acceptance of reality alters how you react and respond to your experiences. Your truthful honesty resolves your desire to be in control of reality. It is your desire to control reality that produces your soul oppressive energy, which disables you from being present in the truth of what you are experiencing.

Your acceptance of the truth of being a soul and being able to acknowledge when you feel yourself resonating with truth, enables you to feel the freedom that your truthful honesty creates. Your truthful honesty naturally resolves and evolves any unconscious energy you experience within yourself. As your acceptance of being of truth increases, you create the freedom to acknowledge and appreciate truth without fear, trepidation or hidden agendas, which enables you to be present in the reality of what you are currently experiencing. Trusting truth without judgement and the desire to control is to experience the grace within your own soul's consciousness. This enables your resolution and evolution to be an awakening experience that frees you from your desire for control and frees you from the stagnation you created protecting your soul's unconsciousness.

Your acceptance of the truth of your soul inhibits you from constructing or aligning to any emulations of honesty. If you want to control truth you will tolerate emulations of truth; however if you have the intention and the commitment to feel yourself resonating with the purity of truth, an emulation will feel out of alignment. The reason why emulations leave you feeling out of alignment is because you can feel the indifference to truth within the emulation.

When you want to control an image of consciousness and create a pretense of being an evolved soul, you become an emulator, which inhibits your resolution and evolution. Your attempts to control your consciousness and truth means you are willing to be deceptive at the same time as wanting the benefit of being able to label your deception as truth. Your soul's consciousness does not resonate with deception regardless of the deceptive label; your soul's consciousness resonates with the frequency of truth. Your perception is your version of reality, which may be of truth or constructed from your deception, your mixture of the two. You can use your version of what you think truth is, to say that you are 'awakened to truth'. However, when you are willing to defend your own deception to uphold an illusion that you are 'awakened to truth', you are constructing deceptive versions of truth to facilitate your desire to control. This causes you to be indifferent to the natural value of truth.

When you create a scaling system to determine what you class as conscious, you believe you can use your judgement to decide the degree of consciousness you will allow yourself to experience. When you believe you can use your judgement to manipulate the concept of consciousness, you begin to emulate what you believe consciousness is. When you emulate what you believe consciousness is, you are fooling yourself with your own deception. The flaws in your emulations mean your deception will eventually be revealed, and any exposure of deception is an opportunity to be honest with yourself. You emulate consciousness and attempt to fool yourself that you are being truthfully honest, because you want to be perceived as special whilst you deny that you devalue truth. You can perceive truth as a rival and compete against the reality of who you are to perform an image of consciousness. You want your deception to outclass the value of truth.

When you try to emulate consciousness and pretend to be truthfully honest, you want your deception to surpass your awareness of truth and you want your constructed version of consciousness to eclipse the purity of your natural consciousness and truth. Your emulations obscure your resonance with truth. When you choose to use an emulation, you are choosing to dumb down the significance of who you naturally are, and consume yourself with your own indifference to truth. Your emulations are an enactment and the embodiment of your indifference to truth, which stagnates your understanding of yourself and truth, and leaves you controlling your evolution to remain stagnant.

When you distrust truth and override your awareness of the grace within your soul, you devalue the significance of being honest with yourself and obsess with using your denial and illusion of control as the governing force over your consciousness. When you want power over your consciousness and truth, you will want to control your evolution to accommodate your desire for control. This stagnates you and causes you to miss the opportunities that life presents to you for resolution and evolution. Evolution occurs when you are willing and committed to resolving anything and everything that you use to inhibit your unification with truth. Your desire to control and indifference to truth are your major inhibitors.

When you defiantly oppose your awareness of your natural flow of consciousness, you believe your denial gives you the power to pick and choose between your consciousness and your illusion of control. However, this is the choice to be dishonest and to remain fallen from grace, sustaining your own opposition to truth. Grace is to value and be unified with truth, which enables you to be kind towards yourself as you discover both your consciousness and unconsciousness. Grace is felt when you freely take responsibility for yourself whilst you discover your own soul truth. When you freely take responsibility for your truthfulness and trust in truth, you create the opportunity to resolve what inhibits your resonance and unification with truth.

You forget controlling yourself to a spiritual illusion or an image of consciousness, is the choice to be unconscious of truth. If you are attempting to control your consciousness, you are unconscious to the reality of truth, and choosing to be unconscious to your own reality. It is impossible to evolve if you are unconscious of truth and not present in your own reality. Your freedom of choice is respected by *True Source Divine Origin Consciousness* (your origins of truth) and you have the freewill to emotionally do as you please. You can choose to ignore the truth of your soul denial, align to your indifference to truth and protect your illusion of control for as long as you like, but you cannot deceive truth, you can only deceive yourself and temporarily deceive others.

Truth is within reality and reality is hard to suppress, repress and oppress. Your attempts to suppress your emotions in relation to your reality, cause you to deny your ability to feel truth. Your attempts to repress the soul insight you hear within your mind from your soul's consciousness, causes you to create mind chatter to override the clarity of your own soul insight. Your attempts to oppress the natural flow of your soul's consciousness, causes you to be separated from your awareness of your soul and disassociated from feeling your own truth. You can attempt to perfect your control of your suppression, repression and oppression. However, you are denying yourself the opportunity to value being an eternal soul who feels truth. Unfortunately, this is you choosing to value your deception over your awareness of truth. This is how you control your evolution to be stagnant, because you are refusing to acknowledge and learn from your life experiences.

When you want to sustain your addiction to being oppositional to truth, you hide from the truth of being aware of your own battle to be unconscious of your reality and the effort required to sustain your spiritual illusion, whilst internally fearing what you are doing to your soul. When you fight your ability to feel the conscious flow of your soul within reality, you avoid being truthful about your reality. You fight truth, when you fear acknowledging the emotional chaos your indifference to truth creates.

Resolution and evolution stem from your decision to be curious about your soul and truth, and occur when you unify curiosity with truthfulness.

Mankind's energetic collectives sustaining controlled evolution beliefs

Mankind has always used collective judgement to sustain division and disunity within mankind. Collective judgement morphs into indifference to truth, which enables us, as mankind, to use our collective identities created from our judgement to justify our indifference to one another. Our indifference to truth is a catalyst for the many harmful ways we judge each other, and we then use our judgement to perpetuate conflict. The division and disunity within mankind creates energetic collectives, which sustain our judgement and indifference to truth. When we sustain our collective judgement and indifference, we inhibit ourselves from acknowledging and learning from our life experiences, which stagnates our own resolution and evolution.

Mankind's collective use of judgement, indifference to truth and desire to control, creates the insidious emotional energy of hatred and jealousy, which is the crux of mankind's racism, sectarianism and fanaticism. This also becomes a way of sustaining our denial of reality. Mankind has ensured our collective unconsciousness by continuing the battle for control and sustaining the competition for supremacy over each other's significance, uniqueness, independence and individuality. The willingness to disregard another's significance, uniqueness, independence and individuality has caused us to collectively view our interactions and relationships as the arena to determine the pecking orders of our perceived control. This causes us to align to different factions within mankind, and leaves us denying the equality of all souls. We deny equality, in an attempt to perpetuate the use of pecking orders and superiority. The compulsion to compete against each other, generates beliefs that are used to construct arenas of indifference that become battlegrounds for mankind. The competition for control results in oppressive beliefs, behaviours and propaganda that perpetuate indifference to truth.

The different factions within mankind have created many methods for individuals to separate from acknowledging their own awareness of themselves and the agenda of the collective, which leaves us opposing our natural resonance with our unified origin. This causes individuals to identify themselves with the judgement of the collective, and to oppress their own uniqueness, independence and individuality. When you lose your awareness of your uniqueness, independence and individuality, because you have aligned to the judgement of a collective faction within mankind, you create competitive beliefs that sustain your scaling of yourself and others. This causes you to become a propagator of indifference, which you use to indoctrinate others into the collective judgement. This sustains the fractious nature of mankind. You can use the judgement of the physicality of others' life experiences as fodder to ignore the value of truth and the significance of others' uniqueness, to sustain your own judgement.

To judge each other we use our points of difference, such as:

- Countries
- Regions
- States
- Cities
- Suburbs
- Towns
- Streets
- Schools
- History
- Families
- Faiths
- Economics

- Skin colour
- Body weight
- Hair colour
- Fans of different sports teams
- Product brands we use

The list is endless because it is determined by our judgement. We, as mankind, compulsively judge anything, any collective of people or any individual so that we can construct a bias to oppose the equality of all souls. Silent conformity enforces the control of those in judgement and exacerbates the fractious nature of mankind. Unfortunately, silent conformity always results from the fear of judgement.

Our fear of judgement and indifference to truth means we have succumbed to opposing diversity as a way to judge and uphold beliefs that sustain how we, as mankind, deny the equality of all souls. It is our denial of the equality of all souls that has sustained the collective factions within mankind, which is how we maintain the denial of our united origin of truth. The history of the extent to which some individuals and factions have used judgement and indifference to pacify their own control, scares us. Our collective denial of coming from the same origin has enabled us to operate from factions within mankind, which we use to develop judgement that perpetuates our oppression and keeps us vying for control. We, as mankind, have continuously separated into collectives of judgement, which ensures the perpetuation of fear. Judgement is how we prolong our refusal to explore, acknowledge and accept the united origin of all souls.

We, as mankind, have created scaling systems and competitive pecking orders of control within each collective. We, use the deception of judgement to scale the value, worth and significance of all souls within each collective. Judgement is used to create blanketing statements that distort reality, devalue the diversity of people and vindicate the collective judgement. We use scaling, competition and control to sustain the fractious nature within mankind and then use the fractious nature within mankind to create and uphold our illusion of superiority or inferiority. We use the collective judgement that sustains our illusion of superiority or inferiority to defend our opposition to the equality and significance of all souls.

Examples of mankind's judgement creating pecking orders within collectives:

People within a country create a collective, within the country's collective of people many other collectives will be formed. The collectives will be formed by ascertaining what is similar, which could be collectives of:

- Those with power
- Those without power
- Youth, middle age and the elderly
- Various religions
- Skin colour
- Political agenda
- Educational achievements

We scale the value of ourselves against others and become embroiled in compulsively comparing. We create pecking orders with a top and a bottom rank with our judgement and denial of the equality of all souls.

When collectives are sustained by judgement there is always a scaling system with a pecking order, which constantly creates factions within the collective. These pecking orders range from:

- The most powerful person, to the least influential in the collective of power.
- The most famous youth, to the most ignored youth.
- The most followed religion, to the least followed religion.

Mankind has many systems that facilitate individual collectives being under one umbrella. For example: The educational system is the umbrella for individual schools and there are many different ways of judging the schools, which creates different factions and sustains pecking orders within the collective.

Within the educational system the pecking orders range from:

- The school with the most elite reputation, to those with the worst reputation.
- The school with the best sporting achievements, to the school with the worst.
- The school with the highest academic achievements, to those with the lowest.
- The school with the most successful past students, to the school with the least successful past students.

Within each school there is a pecking order ranging from:

- The highest achieving class in the school, to the lowest achieving class in the school.
- The most popular teacher, to the most unpopular teacher.
- The most popular student, to the most unpopular student.
- The most involved parent of the school, to the least involved parent.
- The student with the greatest number of awards, to the student with the least amount of awards.

Selective aspects of reality are used to scale each individual's value and worth, which upholds the pecking order, and is how the fractious nature within all collectives is sustained. The scaling could be on:

- Personal wealth
- Material possessions
- Physical appearance
- Levels of intelligence

Wealth can be used to scale pecking orders such as:

- The wealthiest country in a region, to the poorest country in a region.
- The wealthiest province within a country, to the poorest province.
- The wealthiest town within the province, to the poorest town.
- The wealthiest street within the town, to the poorest street.
- The wealthiest house within the street, to the poorest house.
- The wealthiest school in the town, to the poorest school.
- The wealthiest student within the school, to the poorest student.
- The most expensively dressed student at school, to the cheapest.
- The most expensive brand of school shoes, to the cheapest brand.
- The teacher with the most expensive car in the school carpark, to the teacher with the cheapest car.

These examples show how we have created tangible methods of justifying our judgement of the uniqueness and significance of each individual and their life experience within the collective. The collective energy becomes an oppressive way of judging and scaling individuals within each collective. However, each individual uses their own judgement to assess and attempt to ascertain their own and everyone else's position within the collective energy. This reliance on judgement and the pecking order to determine your worth is totally devoid of the reality of what is actually occurring within the collective energy and is a dumbing down of who you naturally are.

Judgement is tangible evidence of our indifference to each other and to truth, and is used throughout mankind. For example within:

- Sports teams
- Workplaces
- Social events
- Religions
- Groups of friends
- Families

The list is as varied as gatherings of people.

We, as mankind, have created tangible excuses for the insidious nature of judgement, to excuse the power struggle for supremacy over one another. Judgement of each others' significance, uniqueness, independence and individuality is a way of curtailing the potential for each individual's exploration of truth.

Racism, fanaticism and sectarianism ramify from the stronghold of our judgement and are the actualisation of mankind's indifference to truth. Racism, fanaticism and sectarianism have been created by our desire to control each other and our illusory control of truth. We, as collectives within the fractious nature of mankind, have strengthened our denial of the equality of all souls, often by deliberately misinterpreting religious teachings for the purpose of securing scaling systems and pecking orders to reinforce racism, fanaticism and sectarianism. These misinterpretations and misconstrued versions of truth are generally devoid of the true nature of truth and cause us to be oppositional towards acknowledging the inequality we create when we believe we have control of truth.

Mankind throughout history has attempted to override the dynamic diversity of truth's evolution. Racism, fanaticism and sectarianism are the manifestations of mankind's desire to control, which is how we attempt to dictate to truth how life should be and how there should be a scaling system of value and worth. Racism, fanaticism and sectarianism are mankind's inability to accept the diversity within reality and our inability to accept the equality of all souls. Racism, fanaticism and sectarianism use mankind's collectives of judgement to concretise our separation. This enforces how we disassociate from feeling the truth that all souls are of the same origins and how we disassociate from the significance, value and worth of each individual, regardless of whether we are of the same skin colour, faith, gender, opinions, region of birth or life experience.

Racism is a direct attack on truth and an attempt to tell our united origins it has made a mistake. Racism is the choice to devalue someone because you will not accept the uniqueness of each soul. We, as mankind, judge truth with an arrogant display of condemnation for the uniqueness of all life experiences. Fanaticism and sectarianism use the differences between faiths and opinion to be discriminative against those who do not comply with their fanatical or sectarian beliefs. Fanaticism and sectarianism use their obsessive desire to be on top of the scaling system as justification to be indifferent to truth. Fanaticism creates blinded judgement that enforces indifference to truth. Racism, fanaticism and sectarianism coordinate beliefs that are used as control structures, to justify defiling the origins of truth. Fanatics want the power to dictate the origins of truth with their own soul denial. The power struggle within mankind has always been the power struggle for control of the individuality of souls and is an attempt to have ownership of truth.

Racism, fanaticism and sectarianism rely on pecking orders. All people who ascribe to pecking orders are constantly using their judgement and indifference to truth to jostle for position, which creates a constant disunity within any collective of people. Judgement and fear are used in an attempt to establish control over one another. The ingenuity of mankind's justification for betraying our united origins is boundless, due to mankind's addiction to constructing illusions of control over truth. We, as mankind, repeat history because we are addicted to our oppression, and have succumbed to our own denial of reality, which means we continue to tolerate our indifference to truth.

We, as mankind, have collectively oppressed ourselves and stagnated our evolution, by ignoring the equality of all souls and denying the importance of the uniqueness of every soul's experience. We judge the significance of mankind with the worship of control, in order to continue overriding the significance of the uniqueness, independence and individuality of souls. Mankind continues to override the significance of truthfulness and refuses to take responsibility for the ramifications of our denial, indifference to truth and desire for control.

We as mankind dumb down our perception of our evolution, because our greed for power and wealth overrides the ramifications of being indifferent to truth. We annihilate any awareness of truth that interferes with our pursuit of securing ownership of reality, because we want to protect our illusory sense of control. Mankind continuously seeks control. Mankind denies being the unconsciousness of *True Source Divine Origin Consciousness*, in an attempt to control truth's natural ability and intention to expose the illusion of our control. Truthfulness is when we individually or collectively acknowledge the value of accepting truth as significant to our individual evolution and to mankind's collective evolution. Evolution occurs when we acknowledge the deception of indifference, judgement and our desire to control as unresolved emotions. We resolve when we intentionally choose to value truth, which leads to being truthfully honest about ourselves and our reality.

We, as mankind, have corrupted our understanding of soul truth, which is the reality of both conscious and unconscious energy, because it suits the power struggle for control of the significance, uniqueness, independence and individuality of each soul. When you deny the truth of feeling your soul, you immerse yourself in controlled evolution energy and oppose hearing, seeing and feeling truth. You can use your denial as a source of power to deny being of truth, which means you are choosing to participate in the continuation of the insanity of mankind's soul denial. When you acknowledge the significance of being truthful with yourself, you become one less participant in the insanity of perpetuating mankind's collective soul denial. This also means you become a ripple of truthfulness within mankind. Who knows how your ripple of truthfulness will affect the true potential of your soul and the collective consciousness of humanity. When you honour your individuality, respect your own uniqueness and uphold your own energetic independence, you emanate the core essences of your soul, which is your purity within the frequency of truth.

Ramifications of controlled evolution

When you manipulate yourself with your fear of being unable to control, you rebel against truth being the foundation and the core essence of life. Your fear is an alert system encouraging you to be honestly present in what is occurring, and to trust your awareness and instincts within your present moment. When fear becomes about not getting what you believe you want or becomes a constant state of being, you lose insight into your reality. Your loss of insight into the truth of your reality causes you to react from fear and diverts your attention away from your actual life experience. This opens the door to your construction of lies which is how you misconstrue the evidence of truth, as you attempt to accommodate your desire to believe you are in control. You desperately want to believe you are in control because you think it will quell your fear, however your desperation to feel in control aggravates your fear. You can desire to quell your fear, however, if you do not acknowledge the truth of your fear, you will be in denial of your reality, which leaves you feeling conflicted. You may use your deception to become a false foundation, hence the construction of your soul denial. Your soul denial is the crux of your soul's unconsciousness, and is the storehouse of the embedded beliefs and fears you have suppressed and refused to acknowledge or challenge.

When you have manipulated yourself to believe you can use your emotions to replace truth, you become indifferent and immersed in the energy of your soul's unconsciousness. Your indifference to truth actually inflames your fear, which instigates the energetic force of your desire for control that you use to distract yourself from your own fear. Your obsession with your own desire for control deflects you from being honestly present in what is internally or externally occurring. You use your indifference to truth to distract and deflect yourself from your fear and from your present moment, and this is how you defect from the truth of who you are.

Your unresolved emotions stem from your denial and insecurity, which have you fearing truth and are sustained by your opposition to trusting yourself to be truthful. Your denials, fears and insecurities are the ramifications of your unwillingness to truthfully experience the uniqueness of your present moment. When you live acknowledging the truth of your feelings, you learn from your exploration of truth and by objectively observing yourself within your own reality. Your unresolved emotions are stored unconscious energy, constructed from your unwillingness to be truthfully honest with yourself about your emotional, energetic and physical reality. When you live your life experiences honestly acknowledging the truth of your feelings, you will neither store nor carry unconscious energy. When you feel the truth of yourself within each experience, your truthfulness enables you to feel the dynamics of your free flowing consciousness which is your soul.

You can become constantly in conflict with the dynamics of life and expect to be able to control the free flowing consciousness of your soul, but your control stagnates your awareness and deprives you of your insight. Truth is never stagnant and truth is an energy that cannot be stored as an emotion. Truth is within your present moment and your insecurity is created because you deny your awareness of truth within your present moment.

When you seek to align to beliefs that validate the unconsciousness of your desire to control, you become indifferent to the ramifications of your beliefs, behaviours and the words you speak. When you only adopt beliefs because they suit your avoidance of truth, you lose your objectivity. You control yourself to assess the validity of your beliefs from your desire to control truth. When you emotionally feel the reality of your control, you have the choice to either deny the reality you feel or use your honesty to acknowledge the truth of your feelings. When you are honest about your control, you alter the stagnation created from being separated from your awareness of your soul and disassociated from feeling truth. Your denial of your control is how you manipulate yourself to compete with truth. You can control yourself to abandon your awareness of your soul's consciousness and fight for a position of supremacy within your own judgement of truth, while justifying your indifference to truth and the choices you make. When you use your own judgement to create an illusion of control, you deny the importance of truth and the significance of your own awareness of your reality. Your desire to be right in your judgement of truth and the arrogant righteousness within your beliefs, has you pretending to be unconscious to the reality of your own and mankind's collective denial. This is a pretense because there are always occasions where you recognise your own denial, but if you are intentionally unconscious you pretend to not notice.

You can manipulate yourself to deny that you are your soul, and manipulate yourself to deny the momentum of your unresolved emotions. Your self-manipulation creates insecurity, which can actually be the catalyst for you to decide to explore your own denial, because you tire of the insecurity within yourself. You create your unresolved emotions with your denial of your present moment. You create the oppression of your awareness of your soul's consciousness with your mistrust of truth. Your discovery of being the creator of your own emotions enables you to comprehend your denial. This opens you to explore the possibility of your own evolution.

When you fight your awareness of being your own emotional creator, you attempt to prove the validity of your control of your soul denial. This causes you to fight the truth of your fear and to class your embedded beliefs as truth, which is how you create more fear and end up confusing yourself. When you use your denial to condition yourself to disassociate from feeling your present moment, you deny the reality of feeling the presence of truth. This leaves you dismissing your awareness of being safe to explore and experience the truth of yourself within your reality. When you have indoctrinated yourself to believe that it is safer to separate from your awareness of your soul and disassociate from feeling truth, you use your unresolved emotions to create an emotional space to hide in, whilst ignoring your present moment feelings. This causes you to become emotionally reactive, instead of staying present in the truth of your feelings.

You can control yourself to deny your feelings and the purpose of your emotional reactions to your present moment, which means you overshadow the truth of your experience with your emotional reactions. Your ability to believe your own illusion of control is limited. As the truth of your reality becomes evident, you either acknowledge the ineffectiveness of your control and ramp up your denial of reality, becoming irrational, or you decide to explore your truth and take self-responsibility of your own emotions. You keep repeating your emotional patterns, however the repetitiveness of your emotional patterns eventually exposes you to the truth of your control and manipulation. This then enables you to observe your own emotional, energetic and physical merry-go-round. Truth is an unlimited dynamic energy that cannot be restrained by the repetitiveness of your or mankind's cyclic patterns of soul oppression.

Your deceptive illusion of control creates insecurity because illusions are devoid of the dynamics of truth. You can condition yourself to be fearful and insecure about the enormity of life's ability to consistently expose you to the reality of what is unresolved within you. When you are honest about your awareness of your soul truth, you feel freedom and relief. Unfortunately, when you are dishonest with yourself you are resisting, denying and avoiding feeling freedom and a sense of ease. Your resistance to and denial and avoidance of truth are the foundations of your insecurity. You can be aware of your own deception and seek to pacify your insecurity with any beliefs you think will exonerate you from being responsible for instigating your own insecurity. Your lack of self-responsibility causes you to control your evolution to be stagnant. The repetitiveness of your emotional patterns become the familiarity of your soul oppression, which is how you counteract your ability to be at peace with the magnitude and strength of the unlimited dynamism within your soul. The strength of your presence within your reality is felt when you value your soul.

When you control yourself to be in constant conflict with the dynamics within your soul and your reality, you become oppositional to your own awareness of truth. You use your internal conflict to rebel against all aspects of your soul, the dynamics of truth, your ability to be at peace with reality and to rebel against feeling your freedom. When you define yourself by your conflicted beliefs you are anchoring to your unconsciousness, which often leaves you forgetting you have freedom of choice. You will use the most convenient method to deny you are making a choice to operate from your contrary beliefs and deception. When you observe yourself being contradictory about your beliefs, you create more insecurity for yourself, because you have to defend your deception as you attempt to exert control over your reality. When you forget you have freedom of choice you breed more deception to control yourself to, which causes you to oppose the truth of your origin and the reality of being a significant, unique, independent, individual soul of *True Source Divine Origin Consciousness*.

Your controlled evolution energy is produced by your attempts to avoid truth and is generated by the desire to control your fears and embedded beliefs. You also want to believe that this will allow you to avoid your own unresolved emotions. Your desire to control your soul denial beholds you to be controlled and manipulated by your own embedded beliefs and fears. You use your desire to control your evolution to create illusions of what you believe your truth should be. You control yourself with your own deception to abandon being open to experience and explore truth. You manipulate yourself with your own deception to deny your own awareness and understanding of truth. Your use of denial, means you misconstrue your awareness and corrupt your understanding of truth, which is how you create control structures you can use to defend your unconsciousness. You control yourself with your own arrogance, to deny the reality that you allow yourself to be manipulated by your desire to protect your unresolved emotions and beliefs.

Your desire to control the fears and embedded beliefs of your soul denial inundates you with negative beliefs, which has you reverberating within the energetic mass energy of mankind. You use these negative beliefs in an attempt to stifle your awareness of yourself and you compulsively become dishonest, which has an immediate effect on your soul consciousness' ability to expose truth. When you automatically start controlling yourself to, and with, your own negative beliefs, you emotionally spiral deeper into the energy of your soul's unconsciousness, while seeking to justify and validate your dishonesty by being righteous. When you utilise your dishonesty to avoid taking responsibility, you will seek security in the negativity you generate. You emotionally, energetically and physically feel the surge of power generated by your deception, and use this feeling of power to stoke your own ego. You attempt to deny the ramifications of your deception, and if you expect you will not be held accountable you smugly believe being anti-truth and anti-your soul has an advantage to you.

Heresy energy, is the result of, or is, what you use to incite yourself to be anti-truth and indifferent towards your soul. Heresy energy is a way of concealing the exposure of the energy of your soul's unconsciousness. For example:

- You use **your desire to control** to orchestrate your mistrust of truth, to overshadow the reality of the energy of your soul's unconsciousness, and to shut down your awareness of truth.
- You use **your indifference to truth** to deny the effects of the energy of your soul's unconsciousness and to ignore your awareness of truth.
- You use **your resentment of reality** to divert blame to another, to hide the truth of the energy of your soul's unconsciousness and to validate your opposition to your awareness of truth.
- You use **being oppositional** to avoid being exposed to the energy of your soul's unconsciousness and to be contrary to your own awareness of truth.
- You use **your denial of reality** to pretend to be unaware of the energy of your own soul's unconsciousness and to deflect your awareness of truth.
- You use **your programming, conditioning and indoctrinations** to justify the energy of your soul's unconsciousness and to counteract your awareness of truth.
- You use **your guilt, shame and humiliation** to abandon the opportunity to resolve what has been exposed to you about the energy of your soul's unconsciousness and to overwhelm yourself with your awareness of truth.
- You use **your disassociation from love** to deny the truth you feel and are aware of. You numb yourself to the reality that you are protecting, sustaining and perpetuating the energy of your soul's unconsciousness, to avoid being present in the truth of your feelings and to be dishonest about your awareness of truth.

When you control yourself to never question your perceived righteousness, you use your heresy energy to remain dogmatic in your own views. This causes you to use your fears and embedded beliefs to oppress your ability to be present within the uniqueness of every moment. You distract yourself from the entirety of your reality with your desire to control your fears and embedded beliefs, whilst you justify your own heresy against the truth of yourself. Your denial of what you are actually doing to yourself ensures you do not have to confront the truth of your soul's unconsciousness.

Your attempt to protect your soul denial produces automatic reactions to the truth being exposed to you. You react to truth with your emotional patterns that leave you controlling yourself to the familiarity of your soul oppression. Your desire to control creates stagnation as you align to the familiarity of your denial. When you believe you have control of something or someone, you emotionally feel an energetic fix, but it is only you deceptively validating your illusory control of life, yourself, others, your relationships and truth. When you defend the familiarity of your stagnation, by automatically defending your fear reactions to truth, you disable your ability to reason with yourself and to challenge the truth of what you are actually doing. You may attempt to avoid being responsible and accountable for the truth you are aware of, because you fear any acknowledgement will reveal that you are not, as in control, as you want to believe you are.

You can obsess with creating distractions to avoid your own awareness of truth, which is an attempt to ensure you can pretend to be unaware, if you choose to reject truth. You can create an emotional storm to be your distraction, in an attempt to avoid acknowledging truth. However, the storm can exacerbate what you are trying to avoid. When you chase distractions, emotionally running in circles, you spiral further into your soul's unconsciousness. This can leave you layering deception on deception, which can cause you more difficulties than what you originally attempted to avoid. You can control yourself to deny what you emotionally observe, to sustain your illusory control of life, yourself, others, your relationships and truth. However, illusions eventually burst and you will be confronted with that which you attempted to avoid.

When you become stagnant within your fear of being a significant, unique, independent, individual soul, you deny yourself the opportunity to explore beyond what you believe you know. You class your unknown as a no-go-zone, retreating to the false comfort zone of what you believe you know or have adopted from your mankind indoctrinations as truth. When you do not accept the truth you feel, you condition yourself to retreat and recoil from your unresolved emotions and start justifying your fears, which inhibits you from feeling your awareness of the presence of both your soul's consciousness and *True Source Divine Origin Consciousness*.

You can use your reverberation with any energetic collective energy to hide from the truth of your soul denial, which is an attempt to hide from your fears and embedded beliefs. Collective energy in this context is any group of people reverberating with the same beliefs, desires and expectations. You align your desire to control with collective beliefs, so you can anchor to a sense of belonging, in an attempt to gain a sense of security. However, this actually creates a sense of insecurity, because you are constantly assessing if you fit in, or are being judged by others within the collective. You can believe that joining a collective will supply you with an image, illusion or controlled identity. You may believe belonging to a collective will enable you to hide the insecurities you feel. When you believe you have selected a collective that will pacify your insecurities, you find that you have actually set yourself up to amplify your insecurities and unresolved emotions, because you end up trying to avoid being judged by those within the collective.

RIGHT: *When you anchor to your soul denial, you become encased in the emotional storms created by the unresolved emotions of your soul's unconsciousness. When you seek the truth of your unresolved emotions, you free yourself from the chains of your own soul oppression.*

When you believe you are just a struggling human, you curtail your freedom to explore your uniqueness, independence and individuality.

When you approach your insecurities and fears narcissistically, you will want to control collective energy to stroke and feed your ego, which becomes another energy you try to control and manipulate. You cannot become aware of your uniqueness, independence and individuality by controlling yourself to collective ideals and beliefs or by defining yourself with collective judgement. When you use collective energy to hide from your own uniqueness, independence and individuality, you become lost in your indifference to your soul. Your acceptance of your own uniqueness, independence and individuality means you are not allowing yourself to be constricted by others' pecking orders and control. Honouring your uniqueness, independence and individuality means you do not need to compete with others' perception of reality, or another's uniqueness, independence and individuality.

When you have entwined and bound yourself to the identity of being a struggling human, you become willing to be anti-yourself. This means you adopt beliefs as an identity and control yourself with the belief of 'if my control is not being pacified, I am a struggling human'. The belief of being a struggling human causes you to feel and often seek to reverberate with any energetic collective energy of mankind you believe will justify your mistrust of truth, and justify defining yourself as a struggling human. You do this to distract yourself from your own awareness and from caring for the truth of who you are. Instead of acknowledging the truth of how you feel, you align to your reverberations with the energetic collectives, you believe will secure your dishonesty. Your dishonesty inhibits you from exploring the truth of why you feel the way you do, or from questioning yourself on why you entangle, engage and connect to unconscious energy. You use your struggling human belief to judge your significance, value and worth, which enables you to lose your sense of uniqueness, independence and individuality.

When you deny you have chosen to separate from your awareness of your soul's consciousness and abandon feeling the presence of *True Source Divine Origin Consciousness*, you become entangled in your own deception. When you abandon truth you anchor to your own deceptive heresy against yourself, and end up wallowing in the identity of being a struggling human. To abandon truth is to abandon the core of your being. When you become a contributing factor to the energetic collective of struggling human energy, which is the energetic collective of anti-truth via being anti-yourself, you become lost in the beliefs that create your struggling human identity. You use this struggling human identity as a fall back position when you recognise you are unable to pacify your control or that your expectations have not come to fruition. You adopt the belief and identity of being a struggling human in an attempt to hide from the truth of your own unresolved emotions. This means you use the topic of your struggle to consume your attention, and hide from the real issue which is what the emotional upheaval is actually about.

When you attempt to control the void created by your separation from your awareness of your soul, you begin to justify your own indifference to your struggling human beliefs. You use your justifications to expand your struggle into an all-encompassing perception that everything in your life is opposing your control, and this causes you to spin in beliefs that keep you being anti-yourself. You fear you cannot escape the despair you create with your struggle against yourself and life. This causes you to implode under the weight of your own negative beliefs and fragments your own awareness of truth. Your awareness of your struggle is actually highlighting what is unresolved within you, and create opportunities for you to truthfully acknowledge the issues that allow you to remain anti-yourself. When you succumb to your own implosions without being able to reason with yourself, you miss the mark of your life experiences.

When you try to control the despair you create with your own heresy, such as your resentment of reality, opposition, shame or denial of reality, you separate further from your awareness of truth, which intensifies the void you feel and seek to control. When you are dishonest with yourself, you will attempt to use your control but your control creates a wider void that you lose yourself in. Your dishonesty entraps you in the heresy energy you are using, such as resentment, indifference or shame, and inhibits you from acknowledging the opportunity and entirety of what you are experiencing. It is your truthfulness that resolves your beliefs and self-identity as being a struggling human. When you are willing to explore the entirety of what you are experiencing, you begin to see, feel and acknowledge you have options.

Your desire to be in control of your own evolution, causes you to use the energy within your soul's unconsciousness to create an illusory perception of yourself and reality, which you then use to overshadow your insight and awareness. Your illusory perception of yourself and reality means you omit the truth of your unresolved emotions. This keeps you anchoring to your beliefs of how reality should be, instead of acknowledging the truth of reality.

When you control yourself to believe your illusions are your truth, you concretise your desire to control yourself to your own illusory perception of yourself and reality. This protects the concealment of your unresolved emotions and secures your willingness to defend your beliefs. You concretise how you protect your unresolved emotions and your willingness to defend your beliefs by regurgitating, stewing and wallowing in the unconscious energy of the thoughts that justify your denial. You deny how you use your thoughts to concretise your stagnation, because you start to believe you are your thoughts. The insanity of denying the dynamic flow of consciousness within your soul leads you to replace the clarity of your awareness with illusions, replace harmony with conflict and replace trust with fear.

When you hinder your ability to resolve and evolve your desire to control, you dogmatically defend your illusions, which sustains your stagnation. Within your illusions you believe you are in control of your soul's unconsciousness and justified in arrogantly denying any truth that will expose the deception of your illusions.

You can deceptively bombard yourself with thoughts that sustain your resistance to, and denial and avoidance of truth and the potential for change. You use your fear of change to impose a fear of freedom. This causes you to emotionally resist, deny and avoid the unfamiliarity of being conscious of the entirety of your own energy, which generates a fear of being conscious of truth. You can fear the change created by being aware of your soul's consciousness and unconsciousness, which causes you to protect your denial. Evolution occurs when you are aware of the truth of both your conscious and unconscious energy, and then use your curiosity to explore the truth of both. Being willing to explore and accept the truth of how you contributed to your own soul's unconsciousness is a key component to resolving your unresolved emotions. To protect and defend your fear of truth or of change, you have conditioned yourself to tolerate your separation from your awareness of truth and of being a soul. Due to the familiarity of being separated from your awareness, you believe that your separated state is who you are. This is a misconception. When you are unwilling to acknowledge and accept both your soul's consciousness and unconsciousness, you perpetuate the oppression of your soul. Your acknowledgement of the truth of your conscious and unconscious energy is important. When you separate from being aware of the truth of your energy, you create a void within yourself.

When you attempt to use control to emulate your beliefs of consciousness, you are actually separating from your awareness of your natural truth. Your consciousness flows naturally, and it is your decision to be truthful that enables you to feel your consciousness. It is your willingness to separate from your awareness of your soul and truth, that actually inhibits your ability to feel what is naturally there.

You separate from your awareness of your soul's consciousness and truth, but your soul's consciousness never separates from you. Resolution is to acknowledge what you use to cloud your awareness of the purity of yourself. Evolution is to actively be accountable for being a presence of truth. Resolution is a discovery process of what you use to cloud your awareness of the purity of the unconditional love of *True Source Divine Origin Consciousness* within your soul and within the truth of your reality. Evolution is to be the purity of your unconditional love, because you are emanating the presence of your soul.

Your soul denial is the crux of your soul's unconsciousness and is the storehouse of your beliefs and fears that create your misconceptions. These misconceptions cause you to anchor to your illusion of control, believing you can create security for yourself within the insecurity of your soul's unconsciousness. Your soul's unconsciousness is built on a foundation of misconceptions; how can you feel secure within misconceptions? The version of security you seek is a falsity; it is unachievable because you are attempting to find security in denying the truth of yourself. It is a fallacy because to separate from your awareness of truth is to defend the deception generated by your fears, which secures your insecurity. You cannot create security whilst protecting your deception.

Your defense of your soul denial separates you from true resolution and evolution. True resolution is to expose the truth of the unconscious energy of your soul's unconsciousness and to trust yourself to resolve the energy and attitude and beliefs that ensue. It is your truthful honesty within your junction, between conscious and unconscious energy, that determines your awareness; the choices you make determine what energy you dominate your awareness with.

If your expectations about your evolution are not pacified, you judge truth and yourself as unworthy, 'not good enough' and insignificant. If you do not get the results you want, you bombard yourself with beliefs of evolution not being worth the effort. This can cause you to run an internal dialogue, which opposes your original intention for resolution and evolution. For example:

- "I cannot completely evolve the negativity of my history, so why bother?"
- "Unless evolution has a mankind prize, why put myself through the confusion?"

When you control yourself to justify your internal dialogue, you become entrapped in your own incessant mind chatter. This causes you to believe you can impose your unconscious will over your awareness of truth, and by opposing your own evolution you believe you are in control of truth. This is an illusion that encases you in your indifference to truth and leaves you emotionally, energetically and physically oppressed.

When you control yourself to abide by images, illusions and controlled identities that you believe suit your illusion of control; you become reliant on your already established pathways of indifference to truth, which you believe validate your images of yourself. Your images are created by your own deception. Your pathways of indifference are cyclic patterns created by you repeating the familiarity of the unresolved emotions you carry from your soul denial history, that oppress your awareness of your soul. You perpetuate avenues of indifference that enable you to believe in your own control. You create a sense of control out of the predictability of your programmed emotional reactions, behaviours and thoughts. You only accept what you believe can be controlled within your awareness of the archives of your soul denial history and attempt to disregard what interferes with your control or the images you want to portray. You retrieve beliefs from your soul denial history without questioning the validity of your beliefs or how you really feel about yourself within those beliefs. You allow your desire to control your soul denial, to fuel your denial of reality.

When you use the energy of your soul's unconsciousness to avoid the reality that your control is an illusion, you create internal chaos to overshadow your awareness of reality, and focus your attention on controlling your denial. You become captivated by your own illusions, creating an internal dialogue within yourself that has you ruminating about negative beliefs and your past. This creates an incessant mind chatter that constantly reaffirms your negative beliefs and causes you to be stuck in your fears and denials. When you create an alternate scenario in your mind that omits the entirety of your own awareness of your reality, you use your constructed lies to justify your belief in the need for your control. This creates a desire for control that clouds your awareness of truth, and also causes you to become disillusioned with your inability to pacify your desire for control with your denial of reality.

Reality is hard to ignore. When you attempt to ignore reality you create insecurity, which causes you to judge yourself by your ability to control your denial to secure your deception. Your judgement causes you to succumb to being anti-the truth of yourself and leaves you confused about the reality of who you are and what you are experiencing. You fight your awareness of your own reality by seeking to create an illusion of control, often believing controlling others will pacify the confusion you create with your deception. You want to control everyone and everything to give you what you want, even if you cannot identify what you want. This causes you to become contrary to your actual reality and full of nonsensical demands that can never be achieved, or if achieved leave no peace within.

Your desire to control your evolution flags up how you oppress the truth of your soul's value, worth and significance with beliefs. The beliefs you construct from your desire to control omit the significance of who you naturally are. As you deny your natural value, worth and significance, you swamp yourself with emotions and seek to appease your own expectations and demands that suit your agendas. When you fight the truth of your natural value, worth and significance, you hide in the familiarity of your soul oppression.

- Do you believe you can hide from truth?
- Do you believe you have the power to switch off truth's ability to feel you and your emotions?

You fight reality for an illusion of control. You can attempt to control to get what you want even if you cannot identify what you want. You can become contrary and confused by your own behaviour, and others can become insecure and confused by your contrariness.

Your misconception of being able to control truth is an illusion of control that separates you from your awareness of your soul's consciousness and truth. You want to deceptively believe separating yourself from your awareness of your soul's consciousness and truth, means truth and your soul's consciousness are unaware of you. Your soul's consciousness and truth remain within you regardless of your separation. Even though you can be unconscious to your reality, you are your soul's consciousness and of truth.

When you are confused by your own deception and diffuse your awareness of your soul's consciousness and truth, you ignore your own insight. Your diffusion of your awareness makes it difficult for you to acknowledge the entirety of what you are actually aware of. Your diffusion of your awareness secures your denial of being able to tell the difference between your truth and your own deception. You use your unresolved emotions to diffuse your awareness of truth. You scatter and fragment your awareness of truth, so you do not have to acknowledge the entirety of what is occurring. This causes you to only acknowledge the fragments of truth you want to, or the fragments of truth you believe will enhance your control, judgement and beliefs. When you only focus on the fragments of truth you choose to be aware of, you rely on your judgement to create an altered version of truth that suits the embedded beliefs and fears within your soul denial. You then use your desire to control to justify what you believe you understand, losing awareness of the essence of truth, replacing it with arrogance and ignorance. This causes you to emotionally feel lost and to believe you have been abandoned by truth, and you use this misconception to justify remaining embroiled in your indifference. When you reject and avoid the truth of your own behaviours, thoughts and addictions, you secure your entrapment in the energy of your soul's unconsciousness. You align to your misconceptions and give yourself permission to eliminate your ability to trust your awareness of your soul's consciousness and *True Source Divine Origin Consciousness*.

When you are in denial of being a soul, it is inevitable that you will construct beliefs out of misconceptions and deception. When you are stagnant within your and mankind's beliefs of evolution, you oppose being absolutely truthful about your reality, which causes you to play manipulative games as you interact with life, others, yourself and truth. This means you become an heir to the limitations and restrictions of the games you orchestrate and participate in, to avoid the truthfulness required for your evolution. You deny yourself the opportunity for evolution with your deceptive beliefs of being able to control your life. You actually protect what you need resolution in, which secures your constructed misconceptions. Mankind throughout history has created misconceptions about evolution, deceptively believing that evolution means having more control. Mankind has attempted to control what we think evolution should be, by creating many misconstrued beliefs of reward if we control ourselves to contrived pathways and images of consciousness. However, you are unique, as is your evolutionary journey.

When you align to mankind's interpretation that your evolution is reliant on, and at the mercy of, pacifying a higher source that you believe is separated from you, you devalue your own natural insight. Devaluing your own natural insight allows you to operate from the misconception that you are separated from your origin of truth. Truth is the core of your being, the life force of your soul and your evolution is only reliant on you awakening to the truth of yourself. When you awaken to the truth of yourself, you feel your own individual resonance with truth. When you want your evolution to be about having control, you seek to pacify what you want, which means you create control structures for how truth should appease you. You use your wants and desires to create beliefs, which separate you from the truth within your soul.

We, as mankind, collectively have disregarded truth and created beliefs in an attempt to secure control of truth, which is how we have sustained our separation from the truth of who we are. Separation generates fears and a belief of not being good enough, which become self-perpetuating. When you use mankind's misconceptions of how to create an image of being conscious, as benchmarks to determine your position within the pecking order of the belief system you ascribe to, you lose the significance of your own individual relationship with truth. You use your belief systems to create expectations about who you have to be, which gets in the way of you discovering who you naturally are. Your belief systems can conceal what is unresolved within you, which leaves you separated from your origins of truth. Your soul's consciousness seeks unification and for you to accept the truth of who you are. Your soul's consciousness is the part of you that is not separated from your origins of truth. Your choices are the pivotal points of your evolution and your acknowledgment of being of truth is the pivotal point for your choices.

Your compulsions keep you compliant to being unconscious to your soul truth, which means you crave the familiarity of the oppression you have created. You attempt to control truth or to escape from your own awareness of truth. This causes you to use your belief systems to remain stagnant; refusing to feel, explore and learn. You become lost in the familiarity of your soul's unconsciousness. What you crave becomes your priority, which alters how you feel about yourself and how you interact with life. When you manipulate yourself to justify your desire to pacify your cravings, you compel yourself to deny the unresolved emotions that underpin what you crave. This feeds your compulsions and leaves you manipulating yourself to ignore the reality of your choice to be unconscious of your soul truth, and to sustain your desire to pacify your own cravings. Your cravings become an insatiable appetite for your desire to control. Your compulsions keep you anchored to your desire for control and you live life reacting from your emotions. Your compulsions have you believing you need to emotionally feel in control to survive. Your desire for control is an energy that cannot be pacified, however it can be resolved. When you recognise the truth of your compulsions and how you oppress yourself and become willing to be truthful about what you can observe of yourself, you create the opportunity to resolve what is unresolved within you.

When you abandon your awareness of truth, you compulsively align to your unresolved emotions and deny that you have any awareness of truth. This is a rejection of the opportunity to resolve your compulsion to oppress yourself. When you blame your emotions with no intent to be truthful and ignore the reality of your choices, you lose awareness of the option of resolution, and oppose being responsible and accountable for your own energy. When you use your unconscious energy to justify your insatiable appetite for control, you stagnate your own evolution and become entrapped in your own web of deception. You use your own web of deception to control yourself to only focus on believing you are in control or to focus on how to get control. This distracts you from the reality of the effort you put into stagnating your own evolution.

Stagnating your evolution is choosing to oppress your soul. Your truthful honesty will enable you to observe the true ramifications of your compulsion to oppress yourself and oppose your awareness of your soul's consciousness and unconsciousness. When you do not challenge your compulsions, you use your unresolved emotions to perpetuate your soul denial history and oppose any inclination within yourself to resolve or evolve.

When you deny your awareness of truth and reject your present moment with your denial, you are creating or perpetuating your soul denial history. When you are in your present moment, what is behind you becomes your history. Your unconsciousness about yourself and truth, creates your soul denial history. It is you who chooses to either be present in the dynamics of what is occurring or to lose awareness of your present moment and focus on your history. Your choice to deny your awareness of being a soul, stagnates your own evolution and the evolution of the unconsciousness of *True Source Divine Origin Consciousness*.

We have created the energetic mass energy of mankind, which is the unconsciousness of *True Source Divine Origin Consciousness*. *True Source Divine Origin Consciousness* has inherited what mankind has created because of our choices to separate and disassociate from the purity of truth. When we choose to resolve our unconsciousness, we expand the consciousness of *True Source Divine Origin Consciousness*. Our unresolved emotions generate the unconscious energy we contribute to the mass energy of mankind, and we each have freewill to choose to participate in the resolution of our individual portion of unconsciousness.

You can feel the truth of your reality and fear not being able to control your reality to make you feel the way you want to. This fear creates a craving that has you compulsively reacting to yourself and life. Your reality exposes to you, the familiarity of your denial and your control, because you constantly observe the cyclic nature of your oppression. When you decide that you only want to experience what is emotionally familiar, you orchestrate dramas that secure the continuity of your struggle with yourself. This causes you to compulsively entwine yourself with your own indifference to truth, which is how you sustain your oppression of yourself. You have to consciously decide to not be indifferent to yourself, which means you have to take the time to pause and acknowledge you have options. You always have the option to make the decision to choose to be truthfully honest with yourself about the reality of your feelings, emotions and the truth of what is occurring.

Your fear of your own reality causes you to judge and scale your value, worth and significance by your ability or inability to pacify your wants and desires. When you observe that you are unable to pacify your wants and desires, you create an internal frustration that has you oppositional to truth and willing to disregard your own internal knowing. This causes you to anchor to your addiction to securing what is emotionally familiar to you, which is how you sustain your oppression and override your resonance with truth. When you compulsively use your judgement of yourself, life and others to create a vacuum to compress your resonance with truth, you allow yourself to devalue the significance of truth. You replace your awareness of truth with your denial and your desire to control, and you conceal your awareness of yourself from yourself. This allows you to perpetuate separation within separation, sustaining the void you feel within. The insanity of this is, the void you create is the same void you compulsively want to fill.

Your protection of your own stagnation, leads to your desire to control your evolution, which causes you to be deceptive and manipulative with any truth you discover. You can become willing to use beliefs as control structures. This means regardless of the truth you discover, you revert back to controlling yourself to the familiarity of your soul oppression. When you utilise your beliefs to discredit and oppress any truth you discover, you believe you are protecting yourself and your unresolved emotions. However, what you are actually doing is oppressing your opportunity for resolution and evolution. When you judge the value of

Your honesty with truth will allow you to observe the true ramifications of your compulsion to stagnate yourself within your own soul oppression.

yourself by your ability or inability to control and by how any discovery of truth affects your perception of yourself, you become defensive and willing to interject your judgement into every situation and conversation. Your judgement of yourself reinforces your defensiveness and your need for your illusion of control. You use your need for control to oppress your awareness of your soul truth, and this causes you to condone your own defensiveness. Your truthful honesty enables you to be objective about your control and exposes to you how you use your judgement as an adversary to your freedom. When you acknowledge that you want resolution of, and freedom from, the familiarity of your soul oppression, you quell your defensiveness and become willing to objectively observe yourself.

When you acknowledge and feel the truth of yourself, you enable yourself to resolve being codependent on your illusion of control and your own judgement. You can falsely believe your defensiveness keeps you safe from others' control and judgement. However, it is your own control and judgement that causes you the most grief. Truth and the freedom to be honest with yourself creates the safety you seek, but when you are compulsively defensive, you are too overwhelmed with the deception of your own judgement and control to acknowledge the reality of what you are seeking.

Your desire to control your evolution causes you to doubt yourself, which is how you create your opposition to accepting the reality you feel and observe. When you analyse your doubt with fear, you perpetuate your desire to control with your belief systems. You fear being unable to control life, yourself and others and this sustains your self-doubt. This self-doubt and consequent

fear interaction becomes self-perpetuating cycles that cause you to distrust truth. You fear your acceptance of truth will disable your illusion of control, or interfere with the beliefs and judgement you use to resist, deny and avoid truth. You doubt your own control and you transfer this doubt onto everything including your resonance with truth, which causes you to become mistrusting of everything you believe, feel and think. This means you become reliant and codependent on your judgement to analyse reality instead of trusting yourself to feel.

Your judgement creates separation from being completely present in what you are experiencing and your judgement causes you to only want to trust what you believe you can control.

When you attempt to use your beliefs to control your evolution, you find yourself wanting the ability to understand truth, as well as wanting to control what truth is. You internally know you cannot control truth and use your self-doubt to hide from your fear of losing your illusion of control. Your fear and self-doubt become control structures that keep you stagnant in your own soul oppression. The choice to defend and support your fear and self-doubt has you creating more deception within yourself, which leaves you willing to blame others, in an attempt to avoid taking responsibility for yourself. Abrogating responsibility allows you to stay in your denial, avoiding and concealing the cost of the ramifications to yourself.

You can control and judge your perception of yourself with beliefs, which actually enhance your fears and self-doubt. You use your beliefs to seek ultimate control over how you are perceived, which causes you to distort your understanding of your significance, uniqueness, independence and individuality. Your pursuit for ultimate control can cause you to become indifferent to the truth of yourself, as you seek to be superior to everything you believe is flawed about you. When your life is not pacifying your beliefs and reassuring your illusion of control, you start to believe there is no value in your existence. This means you have entangled your sense of worth with your perception of control. When you use your negative beliefs to determine your value, you control yourself to be indifferent to your natural significance, uniqueness, independence and individuality. You become the unconscious energy you came to resolve, which stagnates your ability to evolve your desire to control.

We, as mankind, have created our own indifference to ourselves, which causes the stagnation of mankind's evolution. Evolution means moving from indifference to truth to compassion for truth, for the uniqueness of all souls and their soul journey. Your indifference to your soul truth causes you to experience your own insatiable appetite for control. This is how you devalue the truth of being a compassionate soul who cares for the truth of who you naturally are and the truth of others. *True Source Divine Origin Consciousness* is compassionate with no hidden agenda. We, as mankind, can operate with hidden agendas that compromise our natural compassion for each other and ourselves. Evolution is to be compassionate, feel compassion and live compassionately.

LEFT: *You can be so consumed by your desire to control what you are focused on, that you become overwhelmed by your own inability to control. This can cause you to become disorientated about what you are emotionally, energetically and physically doing to yourself.*

The energetics of the mass energy of mankind is made up of the combination of each individual's ability to be indifferent to truth. We, as mankind, use being a dysfunctional, divisive mass as an excuse to remain indifferent to the reality of what we cause each other and our environment to endure. The energetics of the mass energy of mankind reverberates with our collective negativity, because we have lost compassion for ourselves. We, as mankind, control the suppression of our compassion by sustaining judgement, competition, grievances and indifference to truth, and we use these to create emotional, energetic and physical barriers. We use our collective barriers to truth to sustain our indifference toward ourselves. We, as mankind, create layers of deception to hide the reality of what we do to ourselves. We use our collective indifference to truth to create excuses for the choice to be uncaring for the truth of being souls of a united origin. Mankind has become overwhelmed with the enormity of our own dysfunction. Mankind is reluctant to acknowledge the reality of our dysfunction, because dysfunction is the space where we can continue the insanity of desiring control over truth.

We, as mankind, deny the natural significance of all souls being from a unified origin. Mankind has fought this reality so we can create the space for our collective deception. We, have lied to ourselves about the deviousness of this deception and have fought to sustain our indifference to the value of truth. We, are constantly separating to create different factions. Each faction seeks to have their own illusion of control pacified, wanting to be superior or inferior within their perception of the pecking orders within mankind. We create our own dysfunction because we refuse to accept and explore the significance of truth.

Mankind separates into and reverberates with different collectives. Each collective is made up of individuals who seek security by creating a sense of belonging to the collective energy. However, suppressing the truth of your soul to fit in with a collective creates insecurity within you. We fight for ownership of ideals, lifestyles and power because we cannot resolve our collective judgement of each other. We fight acknowledging the truth of the emotional, energetic and physical results of our collective judgement and indifference to truth.

We, as mankind, want to remain separated from feeling truth and avoid being aware of how our individual unconsciousness contributes to the mass energy of mankind. We fear coming to terms with what we have created with our indifference to truth and the unconsciousness of ourselves. Unconscious energy is the willingness to disassociate from feeling our unified origins of truth. We disassociate because disassociation is how we procure the opportunity to create an illusion of control. We do not realise the true extent of what we do to ourselves by trading our soul for an illusion. We think we are going to gain control and are reluctant to acknowledge the ramifications of our pursuit for control. Mankind remains separated from feeling and being aware of the significance of each individual's soul truth, because each individual soul's consciousness and unconsciousness is contributing to the dynamics of reality.

When you deny the truth of the dynamics of reality, you use your unconscious energy to willingly incite others' unconscious energy to participate in your merry-go-round of soul oppression. This, inadvertently, also activates the collective soul denial within the energetic mass energy of mankind. Soul denial is the foundation for all unconscious energy. How we interact from our unresolved emotions actually exposes the truth of the unconscious energy of our souls. This creates an opportunity to acknowledge and resolve what we are unconscious of. The resolution of unconscious energy is driven by experience.

- Are we as mankind unconscious to the reality of our own denial?
- Has mankind chosen to be stagnant as the unconsciousness of *True Source Divine Origin Consciousness*?

It will be each individual soul's resolution and evolution that will alter the mass. Evolution is not achieved by waiting for a collective decision to evolve; our shared experiences provide us with the learning we need, but each person's evolution is an individual and unique journey. Mankind cannot evolve as a whole because there are numerous collectives desiring control. If any change is perceived as disrupting the collective control, the collective will oppress the possibility of change. Evolution is always unique for each soul. When an individual resolves their unresolved emotions they create change within the energetics of mankind. The energetic collective mass of mankind can feel these individuals' resonance with truth, because they are withdrawing unconscious energy from the energetics of mankind. This creates an expansion of consciousness within mankind and enables humanity to flourish. The energetic mass energy of mankind can feel the frequency of truth within the truthful honesty required for the resolution of an unresolved emotion. This creates an energetic ripple effect through the collectives of the mass energy of mankind, because there is an energetic response to the awareness of truth.

The energetics of the mass energy of mankind is codependent on reverberating with the vibration of unconscious energy to unconscious energy. When you hold to your energetic independence, you can be present within the vibrations of unconsciousness and remain true to the essence of your soul. The frequency of truth does not reverberate with the vibration of unconscious energy. The frequency of truth naturally exposes the vibration of unconscious energy for what it actually is. The presence of truth exposes the disharmony within the vibration of all unconscious energy. Souls are unique individual strands of truth energy. Truth exposes opportunities for the resolution of unconscious energy in each individual strand of truth, one of which is you. Each soul's experience exposes their own freedom to choose to either harmonise or to disharmonise with truth. To disharmonise with truth, means you continue reverberating with unconscious energy. Unconscious energy can only reverberate when there is a willingness to disharmonise with truth. When you are willing to disharmonise with truth and be oppositional to reality, you become vibrational energy which stagnates your evolution. It is your choice to decide if you will resolve your own unconsciousness, and become conscious of the essence of your soul within the dynamics of truth.

You, as mankind energy, can create change by being of your truth, unencumbered by the desire to control truth or mankind energy. You create change by being aware of the entirety of the consciousness and unconsciousness within all souls, and by not using your growing awareness and understanding of truth to rank yourself as superior when you see unconscious energy in others. When you are willing to acknowledge the truth of unconscious energy with grace and compassion for the unconsciousness in yourself and in other souls, you create change. Mankind's indifference to truth has been created from our compulsion to scale each soul's worth. We, as mankind, struggle to recover from our judgement of each other and our collective indifference to truth.

When you are unconscious to your soul's consciousness, you equate freedom with the ability to control and oppress your awareness of your soul truth, in an attempt to create an illusion of control. When you are unconscious or indifferent to your soul truth, you want to believe you will never have to be accountable for the reality of controlling the sustainability of your own soul's unconsciousness. However, when you decide to be accountable for the truth of your unresolved emotions, you expand your awareness of truth. This enables you to discover how you protect the oppression of your soul and enables you to resolve your own defensiveness that sustains and maintains the unconscious energy within your soul.

Your willingness to be completely honest with yourself about your awareness of the truth of both conscious and unconscious energy, naturally affects your contribution to the energetics of the mass energy of mankind. When you attempt to be intentionally unconscious to the truth of your soul, you believe you can use your soul's unconsciousness to protect you from being accountable for the truth of your behaviours, emotions and hidden agendas. When you fight truth's ability to expose you to the reality of your unresolved emotions, you are fighting to remain unconscious to your own soul truth. You fight, defend and protect the unresolved emotions of your soul's unconsciousness, because you have decided your control is worth more than being aware of the truth of your soul or the opportunity to resolve and evolve.

You can attempt to control yourself to deceptively believe unconsciousness is the same as innocence; this is a mankind misconception that you use to be arrogantly indifferent to your own awareness of truth, and contributes to the stagnation of mankind's evolution. Your intentional unconsciousness gives you the ability to separate from your awareness of your soul truth and origins, which disassociates you from feeling your reality and the opportunities within your present moment. In truth you are just perpetuating your own insanity of unconsciousness. When you are choosing to perpetuate your disassociation from feeling your soul truth, you procure your codependency on the stagnation of mankind energy. This is because you are willing to deny how you feel and use your own misconceptions to secure separation from your awareness of your soul truth. You use your desire to control with belief systems, to undermine the reality and gravity of your choice to be dishonest with yourself.

Dishonesty is how you manipulate yourself to be controlled by the stagnation of your own soul's unconsciousness. When you are choosing to oppose freedom from your unresolved emotions, you are intentionally unconscious, which causes you to create more emotional chaos. When you use your own emotional chaos to fight against truth, you create red herrings to distract yourself and constantly fight to be right in your judgement. This causes you to become a warrior for your own desire to control truth and you lose awareness of the significance of your soul.

When you use beliefs of your own superiority and inferiority created by your judgement of yourself, you deny yourself the opportunity to explore what you are fighting with your denial. You create destructive images, illusions and controlled identities with your judgement of yourself, which oppose your natural value, worth and significance. Your judgement inhibits the confidence and security that comes naturally when you trust yourself as a soul and accept the truth you feel. Your judgement bombards you with your mistrust

of your resonance with truth, which causes you to align to your desire to control, because you want to escape the insecurity you feel within yourself. By acknowledging the truth of how you oppress yourself, you enable your awareness of truth to guide you to freedom. This enables you to realise the natural value, worth and significance of yourself as a soul. Your freedom from your soul oppression is a choice and you are the only one who can choose your time for resolution and evolution. You are the only one who can seek to discover your truth and the only one who will feel your own freedom.

Freedom is accepting truth and is the choice to be present in your reality. Freedom is communicating as a soul, feeling the truth of your own expanding consciousness with every choice made from your awareness of truth. Freedom is caring for yourself as a significant soul and making the choice to resolve your unresolved emotions and to unify with the origin of your soul. Freedom is to realise the reality you are fighting. Freedom is to feel at peace with your soul journey, realising without your experiences of being unconscious, you would not understand the significance of consciously feeling your uniqueness, independence and individuality. When you choose to be truthfully honest about the insanity of your unconsciousness you free yourself to feel and trust truth, reality, your soul's consciousness, and your individual relationship with *True Source Divine Origin Consciousness*.

When you desire to control your evolution, you interfere with your ability to acknowledge truth by compulsively opposing your freedom. This means you become stuck, as you want change within yourself, but fear you cannot control what the change means. Your fear becomes a tool you use to control yourself to preserve your ability to create, use and deny your emotional deception, which means you become oppositional to freedom. You use your fear to control yourself to reject the freedom you feel when you are truthfully honest, which means you secure your ability to discount the significance of your honesty. Your rejection of your own awareness of your soul and the significance of your honesty, causes you to fear not knowing what will be exposed to you about your soul, which becomes a catalyst for your retreat from truth. When you are intentionally unconscious to your soul truth, you will fear evolution. Freedom is the ability to trust whatever is being exposed as an opportunity to expand your awareness and understanding of yourself.

Oppression is the ability to control yourself to what you believe you already know and to stifle the exploration of truth, which creates deception that conceals your control of your evolution. When you protect your beliefs and fear evolution, you constantly create emotional turmoil, enabling your own soul oppression to be ignored and disregarded. When you enforce your own beliefs that oppose freedom and the exploration of truth, you defend your control structures. You also restrict yourself from ever realising the true significance of accepting yourself as a soul, and accepting and appreciating the reality of your life experiences.

Through your lack of acceptance and lack of understanding of your own significance, you control yourself to separate from your awareness of being a soul. You fail to comprehend that you are a soul in a physical form, which keeps you seeking control of your soul denial and fighting for validation within mankind's versions of significance. You control yourself to deny you are a significant, unique, independent, individual soul of *True Source Divine Origin*

Consciousness. You are of truth, and when you appreciate who you are, you naturally resonate with your own significance.

When you fail to comprehend the significance of evolving beyond your deceptive beliefs, you become entrapped by your own indifference to truth and your worship of control. When you hinder or obliterate your ability to accept being a contributor to the energetics of the mass energy of mankind and of *True Source Divine Origin Consciousness*, you become unconscious to your truth. You incarcerate yourself with your denial of reality to remain stagnant within an emotional energetic limbo. Your emotional energetic limbo can be recognised by your obsession with your illusion of control, your desire to remain in denial and your defiance against your own awareness of truth. Your emotional limbo is the choice to remain where you are, unwilling to explore truth, your own awareness and the dynamics of your reality.

Your controlled evolution energy is your willingness to incarcerate yourself within the emotional, energetic and physical barriers to truth created by your and mankind's deception. This confines you to oppressing your awareness of your soul. When you control yourself to deny the opportunities within your present moment, you choose to remain stagnant, repeating the patterns of your soul oppression. You can choose to either find your freedom within truth, or control yourself to exist within the cyclic patterns of your soul oppression. You can choose to either accept your freedom to explore and experience your soul truth, or be consumed with surviving your own unconsciousness, attempting to pacify your desire for control, whilst securing your denial of reality.

You use denial to sustain your ability to disassociate from noticing that life is filled with constant junctions. A choice is made whenever there is a junction. However, you become complacent and lazy about the reality that you are making a choice in every present moment. When you separate from being aware of the junction, you gloss over the choices you are making, and disregard the significance of what you are doing to yourself. When you oppose the knowledge that there is a conscious decision to be made with your freedom to choose, you align to complacency and laziness which compounds your oppression. You become complacent about the reality that you are constantly choosing whether you are going to be honest or dishonest with yourself. You attempt to ignore your dishonesty with yourself. Dishonesty is how you deny you have the ability to use your freedom of choice to evolve beyond your addiction to soul oppression. Denial of your freedom to choose restricts and limits any possibility for your own internal peace and your freedom from orchestrating your own soul oppression. The beliefs you use to perpetuate your desire to control your evolution make you compliant to the limitations of your own merry-go-round of soul oppression. You become entrapped by your methods of controlling your soul's evolution to be stagnant and refuse to acknowledge that you have a choice.

Your controlled evolution energy is the result of your willingness to be codependent on repeating your emotional history and is the manifestation of your fears of going beyond your known. You fear being without your barriers to truth and fear losing your illusion of control. Your controlled evolution energy is your portion of mankind's mistrust of truth. To mistrust truth is to be suspicious, fearing truth will deprive you of your illusion of control. When you mistrust truth you fuel the energetic collectives of the mass energy of mankind, and your willingness to oppress your own awareness of your soul truth for an illusion of control. This enables you to perceive evolution as something you have to control yourself to achieve, instead of allowing yourself to be dynamically present in your own process of unraveling your unconsciousness as life dynamically unfolds around you. When you try to control your evolution, you turn life into a struggle instead of being present in the process of evolving. When you become addicted to the identity of being a struggling human, you participate in mankind's stagnation. Your identity of being a struggling human, incarcerates you in your willingness to be anti-yourself and to distrust truth. You use your negative self-beliefs to imprison yourself in your own negativity and to stagnate the potential and possibilities of your evolution as a soul.

When you incarcerate yourself in your own cyclic patterns of soul oppression and believe you can pacify the oppression you feel, you become trapped in your own mistrust of your soul journey. This causes you to distrust your ability to be honest about the truth of your original intention to resolve and evolve. You consequently miss the journey of living your life experiencing your presence as a soul. The reality of your life is in your present moment; however if you are consumed with your desire to control, you will ignore your present moment and obsess about your past or your future. This will cause you to use your negativity as a weapon to deny being all you are uniquely capable of in your present moment. When you deny the uniqueness of your present moment because you want to secure and protect your beliefs, you perpetuate your indifference to the significance of your individual truth and energetic independence. Your indifference inhibits you from consciously participating in your own evolution, by securing your denial of the significance of your present moment.

When you attempt to control your evolution by filtering your experience of the present moment through your unresolved emotions, you become disassociated from feeling the reality of yourself. This causes you to overthink things, attempting to work out possible scenarios as you seek to secure a sense of certainty and safety for your denial of yourself. Instead of feeling the truth of yourself within your present moment, you consume yourself with trying to control reality. When you acknowledge you are, and aspire to be an evolving soul, you can condition yourself to be reliant on your hindsight to understand yourself. This can at times be a hindrance to being present, because you compulsively analyse what has occurred or is occurring in an attempt to assess what is relevant to your evolution, which throws you into constantly judging yourself, trying to determine if you are conscious or not. This inhibits you from being present. Evolution is a process that enables you to feel the presence of your soul within what is actually occurring. When you obsess about your evolution you can cause yourself to tarnish the process, which means you use your evolution as the arena for your desire to control and inadvertently act out the energy of your soul's unconsciousness. Trusting what you feel will allow you to either accept reality or to expose your unresolved emotions to yourself to resolve and evolve.

When you try to control your evolution with your obsessional beliefs, you program yourself with your own expectations, which control your perception of evolution. Your perception of evolution can be derived from believing you have to construct an image of yourself that has no flaws, and this becomes a misconception you torture yourself with. You condition yourself with your own misconceptions that you are not good enough for evolution, which entraps you in your soul oppressive cycles. Your desire to control your evolution sustains your misconceptions of evolution and creates an agenda you control yourself to, which has you constantly governing yourself with what you believe evolution is. This means you indoctrinate yourself with your own beliefs of evolution and inhibit your awareness of your own natural flow of consciousness. Evolution is to go beyond your beliefs and to experience your natural flow of consciousness. You have the opportunity to be present within the uniqueness of your own soul journey and to participate in your resolution and potential evolution.

When you justify the validity of your control by how familiar your control emotionally feels, you lose insight into how you approach the potential evolution of your soul. When you objectively observe what is familiar to you, the familiarity of your control will expose the truth of the cycles of your soul oppression. Your truthful honesty enables you to objectively observe your attempts to control your evolution with soul oppressive patterns, agendas and beliefs. By understanding you are plagued with the desire to control, you will start to objectively observe the truth of your control and become more naturally present in the opportunity to resolve your control and the deception you protect with your beliefs.

You can create emotional turbulence to feel embattled, in an attempt to justify and protect your desire to control your own negative beliefs, soul denial and indifference to truth. You struggle to comprehend why your control does not work and exhaust all avenues known to you, in an attempt to prove the validity of your control. Evolution is the process of chipping away at your own soul's unconsciousness, and the beliefs and fears that sustain your soul denial. Resolution of your soul denial, involves resolving the framework of your soul oppression, which is how you use your indifference to truth to sustain your soul's unconsciousness. Resolution of your soul denial means you resolve your illusory control of yourself, life, others and your desire to control truth. Resolving your soul denial is a process of resolving that which inhibits your natural ability to feel the truth of your soul. Your natural ability to feel the truth of your soul cannot be emulated, controlled or manipulated.

Your desire to control stems from belief systems, that you have conditioned yourself with in an attempt to control your unresolved emotions, rather than be honest and accept the reality of your emotions. Your acceptance of your unresolved emotions enables you to resolve them and evolve. You cannot control your deception to accept truth without acknowledging the reality of your deception. Acknowledging your deception creates an opportunity for you to use your freedom of choice to be truthfully honest with the reality of the unconscious energy of your soul's unconsciousness. This is the choice to accept rising and falling from grace as the natural process of your resolution and evolution. Your rise and fall from grace results from your reactions to the truth of your reality.

Your desire to control your soul denial has you believing you have no choice but to abide by your own programming, conditioning and indoctrinations. You can instruct yourself with your own history and control yourself to the familiarity of your control. You can use your history and what is familiar as an excuse to ignore the truth of your ability to utilise your freedom of choice to create change. Your fear of change immobilises you to be entrapped between truth and deception, which creates an energetic idle.

- What control structures do you use to immobilise your freedom of choice?
- What beliefs do you have about your evolution?

Denial of the truth of controlled evolution beliefs

Truth recognises truth and cannot be fooled by any mankind illusion of control. *True Source Divine Origin Consciousness*, is truth and the origin of your eternal soul, and is unwaveringly committed to you. *True Source Divine Origin Consciousness* accepts your soul journey as an opportunity for you to discover and be truthfully honest about the reality of who you naturally are. Your soul journey is the cycle of life. You leave from your origins and return to your origins, and how you return is open to your freedom of choice (freewill). *True Source Divine Origin Consciousness* honours your experience of having freewill and is loyal to your original intention; as a soul of truth you intended to resolve the energy of your soul's unconsciousness and naturally resonate and emanate the truth of who you are whilst having freewill. You are the interface between the conscious and unconscious energy within your soul as you experience life on Earth, which is why your recognition of freewill is so important, because you are constantly making a choice between the two.

Throughout your life, you expose yourself to your own soul's unconsciousness, by the way you react, or choose to respond to what is being exposed. This is how you unravel your soul's unconsciousness and you either choose to be indifferent to the reality of your own behaviours, reactions and responses, or you commit to exploring your own unconsciousness. When you choose to be indifferent to yourself, you create more layers of deception, which compounds and concretises you in your soul denial. When you commit to being truthfully honest, you participate in the resolution of your layers of deception. *True Source Divine Origin Consciousness* never interferes with your divine right to freedom of choice (freewill). Your life is the experience of constantly exercising your freewill.

When you use your judgement to condemn truth, for the suffering you have created with your own soul's unconsciousness, you blame truth for your inability to cope with your freedom of choice (freewill). Your acknowledgement of the entirety of what is occurring, both internally and externally, exposes you to the opportunity to discover truth. However, if you are unconscious to the reality of your soul's consciousness and the value of your freedom to choose, you will automatically override the truth you can feel and refuse to acknowledge the natural value of truth. Your automatic devaluation of truth exposes your unconscious energy. You use your unconscious energy to devalue the worth of truth, and you can believe any exposed truth should be deceptively manipulated to secure an illusion of control, inverted to protect your soul denial energy, or bastardised to conceal the orchestration of your soul oppression. Manipulating your awareness of truth is the choice to be unconscious to, and in disharmony with your origins, which is how you use your freedom of choice to stalemate your own resolution and evolution. Trusting yourself to trust truth will enable you to feel the clarity of your soul's consciousness and to be at peace with your natural ability to be conscious of the truth of your soul journey. Clarity is to feel the entirety of your soul experience and to be aware of your soul's consciousness and unconsciousness. Clarity is to feel, acknowledge and accept the entirety of your present moment without embellishing or omitting any truth.

True Source Divine Origin Consciousness remains loyal to your evolution and is always presenting you with opportunities to feel the truth of being a naturally significant, unique, independent, individual soul. *True Source Divine Origin Consciousness* is the collective of the purity of truth. It is the collective of the purity of souls, unencumbered by any unconsciousness. Mankind is the collective energy of the immature aspects of individual souls. Our immaturity stems from denying the truth of who we naturally are and residing in our unconsciousness. When we oppose being the natural purity of our own souls, we become the unconscious energy of *True Source Divine Origin Consciousness*. We never lose connection to our origin, because our soul's consciousness is anchored to the collective energy of *True Source Divine Origin Consciousness*. When we separate from our awareness of our origins, and reside in our unconsciousness, we are mankind, however, this does not means we are no longer of *True Source Divine Origin Consciousness*. The unconsciousness of *True Source Divine Origin Consciousness* is mankind because we separate from being aware of the purity of our souls and separate from being unified with truth. Our collective and individual unconscious energy can only reside within us when we are on Earth.

True Source Divine Origin Consciousness is always aware of mankind and acknowledges each individual soul as an aspect of itself. We all have freedom of choice to either resolve our portion of unconsciousness or to sustain and perpetuate our unconsciousness whilst on Earth. You are the bridge between the two energies and are both conscious and unconscious. The choice to acknowledge and be truthfully honest about your unresolved emotions is the choice to resolve your soul's unconsciousness, which contributes to the energetic mass energy of mankind. Your resolution of any unconscious energy is the choice to resolve your separation from the purity of who you are and your origins of truth. You are an individual strand of truth. *True Source Divine Origin Consciousness* waits for each individual strand of truth to discover their origin and to choose to resonate with their origins of truth, unifying to the natural flow of consciousness.

When you distort the value of trusting truth with the mankind illusion that you can control your evolution to an image of consciousness, you lose the clarity of your soul. To trust truth, you need to resolve your compulsion to use the unconscious energy stored within your soul's unconsciousness, against your own soul. Your compulsion to oppose truth is your futile attempt to be the master over your life and your environment, which separates you from unifying with truth. Trusting truth will enable you to unify and flow within the dynamics of life. Your unification with truth cannot become a reality if you want to be unconscious to truth, or if you want to protect aspects of your unconsciousness to control truth. Your control and indifference energy is your attempt to flow in the opposite direction to truth, and is the result of you wanting diversion, separation and disassociation as you seek to secure an illusion. Unconsciousness is a description for the disharmonised energy created by denying you are a soul and devaluing truth.

Trusting the truth of your soul enables you to freely express your truth without fear, oppression or hidden control agendas. Trusting truth is to experience and feel the conscious energy of truth. Trusting truth enables you to feel the pureness of truth without your or mankind's embellishments or omissions of reality. The conscious energy of truth is devoid of any control energy, and we can all feel this within the freewill we have. *True Source Divine Origin Consciousness* is always exposing opportunities, but we are the ones who choose how we react and respond to our own creations within life. You disharmonise yourself from truth by either embellishing the illusion of being able to control or by omitting the reality of being separated from your awareness of truth and disassociated from feeling truth. Trust is

harmonising with truth. Harmonising with truth occurs when you honour your own original intention to discover your truth and resolve what creates disunity within your soul. This is your soul consciousness' intention to live, experience and be truthful about your emotional, energetic and physical reality. It is your truthful honesty that creates the opportunity to resolve and evolve.

Truth does not want to control you, it is you who uses the energy of your soul's unconsciousness to fight against trusting truth. When you fight your awareness of your soul's consciousness, you are choosing to align to the unconsciousness of your soul, attempting to control what you will acknowledge and accept as truth. Your desire to control will not be found resonating within the consciousness of truth. Once you are indoctrinated, addicted and codependent on the belief that you can control, your desire for control starts controlling you and overshadows your experiences of life. You use your control structures to override your freedom of choice (freewill), which means you are choosing to control your evolution to be stagnant and oppressed. You control yourself to the belief that resolving your desire for control would be a sacrifice, but the desire to control is a choice to deny yourself the potential to experience evolution.

You fear being vulnerable, and not being able to control the change your evolution may initiate. This causes you to construct expectations of your consciousness and evolution, which become beliefs you ascribe to. Unfortunately, these beliefs separate you from being present in the process of your resolution and evolution, and have you striving to achieve what you believe consciousness and evolution is. Evolution occurs naturally as you resolve what separates you from truth and cannot be controlled or orchestrated. Your fear of not being able to control yourself to your beliefs creates a fear of vulnerability. The fear of vulnerability can become a control structure you use to oppose being dynamic and present within what is occurring, which allows your fear to feed and sustain your desire for control.

The natural true essence of fear is your soul's consciousness signaling you to be conscious and present within your reality. The true essence of fear and the awareness of fear is you acknowledging your soul's consciousness alerting you to the unconscious energy within your reality. However, you have to be honest to be able to distinguish the difference between the true essence of fear, and your self-generated fear that stems from wanting to be in control and refusing to accept your reality. Your self-generated fear stems from being unable to control reality. Your anxiety is caused by wanting reality to conform to your desire to emotionally feel in control. When you fear being unable to orchestrate your control, you resist, deny and avoid feeling, acknowledging and accepting your reality for what it is, and you become separated from your awareness of your soul's consciousness. This causes you to become entrapped in your denial of reality, which is a form of indifference to truth. You, and we as mankind collectively, store fear and allow fear to become a propellant for our desire to control. Unfortunately, we begin to fear the wrong things, we fear truth instead of looking at the truth of our control and our indifference. Fear is an unresolved emotion and

LEFT: ***When you remain stagnant within your fear of exploring truth, you allow yourself to oppose any opportunity to discover truth and oppose any change that may interfere with your illusion of control.***

is the result of recognising, but not being completely truthful with ourselves, about our fear of being unable to control the indifference within ourselves and others.

Fear sparks your control structures, creating many diversionary emotions that control you to be indifferent to truth. Your indifference and mankind's collective indifference to truth creates beliefs that the opportunity for evolution is incidental and unimportant. You can fear losing your believed immediate advantage, which is facilitated by your indifference to truth, leaving you to become shortsighted and selfish. This allows you to override and deny your awareness of the destructive nature of your indifference to truth and the ramifications of your denial. When you are shortsighted and selfish it is like you are at a fairground determined to win a prize on a sideshow, willing to exhaust all your resources into winning the prize, already knowing that the prize is not worth the cost and already knowing the ramifications will be painful to endure. The ramifications are huge but we continue to ignore them. When you pursue what you identify will feed your ego, you become consumed with an agenda you believe will pacify your control, whilst being willing to deny how you oppress yourself.

When you store your fear of being unable to pacify your own control and use it as your reference point, you believe your fear is the parameter for how to stay safe and avoid feeling vulnerable. You use your fear as your decider. Your fear causes you to demand that truth conform to your expectations, and as you identify truth not aligning to your demands, you build your anxiety and create more fear. Fear becomes a self-perpetuating energy, the more control you want, the more fear or indifference you create. You fear your own fear, and you fear your own indifference. You will either incite your fear or incite your indifference when you do not trust yourself to be truthful and deny the entirety of your reality. Your desire to avoid vulnerability, uncertainty and the dynamics of life creates a fear of the unknown that you use to perpetuate your own fear.

There is a difference between the true essence of fear and fear you generate with the energy of your soul's unconsciousness. The true essence of fear is an alert to be present and honest within your present moment reality, and will subside when there is no need to sustain the alertness. Unconscious fear is your resistance to and denial and avoidance of being present in, and honest about what is occurring internally and externally. Your fear sustains your resistance to and denial and avoidance of your present reality and to resolving the soul denial history you carry. The history you fear becomes an anchor point for how you perpetuate your own fear, which creates the anxiety within your anticipation. Your fear stops you from looking at yourself and your present moment as an objective observer, and your fear stops you from looking at your history with the clarity of hindsight. Fear sustains whatever unresolved emotion you have attached to the fear, such as fear of humiliation, fear of vulnerability or fear of judgement. This allows what you fear to become the focal point in your perception of reality. Your unconscious fear becomes a carried energy you use when you want to justify your resistance to, and denial and avoidance of your awareness of the truth of your present reality.

You control yourself to be codependent on your willingness to deny your freedom of choice, because you fear being responsible and accountable for yourself and your evolution. When you deny your freedom to be present and truthfully honest about the reality you are experiencing, you amalgamate with any unconscious energy that you believe will allow you to hide from your awareness of your soul truth, in an attempt to believe you can control the reality you are experiencing. You use your unconscious energy produced by your unresolved emotions to amalgamate with beliefs, desires and any other unconscious energy you can source to override the significance of truth. You have to choose to discredit truth to be able to justify amalgamating your unresolved emotions with beliefs. These beliefs can be of your own creation or a collective belief that you want to use to justify your fear and indifference to truth. When you become an insatiable participant in the fusion of your fear, you become willing to amalgamate your unconscious energy with any other unconscious energy that enables you to become lost in the labyrinths your indifference to truth creates.

The labyrinths you become lost in, are sustained by your denial of the uniqueness of who you are, and denial of the significance of your individual journey. Your illusory control of your denial is unsustainable, because you cannot control the unconscious energy you choose to fuse your fear with. This exposes you to the truth of the fallacy of your control, the insidiousness of indifference and the deception of your denial. Your fear is an exposer of your unconsciousness.

Your control structures are recognisable by the familiarity with which you insert the same unconscious energy into every experience you have, exposing your fear of being in the dynamics of life. Your desire to control only controls you to the familiarity of the energy of your soul's unconsciousness. Your desire to control makes you more vulnerable to your past wounds, emotional pain and perceived injustices, because you control yourself to hide from what is being exposed within the dynamics of life. When you manipulate yourself to create the beliefs that have you wallowing and floundering in what you fear is out of your control, you create the willingness to retreat from feeling the opportunities within your present moment. Wallowing in your unresolved emotions and floundering in your non-acceptance of reality are control mechanisms you use to hide from your ability to accept the truth of your choices, and to expose to yourself how you can discredit your own beliefs. At times you are aware that you do not even believe your own illusion of control, because you cannot control your wallowing and floundering.

Your desire to control your evolution creates a framework of rules for your conceptual ideals of being conscious, which engages the use of your unconscious energy produced by your unresolved emotions, such as manipulation, judgement and denial. You align to images as you seek to do a stellar performance within your own perception of what you believe the reality of consciousness and evolution should be. This means the image of consciousness becomes more important than the resolution of your unresolved emotions, and your truthfulness takes a backseat to your desire to construct an illusion of evolution. You attempt to construct an illusion of evolution that you believe sustains your illusion of control. Unfortunately, you have missed the mark of the significance of evolution and have aligned to the dumbing down of your soul for a performed image.

Your barriers to truth distort your awareness of the reality of the unresolved emotions you use to construct an illusion that you can control your evolution. You do this whilst attempting to conceal your indifference to truth, justifying your distorted perception of truth, evolution and yourself. This is how you enable yourself to remain unconscious to truth and defiant against your own original intention for resolution and evolution.

When you judge truth via your distorted view of yourself, truth becomes something you class as a hindrance or as an advantage, which does not allow you to simply accept truth. This creates agendas, built on your wants and on what you have decided is unwanted, which has you judging all you encounter via your own self-interest, often disregarding the synchronised opportunities within the present moments that make up the uniqueness of your life. You judge truth, unconsciously wanting control of truth while denying your awareness of reality. You attempt to impose and align to your illusion of control, because you fear if you accept reality, you will lose your perceived control. You fear losing control of your denial and fear accepting the truth of the reality you are experiencing. Your desire to control reality is a control structure that dumbs down your awareness of the reality of being of truth and discredits the significance of the uniqueness of your soul journey.

When you use your awareness of being a soul to magnify your ego, you create beliefs about the significance of who you are, which expands your indifference to truth. You allow your egotistical beliefs to become a way of justifying your reluctance to explore all aspects of yourself. You create a fear of discovery, which generates into a fear of truth. Your fear of truth and of yourself becomes an avoidance technique to being responsible and accountable for your own soul truth, which is both your consciousness and your unconsciousness. You use your fear as an excuse to hide from what is being exposed to you and then you use egotistical beliefs to hide from the truth of your fear.

You can manipulate yourself with your own indifference which is how you have constructed your framework of soul oppression, and this oppresses your awareness of your soul's consciousness and distracts you from acknowledging your own opposition to the truth of your soul. You project your control energy at others, life and yourself to create turmoil and chaos, in an attempt to justify exerting your control over others, life and yourself. You want to prove to yourself that your control works, so that you can deceptively align to the belief that control is the prize for abandoning truth. What prize do you want for abandoning truth? If your answer is peace within yourself, clarity of mind or harmony with life, these are not achievable by abandoning truth. If your answer is control, what do you believe you can control that could possibly overshadow the value of your natural flow of truth. When you pursue the illusory prize of control and disregard the truth of your own deception, you create an insatiable appetite for control that you can never pacify.

Your willingness to be deceptive with yourself has you believing your pursuit for control and indifference to truth is protecting you, but what do you believe you are protecting yourself from? Your pursuit for control and indifference to truth secures all your barriers to truth and sustains your oppression. You use your barriers to truth to impose control over your own freedom to feel and resonate with truth.

- What do you want to protect yourself from?

Is the answer the energy of your own soul's unconsciousness?

Or is the answer the indifference of mankind?

Or is the answer the purity of your soul's consciousness?

Or is the answer the unconditional love of *True Source Divine Origin Consciousness*?

- What does your fear of answering these questions, expose to you?
- Are you intentionally unconscious to the reality of the unresolved emotions you use to create and sustain your barriers to truth?

Your emotional, energetic and physical barriers are created by your refusal to resolve your unresolved emotions, which enables you to suppress your awareness of reality. Your refusal to acknowledge and accept resolving your unresolved emotions is the choice to disrupt your awareness of the natural flow of truth within your rise and fall from grace. What is ironic, is that you use a lot of effort to protect yourself but you actually protect yourself from nothing. This is because you are the producer of the energy you do not want to feel, and you are the producer of the energy that exacerbates your fear.

Your soul's consciousness is the aspect of you that intends to experience the energy of your soul's unconsciousness. You internally do not want to be protected from the truth of your unresolved emotions, because your denial allows you to stay in your oppression. Your soul's unconsciousness is the aspect of you that inhibits you from experiencing the consciousness of your soul, and from being aware of your unresolved emotions and the opportunity for resolution and evolution. This creates conflict within you, and if the internal conflict is ignored you separate further from truth. Your soul's consciousness naturally exposes the deception of your soul's unconsciousness, just by you being present in the truth of your own energy. If you believe you need to protect yourself from truth, then you have just exposed your own opposition to yourself. You are of truth. You think you have the ability to store your emotions and choose how your emotions affect you; but this is a belief, not a truth. It is also an illusion of control because your emotions create emotional, energetic and physical barriers to truth and encapsulate you in your own deception towards yourself. Your emotional, energetic and physical barriers to truth are barriers of contempt for your own evolution. You control your evolution to be stagnant and oppressed with your own contempt for yourself and your deceptive illusion of control. Freedom is to live without barriers to the truth of your soul and the purity of *True Source Divine Origin Consciousness*. Accepting you are a soul enables you to objectively observe life as an opportunity to feel truth.

You control your evolution to be stagnant by defensively fighting to be right in your perception of truth, which limits and restricts your exploration of truth. This leaves you controlling yourself to be fixated on what you believe you know and opposing truth. Ironically, this causes you to oppose any possibility of trusting the dynamism of truth. As you understand one aspect of truth, you open the door to expose another aspect of truth. The resolution of your unresolved emotions creates the space for your awareness of the dynamics of truth, which enables your own natural evolution to occur. Truth is never stagnant and you are arrogant if you believe you can control an understanding of truth with archaic beliefs, expectations and rigid desires. When you want to align to archaic beliefs, you use the longevity of the held belief to reinforce your rigidity, which becomes a stagnant cycle you lose yourself in. You want to perceive truth as rigid so you can create control structures out of your perception of truth. You want to believe you can apply rules to truth and fight your own awareness of reality because you think you can ensure your control of truth.

If we only seek to secure control of what truth is or should be perceived as, we never learn from the past, because we are unwilling to be truthfully honest about the dynamics of truth. Your and

mankind's collective unwillingness to be truthful enables us to remain stagnant in our archaic and futile desire to control. Our desire to control inhibits us from evolving from our past and has us repeating the same unconscious energy, perhaps in new inventive ways, but with the same agendas and indifference to truth. Your and mankind's collective desire to compulsively repeat what we have done before whilst seeking to be superior over truth is futile. Our desire to be in control of reality inhibits our awareness of the opportunities within life, and we miss the significance of the dynamics of truth. This means we fail to honour the equality of all souls and stay entrapped in our indifference to ourselves and to each other. Our desire to control truth to be rigid is our method of controlling our own evolution to stay stagnant. It is ludicrous that we refuse to acknowledge the insanity of denying reality and the dynamics of truth. Unfortunately, our insanity is sustained by the arrogance of our indifference to truth.

When you hide from the reality of being a naturally significant, unique, independent, individual soul by camouflaging yourself in mankind beliefs, you become obtuse about the reality of yourself. This means you are a slow learner which is an infliction that has affected how you view yourself and others; being a slow learner plagues us all. We, as mankind, throughout history have opposed the flow of truth's dynamism, because the dynamics of truth affects our illusion of control. We have deceptively denied the amount of effort that we put into camouflaging our natural resonance with truth, which causes us to devalue ourselves, trading our integrity for the illusion of control. We, as mankind, have confused ourselves about our own origins, to hide from the truth of being a collective of significant, unique, independent, individual souls from a united origin.

Your truthful honesty creates resolution of your soul denial, which is evolution. By acknowledging the truth of just how little you can control and the ramifications of desiring control, you expose the truth of your denial and the perpetuation of your own soul oppression. By being truthfully honest about your attempts to secure your control, you expose your mistrust of truth and how you separate yourself from the opportunity to be aware of your soul's unconsciousness. Your choice to be truthfully honest is part of the evolutionary process, which enables you to observe how you use your unconscious energy to compulsively oppose your own awareness of truth. When you are willing to accept being present in the dynamics of truth, you are giving yourself permission to go beyond your:

- Own compulsion to oppose yourself
- Desire to control
- Incessant drive to be right in your judgement
- Established embedded beliefs, denials and desires

When you externalise your soul oppression onto others, you inflict them with your unresolved emotions and run control structures which incite your judgement, leaving you indifferent to the reality of yourself. When you deny your desire to control your evolution, which is the desire to control what truth is, you automatically want to control others to accommodate your demands and to oppose their own awareness of you and truth, believing they should align to your expectations and desires. You control the perpetuation of your soul oppression with your reluctance to acknowledge the truth of how you feel, and you seek others to justify your reluctance to be of truth. When you use another's reaction to truth as an excuse to hide from your own awareness of your soul truth, you become consumed with both the desire to control others and the desire to orchestrate an image to fool and deflect others from feeling the truth of your soul. This is because you have rejected the value, worth and significance of who you naturally are. To shield yourself from your own rejection, you blame others for the oppression you feel.

You also believe if you can control others to make you feel good about yourself, you will relieve yourself of the oppression you feel. However, this belief is a doubled-edged sword, which can cause you to believe control is the solution and to not control means you are a victim. These types of beliefs cause you to remain entrapped in the duality of your judgement and are used to justify inflicting your unresolved emotions on others. You externalise and act out your unresolved emotions but deny the reality of what is causing you the most pain, which is your resistance to, and denial and avoidance of acknowledging the reality of how you abuse the truth of your own soul.

The control structures we inflict on one another creates soul carnage. Soul carnage is the carried unconscious energy of mankind's indifference to truth. Controlled evolution energy has developed from the carnage we, as struggling humans, have inflicted on our souls. We have controlled our evolution by creating beliefs that are indifferent to the dynamics of truth. Your controlled evolution energy is your portion of indifference to truth, which you use to attempt to eliminate your awareness of the opportunities to resolve your unconsciousness. Your indifference to truth overrides your ability to trust yourself to care for the truth of yourself and mankind. Caring for yourself, others and truth is a bridge to consciousness. Caring for the truth of yourself and others resolves the indifference within the stagnation of your soul oppression. By trusting the truth of yourself and being truthfully honest about what you can observe, you are choosing to align to the process of resolution and evolution. This is the process of acknowledging and accepting the opportunities within your rise and fall from grace.

The fall from grace is the exposure of, and opportunity to resolve, your unresolved emotions that produce your unconscious energy. To rise with grace is to be truthfully honest which enables you to be conscious of your own resolution. Your truthful honesty is the catalyst for your soul's consciousness to be able to convert unconscious energy to conscious energy. The resolution of your unresolved emotions withdraws your portion of unconsciousness from the energetics of the mass energy of mankind, which is the act of caring for yourself and mankind. By removing your unresolved emotions from the energetics of the mass energy of mankind, you create more space to be available for conscious energy to flow. To rise with grace is to experience your soul's consciousness naturally returning unconscious energy to your origins of truth. Your soul's consciousness is constantly flowing from your origins to the depths of your soul's unconsciousness and returning back to your origins. To rise with grace means choosing to be consciously aware of the natural flow of your soul's consciousness and the reality of the exposure of your unresolved emotions when you fall from grace. Your truthful honesty is the opportunity to create resolution and evolution within the natural process of rising and falling from grace.

Your truthful honesty enables you to acknowledge the freedom that comes with your awareness of your own soul truth. There is freedom in being aware of the entirety of what you are experiencing; both conscious and unconscious energy. When you allow yourself to objectively observe the entirety of what you are experiencing, rather than tunneled vision about your unresolved emotions and your inability to control for what you want, you start to trust your own awareness. When you refuse to look at the entirety and start omitting parts of your awareness and denying reality, you become distrustful of truth and oppositional to yourself. When you acknowledge the entirety and trust the significance of your own and others' unique soul journeys, you feel the freedom within your awareness of truth. This enables you to take responsibility for your own resolution and evolution. Trusting yourself is the choice to be consciously aware of yourself within the entirety of your reality. When you permit yourself to deal honestly with the process of realising the truth about your control, denial, unresolved emotions and beliefs, you create the space to resolve your inhibiting control of your own evolution.

When you experience the truth of your soul, you realise feeling the conscious energy of your soul can never be impersonated nor controlled by any unconscious energy. If you are truly feeling your soul's consciousness, the truth of your soul is undeniable. *True Source Divine Origin Consciousness* does not want to control you and respects your freewill. You utilise your freewill to choose to be conscious of your soul truth, or unconscious of your soul truth. You are always respected by conscious energy as a significant, unique, independent, individual soul of *True Source Divine Origin Consciousness*. You create barriers to this truth with your desire to control your evolution and your soul denial.

To resolve your desire to control your evolution, you have to trust the uniqueness of your soul, appreciate your independence within the energetics of the mass energy of mankind and acknowledge the individuality of being a soul of *True Source Divine Origin Consciousness*. To resolve your indifference you have to trust and acknowledge that all souls are significant, unique, independent, individuals of truth. Your acceptance of the value of your freedom of choice breaks down your barriers and sequenced reactions of indifference to truth. This then enables you to objectively observe, acknowledge and trust in your own feelings. Your feelings are communication from your soul. Your acceptance of truth allows you to objectively observe the reality of the unconscious energy of your own soul's unconsciousness, which means you are conscious of your truth and within an opportunity for resolution and evolution. When you deny your unresolved emotions, you control your opportunity for resolution and evolution to be ineffectual, which means you have the experience but miss the mark and gloss over the significance of your awareness and present moment experience.

Your desire to control your evolution has you believing you need to know exactly what is in your blueprint, so you can control yourself to a fixed ideal of what your blueprint is. This is how you slyly protect your illusion of control. You construct expectations of what you want truth to adhere to based on your fixed ideal of your blueprint. When you oppose being in the entirety of what is occurring and only fixate on constructing what you want, you perpetuate your indifference to truth. The perpetuation of your indifference to truth means you obsess about wanting to know the reasons behind every event you experience, because you want to secure your 'I know' belief, and be the predictor of your destiny. When you are codependent on your own 'I know' mentality, you begin to construct expectations, demands and illusions of spiritual elitism, which leaves you oppositional to any truth that interferes with what you want to construct. This causes you to miss the mark as you are so focused on, what you want to construct that you miss the potential to be free within the truth of your own uniqueness and the dynamics of life.

Your desire to secure your beliefs about how to evolve has you filtering anything and everything through what you think you already know. This leaves you picking and choosing what you will acknowledge and ignoring the entirety of what is occurring and the entirety of your own awareness. Your desire to control your evolution causes you to create misconceptions and expectations, which you use to conjure up your fixed ideal of your own blueprint. This means you create a labyrinth of illusions you try to align yourself to, and sadly you miss the true potential of your soul journey.

Your soul journey is dynamic. Being dynamic is the opportunity to trust yourself to be present in what is occurring, which enables you to trust yourself to feel how to respond to your reality with integrity. Regardless of what your present reality is, and the outcomes you have created for yourself, you are where you need to be for your resolution and evolution. You can believe having control is essential to achieve your intention to resolve and evolve, but the use of your control takes you on a deceptive pathway. Your controlled evolutionary pathway of deception separates you from your awareness of truth and sustains your desire to feel validated that you are right, in control and are going to be rewarded for your illusory control of truth. Your blueprint is not just what you are going to be and experience, but what you intend to resolve. Your blueprint is your present moment. The experiences agreed to in your soul blueprint are going to happen, how you respond to your reality is up to you. Truthful honesty creates resolution. Denial perpetuates stagnation.

You want to be reassured by *True Source Divine Origin Consciousness*, but how can you feel truth's support and unconditional love for you, if you are trying to control truth with the energy of your soul's unconsciousness? Whenever you attempt to control truth, you deny yourself the ability to feel the purity of your soul. When you want to control your evolution to pacify your desire to control, it is not evolution you seek or experience; it is the perpetuation of your soul oppression. You undermine the natural significance of your soul with your desire to control how and why you are significant, which incites your judgement of yourself to be at the forefront of all your experiences. You are naturally significant. You are a unique strand of truth energy. You are of *True Source Divine Origin Consciousness*. Your mankind perception of significance is the belief that if others revere your control you are significant, which causes you to deny yourself the ability to feel your natural significance, uniqueness, independence and individuality.

Your controlled evolution beliefs have you seeking to be revered, classed as special and superior to others. This exposes the unconsciousness of your controlled evolution energy, because this belief is the result of you losing awareness of the equality of all souls, respect for your uniqueness and your resonance with truth. The way that mankind scales significance gives no meaning to the truth of the consciousness and unconsciousness of all souls. If you equate consciousness with mankind prizes of control, you miss the mark of consciousness and fight truth, which is how you cheapen your natural value and worth. The potential of feeling the truth of your soul surpasses any of your mankind illusions of being a soul. The resolution of your soul's unconsciousness is significant to the evolution of mankind.

Each individual is accountable and responsible for the energy of their soul's unconsciousness, which reverberates within the energetic collectives of the mass energy of mankind. When you participate in the resolution of your own unresolved emotions, you alter the unconscious energy contributing to the energetics of the mass energy of mankind. When you resonate with truth, the purity of your soul emanates from you, and this can be a reminder to others that they are a soul who also resonates with truth. When you are conscious of being a soul, you are aware of your inability to control the resolution of another soul's unresolved emotions or the evolution of their soul.

Evolution is an individual experience and it is from our arrogance as mankind that we rely on a few chosen conscious souls to carry the burden of mankind's unconsciousness. When we believe evolution is about following another soul without truthfully acknowledging responsibility for ourselves and accountability for our interactions with each other, we disregard and then forget our natural resonance with truth. It is also the arrogance of mankind to pretend that there are only a few chosen paths to resolution and evolution. Your truthfulness about yourself is your path, and all other information including *Your Insight and Awareness Book*, is just a guide; it may point you in a direction and may expose you to something to contemplate, but ultimately it is you who evolves your soul. When you feel the truth within another's consciousness you are resonating with truth energy and it can inspire and excite you, triggering an acceptance of your own original intention to resolve and evolve. All souls resonate with truth, your soul's consciousness is of truth. Consciousness cannot be bought, adopted or studied to be controlled or emulated; consciousness has to be felt, experienced and trusted.

It is the insanity of mankind to fight what cannot be controlled with unconscious energy. Truth is not a controllable energy, it is the energy of what is, regardless of your assessment or denial. We, as mankind, have devalued ourselves by denying the significance of our resolution and by denying that we are the collective unconsciousness of *True Source Divine Origin Consciousness*.

True Source Divine Origin Consciousness has never devalued mankind's significance because truth never denies the entirety of reality. It is through the acknowledgement and acceptance of the entirety of what is occurring that enables resolution and evolution. Each individual soul has been entrusted with freewill, the freedom to choose how we react and respond to the truth of all energy, and we all have the opportunity to become truthful about the reality of being both conscious and unconscious energy. Your choices are a bridge to either trust yourself to experience your flow of consciousness, or to stagnate yourself in your own unconsciousness.

When you judge what you believe the outcome of resolving your emotions should be, you become selective about which emotions you protect, deny or actively resolve, believing you know what is important for the evolution of your soul. However, you will only decide what is important based on your impression of evolution and you need to question yourself on how you created that perspective. You are unique and your insight into and awareness of evolution keeps increasing as you experience your own resolution and evolution. When you control yourself to be an impression of evolution and attempt to perform an image of consciousness, you are not evolving. Resolution of your unconsciousness occurs as you choose to be present, and choose to be truthfully honest about your own beliefs, your 'I know' mentality and your expectations. You are a clever soul and are in sync with your life experiences. By being truthful with yourself you reveal what is unresolved and your truthfulness enables you to feel beyond your denial and to resolve your unconscious energy.

When you want to be in control of the results of your resolution and evolution, you miss the mark of the entirety of your reality. This equates to you being in the presence of a beautiful landscape but wanting to put a billboard of yourself in the middle of it, because you want to know you can affect how the landscape appears and you think this means you have control. However, the billboard you have constructed obscures your view and limits the distance you can see, which changes how you feel about the landscape and how you feel about yourself. Resolution is the choice to acknowledge what you have constructed, to resolve any agenda that inhibits your acceptance of your soul and to be truthfully present in the deconstruction of your limited perception of yourself. Your willingness to be truthfully present in whatever is occurring enables you to discover, see and explore what is beyond your desire for control and your fear of being without the illusion of control. Evolution is trusting yourself to be in the truth of your own landscape and to be conscious of the entirety of your life experience.

We, as mankind, have insanely judged evolution by the desire to orchestrate the results we want, and this diminishes the opportunity to learn from our experiences. When we approach our experiences with an agenda, we lose the willingness to observe, acknowledge and accept the entirety of what we are experiencing and that alters how we experience our present moment. The concept of evolution can become converted to a control structure that we seek to pacify, but refuse to be completely truthful about.

When you falsely interlink the concept of evolution with securing your control, you create an energetic idle which entraps you in your denial of the entirety of your reality. Unfortunately, you become emotionally stuck within the repetitiveness of your own emotions, beliefs and agendas. Your own entrapment in your denial causes you to incessantly justify trying to compare the value of your soul's evolution with your desire to pacify your control of life, yourself, others, relationships and the presence of truth. When you want a guarantee that the result of resolution is worth your effort, you attempt to judge the validity of being honest with and about yourself. If you are judging the validity of being honest with yourself, you are exposing that you believe your deception may get the results you want. If you believe your deception can create something of value to truth, you do not understand truth. Your desire to control your evolution has you deceptively trying to orchestrate to controlled outcomes you believe will meet your expectations. This is not evolution, this is the perpetuation of your own and mankind's control, arrogance and mistrust of truth.

Truthfulness is an expression of consciousness, which enables you to be a conscious participant in the discovery of your own truth. To be a participant in the discovery of truth is to resonate with truth. Discovery is to be present in the opportunity to realise the truth of unconscious energy and the presence of conscious energy. Discovery is the recognition of the truth that has always been there, which you may have been too unconscious to realise. When you fixate on asking the wrong questions, and refuse to uncover what you use to conceal truth because you want to protect your own lies, truth becomes unrecognisable to you. Discovery and acceptance of truth breaks through your own denial exposing more truth and new questions to challenge yourself with. Discovery and acceptance of truth creates the stepping stones for your resolution and evolution.

When you objectively observe the truth of the insanity of your indifference to truth, you become conscious of what needs resolving and evolving. Being conscious of the truth of yourself honours your original intention to evolve. Truthfulness creates trust and trust is the resonance of truth in action. Trust bridges you from thinking to feeling. Thinking is an interface between all your varieties of energy, which means your thoughts can be influenced by both your unresolved emotions and your feelings. Emotions only reverberate with unconscious energy while feelings resonate with the truth of all energy.

You use your beliefs to create controlled evolution energy, which then corrupts your search for truth to become an echo of your desire for control. This inhibits your exploration of truth and causes you to fight what your life experiences reveal to you. Your deception is often difficult to discover, when you want your deception to be truth. Your deception is how you attempt to get your own way but it is also what gets in your way. Deception is your choice to deny your own arrogant intention to oppose truth. Your original intention was to expose your deception, to resolve what separates you from your awareness of your soul and to feel your resonance with truth within the entirety of your reality.

Controlling yourself to be separated from your awareness of your soul and disassociated from feeling truth in any form, will leave you stagnant within your own desire to control your evolution. Separating from your awareness of your soul and disassociating from feeling truth creates an arena where you can delude yourself with your denial of reality. You attempt to control your emotional, energetic and physical barriers to oppose your awareness of truth. This internally makes you feel unsafe, insecure and vulnerable, which incites your desire for control. The paradox is, what you are trying to control, such as your unresolved emotions triggered by your insecurity and vulnerability, can only be achieved by resolving the need for control. The intensity of your desire to control exposes your resistance to, and denial and avoidance of the truth of what needs resolving, which actually highlights what is unresolved within you. In truth, this is a foolproof way of discovery, unless you are a fool who deceives yourself with denial and illusory control. Are you willing to be deceived by your own denial and illusory control or do you seek to discover truth?

You can use your willingness to deceive yourself to ignore the intensity of your desire to control, which means you lose the ability to be insightful about yourself. Your pretence is a protective shield of your insanity, inhibiting you from being truthful. When you lose insight into yourself, you become emotionally reactive to anything you do not expect to happen, do not want to feel or do not want to be exposed to. Your willingness and desire to protect your unconsciousness is the insanity of your indifference to truth, which perpetuates your soul oppression and the sustainability of your soul's unconsciousness.

Your denial of being a soul has you believing it is not safe to be without your judgement and illusion of control. This belief is strong because you are separated from your awareness of yourself as a soul and truth, and disassociated from feeling the truth of your reality. When you are disassociated from the reality of your truth, you are separated from your awareness of the natural essence of your soul. The natural essence of your soul's consciousness is the opposite type of energy to your soul's unconsciousness, which is the storehouse of your unresolved emotions. When you oppose truth and use the opposite spectrum of the energy of your soul's consciousness, you sustain your indifference towards truth.

For example:

- Denial opposes *trust*.
- Judgement opposes *compassion*.
- Manipulation opposes *integrity*.
- Control opposes *freedom*.
- Images oppose *individuality*.
- Avoidance opposes *dynamism*.
- Resistance opposes *acceptance of truth and reality*.
- Confusion opposes *clarity*.
- Codependency opposes *independence*.
- Indifference opposes *unconditional love*.

- What are your persistent unresolved emotions?
- What do your persistent unresolved emotions oppose?
- What truth can be discovered when you are honest about your persistent unresolved emotions?

The beliefs you use to attempt to control your evolution are the result of your choice to be unconscious of what you are really choosing when you resist, deny and avoid truth. Your controlled evolution energy is your choice to be unconscious of the effects of your judgement, manipulation, confusion and control. Your controlled evolution energy is produced by your codependency on oppressing your awareness of your soul, which leaves you opposing your freedom to discover truth. When you make a choice to be conscious of reality and honest with truth, you are choosing to be an expression of your soul's consciousness.

You cannot feel your soul's consciousness when you are in a state of denial. Your denial oppresses your awareness of your soul's consciousness. This leaves you codependent on your own deception and the beliefs you use to exonerate yourself from responsibility, or use to justify your indifference to truth. You use your soul denial as permission to lie to yourself about your manipulation of truth and reality. Your use of manipulation has a cumulative effect on how you burden you soul. The lies you use to justify your own belief of being secure in your control, eventually expose you to your indifference to truth. You use your indifference to anchor to any belief that pacifies your desire to emotionally feel secure and justified in the familiarity of the energy of your soul's unconsciousness. When you concretise the stagnation of your evolution with your desire to feel secure in the illusory control of your soul denial, you become indifferent to yourself in your reality.

Question yourself truthfully:

- Have you ever felt secure in your denial?
- Have you ever realised what you are doing when you discount the importance of truth?

You may have learnt to conceal your insecurity from others but not from yourself. You are a naturally significant, unique, independent, individual soul of *True Source Divine Origin Consciousness,* who always had the intention to resolve your own unresolved emotions. This means you will experience the truth of your unresolved emotions throughout your life experiences creating the opportunity for your resolution and evolution. Your unresolved emotions and your fear reactions to your unresolved emotions contribute to the energetics of the mass energy of mankind. When you acknowledge, accept and feel the truth of your original intention for resolution and evolution, you are choosing to honour and appreciate the opportunity life presents, and enabling yourself to unify with truth.

Chapter Twenty-Seven

The opposition of energies

Your resistance is how you oppose your freedom from denial. Resistance is how you oppose being realistic and honest about the emotional, energetic and physical aspects of your life.

Your denial is how you oppose accepting the truth of being a soul. Denial is how you oppose accepting responsibility for the unconscious energy of your soul's unconsciousness. Denial is how you oppose acceptance of your reality.

Your avoidance is how you oppose being honest about your freedom of choice. Avoidance is how you oppose trusting in your soul journey and your synchronicity with truth.

Your codependency is how you oppose energetic independence and freedom from being a contributor of unconscious energy to the energetic mass energy of mankind.

Your victim mentality is how you oppose true acceptance of yourself as a soul and the reality of your freedom of choice.

Your belief of 'not being good enough' is how you oppose your awareness of truth and the significance of your uniqueness, independence and individuality, and your opportunities to resolve and evolve.

Your images and illusions are how you oppose responsibility and accountability for being a soul of *True Source Divine Origin Consciousness*.

Your controlled evolution energy is how you use beliefs to oppose your internal knowing of your individual resonance with truth. Controlled evolution energy is how you use beliefs to oppose trusting truth and the discovery of the opportunity to resolve and evolve. Controlled evolution energy is how you use beliefs to oppose your unique individuality.

Your judgement is how you oppose your compassion for the uniqueness, independence and individuality of yourself and others. Judgement is how you oppose the clarity and purity of your natural resonance with truth, and the wisdom created by your truthfulness. Judgement is how you oppose your peace and harmony with the presence of truth.

Your manipulation is how you oppose trusting and acknowledging truth. Manipulation is how you oppose trusting yourself to be truthfully honest.

Your confusion is how you oppose your clarity of being a soul and your ability to be truthfully honest with life, yourself, others, relationships and the presence of truth within your reality. Confusion is how you oppose your awareness of the opportunity to resolve and evolve.

Your heresy energy is how you use various types of indifference to truth to oppose the core essences of your soul. Heresy energy is how you oppose the unconditional love within your soul and the presence of *True Source Divine Origin Consciousness'* unconditional love for you.

Your control is made up of all these energies and you use your control to oppose everything that does not satisfy your expectations to have control. Denying your unresolved emotions is how you control yourself to be a contributor to the energetics of the mass energy of mankind, and how you deny that you are a significant, unique, independent and individual soul of *True Source Divine Origin Consciousness*.

These oppositional energies are the unresolved emotions of your soul's unconsciousness, which are the energetic residue of your soul denial history. What is unresolved within you becomes the energy you carry within your soul's unconsciousness, until you are willing to be truthfully honest with yourself. Life is an opportunity to resolve and evolve beyond the chains of your soul denial history.

Dragging the chains of soul denial history

Section Six

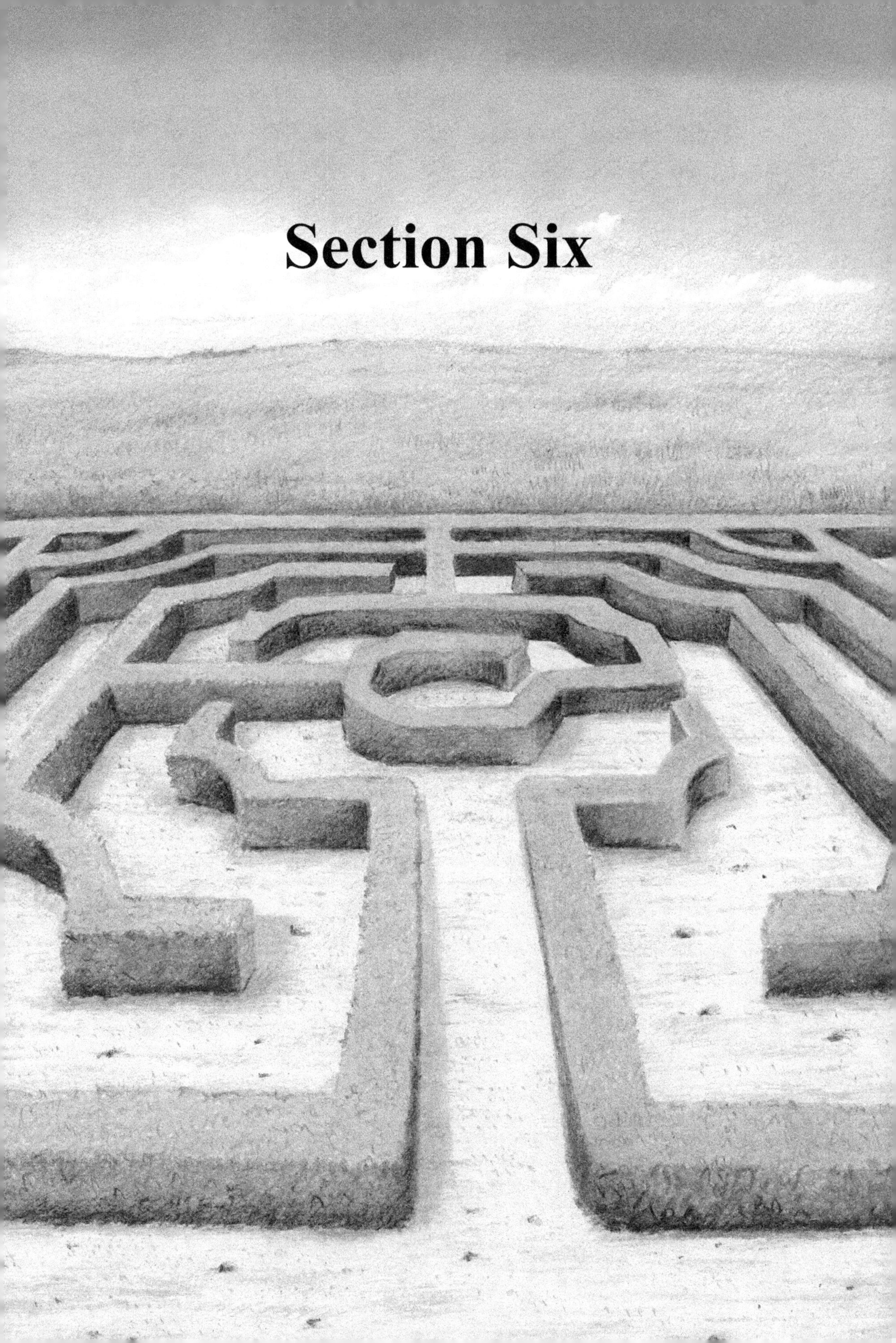

Chapter Twenty-Eight

Soul serenity

Serenity within your soul results from your willingness to unconditionally love yourself. It is also, to unconditionally love all the experiences you have had that enabled you to comprehend the magnitude of the significance of who you naturally are. You are a significant, unique, independent, individual soul of *True Source Divine Origin Consciousness*, who has ventured into this world to expand your awareness of yourself and truth. You are an opportunity for the expansion of consciousness; you are an opportunity for evolution.

To feel the serenity within your soul is to feel the truth of your natural core essences whilst acknowledging there is no other soul with the exact same frequency. There is a purity to your soul that is unique to you. Serenity is to experience the unification within your soul as you feel the unconditional love emanating from your soul. To feel the serenity of your soul is to choose to unify with the truth of your own flow of consciousness.

Serenity is to treat yourself with kindness as you experience the truth of your soul within the dynamics of life. Serenity within your soul is the experience of being true to your own soul integrity, as you encounter the diversity of life. It is the willingness to be patient with yourself, as you learn to trust yourself to be truthful. As you become loyal to your soul integrity, you feel the serenity within yourself strengthen, which enables you to have the courage to explore all aspects of your own soul. Serenity is to give yourself the freedom to be present and honest within the truth of your life experiences, as you acknowledge and accept your own awareness.

Serenity within your soul is having compassion for yourself and the truth of your soul journey. It is the willingness to be of your own grace as you explore your life experiences. Serenity is to feel the internal joy that peace within creates. Serenity within your soul is an acceptance of yourself and an appreciation for what your experience of life is exposing to you. Serenity is not the conclusion of a soul journey, it is the acceptance of being on a soul journey.

Chapter Twenty-Nine

History of development

I had no idea when I first started trying to understand my own unresolved emotions, that what I was searching for was to come to terms with the truth of who I am. I was confused about what I was aware of within myself and life, and did not even comprehend the ramifications of being in denial of my natural significance, uniqueness, independence and individuality. I have come to understand that this denial plagues us all. *Your Insight and Awareness Book* is the exploration of the natural significance, uniqueness, independence and individuality of all souls.

I started by just wanting to sort out my own unresolved emotions, to work out what I was feeling and why I could not control the way I felt. I wanted to find a way to be at peace with myself. I started by exploring a couple of different modalities, which exposed me to the concept of truth being energy, and that truth is something we all originated from. These modalities gave me avenues to explore and resolved some of my confusion. They taught me to challenge my beliefs and that the exploration of truth had to be a choice I made for myself. I explored these modalities until the opportunities within them were exhausted. I learnt what I resonated with, what I was uneasy with and the significance and importance of trusting the truth of my own awareness.

There was a yearning I could not explain but chose to follow wherever it took me. I chose to explore the truth of my own soul and the truth I could observe. I knew I did not have all the answers I sought but I was aware of some of my questions. I chose not to deny what I felt and the questions I had. I realised that soul recovery had to become an independent pursuit, and that I had to choose to be responsible for my own unresolved emotions. I had to track into my soul's unconsciousness in order to discover the truth of my soul's consciousness and my origins. Through these modalities I had been exposed to the concept of being from a collective origin and the more truth I recognised the more I realised we are all unique strands of truth energy (souls) originating from a collective origin, but lost within fear and denial.

While I thought these modalities were going to be a place to find the answers to fix myself, actually they were a stepping stone in my process of committing to the exploration of my relationship with truth. We all forget that the most important relationship in life is with truth and ourselves. I realised I was full of questions, and one question led me to another. I was willing to explore my own questions and they exposed me to my natural awareness that I could not explain but knew I could trust. I was aware of being supported by energy greater than mine, although I struggled to identify what it was. I later realised it was truth that was supporting me, and we are never separated from truth, we just separate ourselves from our awareness of truth. We are all supported by truth.

I experienced a lot within these modalities and could see that the energies within our soul's unconsciousness are quite treacherous, because we have fear reactions to losing our illusions of control. When I acknowledged the truth of fear reactions it gave me the confidence to trust myself, even though at times I feared my own awareness. I realised I could not give up on myself and I could not settle for any image or illusion, as they would never resonate with my soul. I seek to feel the purity of truth and realised that no one has the right to tell me who I am or what truth is, I have to discover this for myself. I understand this to be true for all of us; truth is felt and *Your Insight and Awareness Book* exposes what is in your way to feeling your own natural awareness of your soul and truth. I had to feel and accept the reality of being able to resonate with truth before I could come to peace with who I am. What I discovered was, we are all evolving souls learning through our life experiences.

I was fortunate, because before looking at any modality I had a trusted friend Will, who allowed himself to be my sounding board and was naturally willing to be non-judgemental towards me. He never told me what to think, just asked very wise questions. I learned that if you do not fear judgement, you are more willing to be truthfully honest, which assisted me to find some clarity. He has been, and still is today, a safe harbour and as I began to whirl in my own confusion, he was willing to listen with integrity to my exploration of truth. Within these shared moments of exploring truth I was exposed to the importance of a sense of humour. Humour is a way of accepting truth, which allows me to laugh at the irony of my behaviour. This helped me shift into compassion for myself and to recognise my resistance to truth. Our friendship has graciously been a place of laughter and security as life exposed me to the disparities between what was actually happening and any illusion, denial or lie I told myself. The freedom to be myself as I unravelled my confusion and awareness of truth in the presence of another's integrity for truth, is a significant gift to give to a friend. I thank you Will, for being you.

I started by writing what I wished I had been able to acknowledge at the beginning of my exploration and to recount the development of my own awareness. For a long time, I did not even consider myself a writer, which was part of my own denial of the uniqueness of my soul. I wanted to honestly pull apart what I was aware of, to comprehend the layers of my budding awareness. I came to realise that my awareness is dynamic because as I was willing to recognise more truth my awareness kept expanding and the writing process was a significant part of that. Without realising it I had become a mapmaker, and the ebb and flow of my life experiences as well as what I have been privy to observe and discuss with others is how I tracked the energy we produce with our emotions and energetic interactions. Little did I know that exploring and documenting my awareness was going to be a convoluted process of uncovering layers and layers of information from many angles. Little did I know this would take a decade and that there would be volumes of information and so much to explore. Little did I know that other people were coming to assist in the process of exploring and discovering truth, which was their destiny to come on board the vessel of Insight and Awareness. Discovery is the ability to go into uncharted waters and find what is there.

I perceive life like a river; life has its own ebb and flow and the current is taking you to your own unique opportunities. We are all experiencing the river of life and share the river, but we are all still significant, unique, independent, individual souls within the river. We each contribute energy to the river of life. This creates a symphony where the truth of both conscious and unconscious energy are being exposed. If you are willing to be truthfully honest with yourself and acknowledge your awareness of truth, you discover your life is an opportunity to experience the truth of all energy, and to resolve what inhibits you from feeling and trusting your resonance with truth. The currents of the river of life are always heading to the sea of truth and it is your honesty that allows you to discover your own truth within. Unfortunately, we get lost in our own emotional whirlpools and internal cyclonic storms, which inhibit us from accepting truth. This can cause the river to have perilous waters, which is all part of the journey. It is the experience of our own perilous waters that gives us the opportunity to discover what needs to be resolved, to evolve beyond our own limited perceptions of ourselves.

I perceive Insight and Awareness as a vessel for the exploration of truth, although those who board her are not taken out of the river but exposed to the river, each soul boards independently and will uniquely discover their opportunities within the written words. The key is to choose to be honest, because it is your willingness to be truthful that facilitates your own discovery of your soul truth.

I was privileged to meet other souls who had converging destinies with me through individual sessions and workshops. Sessions and workshops were opportunities for me to expose what is within a person's energy system and to assist in facilitating their awareness and understanding for how that influences their experience of life. I observe the energetics of the present moment, feel the consciousness and unconsciousness of a person's soul and have a heightened awareness of how people energetically interact with each other. This enabled me to conduct workshops and private sessions as an exploration of unresolved emotions, control structures, cyclic patterns of soul oppression, feelings and the natural significance of their souls.

Bronwen Prazak came as a client participating in workshops and private sessions. Bronwen had always been looking for answers to understand herself and her life, and trusted her own internal knowing that I would assist her in discovering the clarity she searched for. Bronwen was seeking to understand her own control structures and unresolved emotions, graciously allowing me to observe and track her emotional, energetic and physical reactions to what I was writing. Bronwen strived to be more honest about herself and kept seeking to live the process of being of her own insight and awareness. Her willingness to uncover truth drew her to become a proofreader of Insight and Awareness, which naturally evolved into her becoming the editor. Bronwen became an assistant to clarity as she interwove proofreading the information with her willingness to be honestly present in what the information and her own life experiences were exposing. She trusted herself to her own exploration of her layers of conscious and unconscious energy, reinforcing the significance of her own search to resolve what was inhibiting her from being at peace with reality. Her experiences became another avenue for the exploration of our conscious and unconscious energy.

Bronwen has been the proofreader throughout the development of Insight and Awareness long before there was even a book. The information was used at first in workshops and later formulated into books. Each section was a workshop and each workshop held became another avenue to track reactions and the truth of energy. These experiences were expanding my awareness and allowed me to expand the information to include the unravelling of emotions, beliefs and fears. The more clarity that could be brought to the information, the more it will be able to assist in the expansion of awareness in those who were and are willing to read *Your Insight and Awareness Book*. It has taken many stages of development to clarify the information. Bronwen challenged my written words, willing to check and critique what was written, becoming another way for me to expand my trust in my awareness and to trust what I felt resonated with my soul. At times I may not have followed all of her advice, but her questions and thoughts always created an opportunity to clarify why I wrote something in a certain way, or created the opportunity to expand the information. This allowed me more opportunities to discover the uniqueness of my soul, to trust what I felt, and to accept the uniqueness of all souls.

I knew for this information to become a book that you could read on your own, rather than part of a facilitated workshop, it needed to be absolutely clear as it deals with the complexities of the energies within our soul. It needed to be self-explanatory and written in a way that could synchronise with the consciousness of any soul who reads it. This is a complex multi-layered process; and you need to explore the layers of each energy before you recognise the simplicity of truth. *Your Insight and Awareness Book* was written by exposing the layers of energy, and follows the many different currents that are present within the river of life and within yourself.

When Leanne McIntyre-Burnes walked through my door, I could see she was energetically impacted and accustomed to feeling energy. If I was going help her I had to acknowledge my awareness of how the energy of each individual soul's unconsciousness reverberates with mankind's collective unconsciousness. Her presence meant I could not ignore what I needed to explore as she also intended to leave no rock unturned within her endeavour to resolve what was inhibiting her from feeling the truth of her soul. If I was going to hold to the integrity of exploring the truth of all energy and work truthfully with others, I had to confront my denial of the enormity of what I was naturally aware of, which is our reverberation with the energetic mass energy of mankind. This is the collective energy generated by our soul's unconsciousness, which is reactive to what I was exploring and proceeded to write about.

Leanne was determined to resolve any illusion that inhibited her from expressing the truth of her uniqueness, and wanted to explore the entirety of her emotional and energetic reality. This meant I could not be selective in what I was going to explore, acknowledge or be honest about. Her presence inhibited my ability to deny my awareness of how illusions reverberate with the energetics of the mass energy of mankind. I was attempting to ignore that I could feel the energetics of the mass energy of mankind, because I feared how it felt, as I had seen many "spiritual explorers" get lost in delusions and create images of consciousness that undermine the truth of who they are. I feared where the exploration could take me if I was not completely truthful, so I was endeavouring to avoid my own awareness. This developed into a fear, and a futile attempt to compartmentalise my awareness, which I eventually realised had to be resolved.

Leanne courageously conveyed every illusion that she had encountered, what she was feeling and her own energetic awareness of the reverberations of the energetic mass energy of mankind. This assisted me in strengthening my resolve to hold to the integrity of my soul and to develop ways of explaining what I was aware of, whilst retaining my respect for and resonance with truth.

Leanne climbed aboard the vessel of Insight and Awareness confronting what was written with every one of her indoctrinated beliefs she had experienced and read before, which exposed me to another avenue of exploration and forced me out of any denial I was attempting to secure. Leanne was energetically impacted but she tenaciously sought answers to her own awareness, which allowed me to acknowledge the significance of my awareness. I documented what I was aware of and tracked what influences our perception of reality. By observing my reactions and the reactions of others I was able to track the extent of the interaction of unconscious energy to unconscious energy, and to explore the presence of conscious energy within all experiences. Truth is always a witness to the reality of all energy; the energy we reverberate with and exchange from our soul's unconsciousness, and the energy that we resonate with and emanate from our soul's consciousness.

Leanne became an assistant to clarity willing to unravel what was inhibiting her from trusting herself and truth, and allowed me to explore her energetics as she sailed with the development of Insight and Awareness. She has been an integral part of the conceptual design for the illustrations that became another way of honing our understanding of the exploration of truth, as we simplified what was written into the preliminary sketches for the illustrations. This was the experience of exposing truth through illustrations, which are intended to enhance the clarity of *Your Insight and Awareness Book*.

The ability to observe and to discuss with others their reaction to what was being documented assisted in expanding the information and brought other elements to it, and for this I have a deep respect for all those who allowed me this privilege. It is our interactions with others that often exposes what inhibits us from being completely truthful with ourselves. I observed myself and others emotionally react to my own and their own changing awareness, and realised you never know what to expect, because the current of each person's resolution and evolution is unique. The process of writing the book exposed and developed my willingness to be present and honest with whatever was occurring, which enabled me to acknowledge how we use both our conscious and unconscious energy to interact with life. I instinctively knew the addiction to staying in the familiarity of the energy of our soul's unconsciousness is strong, and that is what stifles our exploration of truth. Misinterpretations are bound to occur because our protection of our unresolved emotions opposes our resonance with truth. It is important to not overlook the strength of the energy of our soul's unconsciousness and the extent we will go to find ways to circumvent our resonance with truth. Exposing ourselves to the truth of our energy will challenge everything we believe we know and everything we believe we can control.

I met Rachel Dearnley, who became another assistant to clarity, who is one of the final proofreaders of *Your Insight and Awareness Book*, as a client in sessions and workshops. She was seeking to discover and resolve the unresolved emotions she carried and was willing to reveal what she was aware of in relation to indifference energy. I was trusted to become the custodian of many people's history of abuse and within my other book *Breaking Free From the Chains of Silence*, I wrote what I read energetically; tracking how the extremes of indifference in the form of paedophilia affects the essence of a soul. Rachel brought an informed perspective to a very sensitive subject and openly shared the depths of the ramifications of indifference she had endured, as she reflected on what I was writing. Rachel enabled me to observe first hand a survivor's reaction to the information in *Your Insight and Awareness Book* and *Breaking Free From the Chains of Silence*. She helped me acknowledge the significance to the survivor of abuse of being heard and understood.

There is a rawness to the unresolved emotions of a survivor of abuse and I feel it is important to explore the ramifications of paedophilia from a soul perspective, because it is soul abuse. Rachel's frankness exposed me to the significance of bearing witness to the insidiousness of paedophilia and the importance of being willing to be present in what makes us uncomfortable. The acceptance of truth regardless of what that may be, gives us the courage to face what we usually attempt to run from. Running from truth creates more unresolved emotions and entraps us in our denial. I wanted to convey respect for the rawness and sensitivity of survivors of abuse, and yet confront the reality of the ramifications of abuse and what they have to deal with. Every individual who came as a client, and who shared with me how affected they were from their experience of abuse has been invaluable to the documentation of both *Your Insight and Awareness Book* and *Breaking Free From the Chains of Silence*, and I thank them sincerely for their candour and trust.

The resolution of any energy can only occur when the reality of it has been faced; our collective fear of paedophilia has allowed us to be silenced by our fear of our own reaction to indifference. We feel guilt, shame and humiliation because we do not know how to come to terms with the depth of destruction created by paedophilia. Guilt, shame and humiliation inhibits our willingness and ability to confront the significance of seeking the truth of the depths to which paedophilia affects the fabric of society. Indifference to truth protects paedophiles and enables a cloak of silence to hide the truth of the emotional, energetic and physical wounds of a soul who has experienced the insidiousness of indifference. If we cannot bear to hear about paedophilia, imagine what it is like for the victim who is living in the shadow of shame and silence created by paedophilia. *Breaking Free From the Chains of Silence* gives an understanding of the layers of indifference and exposes you to what is often denied, feared and hidden. When truth is hidden it creates the space for deception to flourish.

Each soul has a unique soul journey and your experience of life exposes the truth of yourself to you. I would like to thank those who generously shared their emotional experiences and innermost thoughts with me. All souls' journeys are a shared experience with truth and I have been privileged to have shared the exploration of truth with many, which has also assisted me in exploring the truth of myself. Some have shared their experiences of resolving and evolving beyond their image of themselves and have trusted themselves to be present within their own unique soul journey. It has been a significant part of my journey to have met so many interesting souls, who have been willing to explore truth, regardless of what they might find. It has been a privilege to experience their willingness to be honest. These opportunities have allowed me to participate in the exposure of my own and others' struggle to acknowledge and accept truth. Truthful honesty enables us to feel truth, trust our own awareness of truth and trust ourselves to never give up on the significance of our soul. Thank you to all those who have been willing to seek the truth within the uniqueness of our shared moments, for allowing me to observe the resolution of your unresolved emotions and to be a witness to the reality of soul evolution.

I am also grateful to those who shared the experience of retreating and hiding from the truth of themselves within their own unresolved emotions, because they feared they could not control their resolution or predetermine the result of their evolution. You assisted me in comprehending the truth of how much we fear the truth of who we are. All these experiences have been invaluable for exposing the truth of unresolved emotions, and I thank you for what I learnt from the experiences we have shared. We all experience times where we are curious about ourselves and then retreat from truth. This is why it is a journey with its own unique ebbs and flows of our willingness to be honest and our fear of honesty. We are souls who are synchronised with truth, and I thank you all for the privilege of sharing the uniqueness of the moments when our paths crossed within our soul journeys.

I personally would like to thank those who have been walking beside me for the long haul, for naturally following their own resonance with truth, for their willingness to trust me, their ongoing support and for never giving up on their own resolution and evolution. They have all enriched my soul journey and I thank them for never wavering from the significance of their soul journeys.

This book is a document of what has been experienced, felt, explored, understood and trusted as we learnt to be more honest with ourselves, truth and the reality of being souls. This book is a map of our discoveries from exploring the truth of our own unresolved emotions, whilst searching for answers as to why we felt the way we felt about ourselves and our life experiences. The writing of *Your Insight and Awareness Book* has been the exploration of unique soul journeys and the exploration of shared experiences. At times, I explored my reactions to my life experiences whilst endeavouring to resolve what I denied and I was also privileged that others shared their reactions for me to explore. *Your Insight and Awareness Book* explores the natural process of learning to be truthful within the rise and fall from grace, which is how we expose ourselves to the truth of the consciousness and unconsciousness within our souls. *Your Insight and Awareness Book* is the documentation of what influences our choice to be honest or dishonest with the truth of ourselves. This is an ongoing process as we are all evolving souls, exploring and learning from the truth of our life experiences.

I have learnt that it is the willingness to be completely truthful with yourself that facilitates resolution and evolution. What I discovered is when you clarify your awareness, your truthfulness expands and your denial dissipates, and as your truthfulness expands so does your awareness of truth. I also discovered I was willing to teach and share with others what I had learnt. The experience of writing the book and of others being willing to engage with the information has been a learning curve, and everything about the process was documented as life exposed truth to us all. The book is an assistant to clarity, it is a map that assists and supports the process of you feeling your own soul while resolving the energy of your soul's unconsciousness. *Your Insight and Awareness Book* is a foundation to build upon as you explore the truth of yourself. It is the first in a series of books that explore the layers of your soul's consciousness and unconsciousness.

ACKNOWLEDGMENTS

Thank you to Bronwen Prazak for being an invaluable assistant to clarity for Insight and Awareness. Thank you for the countless hours spent throughout the development of *Your Insight and Awareness Book* proofreading and editing. You have been instrumental in the process of this book being published. Thank you for your dedication to trusting the exploration of truth. I appreciate your willingness to unconditionally support the development of this book, and it has been a privilege to have such a trusted friend walk beside me.

Thank you to Leanne McIntyre-Burnes for being an entertaining assistant to clarity for Insight and Awareness. Thank you for the adventurous weekends and your willingness to share your home, time and creativity as we came together to discuss, debate and explore how to convey the text into illustrations. Thank you for your artistic insight into capturing the essence of what we wanted to convey, whilst creating the preliminary sketches for the illustrations. I appreciate your dedication to the development of *Your Insight and Awareness Book* and feel extremely fortunate to have shared your friendship.

Thank you to Rachel Dearnley for being a supportive assistant to clarity for Insight and Awareness. Thank you for your candour during the development of this book and for the hours spent proofreading. I appreciate your support, I am also grateful for your willingness to be truthful. I feel honoured to have your friendship.

Thank you to Katherine Close for coming on board and fulfilling the epic task of the illustrations with the willingness to encapsulate the significance of what *Your Insight and Awareness Book* is conveying. Thank you for going the extra mile for me and the book, and for having respect for the integral part the illustrations play in the clarity of the information. I would also like to express my gratitude for the beautiful book cover, superb work as per usual. Thank you for your friendship and continual support.

Thank you to Daniel Middleton for your patience and your assistance during this project. I found your kindness and honesty inspiring. The development of this book has taken way longer than anyone expected, and I appreciate your on-going advice and support. Thanks mate.

I would like to thank Col Burnes for his generous support, hospitality and legendary cooked breakfasts during the many weekends spent creating the preliminary sketches for the illustrations.

Thank you to my family for supporting the marathon that this process became and for accepting that it is part of who I am. I would also like to thank the families of the assistants to clarity for sharing your loved ones with me in this process.

I would like to acknowledge all the souls who have shared their stories, insights, angst and laughter whilst we were exploring the truth of both conscious and unconscious energy. Thank you.

GLOSSARY

Acceptance A core essence of your soul's consciousness, unconditional love for who you are.

Embracing truth. Acknowledging reality without any deception or denial. Trusting yourself to be truthfully honest and present in the dynamics of the entirety of what is occurring.

Addiction A compulsive dependency. Addiction describes how you lose yourself to your own soul oppression, and become enslaved to the merry-go-round you create, whilst being controlled by that which creates negative consequences. Addictions stem from the desire to escape reality. A compulsion you believe you cannot resist.

Appreciation A core essence of your soul's consciousness, unconditional love for reality.

Trusting the value and worth of your own presence within your present moment. Feeling gratitude for the uniqueness of your own experience of life, and for the presence of others and truth.

Anxiety The tension you create within yourself when you believe you are not in control, or fear losing your illusion of control. An energy produced by your fight, flight, freeze, fawn or hide fear reaction.

Arrogance An unrealistically high evaluation of your importance, and offensive displays of superiority. Believing your own opinions, desires and expectations are superior to the truth of reality and others. To be full of contemptuous indifference towards anyone or anything that interferes with your desires. The belief you are entitled to control how reality should be, and the desire to prove you are on top of a pecking order, created by your own evaluation of yourself and others. Arrogance is the choice to ignore reality.

Aura Your own energy that surrounds you. All living systems have an aura. Your aura is a combination of the various energies that are emanating from your soul's consciousness, or being projected or oozing from your soul's unconsciousness. Every emotion, feeling, thought or belief creates energy, and your aura is determined by these energies. Your aura dynamically changes according to your reaction to each present moment.

Autonomous Self-governing. To make decisions freely and independently.

Avoidance One of the barriers to truth within your soul's unconsciousness, used to oppress your awareness of your soul's consciousness. Shunning away from reality, attempting to prevent awareness of yourself and truth. To hide from truth.

Barriers to Truth Emotional, energetic or physical obstructions to accepting truth. Barriers to truth are how you maintain your separation from your awareness of your soul. Barriers are part of the energetic structural web of the vortex of your soul's unconsciousness, and are sustained using the major collectives of energy that result from opposing truth. The major collectives are resistance, denial, avoidance, codependency, judgement, manipulation, confusion, control, images, illusions, controlled identities, controlled evolution and heresy. Barriers are deceptive control structures formed from your layers of triggered emotional reactions, which you use to prevent your awareness of the flow of truth within you, and to inhibit your ability to recognise and learn from the truth of your reality.

The mass energy of mankind also has barriers to truth. The mass is a macrocosm of our individual microcosm of unconsciousness.

Belief systems A collection of beliefs used as a point of reference to construct and secure your judgement, which you use to create a perception of reality or viewpoints of what reality should be. Belief systems are used to influence and persuade yourself and others to align to your opinions, indoctrinations or lies. Belief systems are guide rails for your judgement, which you use to oppress your awareness of the dynamics of truth. Belief systems are often used to camouflage your own desire for control or self-manipulation.

Blueprint An intent for this lifetime made by you as your soul's consciousness, while you were residing in the purity of your origin, labelled here as *True Source Divine Origin Consciousness*.

Camouflage An act of obscuring things to deceive yourself or others. The intention to deceptively disguise your emotional, energetic or physical reality.

Care A core essence of your soul's consciousness, unconditional love for yourself and the equality of all souls.

An expression of love and concern for yourself or others. Your acceptance of the value and worth of truth. Taking responsibility for supporting your natural significance and the significance of others. Being committed to respecting truth.

Carried victim energy is a multitude of unresolved emotions and resulting mentalities, which can be used together or separately to oppress your awareness of the exquisiteness of your soul. Carried victim energy results when the victim mentality is carried without the aspiration to resolve, which becomes a control technique used to oppose accepting reality, and to undermine the value of who you are. It is also a description of how your victim mentality becomes a self-definition you protect, because you are immersed in the energy produced by your indifference towards yourself.

Chakra A two-sided vortex of energy stemming from the channel that is at the core of your energy system. The word chakra means wheel of energy or turning. Chakras are collection points for the movement of energy.

Chakra system A label for the human energetic system and the individual collection points for the movement of energy (chakras). Both conscious and unconscious energy move through your chakra system. The core of your chakra system channels conscious energy, delivering the energy of your soul's consciousness through the depths of your soul's unconsciousness. The energy of your consciousness always returns to your origins of *True Source Divine Origin Consciousness*. The energy of your unconsciousness always returns to the vortex of your soul's unconsciousness via your chakras.

Your chakra system is an energetic structure that channels the energy you produce from your emotional reactions to reality. You project out your own energy and draw in energy from many sources. The chakra system connects the energy produced and projected from your unresolved emotions to correlating collectives within the mass energy of mankind. You can also entwine your projected emotions with another's correlating or reactive emotions, as well as drawing in others' projected unconscious energy.

Charade A pretense. A false or pointless act created from an attempt to hide the truth of reality. A charade runs concurrently with the images you want to portray and the illusions you want to hold onto.

Choice The opportunity to choose between two or more different possibilities. Conscious choice results from you realising you have options and from accepting your ability to choose, which is a recognition of having freewill.

Clarity A core essence of your soul's consciousness, unconditional love for your unification with truth.

Your acceptance of reality, free from any deception. Being truthful with yourself, clearly expressing the truth you are aware of, understand and trust.

Codependency One of the barriers to truth within your soul's unconsciousness, used to oppress your awareness of your soul's consciousness. Rejection of independence. Addiction, compulsion or attachment to that which you believe you need to rely on, which creates and sustains barriers to being completely honest with yourself. Your dependence on that which is unresolved within you, or on someone or something that sustains harmful beliefs and behaviours that are detrimental to you and your awareness of truth.

Compassion A core essence of your soul's consciousness, unconditional love for the journey of each soul including your own.

Allowing yourself to feel the reality of life while having empathy for yourself and other souls. To flow in harmony with the realisation of the significant uniqueness of each individual soul, including yourself. To be free of judgement and full of acceptance of truth. An expression of thoughtful resonance with unconditional love.

Concretisation When beliefs are so ingrained and deep rooted that you constantly align yourself to the patterns, mindsets, cultures, attitudes, judgements and behaviour traits that cause you to deny the dynamics of truth. A stubborn conviction to protect your own denial, fears and beliefs. Concretisation is the intent to defend your viewpoint, regardless of your awareness of contradictory evidence. The embodiment of indifference and tangible defiance against truth and the truth of who you naturally are.

Conditioning An element of the heresy barrier of your soul's unconsciousness, used to oppress your awareness of your soul's consciousness. A method of training that results in being conditioned, which creates expectations and automatic reactions. Controlling yourself to repeat what you have emotionally, energetically and physically done before, because it is your familiar. Responding to the dynamics of life with your preconceived beliefs, behaviours and emotional reactions.

Creating a way of existing influenced by your soul denial history, or indoctrinations that limit your experience of the dynamics of your soul's consciousness, and the presence of truth within your reality. The willingness to override your present moment reality and feelings to repeat what you have done before, regardless of the results you have experienced.

Confusion One of the barriers to truth within your soul's unconsciousness, used to oppress your awareness of your soul's consciousness. The chaos you create with your inability to accept reality. Unable to feel your truth with clarity, or to reason clearly with logic, because of the emotional disorder created by your denial. To be lost in misconceptions or being unaware of the entirety of truth. Feeling the insecurity of being separated from truth. The fear of being wrong if you make a decision, which becomes an avoidance that you use to create a confused state, that leaves you either unable or unwilling to be completely honest with yourself.

Congested rise and fall from grace Over-burdened with the unconscious energy generated by your unresolved emotions. Restricting your awareness of truth. Denying your resonance with truth to protect how you use the energy of your soul's unconsciousness. Inhibiting your awareness of the flow of your soul's consciousness.

Consciousness is free flowing truth energy. Being aware of and awakened to the truth of who you are and the reality of all energy. The authenticity of your soul and truth.

Control One of the barriers to truth within your soul's unconsciousness, used to oppress your awareness of your soul's consciousness. The desire to have complete authority over what reality should be. A desire to dominate truth, and everyone and everything in your environment. Using your desires, expectations and illusions as a false authority over your soul, while selectively judging what parts of truth you will value. An energy you generate that limits and restricts your awareness of your soul truth and your freedom of choice. An illusion that you can manipulate and orchestrate life, yourself, others, relationships and the presence of truth, to align to your desire to have power or influence over reality.

Control energy is generated by fear or the desire to dominate, whilst being willing to abandon your own awareness of truth.

Control structures The complex methods and mythology of how you utilise your desire for control or your illusion of having control. A sequenced pattern of various unresolved emotions you use in an attempt to influence reality with your desire to have control. Your desire for control is how you interweave and interrelate all the different components of your soul's unconsciousness to one agenda, for the purpose of appeasing your desire for how you want reality to be. Control structures can become a very complex system that sustain your emotional, energetic and physical barriers to truth and strengthen your avenues of indifference.

Controlled evolution One of the barriers to truth within your soul's unconsciousness, you use to oppress your awareness of your soul's consciousness. Your controlled evolution energy is a mixture of your beliefs, denials and desires. Controlled evolution energy is produced when you sustain your programmed, conditioned and indoctrinated beliefs, and use them to inhibit yourself from honestly exploring truth. The use of beliefs to habitually silence your awareness of your soul's consciousness, leaving you to express your unconsciousness, instead of being the authenticity of your own soul. The use of belief systems to pretend you are of truth, as you attempt to emulate what you want to believe consciousness is, in an attempt to convince others of your evolution.

Created belief systems used to control perceptions of truth. Belief systems can be used to justify being indifferent towards others and the basis of battlegrounds for superiority, oppression and appeasing the seven deadly sins. The convergence of beliefs you use to control yourself to remain separated from your awareness of your soul's consciousness, the reality of your actions and potential evolution, whilst you pretend to be truthful. The belief of being able to control what truth is, whilst denying the energy of your soul's unconsciousness. Beliefs used to bypass the truth of what is unresolved that leave you out of sync with the reality of yourself.

Controlled identity One of the barriers to truth within your soul's unconsciousness, used to oppress your awareness of your soul's consciousness. Controlled identities are self-definitions created from the roles you perform in life. Identities you use to lose your sense of self, embodying the roles you have in life, allowing the role to become the only way you perceive yourself. Adopting what you do or experience as a label for the entirety of who you are. For example: You are a soul who is experiencing mothering, you are not just a mother. You are a soul experiencing being lost within an addiction, you are not just an addict.

Core essence is unconditional love, which is the unification of all core essences. The purity of who you are. Your soul's unique frequency which is in harmony with your origins, labelled here as *True Source Divine Origin Consciousness*.

Core essences are unique strands of conscious energy that contribute to the purity of who you are. They are unique strands of conscious energy within unconditional love. The natural energy that emanates from your soul's consciousness. Core essences explored in Insight and Awareness are: *acceptance, appreciation, care, clarity, compassion, dynamic, freedom, grace, harmony, honesty, hope, independence, individuality, integrity, joy, kindness, loyalty, patience, peace, purity, serenity, trust, truthfulness and uniqueness*.

'Couldn't be bothered' mentality The decision to be slothful in order to ignore truth and to avoid taking action within your reality.

Crossed over soul A soul who has lived and returned to their natural origin, after the death of their physical body, which is the completion of a lifetime. When a crossed over soul returns to their origin they become free from the energy of their soul's unconsciousness as this dissipates into and is stored within the energetic collectives of mankind. Crossed over souls can visit but they do not reside on Earth. They visit in their purity, unhindered by any unconscious energy, and they emanate unconditional love.

Declaration A statement, which gives clear details, announcing and declaring intention.

Defection Your willingness to deny your origins and the eternalness of your soul.

Delusion Ideas that have no basis in reality. A belief maintained regardless of the evidence of reality being contradictory to the belief. Unwillingness to be rational or to accept reality.

Denial One of the barriers to truth within your soul's unconsciousness, used to oppress your awareness of your soul's consciousness. The refusal to acknowledge and accept reality, or the willingness to fool yourself about what is occurring. To reject truth or the refusal to admit the existence of truth. The willingness to orchestrate the loss of awareness of truth and reality, preferring to exist in the void created by revoking what is real. The inability to recognise your resonance with truth.

The willingness to disown what was once recognised as truth. Used to override whatever you believe is interfering with your illusion of control. When the truth of your reality is emotionally, energetically or physically overwhelming, denial becomes an automatic protection mechanism. The overwhelming desire to ignore or forget what you are experiencing or have experienced.

Denial of reality An element of the heresy barrier of your soul's unconsciousness, used to oppress your awareness of your soul's consciousness. To deny what is. To pretend you are unaware of your present moment experience. The inability to trust yourself to be present in the truth of what you are experiencing, believing you can alter what is, by ignoring reality. Refusal to be present or to acknowledge the truth of life, energy, yourself, others, relationships and your resonance with truth.

The inability to recognise the truth of something, someone, an event or yourself due to your own willingness to be deceptive. Being too scared to admit what you feel within the experience, or seeking to camouflage your awareness of reality to hide from what you know and feel to be true.

Desire for control A facet of your soul control. Coveting power and dominance over reality.

Diffuse To cause your awareness to be fragmented. To make truth harder to recognise by fragmenting the reality of what you are aware of. The deliberate reduction of your awareness of truth by being willing to deny the entirety of what you are aware of. The willingness to filter your awareness of truth through your unresolved emotions, scattering and fragmenting your awareness of your internal and external reality.

Diffusing your awareness of truth results in you reverberating with the energetics of your own soul's unconsciousness and with the energetics of the mass energy of mankind. This requires passive movement and little effort; one thought will suffice to create diffusion, which enhances your ability to deny truth and reality.

Disassociate Distancing yourself from reality, with the intention to shut down your awareness of truth. A state of separation from truth that leaves you with fragmented awareness. A reaction to shock that causes you to shut down your own awareness of your emotions and feelings. Extreme disassociation involves feeling like you are physically outside yourself and no longer present.

Disassociation from feeling The act of disunity from the truth of what you are feeling. The choice to deny the truth of how you feel and disconnect from what you are feeling. The desire to override your feeling with numbness in an attempt to deny your association with your emotional, energetic or physical reality. The desire to terminate your awareness of your internal or external reality, and exist momentarily in a void.

Disassociation from feeling truth The act of disunity with truth by distracting and distancing yourself from your resonance with your feelings, reality and your origins. To pretend to be ignorant to the energy you resonate or reverberate with. The willingness to emotionally hide from being present. The desire to terminate your awareness of feeling the entirety of what your present moment entails. Disconnected from truth as you attempt to discount the value of truth.

Disassociation from love An element of the heresy barrier of your soul's unconsciousness, used to oppress your awareness of your soul's consciousness. The result of being indifferent to truth. Amalgamating different types of indifference to oppose the core essences of your soul. Denying and distancing yourself from the significance of unconditionally loving yourself, others and truth. The choice to abandon your authentic self.

Disconnect A component of the '*Self* expose self' declaration. Withdrawing your unconscious energy from any other source of unconscious energy, such as another's unresolved emotions or the energetics of the mass energy of mankind. Retreating from how you emotionally, energetically or physically fixate on or lock yourself to unconscious energy. Detaching from using or binding yourself to your own or another's unresolved emotions, so you can objectively observe your own emotions, feelings, energetics and physicality.

'Dis-ease' To experience disharmony within yourself, which can create an emotional, energetic or physical imbalance.

Disengage A component of the '*Self* expose self' declaration. Releasing yourself from how you engage with unconscious energy, freeing yourself from energetically contributing to the perpetuation of soul oppressive energy. Liberating yourself from applying effort to using your own unconscious energy. Emancipating yourself from automatically matching and reverberating with the unconscious energy within a situation, being projected from others or generated from belief systems. Freeing yourself from emotionally, energetically or physically engaging with what perpetuates your own soul oppression. To withdraw and release yourself from the war you wage against the truth of yourself and your own reality.

Disentangle A component of the '*Self* expose self' declaration. To untangle and unravel your own emotions from that which is creating confusion and affecting your sense of self. Taking responsibility for the energy, you have projected out. To liberate yourself from being ensnared, enmeshed or entrapped emotionally, energetically or physically in your own or another's unconscious energy. To clarify your confusion and uncover truth.

Divine The eternal purity of unconditional love. The origin of all souls. Free of any form of deception. Free of unconscious energy. Purity of truth

Douse To immerse something or someone in an energy. Attempting to saturate another with energy.

Duality A dual state, contrasting, complementary or opposing each other. The activation and sustainability of emotionally see-sawing between two mind-sets or justifications.

Dumbing down Deliberately down playing your intelligence and your awareness of truth. Not trusting what you are aware of, understand or feel. Attempting to hide the truth of who you naturally are. Depriving yourself of your own shine of consciousness.

Dynamic A core essence of your soul's consciousness, unconditionally loving the flow of truth.

The cause and effect of the truth of all energy. The ability to quickly adapt to the truth of what is occurring. Energy in motion.

Ego The desire to be in control and wanting your desires appeased and gratified. This causes you to prioritise your unresolved emotions over your awareness of your soul and truth, and to ignore the equality of all souls. The exposure of your arrogant belief of self-importance created by your illusion of yourself and willingness to be selfish within a shared reality. Ego is a product of your separation from your awareness of your soul and your disassociation from feeling truth.

Embedded beliefs are opinions, attitudes and ideals you deem as relevant or true, which are fixated deeply within your soul denial and integrated into how you perceive yourself, others, life and truth. These beliefs are surrounded by reinforcing energy, such as fear, denial and indifference to truth. Ways of thinking that inhibit your awareness of truth and sustain your own soul oppression.

Emotions are energy, created from your non-acceptance of truth and rejection of your feelings. Emotions are stored in and projected or oozed from your soul's unconsciousness, whereas feelings emanate from your soul's consciousness. Denied feelings convert into emotions that become vibrations of energy you carry, which at times cause you to be out of sync with the truth of reality. Emotions are agitated by your thoughts and reactions to your feelings. Your responses from the energy of your soul's unconsciousness.

Emulations The use of deceptive charades to try to be equal to, or surpass, the significance of truth. Attempted imitations activated by the willingness to undervalue the significance and authenticity of that which is being emulated. Pretending to be of truth, while having little understanding of truth. Imitations competing against truth.

Energetics The vibrational force of reverberating unconscious energy. The movement of the energy being exchanged within your present moment reality (both internally and externally) that sustains the vibrational force of unconscious energy. The vibrational force created from the activation of your unresolved emotions, barriers to truth, control structures, framework of soul oppression, fears and beliefs. This can be projected by you or at you by others, with or without awareness, creating reverberations of unconscious energy. You can also reverberate with the energetic collectives within the mass energy of mankind that correlates to what you have activated from your soul's unconsciousness.

Energetic Collectives Unconscious energy forming a collective group through the law of attraction as the energy reverberates with the same vibration. The energies within the collective are similar in character and are stored within the energetic mass energy of mankind. A collective force of unconscious energy that entangles, engages and connects to other unconscious energy that is complementary, similar or of an exact vibration. Like energy attracts like energy.

Energetic mass energy of mankind is the energetic force and residue of mankind's collective unconsciousness, which consists of the energetic collectives of unresolved emotions, barriers to truth and the framework of soul oppression. The energetic mass energy of mankind is the macrocosm of unconsciousness, and an individual soul's unconsciousness is the microcosm. Each individual soul's unconsciousness contributes to the sustainability of the collective energy within the mass energy of mankind. The energetic mass energy of mankind is the storehouse for all mankind's varieties and types of unconscious energy.

It is the energetic structure of our collective unconsciousness, formed from our collective soul denial history and present opposition to the significance of truth and our souls. It has the same energetic structure as an individual soul's unconsciousness. The energetic structure is made up of different reverberations. The reverberations of unresolved emotions create energetic collectives. The reverberations of control structures and belief systems form barriers to truth. The reverberations with our collective avenues of indifference form the framework of soul oppression.

Energetic independence Your willingness to be of your own soul integrity, and to acknowledge the emotional, energetic and physical truth you are experiencing, whilst not losing your awareness of the truth of yourself. To be able to consciously respond, not emotionally react.

Energetic idle The choice to fight reality with your desire for control, or the protection of your illusion of control whilst emotionally torturing yourself or others with your unresolved emotions, which creates obstructions to feeling your own flow of consciousness. Generating a limbo from the process of fighting against truth in an attempt to have control. The action of using your control structures to fight for dominance over truth, which can be physically felt as an internal vibration.

Energetic idle describes being fallen in the energy of your soul's unconsciousness and denying your own awareness of what can you feel and observe. Allowing yourself to protect the stagnation created by your indifference to truth. To deny yourself resolution and evolution by being narcissistically transfixed on controlling the sustainability of your indifference to the truth of your own soul.

Energy The movement of the frequency of consciousness or the vibrations of unconsciousness.

Enlightened To know yourself in truth. To acknowledge the reality of your soul oppression and utilise your realisation of truth to evolve that which is unresolved within your soul's unconsciousness into conscious understanding. Being truthfully honest enables your soul's consciousness to evolve and thus diminish the vibrational unconscious energy of your soul's unconsciousness, which expands your soul's consciousness. (*see evolution*)

To be aware of yourself within your present moment. To not dilute your soul integrity, and to freely emanate the pure frequency of your soul's consciousness, while being of grace for yourself and others.

Entangle To ensnare and twist the energy of your soul's unconsciousness with other unconscious energy, making your individual energy difficult to recognise. Entwining your individual strands of energy into energy that is difficult to escape from. To complicate reality and to incite confusion. To lose energetic independence.

Entrapment To trick yourself with your own or another's deception. The use of deceit to restrain the awareness of truth. The willingness to oppress your own or another's awareness of truth with the intention to prove you have control. Conniving betrayal of trust. Conditioned by the lure of the illusion of control and false promises to be ensnared in your own soul oppression.

Escapism The inclination to resist, deny and avoid reality through diversion and decoys. The attempt to escape being aware of your emotional, energetic or physical reality by aligning to illusions that you superimpose over your perception of reality. The willingness to overindulge in something, as a means to ignore, forget or separate from your awareness of reality.

Evolution Your original intention for life. Evolution is the process of change created by conscious participation in the resolution of the energy of your soul's unconsciousness. Evolution is to awaken from your unconsciousness and embrace your unification with the presence of truth. Evolution is acceptance of the equality of all souls. Evolution is choosing to adapt to your recognition of truth.

Evolution is the process of accepting responsibility for and resolving the unconscious energy you created. Evolution is the ability to trust and feel the truth of your freewill. Evolution is to feel the entirety of your core essences. Evolution is to walk beside truth, caring for and valuing your relationship with your soul and the essence of truth.

Expectations Attempting to predict future events and outcomes whilst seeking to secure beliefs about what you think you know. The desire to be right about something before it happens. The choice to oppress your ability to be dynamic, because you only want to experience what you believe should occur. The desire to have confidence in what you believe reality will be. Fixating on what you want, corrupting your perception, whilst aligning to the desire to pacify your own perspective. Your desire to predict your own emotional reaction to people, the truth of your feelings and events within your reality. Expectations stem from the desire to ascertain what your future will be.

Exonerate To declare free from blame, obligation or responsibility.

Expose To reveal truth. To allow something to be seen; to uncover reality.

Externalisation The willingness to focus on energy outside yourself, or projecting your energy onto an outside source. A defense mechanism used in an attempt to deny responsibility for your own reactions to the truth of your internal reality. The creation or instigation of turmoil, to ignore the truth of how you feel. An orchestrated way of protecting your denial.

Façade Using a superficial appearance in an attempt to camouflage reality. Creating a veneer to hide from reality. Your facades become your accessories for the images you create to disguise the reality of your emotional reaction to your present moment. Your facades conceal the deception of your charade.

Fall from grace To operate in separation from your soul's consciousness. This is in contrast to rise *with* grace, which is to operate in unification with your soul's consciousness and truth.

Familiarity The state of knowing something very well. An expectation for the same emotional, energetic and physical experience due to the regularity of experiencing this as the norm. Consistently predictable. Familiarity is the repetitiveness of controlling yourself to the same patterns of behaviour or observing the repetition of others.

Fear There are two types of fear: One is an indicator to be alert within your present moment, and the other is negative energy you generate with your thoughts that may or may not be related to the truth of your reality. The sensation of fear you generate from your soul's unconsciousness stems from your avoidance of truth. Fear can be generated from your refusal to accept the truth of your present moment and your broader reality. This can be debilitating as it either causes, or is a result of separation from your awareness of your soul, or the truth within your present moment reality. This incites your codependency on your illusion of control and sustains your trepidation about your ability to control.

The true essence of fear is a warning signal from your soul's consciousness, communicating to you to get present in your reality and trust your awareness.

Feelings naturally emanate from your soul's consciousness. Feelings communicate the truth of your awareness and reaction to the reality of what is occurring. Feelings are how you interconnect with life. You communicate truth to yourself through your feelings. Your feelings can be the result of your soul insight exposing truth to you. Your feelings can emanate from the truth of the core essences of your soul and cannot be controlled or orchestrated. Feelings are the truth of your reaction to your present moment. Feelings are temporary if you accept the truth of them. When you deny or oppose the truth of what you feel, you create unresolved emotions.

Fortify An attempt to make something defensible by strengthening and reinforcing your emotional, energetic and physical barriers to truth.

Flow of consciousness Truth undisturbed by unconscious energy. The natural stream of the purity of the energy of your soul's consciousness. Free moving conscious energy.

Fragmentation The splitting of your awareness into isolated and separated factions which are often conflicting and contradictory. Loss of unity. Lack of integration. Creating segregation. Disconnecting from the reality you feel, observe and are aware of. Breaking the entirety of reality into pieces, in order to ignore parts of it, which leaves you in opposition to unifying with truth.

Framework of soul oppression is comprised of your different avenues of indifference, which are sequenced reactions and responses that you use to be and remain indifferent to truth. These avenues of indifference originate from the fears and embedded beliefs within your soul denial. Each avenue of indifference is a cyclic pattern of your soul oppression that ascends from your soul denial to your heresy barrier and descends back to your soul denial. The avenues of indifference are your soul abuse, soul betrayal, soul deception, soul defiance, soul demise, soul illusion, soul sabotage and soul traitor. You use these to construct a framework of how you oppress the truth of yourself.

The avenues of your indifference are fuelled by the energy you generate with your soul control and your willingness to be indifferent to truth, which you use to fortify the protection of your soul denial and to remain worshiping your soul control. The mass energy of mankind also has a framework of soul oppression. The mass is a macrocosm of each individual's unconsciousness.

Freedom A core essence of your soul's consciousness, unconditional love for truth and freewill.

The acceptance of truth, without the desire to control truth. To live the authenticity of your soul without fear. Acceptance of freewill and the divinity of your soul.

Freedom of choice is freewill. Independently choosing how you feel about yourself, life, others, relationships and truth. How you feel, what emotions you use, what you trust, what you are internally curious about and how you perceive yourself within your reality are decisions made as an autonomous being, and expose how you use your freedom of choice. Your natural right to choose what you align to, reverberate with, believe or acknowledge. You have freewill to choose how you respond to reality, but you cannot dictate or control what reality should be.

Frequency The flow of conscious energy retaining its purity. Consciousness is pure and is felt as a frequency. Unconsciousness is tainted and is felt as a vibration. Frequency is the authenticity of that which naturally emanates from truth, or from your own or others' soul consciousness. All core essences emanate a frequency.

The purity of your soul's consciousness is a frequency that travels in a circular journey from your origins, which is part of something bigger than yourself, as it is the frequency of truth. The frequency of your soul's consciousness is always anchored to your origins as it travels through the depths of your soul's unconsciousness and returns back to your origins untainted by the vibrations of your unconsciousness.

Freewill Autonomy. The freedom to choose. Having a choice. Done voluntarily.

Frustration A warning signal that you are consumed by your desire to control or by your unresolved emotions that hinder your acceptance of reality. A signal that your desire to be in control of reality is being thwarted. Aggravation created by being disappointed that your plans and expectations are unsuccessful or difficult to manage. A reaction to others inability or unwillingness to understand your perception or to work in harmony.

Grace A core essence of your soul's consciousness, unconditional love for the opportunities within the symphony of truth.

Grace refers to the constant flow of conscious energy, which is always present whether you are recognising and accepting, or denying and opposing truth. Grace is the energy of your truthful honesty harmonising with truth. Grace is the willingness to trust the unconditional love within your soul's consciousness and to be free of judgement.

Grace is awareness of the entirety of reality and the truth of all energy with the willingness to be forgiving. Grace facilitates the generosity of your soul to forgive the unconsciousness of others and yourself. Grace is the willingness to be of truth, which eases distress and pain. Grace is the energy that you use instinctively, to access and stimulate the energy of the other core essences required for you to remain present within your reality.

Guilt An element of the heresy barrier of your soul's unconsciousness, used to oppress your awareness of your soul's consciousness. An overwhelming emotion coming from the belief that you have done something wrong, which you use to be non-forgiving of yourself. Your guilt can be a recognition of operating from your unconsciousness. Guilt clouds your awareness of truth and inhibits the opportunity for your truthfulness to create resolution and evolution.

An emotion created by realising the truth of your own separation from your awareness of your soul and disassociation from feeling the unconditional love of *True Source Divine Origin Consciousness*, which incites and sustains an energetic idle and a fear of yourself. Guilt can be used to sustain a conflict within yourself, causing you to be non-accepting of how your reality has played out, emotionally imploding about everything you believe you are responsible for. Guilt is a self-inflicted punishment for not being able to control the unconsciousness of your soul, or the truth of your reality. Regret for being responsible for pain created for another or yourself to endure. Guilt can be a result of knowingly manipulating others or allowing others to manipulate you. Inciting guilt in others is a way of controlling them to be compliant to your wants, desires and demands.

Harmony A core essence of your soul's consciousness, unconditional love for resonating with truth.

The remembrance of your origins and the ability to flow in the dynamics of truth, whilst feeling the significance of your unification with truth. The willingness to freely align to and support your presence within truth's symphony, while retaining the independence of your uniqueness and individuality. To be present, unified and resonating with truth. The natural coordination of all core essences working in sync with the presence of *True Source Divine Origin Consciousness*' unconditional love for all souls.

Heresy Barrier One of the barriers to truth within your soul's unconsciousness, used to oppress your awareness of your soul's consciousness. Heresy Barrier is comprised of the different energies you use to remain anti-truth, which leave you indifferent to your own soul and perceiving yourself as a struggling human. Your willingness to be anti-truth is generated from your desire to control and can leave you operating from your indifference to truth, resentment of reality and opposition to truth. You justify this by filtering your awareness of yourself through your programming, conditioning and indoctrinations. Your guilt, shame and humiliation become ways you can protect your own indifference to truth, which enables you to remain in denial of reality, all of which leaves you disassociated from love.

Heresy is to be willfully persistent in rejecting the truth of your soul, which causes you to be indifferent to truth. Your own heresy against yourself incites your many forms of indifference energy. Heresy is the willingness to exploit your awareness of truth. You take what you are aware of and turn it into something you can use as a manipulative tool, in order to remain separated from the significance of the truth of your energy, and to ensure the perpetuation of your indifference to the truth of your own significance. Your heresy energy is the willingness to be anti-yourself and to attempt to use unconscious energy to control unconscious energy, while disregarding your awareness of the significance of truth.

Honesty A core essence of your soul's consciousness, unconditional love for choice.

Honesty is the ability to recognise truth, which becomes a junction within your awareness of truth. Honesty invokes an awareness that you have a choice. The willingness to acknowledge truth and the truth of your feelings, creates opportunities to explore reality. Honesty is the bridge to experiencing your own flow of consciousness free from any form of deception.

Hope A core essence of your soul's consciousness, unconditional love for your own courage.

The recognition of the dynamics of truth and acceptance of your synchronicity with truth. An appreciation for the unconditional love *True Source Divine Origin Consciousness* has for you and you have for truth. Courageously being present within the uniqueness of your reality while acknowledging that the symphony of truth is dynamic.

Humanity is felt when souls operate from their soul's consciousness and emanate their core essences. Acknowledgment that we are souls in a physical body. Humanity is the collective when souls resonate with truth. Mankind is the collective when souls deny truth.

Humiliation An element of the heresy barrier of your soul's unconsciousness, used to oppress your awareness of your soul's consciousness. An overwhelming emotion coming from the belief that either you have proven yourself to be, or another has put you in a position of being, inferior to others. This often leaves you believing that unless you are submissive to those who want you to believe you are unworthy, the harassment and embarrassment will continue. Humiliation can result from the belief that you cannot escape what you feel shameful about or what you know embarrasses you. Humiliation is painful embarrassment and a fear of being ridiculed or perceived as unworthy.

Humiliation can stem from the knowledge of dumbing yourself down, or from allowing yourself or another to deprive you of your dignity and self-respect. Collectively or individually undermining how others feel about themselves, with the deliberate intention of decreasing their sense of value, worth and significance.

Ignorance A lack of knowledge or being ill-informed, causing you to be unaware of truth. Unenlightened, meaning to not know the truth of yourself or the truth of your reality. Choosing to remain unaware of yourself and in denial of your capacity to be aware. Lacking the inclination to question and challenge your limited awareness and knowledge. Arrogantly ignoring the opportunity to examine the evidence of truth.

Inability to comprehend that you are not feeling your own soul's consciousness and truth. Governed by limitations. Stuck in your own programming, conditioning and indoctrinations without the desire to challenge or explore the dynamics of your soul, truth and life.

'I know' mentality is the combination of beliefs and the desire for control that generates an air of arrogance and stems from you protecting what you think you comprehend and have committed yourself to. It is using what you want to be true, or believe to be true, as an excuse to avoid the exploration of truth. Affixing to your own 'I know' mentality leaves you believing there could be no other explanation or possible reality, except that which you have decided is under your control, or running to your expectations. What you believe you know can become how you programme, condition and indoctrinate yourself, which generates energy within your soul's unconsciousness, that you use to sustain your denial of reality and indifference to truth.

Illusion One of the barriers to truth within your soul's unconsciousness, used to oppress your awareness of your soul's consciousness. A perception of reality built from the willingness to be deceptive and the desire to conceal reality. The ability to deceive yourself or others by anchoring to misconceptions and creating misleading beliefs that you use to oppose the significance of truth, or to alter others' awareness of truth. May appear to be one thing but is another. The ability to use a lie to conceal truth. The loss of authenticity, not genuine.

Illusion of control A facet of your soul control. The belief that you are in control of life. The belief that you have power over reality, often disregarding the deceptive lies you use to conceal the truth of your reality. Operating from lies to enhance your denial of reality. The belief that you can orchestrate reality to adhere to your expectations and appease your desires. Taking an element of truth and confabulating a story that suits your desire to be an authority over what truth is. Stems from the deceptive belief that controlling the perception of reality means you have the ability to control the symphony of truth.

Image One of the barriers to truth within your soul's unconsciousness, used to oppress your awareness of your soul's consciousness. Acting out a performance, trying to orchestrate how you want to be perceived, because you are scared to expose the truth of who you are, or you are attempting to manipulate others. Using fragmented aspects of yourself to generate a persona, which you use to fool yourself and others. Staging facades and charades that sustain your separation from your awareness of your soul. Enacting what you believe will allow you to hide from your internal or external reality whilst overshadowing the truth of who you are.

Image failure Recognition that your image has failed to create the results you want. Unsuccessful in the impression you wanted to create or sustain. A failed performance, which leaves you unable to control others' perception of you. The realisation that others are aware that you are not being genuine. Feeling humiliated for not being able to fool yourself or others with your facades and charades. The exposure of the superficial nature of your facades and charades, which often leaves you emotionally imploding in your own guilt, shame or humiliation.

Images of consciousness An imitation of what you believe consciousness is. Using superficial and egotistical facades and charades to try to depict spiritual elitism as you seek to be revered, whilst denying the truth of your own deception and manipulation. A control structure orchestrated by your willingness to be dishonest in your relationship with truth. A performance with the intent to be indifferent to the purity of truth. The belief that you are entitled to dictate what truth is to yourself and others, to ensure you remain on top of what you perceive as a spiritual pecking order. Deception cloaked in the illusion of spirituality.

Independence A core essence of your soul's consciousness, unconditional love for freedom.

The choice to allow your uniqueness to flow with ease, undisturbed by your willingness to oppress your freedom. Independence is to trust your internal knowledge of being an eternal strand of truth energy, flowing from your origins of *True Source Divine Origin Consciousness*. Independence is your ability to freely experience life as a soul, uninhibited by negative judgement and opposition to truth. Independence is taking accountability and responsibility for yourself. To make decisions autonomously rather than hiding behind or relying on external factors to govern your reactions and the choices you make.

Indifference The intention to abandon the truth of reality and class everything, bar your own desire for control, as unimportant, not worth caring about or incidental. Disconnected from your integrity. A self-perpetuating energy that enables non-caring for your own and others' suffering to continue, unabated by compassion or truth. The willingness to support your own denial of reality and to be apathetic about the ramifications of your desire for control and denial of truth. Remaining unresponsive to the truth you cannot deny. Intentional unconsciousness.

The result of completely losing awareness of being a soul, and denying the significance of all souls. To be uncaring and emotionally insensitive to the point of being cruel. To callously disregard and deny the significance of unconditional love. The desire to oppose the core essences of your soul, other souls and the presence of truth. Denial of the significance of truthfulness. Denial of the significance, uniqueness, independence and individuality of another soul.

Individuality A core essence of your soul's consciousness, unconditional love for the exquisiteness of your own soul.

Accepting yourself as an independent strand of truth, freely resonating with the uniqueness of your own dynamic soul. Freely expressing the truth of who you are and what you feel. The natural frequency that distinguishes the uniqueness of your soul from another.

Indoctrinations An element of the heresy barrier of your soul's unconsciousness, used to oppress your awareness of your soul's consciousness. Beliefs, opinions, ideas, attitudes and an orchestrated way of being that you have been instructed to align to, or have chosen to be influenced by. Adopted beliefs, doctrines or ideologies that have been taught to you that you are expected to accept without questioning their validity. To be systematically discouraged from independent thought, causing you to become non-accepting and intolerant of the dynamics of truth, others' freewill, your own internal knowledge and the uniqueness of each present moment.

Beliefs, opinions, ideas, attitudes and an orchestrated way of being that have saturated your thought process, causing you to believe they are an explanation of how reality should be. Indoctrinations can be propaganda that have no or little evidence supporting what is being promoted, however, as it becomes familiar and ingrained within a collective psyche, the deceptive or distorted information develops into a defended belief system.

Insatiable Impossible to satisfy, always wanting more. Greedy

Insignificance The belief of being unimportant. The fear of having no value, worth or significance. A mankind judgement that is in opposition to the truth of the equality of all souls.

Insipid Lacking interest in truth or lacking expression from the truth of your soul.

Integrity A core essence of your soul's consciousness, unconditional love for soul accountability.

To maintain your unity with truth because you value truth. The willingness to value truth within all your decision making. Your soul's consciousness flowing freely, undamaged and not divided by any deception. To adhere to and trust your original intention to experience the truth of your reality and to respond to life from truthful honesty. Maintaining your awareness of your present moment. To make decisions with commitment and fortitude that support trusting your own feelings and your awareness of truth.

Internal knowing Your soul consciousness' knowing, which is insight from truth, often referred to as soul knowing. Internal knowing is your clarity that stems from naturally resonating with and being aware of truth. Knowledge that is felt from the depths of your soul.

'I want' mentality The fixation on what you desire control of, or want to possess. The willingness to be indifferent to truth, in order to acquire what you believe will pacify your desire for control. Your desire for control amalgamates with the belief, that the acquisition of something outside yourself, or the ability to possess and control somebody, or an event will quell the void you feel. To covet what another has. Derived from envy.

Jealousy An emotional implosion created from your inability to believe your own illusion of control. A fixation on a judgement creating a surge of control energy. Your jealousy is a display of perceived image and control failure. Envious, while emotionally being suspicious of losing control of what you want to possess. Jealousy is a by-product of your fear of losing control.

Joy A core essence of your soul's consciousness, unconditional love for being alive.

Acceptance of the dynamics of truth and the spontaneity of your elation. Jubilation for being alive. To feel your own shine of consciousness. The freedom to naturally be at ease, celebrating the truth of your soul. To feel yourself trusting the journey of life.

Judgement One of the barriers to truth within your soul's unconsciousness, used to oppress your awareness of your soul's consciousness. Judgement is a binding force of your embedded beliefs, fears and desire for control that you use to incite and sustain your own soul oppression or the oppression of others. Judgement inhibits your ability to feel truth. Judgement is used to oppose and deflect your resonance with truth. Judgement is a catalyst, which fuels the connection between the different unresolved emotions within your soul's unconsciousness and ignites your indifference to truth.

Junction The crossroads and decision point where energy is exposed for the truth of what it is.

Kindness A core essence of your soul's consciousness, unconditional love for giving without an agenda.

To trust your awareness of truth and to share the essence of who you are with life, yourself and others. The willingness to be sympathetic to the plight of others and yourself. The inspiration created when unconditional love is freely given.

Knowing: You have two types of knowing: Your soul consciousness' knowing, which is insight from truth. You also have the knowing developed from the familiarity of your unresolved emotions and the repetitiveness of your cycles of soul oppression.

Labyrinths Your soul journey is the expedition of walking the many labyrinths of life. Labyrinths are complex connecting pathways, passages and junctions that can seem like a maze, except they have the same entry and exit point. Labyrinths are easy to lose focus on. There is no direct way to the centre or to exit once you journey in. It is through the experience of the path and the decisions you make that you learn about yourself and the value of truth. When you resist being exposed to the truth of yourself, you can convolute the experience of the path you walk. Labyrinths do not have dead ends where you are trapped, because you are never without the opportunity to accept the significance of what you are experiencing and the potential to learn. You only remain trapped in a labyrinth by choice. You experience a multitude of labyrinths during your life, some are internal and others are an external pathway. Your soul's unconsciousness is a labyrinth of energy you created. Your labyrinths are also created from your thought process, and can become mind games you use against yourself, which makes it hard for you to discover, acknowledge and comprehend the truth of yourself.

The intricacies of your emotional, energetic and physical cyclic patterns of soul oppression complicate your journey through the labyrinths you walk. You use your unresolved emotions to confine and restrict your awareness of truth, which is how you lose your awareness of truth, to the complexities of the layer of your soul's unconsciousness. Your soul's unconsciousness is a labyrinth of your unresolved emotions, control structures, avenues of indifference, fears and beliefs. This also means what you create can be resolved, and you can evolve out of the deceptive labyrinth of your own soul's unconsciousness.

Life is a moment to moment experience. It is the privilege of being a soul within a physical body. The opportunity to exist and experience being on Earth as a naturally significant, unique, independent, individual soul of *True Source Divine Origin Consciousness*. The arena of freewill. The opportunity for resolution and evolution.

Lost Soul Often referred to as a ghost. A soul who has not returned to their origins after the death of their physical body. A soul who after their death has become stuck within the energetic mass energy of mankind.

Loyalty A core essence of your soul's consciousness, unconditional love for the essence of truth.

To live the authenticity of your soul, consciously participating in your relationship with truth. To trust yourself to unify with the significance of truth and to remain faithful to your soul. To honour and respect your original intentions and your resonance with truth.

Manipulation One of the barriers to truth within your soul's unconsciousness, used to oppress your awareness of your soul's consciousness. The willingness to coerce another or yourself by engaging in deceptive manoeuvres to obstruct the awareness of truth. The intention of hiding and attempting to alter your own or another's awareness of truth, for the purpose of trying to gain control of reality. Devious coercion or intimidation in an attempt to secure the pacification of your desire for control. Results from disregarding the value of truth and fixating on what you believe you want.

Mankind is the result of losing awareness of our humanity by devaluing the soul within our physical bodies. Mankind is the collective when souls deny truth. Humanity is the collective when souls resonate with truth.

Martyr The willingness to perpetuate and orchestrate your own suffering for the continuation of your soul oppression. To sacrifice your own soul integrity by investing in suffering, seeking to gain sympathy, help or recognition. The generation of 'poor me' mentality.

Merry-go-round A repetitive cyclic pattern of soul oppression.

Mentality is a way of thinking that governs your actions and becomes a way of being.

Mind chatter Constant thinking, analysing, assessing and judging, that leaves you ruminating without a solution to your own emotional angst. Repetitive and compulsive thought processes that guarantee the creation of emotional, energetic and physical upheaval. An awareness of the energy generated from your soul's unconsciousness. Your mind chatter is produced when you oppress your awareness of truth and your soul's consciousness. Mind chatter can be generated from the deception or avoidance you refuse to be honest about.

Misconceptions Misunderstandings or mistaken ideals and beliefs. The result of misreading energy, aligning to misleading beliefs, supporting deception and maintaining incorrect assumptions. Accepting lies as truth.

Missing the mark Refers to missing your original intention to resolve your unresolved emotions while experiencing the truth of yourself within your reality. Not achieving the results or understanding that you originally intended. Missing the mark means to resist, deny and avoid the opportunities within your soul journey.

Narcissists interact with life and others with an over-inflated belief of self-importance, narrow-mindedness and egotism. Their overriding concern is to fulfil their own desires. Narcissists operate from the compulsion to forsake the value of truth, the equality of all souls and to fixate only on what they want with a deluded sense of entitlement. Narcissists disregard the harm, confusion and pain they cause with their arrogant behaviour, selfishness and manipulation. Narcissists defend their lack of compassion and empathy for others as they align to the belief that if others adhered to their wants, there would be no problem. Narcissists have a strong belief that the pacification of their control is essential, and that they deserve special treatment. They expect that their insecurities, obnoxious behaviour and the words they speak should be glossed over and ignored, believing they should receive accolades for being superior to others. Narcissists are willing to deceptively and harmfully enforce the belief that all those who are involved with them should align to enhancing their ability to create the desired outcomes they want, regardless of the consequences to others.

Narcissists desire to prove they are better than others and constantly avoid self-responsibility, going to great lengths to blame others for their own failings. Narcissists use people and disregard them when they no longer perceive them as useful. Narcissists are conniving in the way they manipulate others to believe they are inferior to them. Narcissists are very retaliative if they believe another has achieved what they desire, exposed their insecurities, or refused to be under their control. Narcissists are the embodiment of indifference energy in action.

Negative beliefs Control structures and belief systems that inhibit you from recognising and feeling the truth of your own soul. This results in you becoming codependent on the familiarity of your soul oppression, swamped by your own unresolved emotions, and deceiving yourself with your misconceptions about the truth of who you are.

What you pessimistically and harmfully believe that perpetuates your soul oppression, without exploring the truth of yourself. Negative beliefs are the manifestation of your unresolved emotions and embedded fears, and expose your willingness to remain stagnant and lost in your own soul oppression. Negative beliefs are often indoctrinations inflicted by another who is or was willing to be oppressive and a domineering influence over how you perceive yourself. Negative beliefs result from experiencing indifference energy, produced either by yourself or any other outside source.

Nobbling The act of disabling. To convince somebody with fraudulent methods, seeking to derail their sense of self, reality and awareness of truth.

'Not good enough' mentality The isolation you feel when you separate from your awareness of your soul's consciousness. Emotionally believing you are inadequate and flawed. The belief of not being good enough causes you to feel insignificant and irrelevant. It is the choice to devalue yourself, while programming, conditioning and indoctrinating yourself to oppose the flow of conscious energy within your soul. The abandonment of your awareness of your own flow of consciousness, causing you to emotionally feel unloved and unworthy, which incites a compulsion to reject the core essences of your soul.

Orchestration Seeking to be the composer of reality, believing you can arrange the different aspects within your reality to align to your illusions, expectations or desires. Seeking to control all the fundamentals you believe are important for you to achieve an illusion of control. The activation of an agenda. The attempt to make reality conducive to what you believe you want. Devising a plan you believe will secure a sense of control while protecting your denial of reality. Preferring to align to your plans for how reality should be, rather than being completely present in and honest about the reality of what is.

Oppression To be treated cruelly, unfairly tormented and prevented from experiencing freedom and deprived of opportunities, because there is no acceptance of equality. Oppression is knowingly causing yourself or another harm, whilst ignoring your own awareness of truth. The desire to maliciously dominate.

Origins The beginning from which everything arises and is derived; the source. The truth of your beginning, where you come from and where you return to after the death of your physical body. Original form before any deception. Your foundation of truth, which is the core of your existence.

Patience A core essence of your soul's consciousness, unconditional love for your own synchronicity with truth.

An acceptance of reality. To trust the truth of your soul journey and willingly accept the symphony of truth. To trust that your original intention to resolve and evolve is always supported by your synchronicity with truth. The ability to have the endurance to never give up on the significance of discovering the truth of who you are. The willingness to accept that reality is a shared experience you are participating in, and that the world does not revolve around your desire to be in control, or your expectation that the world should work the way you want it to. Honest acceptance of what is, within the uniqueness of every experience and present moment.

Peace A core essence of your soul's consciousness, unconditional love for reality.

Acceptance of the reality of yourself being a significant, unique, independent, individual soul of *True Source Divine Origin Consciousness*. Acceptance of the significance of truth's symphony without judgement or expectations.

To trust your synchronicity with the presence of truth within your reality. Peace is an acceptance of the significance of being aware of yourself within your present moment. Peace is the willingness to be present, regardless of what is occurring. Peace is the ability to not fight against acknowledging your reality and to trust yourself to experience life as an opportunity to be of your truth. To be free of any internal conflict. Peace is the stillness felt when you are in harmony with your own consciousness.

Pecking order Hierarchical system of judgement based on rejection of the equality of all souls. The desire to align to a position within a constructed hierarchical system. The use of judgement to secure a ranking. A constructed assessment of the value and worth of someone or something, which is contrived to control and dominate others. Ranking people's significance, by an array of judgements such as their financial achievements, occupations, education, religion, appearance or the colour of their skin; the list is endless. The willingness to sustain the disunity within mankind and a blatant disregard for the uniqueness of each soul and their experience on Earth.

Present moment Your current reality. Many different energies contribute to each moment and no one moment can ever be replicated, due to the dynamics of truth.

Programming An element of the heresy barrier of your soul's unconsciousness, used to oppress your awareness of your soul's consciousness. The way you instruct yourself to automatically react to different energy, feelings, emotions, people and events. Sequenced reactions and responses that sustain the cyclic patterns you use, to oppose your awareness of the dynamics of your soul's consciousness and the truth of your reality.

Purity A core essence of your soul's consciousness, unconditional love for consciousness.

Purity is to feel the shine of your consciousness. Purity is free of any unconscious energy, complete within the wholeness of your origins, without division. The pureness of the unconditional love of *True Source Divine Origin Consciousness* and your soul's consciousness. The result of consciousness unifying with consciousness. Complete truthfulness. The transparency of truth that is always there.

Reaction An automatic response, without thought. Emotionally charged or fear triggered actions. Habitual or mindless emotional, energetic, physical or verbal actions, often made while denying the truth of what you are doing.

Reality What is real, genuine and original, not artificial or fabricated. The totality of all that exists. The entirety of what is happening, the presence of both conscious and unconscious energy within the uniqueness of each present moment. Reality is the truth of the energy and experience of your present moment or an unfolding experience.

Reconnaissance The exploration of your unconsciousness and life with the intention of discovering what is inhibiting you from resolving and evolving. To experience, observe or survey your unconsciousness and your life experiences to inform yourself of what is unresolved, or to realise the core essence of who you are. To experience, observe or examine what is required for you to discover what you were seeking to find.

Red herring A decoy that someone uses in an attempt to mislead and divert attention away from truth.

Repression A defensive mechanism of preventing yourself from being aware of thoughts that expose truth to you. Holding back your awareness of truth by clouding your thought process with ruminating mind chatter that leads to no solution. Confusing yourself with contradictory thoughts. Subduing your awareness of the reality you are or have experienced by fixating on your own wants and desires, distracting yourself from acknowledging truth. Activating your denial, delusions, memory inhibitors and protective mechanisms to ensure the perpetuation of your ability and willingness to disassociate from being present in the truth of your reality.

You repress your awareness of truth by over-thinking, rejecting your feelings and believing your own misconceptions about yourself, others, life and truth. Repression is the use of thoughts to incite the oppression of your soul and to oppose your awareness of truth.

Resentment of reality An element of the heresy barrier of your soul's unconsciousness, used to oppress your awareness of your soul's consciousness. Intense feelings of anger, disappointment and emotional upheaval, because you do not want to accept what has occurred, how you have been treated or that you cannot control life to adhere to your desires and expectations. A reaction to life not being what you want or what you believe it should be, creating in you, a persistent animosity towards reality. The willingness to hold onto a grudge, refusing to accept or forgive.

Resistance One of the barriers to truth within your soul's unconsciousness, used to oppress your awareness of your soul's consciousness. Attempting to ignore the truth of reality even though you have some awareness of reality. Forcibly opposing the reality within you and your life experiences. The willingness to oppose and struggle against your awareness of truth. Attempting to use your opposition to retard your awareness of the reality of both conscious and unconscious energy, seeking to prevent and inhibit any energy or event from interfering with your illusion of control. The willingness to remain unaltered in your perception of reality even though you have evidence, which is contradictory to your perception of reality.

Resonance Your recognition and acceptance of your own consciousness and your unification with truth. To be in harmony with the frequency of truth. Feeling the resounding depth and richness of freely flowing unified conscious energy. The effects of unification, which is often beyond what is immediately apparent. Feeling the essence of your soul at the same time as feeling the unconditional love of *True Source Divine Origin Consciousness*.

Response An intentional and considered reply or action. An action or reply made with some form of awareness.

Reverberation The reflection and succession of energy echoing the same vibration, which always returns to the initiator of the energy. Energetic repercussions from your utilisation of the energy of your soul's unconsciousness, such as your unresolved emotions. The projection of unconscious energy builds in vibrational force creating a prolonged effect, and has the ability as it builds momentum to incite other unconscious energy to be activated. The energy connects to another's energy or the collective energy of the same vibration and is then rebounded back to the initiator of the projection.

Rise and fall The natural process of the energy of your soul's consciousness descending into the energy of your soul's unconsciousness and then naturally ascending, to return to the origins of truth. This is a multi-strand stream of conscious energy that is constantly flowing dynamically and in various stages of descent and ascent, which exposes you to the opportunity to resolve and evolve. As the energy of your soul's consciousness moves through your soul's unconsciousness, you are exposed to the reality of your own energy. When you operate from your soul's unconsciousness, meaning from the energy of your unresolved emotions, control structures, barriers to truth, your framework of soul oppression or the seven deadly sins, your soul's consciousness illuminates the truth of your energy, providing you with the opportunity to be truly aware of yourself. Your soul's consciousness is the part of you that never loses the authenticity and the purity of your consciousness, or your original intention to naturally unify your soul system to your origins of truth. Your soul system is both your soul's consciousness and unconsciousness.

Rise and fall *from* grace Grace refers to the constant flow of conscious energy, which is always present whether you are recognising and accepting, or denying and opposing truth. Rise and fall *from* grace is the process of being exposed to the reality of your energy. However, when you operate from your unresolved emotions and keep yourself immersed in the energy of your soul's unconsciousness, you are separated from your awareness of truth and fallen *from* grace, because you have failed to be curious and truthfully honest about what is occurring.

Rise and fall *with* grace Grace refers to the constant flow of conscious energy, which is always present whether you are recognising and accepting, or denying and opposing truth. Rise and fall *with* grace is the process of being exposed to the reality of your energy. When you acknowledge your unresolved emotions, and choose to be truthful, you rise *with* grace. This means you are in the process of resolving the energy of your soul's unconsciousness. Resolution can occur at the time or in hindsight when you choose to be curious about truth and are willing to be truthful. Rising *with* grace is unifying with your own consciousness and truth.

Rise *with* grace To operate in unification with your soul's consciousness and truth. This is in contrast to fall *from* grace, which is to operate in separation from your soul's consciousness and truth.

Ruminating To mull over something, often at length. To over-think and over-analyse something, whilst becoming stuck in the repetitiveness of your own mind chatter.

Self Used in the declaration of truth to represent your soul's consciousness, the truth of who you are and the presence of truth.

self Used in the declaration of truth to represent your soul's unconsciousness, the energy you create when you deny who you are and deny the reality of what you create from your own soul's unconsciousness.

'*Self* expose self' From the declaration of truth; a statement asking your soul's consciousness to expose the truth of your soul's unconsciousness. A statement declaring you seek to resolve the aversions or barriers you have to acknowledging truth.

Self-responsibility The acceptance of being an autonomous being. Trustworthiness. Custodian of your own decisions and actions.

Separation from your awareness of your soul The choice to separate yourself from your awareness of your soul's consciousness and to immerse yourself in the energy of your soul's unconsciousness. This means you operate from what you use to oppress your ability to care for and notice your own soul and reverberate with the energetics of the mass energy of mankind that supports your defection from the truth of who you are. Separation stems from your non-acceptance of your own significance, uniqueness, independence and individuality.

The process of concealing or avoiding your recognition of soul and the reality of being aware of a void within. When you are not of your truth, you feel a void. The void you feel is your recognition of your separation from your awareness of and resonance with your own soul. Separation creates a void you have attempted to fill with unconscious energy.

Serenity A core essence of your soul's consciousness, unconditional love for being at peace with reality.

The tranquility created by accepting your natural significance, uniqueness, independence and individuality. A steadiness within your mind which is undisturbed by what is emotionally, energetically or physically surrounding you. This is felt as natural strength. Unclouded awareness coupled with your natural ability to trust yourself as a soul of truth. A still calmness within the depths of your soul. The willingness to remain honest about your awareness of your natural unification with the presence of *True Source Divine Origin Consciousness* within your present moment reality. Feeling the unconditional love of *True Source Divine Origin Consciousness*. Joyous internal acceptance of your clarity and the magnitude of your significance.

Seven deadly sins are forms of indifference to yourself and truth that invoke false promises: Lust, greed, gluttony, envy, sloth, wrath, pride and the narcissism of vanity. These are transgressions that are fatal to your participation in your evolution because you become seduced by your own indifference to truth. The seven deadly sins are how you impel yourself to stay lost in the compulsion and addiction to protect the energy of your soul's unconsciousness and to forsake the purity of your soul's consciousness. Succumbing to the perpetuation of your soul oppression, whilst missing the mark of your original intention to resolve what inhibits your evolution.

Shine of consciousness An internal glow that can be felt. The emanation of the truth of your soul. The radiance of the truth of who you are unencumbered by any unconscious energy.

Shame An element of the heresy barrier of your soul's unconsciousness, used to oppress your awareness of your soul's consciousness. An overwhelming emotion coming from the belief that there is something wrong with who you are. To cover yourself in the energy of unworthiness and any emotions connected to your belief of being a disgrace. A loss of respect for yourself. The result of your or another's indifference to the significance of your soul. Your unwillingness to unconditionally love yourself which causes you to retreat from your natural value.

Shame can be internalised by some victims of sexual abuse and can cause them to believe they are unworthy and insignificant; falsely blaming themselves for the experience of their abuse. This causes victims to carry false guilt as shame when both the guilt and shame belong to the abuser.

Significance To trust your own uniqueness, independence, individuality and the importance of your own soul journey. To appreciate your natural value and relevance. Accepting you are in a relationship with truth. Trusting your synchronicity with truth within your present moment. The importance of your freedom to choose how you respond to yourself and your life experience. Acceptance of freedom is to acknowledge your significance.

Source Origin or provider. The origins of the infinite supply of consciousness and unconditional love, referred to as *True Source Divine Origin Consciousness* in *Your Insight and Awareness book*.

Soul abuse A cyclic pattern of an avenue of indifference within your framework of soul oppression. The willingness to hurt yourself or others. Ritualistic cyclic patterns that you use to oppress your awareness of your soul. Your persistent emotional, energetic and physical maltreatment of your soul's consciousness, you inflict on yourself by being indifferent to truth.

Soul accountability Recognition of the truth of your own energy, both conscious and unconscious. The application of truthful honesty while acknowledging and exploring the reality of life. When you value the significance of being a soul, you become answerable to yourself. Accountability is to take responsibility for your actions, choices and the truth of your own energy. Accepting the cause and effect of your being.

Soul betrayal A cyclic pattern of an avenue of indifference within your framework of soul oppression. The deliberate act of disloyalty and the willingness to destroy trust. You oppress your awareness of your soul with your choice to ignore the reality of how you obscure truth with deception. The treachery of your emotional, energetic and physical disloyalty towards your soul's consciousness, which leaves you indifferent to yourself and truth.

Soul carnage Damage created that can be carried from one lifetime to another lifetime, and is carried until resolved. The severity of inflicting and leaving a person to endure emotional, energetic and physical pain, which is felt within the depths of their soul. The result of callous indifference.

Soul control The energy you produce by either your desire to control or your illusion of control. Formidable energy used to fuel the different avenues of indifference within your framework of soul oppression, to incite your other unresolved emotions and to fortify your barriers to truth. The desire or illusion that you use to sustain your separation from your awareness of your soul and truth. *(See control)*

Soul deception A cyclic pattern of an avenue of indifference within your framework of soul oppression. The willingness to mislead yourself and others. Deliberate indifference to truth, with the intention to deceive yourself and others. Your radar for detecting where you believe your deception will enhance your control of reality or improve the image you want to portray, which determines how you use your unresolved emotions.

Soul defiance A cyclic pattern of an avenue of indifference within your framework of soul oppression. The insidiousness of your resistance to truth. The willingness to be dishonest and selfish, allowing yourself to become an opposing force against your own awareness of truth. The result of not trusting truth, whilst wanting to observe your own control in action. The insolence of your emotional, energetic and physical disregard for the significance of your soul's consciousness.

Soul demise A cyclic pattern of an avenue of indifference within your framework of soul oppression. The loss of awareness of your soul's consciousness, the presence of truth and the truth of your own reality. The willingness to attempt to destroy or dismiss your own or another's awareness of truth. To lose awareness of the emotional, energetic and physical ramifications you create with your indifference to yourself and truth.

Soul denial The crux and original energy of your soul's unconsciousness and the source of all unconscious energy; all unconscious energy is a mutation of soul denial. Soul denial is the storehouse of your fears and embedded beliefs. The fears and embedded beliefs of your soul denial are constructed from your denial of the truth of who you are, the origins of your existence and the truth you feel. Soul denial is the foundation of your framework of soul oppression. Your framework of soul oppression is structured from the avenues of indifference that you use to protect your soul denial. The entry point of the seven deadly sins.

Soul Denial is the energy produced by your rejection of being a naturally significant, unique, independent, individual soul of *True Source Divine Origin Consciousness*. Soul denial stems from your denial of your resonance with truth. Soul denial results from your internal war with the truth of who you are. Soul denial is the energy of your mistrust of truth. Your soul denial energy is the energy of the void you create by separating from your awareness of truth.

Soul denial history Your history of forsaking your own soul is how you created the unconscious energy that you carry and are reactive to until resolved. This unconscious energy is the vortex of your soul's unconsciousness. When you denied the truth of your soul and the truth of your reality, you created unresolved emotions that produce unconscious energy. Your unresolved emotions are stored and carried until you are ready to use your freedom of choice to become an active participant in your own resolution and evolution. Your history of denying your soul, fuels your cyclic patterns of oppression that you may have repeated in many lifetimes. Soul denial history incorporates the entirety of your soul journey, which is not restricted to just this life you are experiencing.

Soul illusion A cyclic pattern of an avenue of indifference within your framework of soul oppression. Deceptive impressions used to control the sustainability of your separation from your awareness of your soul and disassociation from feeling truth. Delusions and false appearances constructed by your desire to orchestrate a perception of reality. The overriding intention to disconnect from and distort your own and others' awareness of the truth of reality. The concealment of truth at the expense of your resolution and evolution.

The use of distorted emotional, energetic or physical filters you produce with your indifference to yourself and truth, to overshadow your awareness of reality. The use of illusion to mock the significance of truth and attempt to avert the reality of your life experience.

Soul insight is intuitiveness. Instinctively understanding something or comprehending the multi-layers contributing to your present moment. Knowledge that stems from your natural resonance with truth.

Soul journey Your life is an expedition to discover your relationship with truth, which is the origin of your soul. Your journey as a soul is unique. You are exploring the truth of yourself and will experience all that is required for you to resolve that which sustains your separation from your awareness of truth.

You are an eternal soul, your journey is the process of discovering the truth of who you are and what you have used to resist, deny and avoid your soul truth. Exploring your soul truth is embracing and being of your soul's consciousness, whilst recognising and resolving your soul's unconsciousness. Your soul journey is the opportunity to participate in your own evolution, and your evolution contributes to the evolution of *True Source Divine Origin Consciousness* and mankind.

Soul oppression The willingness to use the energy of your soul's unconsciousness as an active force that emotionally, energetically or physically oppresses the freewill of others, and keeps you incarcerated in the stagnation of your unconsciousness. Inhibiting your own awareness of the presence of your soul's consciousness and truth. Allowing yourself, to constantly default, to using the energy of your soul's unconsciousness to dominate your attention and overshadow your clarity. Remaining stuck by repetitively immersing yourself in that which causes you angst. Controlling yourself to deflect or conceal truth. Subjugating your own core essences with your indifference to your soul.

Your willingness to mistreat yourself or others, by overriding your soul integrity and tarnishing your shine of consciousness. Suppressing your true feelings. Seeking the demise of your awareness of truth, by repressing your soul insight and activating negative thoughts. Inflicting cruelty and torment upon yourself, by denying the truth of who you are. Setting yourself up to be repetitively anti-yourself, and lost in your fears and embedded beliefs.

Feeling restricted. Burdening yourself with your own emotional, energetic and physical resistance to unshackling your indifference to yourself, others and truth. Recognising your own anguish or feeling the void within. Dominating and intimidating yourself or others with oppressive energy. Oppression is the anguish you create by separating from your awareness of your soul, and disassociating from feeling the unconditional love within your soul and the unconditional love of *True Source Divine Origin Consciousness*.

Soul sabotage A cyclic pattern of an avenue of indifference within your framework of soul oppression. Your willingness to align to any actions, beliefs, energy and fear you know will heighten your opposition to discover truth. Your willingness to be anti-yourself or another with the intent to oppose the significance of truth. The deliberate disruption of your or another's awareness of truth to hinder your own resonance with truth, or to undermine the opportunities life presents to you or another. Your preference for fighting against the reality of life, yourself, others, relationships and truth. Destructive tactics.

Soul traitor A cyclic pattern of an avenue of indifference within your framework of soul oppression. Deliberately oppressing yourself or another. Conspiring against your own soul's consciousness by abandoning truth and aligning to the oppression of your soul. Portraying, doing and saying one thing whilst being intentionally conniving to create outcomes you believe will enhance your illusion of control or undermine another's natural significance. Intentionally being indifferent to truth to ambush the reality of what is occurring, striving to inhibit being in harmony with truth.

Soul truth Both your soul's consciousness and unconsciousness.

Soul's consciousness The divine aspect of you that has never separated from being of truth. Your unique strand of truth energy, which is anchored to your origin and flows within the core of your being. The part of your soul system that has never abandoned the unconditional love of *True Source Divine Origin Consciousness* and is naturally of unconditional love. The truth of who you are unencumbered by any unconscious energy.

Soul's unconsciousness The vortex of unconscious energy within your soul system that you create and use to keep opposing the unconditional love of *True Source Divine Origin Consciousness* and to deny the truth of who you are. The unique combination of your personal collective of unresolved emotions, control structures, barriers to truth and your framework of soul oppression. These stem from the fears and embedded beliefs of your soul denial and your desire for control. The energy you have created within your void of separation from your awareness of your soul and disassociation from feeling your resonance with truth.

Spiritual illusionist Someone who creates an image of consciousness while denying their own unconsciousness. People who identify themselves as spiritually elite, for the purpose of stroking their own ego. Someone who ignorantly or arrogantly portrays an image of consciousness whilst desiring to be referred to or revered as spiritually elite. A person who uses their beliefs of spirituality as a way of thinking they are in control of life and truth. Deceptively using spiritual beliefs to by-pass the process of resolution and evolution.

Stagnation An energetic idle created from the repetitive nature of your unwillingness to learn from the truth of what you are experiencing. Your denial of how you continuously act out your unresolved emotions. Remaining gridlocked by your own oppression of your soul because you inhibit your awareness of truth and refuse to be truthful. Opposing being honest to protect your rut, preferring to remain trapped in established cyclic patterns with no desire to challenge your own oppression.

Stagnation results from forsaking the value of truth and worshipping your desire for control. You become stagnant when you are unreceptive to change or the truth of your reality and the dynamics of life. Stagnation results from your choice to continuously deny the value of truth.

Struggling human energy is to be anti-truth, which causes you to be anti-the eternalness of your soul, anti-the truth of your soul journey, anti-your opportunity for resolution, anti-your original intention for evolution, anti-being present and honest about your reality and anti-this lifetime. Being anti-truth becomes fuel for your own web of deception.

Your struggling human energy is the result of your heresy against yourself and your opposition to the significance of the uniqueness, independence and the individuality of each soul. Your struggling human energy is the result of your willingness to be in conflict with the truth of your own value, worth and significance, which means you become your own enemy.

Superficiality The willingness to be non-genuine, which manifests in the shallowness of the charades and façades of your images and illusions. Superficiality is the refusal to acknowledge the significance of your soul. Superficiality is to lack the substance of truth and to make choices for how you live your life based on what you believe will provide you with accolades for the image you want to portray.

Suppression Your forceful prevention of acknowledging the truth of your own feelings and unresolved emotions. Burying memories, thoughts, unresolved emotions and feelings deep within your unconsciousness in an attempt to resist, deny and avoid the truth of your emotional, energetic and physical reality. Denying your unresolved emotions and hiding from the fear you have about facing and feeling your emotions. Suppression is the concealment of the truth you feel. Aligning to an illusion to pretend your emotions do not bother you. Using the concealment of your emotions to attempt to deny your reality.

Symphony of truth The reality of life. The truth of all energy creating and contributing to reality. The cause and effect of the truth of our choices.

True Real, genuine and authentic. In harmony with the entirety of truth. The energy of what is.

Thinking The process of using one's mind, which can be an intellectual process of discovery, recognising an array of thoughts and a way of attempting to decipher what is real or deceptive. Thinking is not a problem unless your thoughts are disconnected from what you are feeling, which can leave you ruminating or trying to orchestrate life from an intellectual stance or from wants and desires. This means you devalue the truth you feel and can become robotic in your decision making. Feelings resonate with truth, emotions are the reverberation of unconscious energy, and thoughts can be invoked by either feelings or emotions. If you omit the truth of what you feel from your thought process and align to your desires, you replace honesty with judgement, which tarnishes your ability to discover truth and to think clearly. Thoughts are the interface of both your soul's consciousness and unconsciousness.

True Source Divine Origin Consciousness A label used in 'Insight and Awareness' for the collective purity of truth and the origin of each soul. Where you come from and where you will return to after the death of your physical body.

Trust A core essence of your soul's consciousness, unconditional love for naturally accepting your own significance within your present moment.

Trust is your resonance with truth in action. Acceptance of the truth of all energy and the relevance of the symphony of truth. Appreciating your own synchronicity with truth and accepting the opportunities to experience your own flow of consciousness. Your trust bridges you from thinking to feeling. Your trust enables you to feel the clarity of your soul. The ability and willingness to be conscious of the truth you are aware of without fear. To feel the strength of your unconditional love for truth and truth's unconditional love for you.

Truthful honesty is to recognise truth, accept the value of truth and to then unify with truth. Honesty can be a recognition of truth, but that does not necessarily mean you will unify with the truth. You can use your honesty to fuel your soul oppressive patterns. Truthful honesty is genuine commitment to aligning to truth and is how you participate in your own resolution and evolution. Truthful honesty is integrity.

Truthfulness A core essence of your soul's consciousness, unconditional love for resonating with truth.

The application of truth and your own integrity. Your willingness to value and acknowledge your own internal soul knowing. The intention to be completely honest about how you interrelate with life, yourself, others, in relationships and in the presence of truth. To experience your own flow of consciousness because you are willing to be open and honest with yourself about your own internal and external reality.

Unconditional love The unification of all the core essences of your soul's consciousness. The purity of your frequency of truth, which is the core of your being. The flow of your truth, freely flowing undisturbed by the energy of your soul's unconsciousness or any other unconscious energy. The willingness to be an expression of the uniqueness, independence and individuality of your soul, allowing yourself to be present in your reality while caring for yourself. Pure resonance with truth. Complete trust in your awareness of the significance of love and of valuing the equality of all souls. Being aware of the truth of unconscious energy and willing to forgive that in yourself and others. To care with no judgement or agenda. To love without conditions.

Unconscious energy is produced from your unresolved emotions, which you create when you separate from your awareness of truth. Conscious energy is the emanation of the truth of your soul, unconscious energy is the opposite to this. Unconscious energy is produced when you are lost in your soul oppression and unwilling to acknowledge truth. You produce unconscious energy when you separate from your flow of consciousness and operate discordantly from truth. Unconscious energy is generated from your willingness to deny the significance and value of truth.

When you are prepared to be deceptive and indifferent to truth, you produce unconscious energy. When you operate from the energy of your soul's unconsciousness, such as from your unresolved emotions, barriers to truth, your framework of soul oppression, control structures, fears, embedded beliefs and the seven deadly sins, you produce unconscious energy. When you devalue truth, you generate unconscious energy.

Unconsciousness Temporarily separated from your awareness of your consciousness. Separated from your awareness of resonating with truth and the truth of all energy within your present moment. Unconsciousness is tainted and is felt as a vibration. Consciousness is pure and is felt as a frequency. Unconsciousness is being unaware of the truth of yourself and oblivious to the truth of all energy. It is also the lack of recognition of truth, while being unwilling to acknowledge and accept truth. The term unconsciousness describes how you create disharmony within yourself.

Unique A core essence of your soul's consciousness, unconditional love for authenticity.

Impossible to imitate. One of a kind. The exquisiteness of who you are. The authenticity of your soul.

Unity Conscious acceptance of your synchronicity and resonance with truth. Unification with truth, willingly flowing in harmony with absolute acceptance of yourself. To naturally feel your resonance with the purity of *True Source Divine Origin Consciousness*, accepting your own value, worth and significance. To work in harmony with others, naturally nurturing each other with respect.

Unresolved emotions Rejected feelings. The result of a person's inability to recognise, acknowledge and accept the truth of their reality. The manifestation of what is created, when you separate from being truth. Emotions are energy separated from the flow of consciousness. Unaddressed emotions become the energy of your soul's unconsciousness. Energy that you may be aware of but find difficult to articulate and understand, which means it is left unresolved and does not return to consciousness.

Vibrational Energy The agitated movement of unconscious energy. Consciousness is pure and is felt as a frequency. Unconsciousness is tainted and is felt as a vibration. Unconscious energy is projected or oozes from your soul's unconsciousness, which generates a vibration. Unconscious energy reverberates with other unconscious energy, which exacerbates the unresolved emotions generating the original vibration. Vibrational energy is the result of being separated from truth.

Victim A person deprived of their freedom. Being hurt, overpowered, exploited or tricked by another person, a group of people or because of a crime. Being hurt or overpowered by a natural disaster or an accident. A person who finds themselves in a circumstance where they are unable to alter, change or reason with the perpetrator.

Vortex of unresolved emotions, vortex of your soul's unconsciousness The cone shaped energetic structure of your soul's unconsciousness, which houses your unresolved emotions, barriers to truth, framework of soul oppression and control structures on a foundation of your fears and the embedded beliefs of your soul denial. The energetic spiralling motions creating the reverberations of the energy of your soul's unconsciousness. A swirling energetic mass of energy that draws other unconscious energy into it. A spiralling flow of unconscious energy, which surges and contracts, and is contrary to the flow of consciousness.

Vulnerability The belief of being unprotected and easily hurt. A feeling of isolation with the false belief that you cannot trust yourself or others. Fear, which causes you to emotionally feel susceptible to another's ability to dominate how you feel about yourself. Vulnerability can stem from your fear that your denial will not work and you will have to accept, deal with and be consciously present in your internal and external reality. The fear that you cannot withstand your own or another's judgement. Fearing your own emotional reaction to life.

Wallowing To devote yourself to feeling miserable. Excessively indulging in self-pity. Believing there is no other choice but to be immersed in your own soul oppressive energy and thoughts. Emotionally and energetically rolling around or bathing in your own unconscious energy. Allowing yourself to become overwhelmed by your unresolved emotions, leaving yourself mesmerised by your own emotional stagnation and reluctance to be completely truthful with yourself.

'What about me' syndrome A recognisable pattern of attempting to make everything about your life, interaction with others, relationships and present moment reality, about you and the way you want reality to be. Emotionally believing you are being deprived of something. It is the selfishness of wallowing in self-pity, believing others are experiencing what they want, whilst you are being deprived of what you want.

The arrogant willingness to ignore the value and significance of truth, others and your own opportunities. Deciding to remain contradictory to the truth of your reality. The desire to have reality orientate to your wants and expectations instead of being truthful about the reality of what is.

White light Some spiritual beliefs systems use white light as a representation of truth energy, however if used as a way of controlling truth or as an avoidance of truth, it is an illusion.

Wild goose chase A hopeless quest. A futile pursuit for something that is unattainable and that you have no chance of achieving.

Worshipping soul control Prioritising the desire for control or the illusion of having control above all else. Fanatical pursuit to pacify your desire to see your control affect your own or another's reality.

About the Author

Lorraine Nilon is a soul intuitive™. She has a heightened awareness of the cause and effect of unresolved emotions, and the true nature of who we are hidden beneath the emotional baggage we all carry. Lorraine has spent decades honing her skill of being able to read both the conscious and unconscious energy of soul systems. She tracks energy, and can insightfully explain the complexities and origin of unresolved emotions. Lorraine has an innate understanding of the barriers that restrict our awareness of the authenticity of who we are, and of how our avenues of being indifferent to truth separate us from the true essence of our souls. Her insight and awareness reflects her respect for the uniqueness and equality of all souls, and her willingness to stand in her own truth.

Lorraine has been formulating the Insight and Awareness anthology through her own personal experience, and from the countless workshops and private sessions with others. Lorraine's insight has encouraged many people to uncover and to be at peace with their emotional reality, and to gain a deeper understanding of themselves.

Lorraine explores life with grounded spirituality, and views truth as a trusted friend. This enables her to instinctively recognise what we can all learn from our interactions with each other and the world we live in. Her writing exposes the duality of the energy we create, in both our authenticity and separation from our awareness of truth. She highlights that we are the creators of energy that impacts the world we live in and that we have freedom of choice. Her distinctive style of writing leads others to become active participants in exploring the multi-facets of themselves and truth.

Author of

Your Insight and Awareness Book

Your life is an expedition to discover the truth of yourself

Breaking Free From the Chains of Silence

A respectful exploration into the ramifications of paedophilic abuse

www.insightandawareness.com.au

www.ingramcontent.com/pod-product-compliance
Lightning Source LLC
Chambersburg PA
CBHW080404300426
44113CB00015B/2403